THE ACCIDENTAL IMMIGRANT

THE ACCIDENTAL IMMIGRANT

A Memoir

JERZY GŁÓWCZEWSKI

Translated from the Polish by Danuta and Stefan Waydenfeld

New York—Warsaw—New Canaan

Library of Congress Control Number:		2007904370
ISBN:	Hardcover	978-1-4257-8270-2
	Softcover	978-1-4257-8268-9

This book was printed in the United States of America.

To order additional copies of this book, contact:
Xlibris Corporation
1-888-795-4274
www.Xlibris.com
Orders@Xlibris.com

38170

Contents

Part Three:
My America—An Uneasy Choice

Abbreviated Key to the Spelling and Pronunciation of Polish

Polish spelling is to a great extent phonetic; one letter of the alphabet corresponds to one sound. In English pronunciation some of its letters are pronounced:
a – like *cut* , c – like *Switzerland,* e – like *let,* g – like *go,* i – like *feet,* j – like *yet,* ł – like *why,* ó and u – like *boot,* w—like *van,* y – like *fit,*

There are no letters *q* and *v* in Polish alphabet.

Some sounds, however, are marked by combination of two letters: ch – like *huge,* cz – like *chin,* dz – like *beds,* rz – like *pleasure,* sz – like *ash.*

In addition, some Polish consonants are divided into "soft", "hardened" and "hard", represented by letters with accents like – **ć, ś, ź, ż, ń.**

Example: Author's name should be spelled Yesi Glovchevski

In memory of my mother and her indomitable spirit.

Endorsements

The Polish edition was well received by Polish and American authors:

"Formidable story by an excellent story teller."

—Stanley Cloud, *The Question of Honour* (A. Knopf)

"The book is written in a beautiful, colorful language, full of passion."

—Ryszard Kapuściński (A. Knopf)

"The part Poland had played in the Second World War needs to be told. Główczewski tells it very well indeed."

—Richard M. Watt, *Bitter Glory* (Simon & Shuster)

"Amazing memory for detail . . . wonderful immediacy of storytelling . . ."

—Julia Hartwig (prominent poet)

"The author is driven by a complex of impulses once so characteristic of Polish intelligentsia . . ."

—Anna Przedpelska (translator of English literature)

"The eventful life of his family and his friends reflect the history and life at the time of violent changes . . ."

—Andrzej Roman (journalist, author)

"He who was in New York on 9/11 and who had earlier worked in Arab countries understands the underlying causes of recent events . . ."

—Czesław Bielecki (architect, author)

"The memoir illustrates the depth of author's professional passion, courage, inexhaustible spirit and the sense of humor."

—Bożena Steinborn (art historian, author)

Preface

Recently, coming to the end of writing the reminiscences of my life, I decided to look up books on the life and impressions of other newcomers to USA. I took to visiting big and small New York bookshops, asking for memoirs and recollections of past or present immigrants. To my great surprise, my inquiries were met with astonished glances from shop assistants and their immediate anxious search in the Internet. With thousands of titles flooding the market, in a country where a large percentage of inhabitants had been born abroad, we found maybe a dozen or so memoirs describing the fortunes of new settlers. I was once even given an impromptu explanation of the phenomenon. "Immigrants don't write memoirs, because most probably don't speak English," said a helpful young shop assistant, spreading her arms in a gesture of helplessness. "I am sorry, but this is the truth," she added in Spanish.

By chance, not long ago, I came across a letter I sent in 1969 to my aunt, Professor Maria Bernhard, who was visiting Paris at the time. It spoke of the controversy in our family, of which I learned recently, caused by our decision to settle in America. Such a topic must have been discussed in many other families at the time, in all oppressed countries of Central-Eastern Europe. Yet even now, in the new postcommunist era, debates concerning immigration to USA are taking place among many people. Thus, obviously, immigration and its associated problems and consequences are an ever-pertinent topic, hardly reflected in any kind of literature. That letter alerted me to the fact that, depending on circumstances, one person's decision to immigrate may cause other peoples' resentment and even anger.

The decision to leave one's country of birth and its traditions ingrained in its history is difficult to understand by anyone who did not go through such a heart-wrenching experience. There are as many of these cases as there are emigrants. Had more been recorded, they might have opened a treasure chest of fascinating stories or film scripts, a true Pandora's box of surprises, struggles, tragedies, and happy endings.

On the one hand, this melting pot of diverse ethnic, racial, and cultural characteristics and traditions does sometimes bring phenomenal results, as manifest by present day America. On the other, it may create tensions, misery, and hostility, as seen recently in France or in the United States during the struggle for civil rights. And yet tight controls of movement of people across borders create dissent and frustration that can be either quelled by force or drowned in a tsunami of nationalism and bigotry.

And thus, in order to encourage others to share their experiences, I begin with my own story. As the descendant of Polish landed gentry and of a French officer of Napoleon's army, who had settled in Poland after the retreat from Moscow, I grew up in a strongly patriotic cosmopolitan family. The family's story, as far back as I can trace it to the middle of the eighteenth century, spans the most turbulent years of European history: the collapse of the Polish-Lithuanian Commonwealth under an elected king; the three partitions of Poland between Russia, Prussia, and Austria; three national uprisings against tsarist Russia; domestic unrest of the underprivileged against the upper classes; two revolutions; two world wars; the Holocaust; mass expulsions and compulsory relocations of the population; Communist rule with its oppression; and the struggles to regain freedom.

Emigration to a foreign country was, however, never considered an option. This might have been the consequence of the families' origins: both my own and my wife's families were of mixed stock, native Poles and immigrants happily settled in Poland two centuries ago.

All that was about to change with the outbreak of the Second World War and, for us, it resulted in a sad aftermath. Briefly, in 1945 Poland was betrayed by the Allies and relegated to the Soviet sphere of brutal dominance. Personally, I was lucky to survive various close calls. I often wandered how threatening were these moments and was I in real danger?

As it happened many times in my life, the answer appears in unexpected times and from most unlikely quarters. When I was putting finishing touches to this memoir of mine, a letter, dated February 16, 2007, arrived from the Institute of National Memory in Warsaw to the effect that the State Committee Tracing Crimes Against the Polish Nation, certifies that I am a person who suffered injustice as defined by the law dated December 18, 1998. It also informs me that a list of pertinent secret police files and microfilms is available for my perusal. I will attend to this in due time. In the mean time life goes on . . .

Part One

Unruly Boy, War Exile,
Desert Soldier, Fighter Pilot
1939-1946

1

No Peace at Any Price

It's a beautiful summer morning in 1939. The apartment telephone rings; Mother is calling from her office. She tells us to come over right away; she wants to show us something. On the conference table is a large newly opened cardboard box. It had arrived from the Polish Ministry of Military Affairs a few weeks ago with instructions not to open it until further notice. The notice has just been received. The box contains the original design for a poster showing a Polish soldier in a steel helmet aiming a rifle with affixed bayonet at an outstretched arm with a swastika on its sleeve. Scrawled in red on the poster are the words *Wara!—Hands Off!*

That day is engraved in my memory. It was the tenth anniversary of my father's death in a car accident and the beginning of hard times, for part of which I was personally responsible. Relieved of the paternal presence and a guiding hand, I soon became an unruly brat. Despite of my having additional tuition at home, I was threatened of being expelled from one school after another, creating serious domestic problems. Almost simultaneously with my father's death, the New York stock market crashed, triggering a world crisis. Father's dream of expanding his business had to be shelved. But on the very day of his funeral, Mother unexpectedly made a decision born of necessity: inexperienced as she was, she would run Father's business herself. Her self-imposed transformation from a happy-go-lucky young woman, the toast of Warsaw's society, to the director of a lithographic company employing many people caused bewilderment and disbelief among her family and friends. Supported by her sister Maria, herself an emancipated young woman and a student at Warsaw University, my mother, Ziuta (short for Józefina), eventually succeeded. Following her second marriage, my younger brother, Andrzej, and I were sent to a strict school for problem boys in Chyrów, run by the Jesuits.

Now, Mother orders the poster to be quickly printed. We stood there in her office, staring at the large red letters with some foreboding.

Events have been moving fast. It was only six months before, when as a student at Chyrów, a Jesuit boarding school for problem boys, I learned about Hitler's abrogation of the nonaggression treaty and of his territorial demands on Poland.

The Polish response came in April. The entire Chyrów student body and staff were assembled in the large auditorium, with a radio receiver and loudspeakers on the stage. After a few bars of Chopin's polonaise, the foreign minister Józef Beck addressed the nation from our parliament, the Sejm. Point by point, he rejected Hitler's demands, declaring in no uncertain terms that Poland would never accede to them and, if need be, was prepared to defend itself. He concluded with words still clear in my memory: "In Poland we don't know the concept of peace at any price . . . Only one thing is priceless in the life of states and nations," he continued, "and that thing is honor." When he finished, we all rose to our feet and applauded wildly. We did not realize, however, that we were now standing on the brink of the abyss of war and no longer in command of our fate as we so desperately wished to believe. It is five thirty in the morning, Friday the September 1, 1939. We are woken by the sound of sirens and distant explosions. We run out on the balcony in our pajamas and look at the empty streets. Several men with armbands run by, pointing up. Tiny airplanes glitter against the morning sky. There are more explosions, louder and closer. Soon the airplanes are surrounded by white puffs of smoke from bursting antiaircraft artillery shells. Mother and Witold, our stepfather, stand behind my brother and me. The alarm is called off. I rush out to a kiosk to buy the *Kurier Warszawski*, the morning newspaper, but there isn't a word about war. By breakfast, however, preceded by the rousing tones of the national anthem, President Ignacy Mościcki addresses the nation:

> Citizens of the Republic! Last night, our historical enemy initiated aggressive actions against the Polish State . . . the entire Polish nation, blessed by God in its just and sacred struggle, will shoulder to shoulder march as one with its army into battle and to total victory.

Witold tells us to be calm, to keep to our daily routine, as he proceeds to dress for work with great care. He whistles as he carefully knots his grey striped silk tie. He deftly folds a white handkerchief and puts it in his breast pocket. On his way out, he picks a white carnation from the vase in the hall and puts it in his buttonhole. He smiles and says, "We shan't give in, shall we?" He kisses Mother good-bye, puts on his gray homburg, and leaves. Mother instructs one of the servants to buy sugar, flour, dry pasta, lard, and other foodstuffs. Andrzej is making room for the provisions in our cellar-cum-bomb shelter. Soon we hear the sirens whining again. The radio, which is on all the time, utters baffling words, "Attention, attention, approaching, 17-chocolate" or "Adar-ma 23."

My friends and I had planned to go to the cinema that night to see a picture featuring the sexy French actress seldom absent from our thoughts. But in the wake of events, we revised our plans and went instead to see the film playing at the Palladium, starring Edward G. Robinson and depicting the unmasking of a Nazi organization in the United States and the ferreting out of German spies. Afterward, we argued about its merits: was it only a paranoid fantasy? Or could Americans really ever support Hitler? There were no answers to our questions. On the way home, we passed people digging air-raid trenches in a public square.

On Saturday, September 2, I wrote in my diary, "A morning newspaper carries on its first page our Hands Off poster. Today the citizens of Warsaw suffer eight more air raids. The radio says that Polish forces have destroyed one hundred German tanks and thirty-four planes. The Kraków newspapers still give no news about the war being waged on Polish soil, though Kraków had apparently been bombed. I notice a photograph: a crowd on the beach in Tel-Aviv watching a small ship at sea. The caption reads, "Jewish Achaeans forced to land in Palestine." A Greek freighter flying the Panamanian flag and carrying 850 Jewish refugees from Central Europe, abandoned by its captain and crew, runs aground near Tel Aviv, its decks crowded with Jews, the eternal wanderers. The ship has been roaming the high seas for several weeks unable to obtain permission to disembark its passengers anywhere. Was it a tragic or happy event? Almost surreal story bringing us closer to a distant land on a fateful day.

It was a largely sleepless night. At 11:15 a.m. on September 3, the radio announced that England and France had declared war on Germany. All over the city, jubilant people, even total strangers, joyously hugged one another. Poland had by now fought against Hitler for fifty-four hours without any assistance from the West. We join the crowds in front of Branicki Palace, the seat of the British embassy. In front of the courtyard, protected by a high iron fence, people gather, strewing flowers over the pavement. Loud cheers in honor of His Majesty King George VI, Prime Minister Chamberlain, and Ambassador H. W. Kennard reverberate down the street. I have to hurry home. Witold had promised to take me on my first visit to the suburban residence of Zygmunt Leppert, co-owner of the chemical plant where Witold is managing director. While my stepfather is to discuss urgent business matters, I am eager to meet Mr. Leppert's daughter, Lala, said to be very pretty.

Monday, September 4. Yesterday's exultation, caused by the declaration of war on Nazi Germany by our allies, has given way to sadness. The garrison at Westerplatte in the Gdańsk harbor is holding on under point-blank bombardment by the heavy guns of the battleship *Schleswig-Holstein*, which, a few days before the start of the war, had sailed into harbor, ostensibly on a courtesy visit. The Germans have sunk the American liner *Athenia*, and hundreds drowned. Canada has declared war on Germany; Egypt has broken off diplomatic relations with the Third Reich.

The following evening, Mother summoned us for a talk. Volunteers are needed to help build fortifications. Mother looks at me. "You and Witold must go at once." Andrzej, who is fourteen, insists on coming with us. But the situation radically changes on Witold's return. He tells us in a state of severe agitation that all government personnel have been evacuated. At 9:00 p.m., the radio reports another major Polish defeat followed by an exhortation by the government spokesman to dig defenses. "Take up your spades, gentlemen, take them up now." But soon after, he issues new instructions: all able-bodied men, capable of bearing arms, are to leave Warsaw immediately and go east, where a new army would be formed and a new line of defense on the Bug-Narev rivers be organized.

Mother switched the radio off. Mournful silence reigned for a while. Witold admitted that he had discussed such an eventuality that morning with Zygmunt, whose nephew, André, was keen to leave Warsaw and join the army. Eventually, a decision was reached that my stepfather, his younger brother Mietek, André, and I would leave that night in our car. At the last moment, my paternal uncle Józef joined the group; an architect at the Ministry of Foreign Affairs, he had been ordered to report at the evacuated Ministry somewhere in Lublin, southeast of Warsaw. An argument followed whether it was prudent to leave my mother and my younger brother behind. She refused, however, to abandon the house and the printing works. "You are needed in the army, I am needed here," she declared. "I have to stay; Andrzej will help me. Stop wasting time now. Go! It's already past midnight."

The irresponsible radio broadcast calling on able-bodied men to leave Warsaw had tragic consequences. Crossing the bridge, we move at a snail's pace, part of a desperate mass of humanity: in cars, trucks, horse-drawn carts, on bicycles, and motorcycles, all laden with suitcases, bundles, and bags. A full moon shines on the chaos. It takes us four hours just to get out of the city.

The road is still congested with all kinds of vehicles and crowds of people on foot, all laden down by their possessions. Suddenly, as we near the small town of Grabów, several low-flying planes roar overhead, strafing people on the road and surrounding fields. We drive the car under a tree and dive into a nearby ditch. Shouts of terror, calls for help from all sides fill the air. The bullets miss our car. Right in front of me, maybe ten feet away, there is a girl lying motionless, her white frock slowly turning red. There is no one with her. The attack is over, there are bodies all over the field, and some are moving. I feel, suddenly, that neither the world nor I will ever be the same again.

We arrive in Lublin. Józef is searching for his ministry only to find out that it is now billeted at Klemensów, Count Zamoyski's residence, not far from Zamość, a sixteenth century town built by the count's ancestors. We are lucky to get forty liters of gasoline.

But we are not as lucky in our search for the army recruitment centre. Nobody in Lublin seems to have heard of it. We reach Zamość in the afternoon and park in the market square to stretch our legs. The town, with its magnificent Renaissance architecture, is nearly empty. As we look for somewhere to wash and refresh ourselves, we spot a Jewish youth with long side curls. Wearing a yarmulke and a white apron, holding a white napkin in his hand, he looks just the ticket. He beckons us to a corner building, "This way, gentlemen, please."

A place to rest? Something to eat?

We followed him under a cool arcade with the Polonized sign Fersztendik above leading to a dark tavern with a high vaulted ceiling, furnished with long wooden tables and benches, lit with candles set in bottles encrusted with layers of wax. The counter and shelves behind the counter carry a varied selection of bottles, vodkas, wines, and series of other drinks.

Suddenly, Witold whispers, "Look who is coming, but discreetly. Old Yankiel is alive and staring at us." This is a reference to the character of an old Jewish innkeeper in *Pan Tadeusz*, an early nineteenth-century epic poem by Adam Mickiewicz. A figure with a long white beard, dressed in a black caftan approaches our table, inquiring whether everything is in order. With arms folded on his chest almost in a gesture of supplication, he turns to us. "Would you do me the honor and taste one of my oldest bottles of Tokay?"

He wants to know all the details of what we had seen on the roads. As we recount our experiences and warn him of the imminent crossing of the Vistula by German forces, he shakes his head and smacks his lips in apparent disbelief. But when we ask him whether he is planning to flee to the east, he looks up, thinks for a moment, and says resignedly, "That would change nothing, sir, nothing at all, God's will cannot be changed, everything that has happened and all that awaits us had been preordained a long, long time ago. Please, gentlemen, drink this old wine, so you may remember me when I am long gone."

The man's words haunted us; they seemed to prophesy nothing but doom. Driving southwest, we remained silent for a long time. We passed, at dusk, through an imposing gate leading to an avenue of old linden trees and stopped in front of Count Zamoyski's large, late baroque palace. A footman in a striped waistcoat opened the door of our car and asked us in. Filthy and bedraggled, we entered the hall and waited round a large table, as Józef followed the footman further inside. He quickly returned to announce that Count Zamoyski was out, but one of his relatives insisted that we be the count's guests for the night. The footman helped with our luggage, somebody else took care of the car, another servant led us upstairs, and in no time, washed and refreshed, we were shown again downstairs to a large drawing-room with a fireplace and with hunting trophies displayed on the walls. A number of well-dressed people were gathered there. For the most part, they chatted quietly, save for one young man who, in a high-pitched voice, loudly related his hunting adventures, roaring with laughter at his own witticisms. A tall, elegant man dressed in English tweeds introduced himself as our host and apologized for not being able to offer us longer hospitality. Pointing to the gathering, he said, as if to justify himself, "Family, kin, relatives . . ." In the dining hall with dark paneling, we were more than twenty around the table. Servants with white gloves changed plates and then stood round the walls. The contrast between our journey and this dinner was incredible, but I was too tired to take it all in. I hardly heard the loudmouthed cousin saying, "And imagine, he had the gall to tell me that there is no more gasoline left! Incroyable, n'est-ce pas?"

The following morning, Józef advised us to proceed in the direction of Lwów. He had heard from his ministry colleagues that all army units have been ordered to concentrate in the Lwów region, where a strong defensive stance was to be taken. The supply routes for the western Allies through the Black Sea were to be protected by friendly Romania. The plan was to pin the Germans down to give our allies time to start an offensive in the west. Witold, Mietek, André, and I reached Lwów without major delays. A city, which, like Rome, was built on seven hills, Lwów had been the cradle of a multiethnic Polish culture in the southeast of Poland since the fourteenth century. Inhabited by Ukrainians, Jews, and Armenians, as well as by native Poles, it was a center of commerce, arts, and science. As for accommodation, there was, needless to say, none available, neither in the Georges nor in any other hotel. But everywhere we turned, in cafés and hotel lobbies, Witold ran into acquaintances, rather lost yet strangely calm, not giving in to panic. But when Witold and Mietek went to the garrison headquarters to inquire about recruitment, a major with bloodshot eyes looked at them contemptuously and slurred, "Gentlemen, please, what recruitment center? Just look around you."

As we wandered aimlessly through the streets of Lwów, Witold, silent and distracted, seemed to have come to a decision. He drove us without warning to a large residence not far from a beautiful baroque Jesuit church. No sooner had he rung the doorbell to a second floor flat than we were greeted with squeals of joy coming from the salon; the whole Leppert family were there, having arrived the day before. The apartment belonged to the Schiffmanns. Mr. Schiffmann was Leppert's company agent in Lwów. His wife, a Jewish Hungarian lady, was at first not amused by the prospect of taking in yet more stragglers. All the same, both proved to be exceedingly gracious hosts to our entire Warsaw contingent over the next five days. Lala's older brother Władek and I were sent to the post office to inquire about sending a telegram, but the telegraph service was temporarily suspended. The radio news from Warsaw was shocking: the mayor was calling on all owners of cars and taxis to assist in the removal of corpses from the streets. The German Polish-language radio station appealed to Poles in Warsaw to cease their "pointless resistance." Great sadness and anxiety overcame us as we pondered the fate of our families.

By September 13, Lwów was fully under siege. Dorniers and Heinkels rained bombs upon the city, already enduring constant tank gunfire. Witold and Zygmunt came to the conclusion that if we stayed any longer in Lwów, the likelihood of our being able to get out of the city would grow slimmer by the hour. A rapidly growing sense of impending doom was in the air. At three o'clock in the morning, we all bid farewell to the Schiffmanns, who chose to stay put; and the eight of us, in two cars, made a dash for the Romanian border. We got used to the sound of bombs exploding in the distance. Lala Leppert and I flirted, as teenagers will; surreptitiously, we held hands, fascinated by one another. That the grown-ups were oblivious of these goings-on provided further satisfaction. Later that day, and only forty miles from the Romanian border, we stopped in a village and were allotted quarters in peasant huts, but Witold decided to look for better accommodation so that eventually we stayed in a manor house owned by the Beigerts, a German family long settled in Poland and willing to claim us as relatives should the Nazis catch up with us.

On Sunday, September 17, we were still undecided whether to proceed further or whether to tarry a bit longer, and might have continued to dither, had it not been for the news brought by Herr

Beigert that Soviet forces had been seen in a nearby village! The news shocked us to the bone, but it also decided our fate. Approaching the bridge on the river Dniester, we had a stroke of luck: we caught up with a Polish military convoy of trucks and staff cars all loaded with equipment and personnel including a large number of airmen in their blue uniforms. Having crossed the river, we drove along its bank; and as we emerged from the forest, the town of Horodenka appeared before us. However, the town was under bombardment; and we saw parts of it engulfed in flames. We waited near a small bridge until German airmen finished their grim task. We then managed to cross the town without any mishaps and, having rejoined the column of airmen, headed for the frontier post. On the Romanian side, the border guards seemed utterly bewildered by the appearance of the convoy. They obviously had no idea what to do, so they refused to lift the barrier and disappeared, seeking orders. As we waited, a man, clearly on the run, dressed in a mix of civilian clothes and army uniform, drove up on a motorcycle from the Polish side. Apparently, within minutes of our passing Horodenka, Soviet Army units drove into the market square and announced the liberation of Western Ukraine from the oppression of Polish landowners and bourgeoisie. They declared that, jointly with the German army, they had wiped Poland—that monstrous bastard spawned by the Treaty of Versailles—off the map. The motorcyclist had not listened any longer. After some delay, the barrier was raised; and we crossed into Romania. "My god, we are the refugees," whispered Witold, resting his forehead on the steering wheel. A storm was brewing and it began to rain.

2

The Odyssey Begins

At daybreak of September 17, 1939, the Red Army, nearly one million strong, crossed the entire Soviet-Polish border. It soon penetrated deep into Eastern Poland from Lithuania in the north to Romania in the south, joining hands with advancing German Forces. Some time before that, the Polish High Command had ordered its troops to cross the border to Romania where the new resistance against Nazi aggression would now be based. Rendered impotent by the Luftwaffe, the Polish Air Force flew whatever it could muster to Cernauti, in northern Romania. The aircrews were told that they would find there new warplanes provided by England and France, which would allow them to go on fighting. When the airmen arrived, however, the situation was very different from the one they had expected.

Germans and their Soviet allies meet in Poland

Ignorant of these developments, we too, part of the horde of exiles, and having filled the tanks with gasoline and holding bags of grapes, took off for Bucharest.

The drive was slow and torturous, the roads all muddy after the heavy rain. We were motivated, it seems, by an unconscious will to survive the awfulness of it all. To pass the time and, no doubt, as a means of escape, I began obsessively to sketch Romanian soldiers. I was fascinated by the disparity in appearance between the elegant officers and cavalrymen, clearly wearing mascara and makeup, and the unwashed, bedraggled common soldiery sporting steel helmets from another military era in addition to assorted civilian caps and hats.

Our odyssey kept presenting us with surreal contradictions. We reached Falticeni, a small town with a largely Jewish commercial quarter, which made a reasonably good impression on us. Eventually, accosted by a rather meddlesome and insistent guide, we were taken to a big, kitschy villa set in a large garden and owned by a nouveau riche Jewish couple named Haras. The walls in the house were covered with paintings in elaborately carved, gilded frames displaying a variety of female nudes, mostly bathing nymphs. Improbably, the housekeeper was a large Negro woman, dressed in a long blue skirt and white apron with a white kerchief

tied round her head. How this look-alike Mamie of the *Gone with the Wind* film fame, found herself in a Jewish household in a provincial Romanian town, remains a mystery to this day.

A week later, after a whole day of queuing, and with the help of a fairly modest bribe, we obtained the required permit to proceed. We left straightaway, passing through Ploesti, the centre of the Rumanian oil industry, and arrived in the capital filthy and jittery about our next move. A few days before, a member of the Iron Guard, a Fascist political party, had assassinated Romania's Prime Minister, Armand Calinescu. So now, gendarmes in white caps and gloves were gallantly directing the traffic of mourners, among whom we were willy-nilly counted.

The Polish consulate in Bucharest was virtually under siege: a multitude of Polish exiles on the verge of rioting crowded the place, clamoring for passports. Zygmunt and Witold decided to apply for French visas as well. Returning to Poland in the wake of the Soviet invasion and the defeat of the army seemed out of the question, and we all had French relatives to whom, we thought, we could appeal for help.

All kinds of gossip and rumor about what was happening in Poland were circulating among the refugees. We were now gripped by a pervasive uncertainty and the sheer horror of the past two weeks finally began to get through our previous emotional anesthesia.

A Romanian police officer, Augustus Schmidt, whom we had befriended, talked us into going west to Timişoara, where he would introduce us to his cousin, Alexander Rode, the man in charge of the traffic department there, who might be able to grease some wheels to our advantage. Witold generously gave Schmidt two hundred lei for his troubles, but the latter was not amused. "What I'm proposing to do for you is worth far more," he protested. To maintain good relations, Witold acceded to his demand.

In Timişoara, an industrial town not far from the Hungarian and Yugoslav borders, we seemed at first to have done nothing save frantically write letters and postcards to every soul whose whereabouts we had known at the beginning of the war. With every passing day, we were getting more and more desperate for news of our families; we kept going to the consular offices of neutral countries in an effort to get them to place our missives in diplomatic pouches. We sent telegrams, reply prepaid. But no replies were coming from Poland; the silence was unnerving. So now, we started writing to France as well.

At last, we got a letter from Antek Bernhard, my godfather, who as a French citizen had obtained a job in Paris four years before. He wrote that he was now in the French army and that his apartment was at our disposal. We momentarily saw light at the end of at least one tunnel. In the meantime, the French visas had also arrived at the consulate. At the beginning of November, we learned that our permit for sojourn in Timişoara was about to expire. Being totally at the mercy of the bloated Romanian bureaucracy, we just had to keep our petty tormentors sweet and in clover. Various clerks unashamedly demanded ever more gratuities to expedite "the process." As we labored to extend our stay in Timişoara, Romanian troops were already marching through its streets. Its Hungarian residents, who called the city Temeshvar, disdainfully turned their backs on the passing soldiers. Our friendly acquaintances advised us that a grave political drama was in the offing and that it might be advisable for us to move on. But where to was the conundrum. Zygmunt Leppert considered France to be the only possible destination for his family. As a reserve captain of the horse artillery from the Polish-Bolshevik war of 1918-1920, he was anxious to reenlist. He even left Warsaw with his uniform, breeches, high boots, and a saber packed in a bag, prepared for all eventualities. Now, his sister-in-law was pulling strings at the Quai d'Orsay, the French foreign office, to expedite our visas. These at last arrived along with foreign currency permits. The Lepperts and Mietek were now free to start on the next lap to France, but Witold decided not to venture any further afield. He, André, and I would head for Bucharest intent on returning to Poland as soon as it became possible.

To make the farewells less painful, on one of the last nights, Zygmunt invited us all to a nightclub. "Who knows what is in store for us," he said. "Let's enjoy ourselves while we can." He suggested the Five Violettas show in the Victoria Hotel. But would it be suitable for "the kids," i.e., Władek, Lala, and me? After all, this was a real topless nightclub show. To be on the safe side, two male grown-ups were delegated to first explore the situation on their own. In the morning, we showered them with questions. Mietek just shrugged his shoulders and with a blasé expression said, "Well, I see no problem, just a lot of bare breasts." We went there after dinner.

In Bucharest, we found ourselves again in a whirligig of indecision. Our letters to Warsaw had gone unanswered and, in so far as we were concerned, no news was decidedly bad news. The expiry dates of our French visas and foreign currency permits were rapidly approaching. We kept sending letters and postcards, some on Red Cross forms. We visited American, Swedish, and Swiss consulates asking them to pass information through their diplomatic channels. All in vain. Eventually, we decided that, in the absence of news, we would leave for France on the last possible day, on December 18. Then, suddenly, we received a letter from the Lepperts; they got to France without difficulty. And we got a cable from our man in Timişoara that some mail had arrived there for us from Warsaw, and he forwarded it by express post to our hotel in Bucharest. That afternoon, we were on tenterhooks. No sooner had the receptionist called us than we dashed to the foyer, stumbling over each other. One envelope contained five postcards addressed to Witold and me, to André, and to Major Skarżyński, a distinguished Polish Air Force officer and family friend whom we met on the border crossing and again in Bucharest. Relatives in Warsaw advised us to hurry home; those in France cautioned us not to believe a word of such messages. The exhortations to return, they said, were for the benefit of German censors who had dutifully stamped every envelope to leave us in no doubt of their vigilance. But Mother enclosed in one letter an opłatek—the thin white wafer traditionally shared by all at the beginning of the Christmas Eve dinner. We took it to be a clear message from her: stay in Romania, at least through Christmas.

Our friend, Major Skarżyński, has been working all along for the Polish government in exile in Paris overseeing the transfer of Polish airmen, aircrew, and technical personnel to France and England. Already, in the autumn of 1939, the Polish government had sought the support of the Polish diaspora in their fight against Nazi Germany. By land, across Yugoslavia and Italy, by sea, through Casablanca and Algiers, thousands of fighting men were being moved to southern France.

The expiry date of our French visas came and went. We applied for and received permission to extend our residence in Romania for another year. We had to organize our life. With money running out, we moved in January from the hotel to a small, inexpensive, vermin-infested boarding house where Witold, André, and I shared one room and a common lavatory and bath at the end of an unheated corridor serving all the tenants. In the severe winter of 1940, the cheap Romanian building offered no protection.

At the same time, Helena Barysz, the energetic and devoted teacher of classics, organized a school for the displaced Polish children. Thus, after a three-month hiatus, I returned to school. The Polish Cultural Center in Bucharest had a well-stocked library; and there, I started to learn English and German. The older generation kept arguing about the causes of our calamitous defeat in September 1939 and the political situation in the West.

About this time, shocking news started arriving from France reflecting the despair of our fellow countrymen who had managed to reach that country. Their arrival in France provoked local animosity and attempts to form a new Polish army there were met with disdain. We found it difficult to give credence to these reports. Those people went there to fight the war—not as unwanted immigrants. My other uncle, Felix, who had enlisted in the French army at the beginning of the war, wrote that French troops were demoralized and none of them wanted to risk their life "for Danzig." The general mood was grim. In addition, rumors had it that it was becoming increasingly difficult to transport thousands of new Polish volunteers there. All the same, Witold, André, and I did volunteer; after all, this had been our goal upon leaving Warsaw four months earlier. But after a perfunctory examination in a Polish army recruitment center in Bucharest, I was rejected as a minor. As the guardian of a minor and in poor health at the time, Witold fared no better. Only André managed to enlist. And so one frosty morning, Witold and I saw him off at the railway station. He was one of a score or so volunteers sitting together in a coach in stunned silence. Most of the young men, obviously soldiers, though wearing all kinds of civilian clothes, must have escaped from Romanian internment camps while the authorities looked the other way. They pretended not to know one another while their destination was perfectly obvious.

Perhaps to escape from all the problems, I became wholeheartedly involved in my schoolwork. The Polish school in Bucharest, as well as some other educational establishments for refugees in Romania and Hungary, were subsidized by the Polish government in exile, helped by the U.S. Fund for Polish Refugees. From this point of view, we were lucky. But the ugliness of the times caught up with us one sunny spring afternoon.

Four of us students, including two girls, Irka Zucker and Roma Gold, were walking along the Bratianu Boulevard. Suddenly, we were confronted by some thugs of the "Garda de Fier," the Iron Guard. Their menacing gangs could appear anywhere out of the blue. Following the Fascist coup of November 1940, when Romania joined the Berlin-Rome axis, these gangs would virtually rule the streets. The hoodlums in their paramilitary attire of black trousers, bright green shirts, and black ties surrounded our small group, started pushing us around, and reviling us for associating with Jewish girls. They were soon joined by some seemingly hostile onlookers. I do not quite remember how it started, but without thinking, automatically and with all my strength, I punched one of the louts on the jaw. As he fell backward into the crowd, my buddy tackled another one. After a brief scuffle, the gang took refuge among the spectators while we quietly walked away through the parting crowd, hand in hand with the girls.

In June, Soviet troops annexed the eastern provinces of Romania: Bessarabia, and northern Bukovina. We discussed these events at school. In the wake of the Red Army's invasion of Poland, the Baltic

States, and Finland; the Soviet Union was no less to be feared than Nazi Germany and Imperial Japan. In the meantime, Romanian refugees were streaming into Bucharest from the Soviet-occupied lands, their horrifying stories nearly identical to those of the Polish refugees still occasionally arriving from the Soviet-occupied parts of Poland.

Meetings were organized to discuss the political situation. The principal organizer and soul of these functions, which Witold attended, was Piotr Wysocki, an army lieutenant whom I remembered from Warsaw, where he wore only civilian clothes. He was a handsome stocky man, with dark hair. Lively and good-humored man of sharp wit whom I greatly admired. Various observations led me to believe that Witold too was involved, as were also some of our dining companions. I should have noticed earlier that something have changed in our daily life. In the spring we moved to a modern apartment building with American elevators and a dark blue Mercury sedan in the garage. Witold would disappear for several days not divulging any details. There were, it appears, some ulterior motives behind our extended stay and life style in Romania, of which I had not been aware.

(It was only after the war that my suspicions were confirmed by Witold and Piotr's brother in law, who served in the same capacity in the US Army; Piotr was indeed working for the Second Bureau of the Polish High Command, i.e., the army intelligence, with vast network in occupied Europe).

Now that France had surrendered, I was anxious as to the fate of the Lepperts. Then Italy entered the fray. Would Poland ever regain her independence? The mood among Polish exiles in Bucharest and the Francophile Romanians was bleak.

Our hospitable Romania was herself on the brink of catastrophe, through more than one source. One night in October, I was alone and asleep in our apartment when I was suddenly thrown out of bed by an unknown force and the contents of my bookshelf tumbled after me. This was the first of several earthquakes that would rock Romania that year. Buildings crumbled; a twenty-floor tower close to our apartment block was now an ugly heap of rubble. A large hotel caved in like a house of cards; among the victims were apparently many of its resident German Army officers. Another elegant hotel, Athenée Palace, cracked vertically in half. It would appear that after all the territorial losses, Romania now attracted the attention of mother nature, which conspired to bring about the downfall of the country. German soldiers in their grey-green uniforms have already been strutting through the streets of Bucharest for some time, relaxed, crowding the pavements, talking loudly, and laughing raucously. The cinemas were now showing mostly German films, though we were lucky enough to catch Judy Garland in *The Wizard of Oz*.

Suddenly, one evening, we had a visit from the Gestapo. This happened a few weeks after Witold had moved us swiftly and surreptitiously from our apartment to a small, obscure hotel. In our school, there had been some quiet good-byes but no discussions. Menace and foreboding hung in the air. My consolation was Liliana, the pretty daughter of the porter/receptionist, with whom I flirted with in Romanian. One evening in November, she knocked on the door of our room. Glancing nervously over her shoulder, she whispered that there were some gendarmes coming up the stairs, and ran out of the room. Soon after, three men came through our door, an Iron Guardsman—with the notorious green shirt under his overcoat—and two men in civilian clothes, one a Romanian interpreter, the other a German, and as we found out, an officer of the Gestapo. Witold was fluent in German and spoke directly to the Gestapo man. The German was in an inquisitive mood. Witold must have impressed him, as soon after, they seemed to be exchanging pleasantries. Nonetheless, the German left us in no doubt that he expected us to appear at a given address the following day for further questioning. As the trio were leaving the room, the German turned round and casually suggested that it might be advisable for either of us not to leave the hotel until the appointed meeting.

No sooner had they stomped down the stairs than Witold went to the telephone, dialed a number, muttered a few words, and quickly put the receiver down. He sent me downstairs to fetch the receptionist, who must have been in the know, as he was already on his way up. Witold asked him to call a taxi and handed him a parcel, but the receptionist mentioned that there might be a problem, as the Iron Guard were still downstairs, presumably left behind to keep an eye on us. After some ten minutes, the phone rang; the porter was calling to say that a taxi was waiting for us at the service entrance round the corner and explaining how to get there from the second floor, bypassing the main hall. We jumped in the cab; and as we turned the corner, I caught a glimpse of Liliana walking with the Iron Guard the other way, clearly flirting with him to distract his attention.

We spent the night at the Glinickis, fellow Polish refugees. No one slept, not just for the lack of room. Witold and Zbigniew Glinicki kept whispering and making phone calls. At six o'clock in the morning, we were already at the railway station where a strange old man in a big black fur hat gave us an envelope containing tickets. We pushed our way into a third-class carriage, already jam-packed with peasants laden down with sacks of maize, baskets of vegetables, with squawking chickens under their arms. Wanda Glinicka's father, a former cavalry colonel of WWI, was also in our party. I could not believe my eyes. This smart military man, always straight as a ramrod, his hat at a rakish angle over his silver hair, his moustache perfectly groomed, appeared to be in disguise now. He was wearing a black beret pulled down over his ears; he was stooping, drawing his head into the upturned collar of his overcoat. His moustache was drooping right down to his mouth. Witold winked at me, smiled, and whispered, "He's being conspiratorial; it reminds him of the thrills of the old days." Anyway, we did not look any better with our thick woolen caps, long scarves wrapped round and round our necks, hands in pockets. To complete our disguise, we tied our suitcases and bags with lengths of string, thus adding to their already battered appearance. The greatest surprise, however, awaited me as the train pulled out and Witold, at last, told me where we were heading—it was to the port city of Constanța, from where we would attempt to sail for Istanbul.

The large customs hall of Constanța's maritime terminal was crammed with shabby looking passengers, our look-alikes.

Romanian customs officers scrupulously went through every piece of luggage, themselves carefully watched by Iron Guardsmen wandering amidst the tables piled with the contents of trunks, suitcases, and bundles. Our possessions dutifully turned upside down, we were at last waved aboard the brand-new and sparkling white MS *Transylvania*.

It was almost as if we found ourselves in another world. In our two-berth cabin with clean sheets, a plate of fresh fruits, and a bottle of mineral water on the table, we fell on our beds in profound relief. Witold considered it prudent to stay in the cabin until the ship left port, and locked the door. Without intending to, I must have fallen asleep and was startled out of a nightmare by the loud blasts of the ship's horn as the *Transylvania* was pulling away from the dock. As we were later going to the dining room, Witold put his arm round my shoulders. "You have no idea," he said, "how hairy our escape was; we just have God to thank for slipping through their fingers." After dinner, we strolled on the upper deck, happy to keep bumping into old acquaintances. We watched the glorious sunset on starboard, the sea a shimmering expanse of orange and gold. The coastline quickly disappeared; we were sailing due south.

By sunrise, we reached the Bosphorus. I don't know who had organized our journey, but we seemed to be guided by an invisible hand. In Istanbul, we went by ferry to the other side of the strait and stayed for two weeks in a charming pension with stunning views of the city. We sometimes pondered how serendipitous our lives as refugees have been since we had left home. Here, we were hoping merely to survive, yet finding occasion to take rowboat excursions to the coves of the Marmara Sea, to tour old Constantinople, and visit Ottoman palaces. In this two-week interval, we neither dwelled on the past nor anticipated the future.

It was said that we were now waiting for a further voyage to Cyprus. The morning of our departure came, and Witold and I, together with other refugees, boarded a train on the Asiatic side of the Bosphorus. The initial phase of the journey across central Turkey took over twenty-four hours so that in the early afternoon of the following day, the train left the snowy plateau, crossed the Taurus Mountains, and arrived in Mersin, a small sunny, Oriental-looking port, beautifully situated between the Mediterranean coast and hills covered with citrus groves.

There we joined a few hundred more Polish refugees awaiting transport to Cyprus, where apparently the British had prepared special camps for us. Among our acquaintances there was Mme Grabowska, a stunning platinum blonde woman I had come across during one of our meetings in Bucharest. She was with her husband, a handsome man who had, just before the outbreak of the war, returned from the World's Fair in New York. I was, for the first time, learning about America from him while secretly flirting with Madame. The husband was very critical of President Roosevelt for not joining the war. "What is America waiting for?" he kept saying. "Have they given up on Europe? There are many Nazi sympathizers there; there is also open anti-Semitism. And their brutal treatment of Negroes is appalling. Do you know that they publicly torture and hang, and even burn alive minor offenders or even innocent people just because their skin is not white? Lynching, they call it. So there you are, you can draw your own conclusions."

I listened to these stories with an open mouth. Somehow, they did not fit my image of America as seen through my favorite films. Even all the cowboys and gangsters seemed inoffensive compared with these outrages. It seemed that it was much worse than our own excesses of arrogant radical nationalist gangs. Still, because of the closeness of the platinum blonde beauty, the two-week wait in Mersin felt to me like a vacation. For others, the prospect of being soon locked up in a camp in Cyprus was not very inviting, but it did not seem that we had any choice. Once again, it was up to the invisible hand.

At the beginning of December, a freighter dropped anchor in the harbor. Lively speculation as to its identity and mission continued until a barge started ferrying our desperate crowd group by group to the ship. It was only on nearing the vessel that we discovered that it was flying the Polish flag and that it was the SS *Warszawa* of the Polish merchant marine; it had been sailing the waters of the Eastern Mediterranean when the war broke out.

Needless to say, the ship was ill-equipped for the task in hand, her amenities being hardly suited for this mass of humanity, but no one was about to complain. As we gathered on the deck of the *Warszawa*, a member of the crew recalled the heart-rending efforts of Jewish refugees attempting to reach safe haven in Palestine before the war in spite of the British blockade. It seemed to me that I had heard that story some time ago, but could not remember when.

The following morning, at dawn, to our momentary bewilderment, we dropped anchor not in Cyprus but in Haifa; but by now, we had become used to the twists and turns of fate. As the ship made her way through the emerald waters into the harbor, its portside slowly turning toward the shore, we all ran toward the rail, trying to catch a first glimpse of the whitewashed town and the green hills beyond.

As we descended the gangway, British military policemen, with white belts and the letters *MP* on their armbands, directed us to a building where at the entrance, a large group of civilians, Jewish immigrants from Poland, greeted us in Polish with loud cheers. I was struck by the informality of the place. Some of the local people greeted us with a smile as long-lost friends, while others wandered anxiously amongst us, hoping that perhaps someone here came from their town or village and might have news of their relatives. They carried faded old photographs and bits of paper with the names of their kin left behind in Poland, hungry for any scrap of news yet fearing to learn the worst. An old man with a white beard, wearing a black hat and collarless shirt went up to Witold. He was selling knickknacks from a box, which he carried in his trembling hands.

"I emigrated here from Białystok five years ago," he said. "I was a history teacher then; here I am too old, and there is no work for me. Let's hope life will be kinder to you." So that might be the fate of exiles, I thought. How sad.

By then, we knew that in Palestine we would find the Polish Army recruiting unit. Finally, after fourteen months, we have arrived at our destination.

Even before the Nazis had invaded France, the French decided to strengthen their Middle Eastern command in order to protect the oil fields from a possible German attack. The few and under strength French battalions under General Weygand's command included units of the Foreign Legion, many Poles among them. Because the French army was apparently having difficulty absorbing the ever-increasing number of Polish volunteers reaching France, General Sikorski, head of the Polish government in exile, sought to channel some of his troops to Syria, a French mandate at the time.

The command of the newly formed brigade was entrusted to Col. Stanisław Kopański, familiar with the French army organization from the time of his studies at the Paris Military Academy. The brigade was to be based in the barracks of the French Foreign Legion in Homs, Syria. Soon the ranks of the Polish Independent Carpathian Brigade had swelled to nearly four thousand men and officers. Their only motivation was to be ready to fight the Germans, and it was their extraordinary loyalty and discipline that enabled the Brigade to put up with the vagaries of the French bureaucracy. Homs, a small town with its history reaching back to antiquity, was situated on a desert plateau renowned for its unbearable heat and frequent sandstorms. The Poles were issued with heavy woolen uniforms and fed mostly fried rice, enriched now and then with frozen, fatty mutton dating back, as proved by the stamps on the carcasses, to as early as 1917. Their water was brackish, hardly fit for drinking, their daily ration of wine (half-liter a man) vinegary. The arms and vehicles promised by the French were slow in coming and, when they finally arrived, were antiquated, relics of the World War I issue.

In the meantime, the situation on the Western Front was changing dramatically. The French Army was, by then, utterly demoralized and infamously melting away. After France surrendered to Germany on June 19,1940, thus ending the "phony war," the newly appointed commander of the Army of the Levant, General Eugene Mittelhausser, issued a proclamation ending the armed struggle against Germany. He requested Colonel Kopański to disarm and disband the brigade. When the colonel refused, Mittelhausser placed him under house arrest. In an ensuing showdown, the Pole warned the Frenchman that the brigade would take up arms, and that the general would thus be responsible for the first ever armed conflict between the French and the Polish troops. Thus warned, Mittelhausser grudgingly conceded. Colonel de la Villéon wrote later, "I witnessed the acute conflict between the two men, of whom only one acted as befitted an officer. Regrettably it was not the French general."

For three days, starting on June 26, 1940, with British approval, the brigade wended its way with its arms and vehicles from Homs across the Golan Heights to Palestine, then a British protectorate, its ranks now swelled by Poles of the French Foreign Legion, whom the French labeled as deserters and deprived of all emoluments due for previous service. Some French officers saluted the Poles as they were leaving.

The British High Command regarded the arrival of the Polish troops as a godsend. The British forces in the Levant were inadequate. All that General Wavell had under his command were roughly eighty thousand troops dispersed throughout Palestine, Egypt, the Sudan, and even Somalia and Kenya. And it was only after Italy declared war on Britain in June 1940, threatening the Suez Canal, one of the vital arteries of the British Empire, that the gravity of the situation became obvious.

In Haifa, Witold managed to get in touch with Piotr Wysocki, who was now about to be transferred from Palestine to Egypt. Between them, they decided to settle their dependants, Piotr's young wife, Zosia, and myself in nearby Tel-Aviv. Witold was conditionally accepted into the army, but I had to promise him to complete my high school education before joining up.

We moved to a rented apartment at 5 Raines Street, a pleasant street of low-rise buildings. Long balconies ran the length of the exterior walls. Front yards were ablaze with rich Mediterranean flora. Chameleons and praying mantises lived in our garden.

At the time, the population of Tel-Aviv was mostly composed of Jewish immigrants from Poland. There were even Polish signs on the storefronts, and you could get around with Polish language only. The town was also a refuge for Polish prewar ministers and dignitaries. At long last Witold and I were able to register as army volunteers. Though in the past, Witold had been rejected as physically unfit for military service, he was now accepted but given category D, i.e., "Temporarily fit for military service, pending reassessment." He was posted to an auxiliary unit of the brigade at the base in El Latrun in the Judean hills.

I was granted deferred enlistment, pending graduation from high school later in the year. As it happened, this was the same school I had attended in Bucharest, now miraculously transplanted to Tel-Aviv with the same headmistress and many of the same teachers and students. Witold also made sure that I received a grant for my living expenses from the Polish Refugee Fund to supplement the allowance he assigned to me from the pittance he would receive as a private in the Polish army.

Tel Aviv bus- student ID

Now I was more than happy. At last, I had been taken seriously by the military authorities; and I was now secure in my belief that I could face the future, whatever it had in store for me. Perhaps this was an unconscious escape from the stark reality of my situation. After all, I was hopelessly cut off from my family, my home. I did not even know whether they were alive or dead. My stepfather, the man whom I had regarded as my role model and anchor, was no longer there for me to depend on; I was now virtually on my own. In a nutshell, I found myself at the age of eighteen independent, though not quite grown-up, yet resolute, subject to forces I could not control and often not understand, refusing to dwell on the chaos of uncertainties facing me. The experience gleaned in the year and a half of exile has taught me that nothing, either good or ill, could be taken for granted, that nothing was ever assured. Cheerful optimism was just as justifiable as glum pessimism. One simply had to ensure one's survival through enduring stoicism. I had made peace, or so I thought, with my lot in life.

In my imagination, I was already shedding my identity as a useless young civilian and entering maturity as a warrior constantly in demand. For the time being, however, I had to expand my excess energy on the Tel-Aviv beach. On the first day, in a sudden flash of memory, I recognized the scene. About a hundred yards from the shore were the rusty wrecks of the two small, single-funneled freighters that had transported Jewish refugees and had been abandoned by their crews only to drift in shallow waters. As victims of shipwreck, the passengers had to be accepted by the authorities in spite of British restrictions on immigration to Palestine. But of course, these were the very ships that the Polish sailor had talked about and that I had seen on the photograph in the Kraków newspaper a day after Hitler had invaded Poland. I remembered now how the paper had referred to the desperate asylum seekers as "Jewish Achaeans" and "eternal wanderers." My younger schoolmate, Renata Zenwirt, a refugee from Kraków, and I swam out to have a look at the wrecks and dived into the sunken ship's interior. Later, when I told my mates what I

knew about the history of the ship, no one showed any particular interest.

At the time, I was rather politically unsophisticated; but I began to understand that the politics of my school, of its administrators, teachers, and students were largely liberal. So it was, that one May evening, the school commemorated the sixth anniversary of Marshal Piłsudski's death. Poems were recited and marching songs of the First World War's Legions were sung. I was chosen to read an abridged story of the marshal's life written by Janusz Jędrzejewicz, our math teacher and the minister of education in the early 1930s during the marshal's lifetime. Many Polish Jews, now residents of Tel-Aviv, joined in the celebration. They had held the marshal in great esteem as a champion of freedom, who brought Poland's independence in 1918 and who preached self-determination for ethnic minorities in Poland and sought their representation in the Parliament.

About that time Piotr Wysocki came from Egypt. There would be nothing special about this visit except for my first personal talk I had with him over a glass of orange juice. He asked if I ware aware of the so called facts of life. I blushed. He suggested, that now, when I was about to go to war, some information about the lurking dangers might be in order. He wanted to introduce me to a nice lady who could be my teacher. I politely declined the offer. He looked hard into my ayes and whispered: "well . . . I thought you would agree . . . never mind. There is something else that I want you to know. Not long ago a strange incident occurred, which may have repercussions for the conduct of the war. Rudolf Hess, high Nazi official and deputy to Adolf Hitler, flew his plane to Scotland. This was no accident. It looks that this was prearranged by some people who want to change the Allied strategy in this war. Be alert, because the change may not be too bad for our cause." For some time I wandered why was he telling me this story? This was a little above my head, and I soon became busy with my own life which was about to turn a new corner. After several anxious weeks, I was called up on July 8, 1941, and given the paybook and my personal army number. I left my civilian clothes at the Cyprus refugee aid collection point and my sketchbooks with our fellow fugee Wanda Glinicka. (Unexpectedly, they reached me in 1986 via mail from Portugal, posted by Wanda's sister. She explained in her letter that Wanda, on her deathbed in Durban, South Africa, obliged her to find me and return the drawings). My female schoolmates bade me a jolly farewell as if I were going on a special vacation, while the younger boys were green with envy as they were still tied to their school desks, not yet ready to join the forces. Nobody seemed to remember that one was actually going to war with all its inherent hardships and dangers. The future seemed to be full of promise and excitement. I was thus preparing to go off to war with little understanding of the complexity and barbarism of the world which I was about to enter.

Jerusalem (author's sketch)

3

The Homeless Army

In mid-July 1941, I found myself in the company of other raw recruits at the back of an army truck speeding along the Haifa highway. A vintage Citroën, it was a relic of the equipment received by the brigade the previous year in Syria, which its CO refused to return to the French. I was not sure whether my mates, most of them volunteers from among the Polish-Jewish population of Palestine, were recent newcomers to the country like myself or whether their parents had been prewar immigrants. Before long, we were all clambering out of the truck at Kahyat Beach, south of Haifa, where our platoon would undergo the rigors of basic training.

Khayat Beach
(frontal view: A. Schneider)

My Jewish buddies explained to me the idea of a "national home for Jews" and their hopes for its establishment in Palestine. I learned that there was stiff opposition to this intended immigration of thousands of new residents by the ancestral residents of these areas. There were many fragmented Arab religious and tribal groups who vied for power while preparing to free the country from the British, at the same time collaborating with them to stop the influx of European Jews fleeing the Nazis. A large conflict was in the making.

While we felt that we were only playing soldiers, the threat of a German landing in the area was quite real. Europe had already succumbed to the Nazi might; Hitler's army had just launched a devastating offensive against the Soviet Union while, in North Africa, General Rommel's army was rapidly advancing across Libya toward Egypt. As part of our training, we went on night patrols along the sand dunes and beaches of the Mediterranean Sea, sometimes accompanied by the highly experienced and savvy former soldiers of the French Foreign Legion briefly posted at the Kahyat Beach camp. There was nothing they did not know about surviving in the desert, having all served in Morocco and Algeria. One grizzled sergeant had even known service in Indochina. Every one of them was a superb guide; and to us, impressionable as we were, they presented the quintessential model of martial valor. They would soon be joining the main force of the brigade at Mersa Matruh in Egypt.

In mid-August, on short notice, our platoon was entrained and sent to Alexandria for yet more training. We traversed the hot northern Sinai, arriving at the Suez Canal early in the afternoon. Aboard a large ferry, we crossed the smooth waters of the canal and boarded another train, which took us through the green belt linking the Canal Zone to the Nile Delta. We traveled through the beautiful, peaceful Egyptian countryside with its lush green vegetation, its groves of date palms, its mud-colored huts, and the unhurried beasts of burden: camels, donkeys, and *gamousas* or water buffaloes. The deep blue of the cloudless sky almost imperceptibly changed to yellow then to orange, and the palm trees first faded to brown, darkening to black against the nearly mystical radiance of the sunset. The magic of that train ride would stay with me for the rest of my life.

It was dark when we disembarked in Benha, while the train went on its way to Cairo. We had to wait for our connection to Alexandria, which was not scheduled to arrive until early morning. Across the station square, there was a NAAFI canteen crowded with Australian, South African, and Polish soldiers. The Poles were huddled in one corner; and we joined them, eager to listen to their stories. Ordered urgently to return to their units west of Alexandria, they assumed that something serious was afoot and were looking forward to at last a significant engagement with the enemy.

At dawn, we reached Alexandria, where a bus was to take us eastward on a short drive along the Corniche, a waterfront boulevard, to a sandy camp of many tents, surrounded by large cactus hedges and tall date palms. We were in Sidi Bishr, an auxiliary command camp of the brigade. A few days after our arrival, we heard on the camp radio that between August 18 and 27, the brigade had been ferried by the British navy to the stronghold of Tobruk, now under siege.

There were two interpretations of the siege of Tobruk, the protracted and brutal struggle between the Axis and the Allied powers for hegemony in North Africa. The German and Italian High Command considered the elaborate defensive measures taken by the British and their allies to be a costly nonsense, and they mocked the Allied troops for being "self-maintained prisoners of war." For their part, the British believed that by tying down large numbers of enemy troops, Tobruk was crucial to their strategy of defending the Suez Canal. Eventually, it proved to be a turning point in the history of the Second World War. The war rolled back and forth along the north coast of Africa; and Tobruk became a symbol of the gigantic struggle, as here, for the first time, the Allies stood up to the invader.

A Libyan port with a single dock on a deep, narrow bay, Tobruk was mainly an expanse of craggy desert, gently inclined toward the sea, and cut by a number of deep ravines providing natural anti-tank defenses.

In April 1941, General Rommel had launched a surprise attack on the British forces in Libya. But Rommel's frontal assault on Tobruk failed.

In June, two months into the siege, the Australian government began to put pressure on the British to withdraw the exhausted

Australian troops from Tobruk. In late July, London approved the withdrawal of the Australians and their replacement by the British Seventieth Division and the Polish Independent Brigade. Secrecy being paramount, however, the brigade itself was kept in the dark. It was a fact that Italian and German spies were thick on the ground in Egypt, where certain nationalist political factions were sympathetic to the Germans, denouncing the British as colonialists.

So it was, that around September 1, 1941, exactly two years after the Nazi invasion of Poland, the Polish Army was poised once again to face the Germans, this time in distant Africa. The troop transfer operation came to a sudden end on October 25, after the Royal Navy had suffered heavy losses through air attacks.

While all this was happening in Tobruk, in Sidi Bishr, we continued to suffer for over three months the unbearable tedium of camp life and the daily routine of training. The position of the camp in the middle of nowhere left us to rely on our own two feet. Perhaps we were intentionally being forced to get used to the conditions of war in the desert. To be a foot soldier in a desert war is a tough job.

Every day, between sunrise and noon, we would march for miles, wearing pith helmets with rifles on our shoulders and full infantry kit on our backs. At midday, we would rest under shady date palms, guzzling water from our flasks, and eating fresh dates bought from little barefoot boys following our platoon.

Back in camp, there was no rest. First we had to clean our rifles and other equipment, a chore difficult on windy days, sand getting into every nook and cranny. Around five o'clock we would return to the mess hall for supper and then rejoin our squads for roll call and prayers. Upon a signal, our platoon would dash to the parade square and line up in two rows facing the lieutenant and the platoon sergeant. First there would be announcements and then the sergeant would yell "Attention!" followed by "those of the Mosaic faith step aside." At the shout of "at ease!" we would doff our caps and sing the old hymn "Oh Righteous Lord,' kindly bless our daily chores and, as we fall asleep, let our dreams praise you too." Our singing was the butt of jokes throughout the camp for its singular ineptitude.

With our Jewish comrades absent, the rest of us could not sing a single note in tune. Major Jankowski would work himself into a fury and spew invective at the sergeant, who in turn would scream at us and order us to practice singing during the afternoon break. But our practicing would only make matters worse: cooks would wander out of the mess hall, banging pots and pans, as we tried again and again to find the right rendition of some of the popular songs. It was Pinkus Litwin who put an end to our two-week-long nightmare. One evening during the roll call, he stepped forward, stood at attention, and timidly addressed Lieutenant Kruczyński, "The hymn that is sung daily, sir, speaks for everyone. Why can't Jews participate? There is only one God for us all. We respectfully request that we be allowed to sing the hymn with the rest of the platoon, sir!" He quickly stepped back into place. The lieutenant only smiled and barked at the sergeant, "Carry on. Everybody sings from now on!" We all felt that we had crossed an important threshold: henceforth the platoon would be truly as one.

Sidi Birsh, Egypt—The "Polish aristocratic/ Jewish" platoon section (from left: count J.Badeni, Lt. Kruczynski, author, Mjr.Jankowski, J.Ernst, Sgt.Jeziorny, P.Litwin, R.Harold, A.Schneider, count S.Badeni)

At the completion of our training at Sidi Bishr, I was picked to join a select group of soldiers sent to a camp at Agami, just west of Alexandria harbor, supposedly to await transfer to Tobruk. Unaware of the fact that troop exchange in Tobruk had been halted, we assumed that we were next in line. For the following three weeks, we were assigned to guard duty at the docks, being otherwise left to twirl our thumbs. Our neighbors in the next camp were Indian troops, the fourth infantry division from Punjab, I believe. We were intrigued by their exotic customs. We would walk past their quarters and watch them from a distance as they sat in front of their tents and ritualistically combed their long black hair. They would then tie it with a yellow band on top of the head and proceed slowly and meticulously to wind their khaki turbans around it. Friendly and polite, they struck one as being really elegant, their shirts and shorts always impeccably ironed, as if always ready for parade. They smiled at us, showing rows of shining white teeth contrasting with their black beards and swarthy faces. Their British officers, on the other hand, were the very picture of haughtiness and arrogance: those blond young lieutenants in their short camelhair coats and tan riding boots, the habitués of "officers only" cafés and bars in Alexandria hotels. Clutching canes or flywhisks under their arms, barking orders through their clenched teeth, they moved stiffly through the ranks. Here was Imperial British India writ small!

Alexandria in those days was abuzz with dozens of languages, spoken in a variety of accents. As one walked in the streets, one was struck by the great variety of people: here you saw a member of some foreign regiment done up in truly exotic military regalia; there Scottish soldiers in kilts; other more usual uniforms of all types as well as civilians sporting red fezzes, white turbans, or Panama hats; some women in colorful attire, others clad in black.

I had first visited Alexandria on a weekend pass when still posted to Sidi Bishr. Our entire group had at long last been granted a day off. While getting ready, I asked whether anyone had a map of the city. As we strolled along the highway toward the tram stop, Józek Ernst sidled up to me and whispered conspiratorially, "What do you need a map for? Stick with me, I know my way around, I'll show you a thing or two." Józek was quite a bit older than the rest of us, and we were surprised, for instance, to learn that he spoke Arabic, or at least what passed for Arabic—he knew how to haggle with the little Egyptian rascals who sold us dates and fresh figs. When I think of it now, he must have been one of the volunteers who had emigrated to Palestine before the war.

From Sidi Bishr, the ride in a yellow and blue tram took a little more than thirty minutes. The last stop was Ramlah Station, on a square

with tall palm trees at its center. Impressive apartment buildings surrounded the square on three sides; the fourth offered a vista of the Corniche and the sea beyond. We wandered about, gawking at windows of luxury goods stores and at patrons of the large café terraces, relaxing in wicker chairs arranged round tables placed in the shade of colorful parasols. At Pastroudis, the black faced Nubian waiters were resplendent in their red fezzes and white galabiyas—long white caftans—tied with red sashes. One would encounter smart looking Egyptian Officers and other ranks in exotic uniforms. Men in civilian strolled the pavements, wearing straw hats and off-white linen suits, or dark-red tarbooshes with black tassels; elaborate, unbuttoned waistcoats on collarless shirts, and baggy black trousers tapered at the calf—all relics of Turkish fashions from before the last war. The latter was predominantly the attire of small shopkeepers standing at the doors of their premises and inviting passersby to come inside. Women wore fashionable silk or cotton dresses of the latest European design and brightly colored hats. Other ones were, in contrast, completely wrapped in black shawls; some of the older ones had their chins tattooed and lower lips blackened.

Haggana camel guard

Side streets were jammed with wagons and pushcarts brimming with leather goods, fruits, or vegetables. The loud voices of vendors praising their wares added to the din of radios played in the shops at full blast. Somehow, we managed to return to the starting point of our stroll and noticed a roller-skating rink off the square. Some of our party decided to test their skills, and soon others grew bold enough to join them. Józek nudged me and said, "What's the point of this tomfoolery on roller skates? Just a waste of time!" and pulled me along, using his elbows to make his way through the crowd. Once outside we walked briskly toward Ramlah square and turned left onto the main artery of the town, Boulevard Saad Zaghoul.

Józek obviously knew where he was going, for he stopped in front of a lavishly appointed corner delicatessen. The large sign in gold letters on dark green background read Lappas. Inside, hidden behind shelves of canned goods, was a kind of bar with a counter displaying jars of pickled tomatoes, gherkins, artichoke hearts and olives. The shelves behind the counter, all along the wall, were packed with bottles of spirits and other alcoholic drinks. Józek clapped his hands and called out in Polish, "Lappas, dwa razy Tata z Mamą" or Dad and Mum, twice. The barman brought out two glasses and poured equal quantities of a clear spirit and black cherry syrup into each of them. Józek grabbed one glass and nodded to me to follow his example. Since I was not partial to strong alcohol, I demurred. Józek shrugged his shoulders and gulped the contents of my glass as well.

We went outside; he was now walking slowly, staring languorously at passers-by, turning his head now and then to have a better look at a passing woman. We approached a square with a statue of a turbaned horseman, Mohammed Ali, the founder of the royal dynasty and the father of modern Egypt. We continued walking aimlessly while our surroundings were getting increasingly shabbier. Most of the male passersby now wore galabiyas and small white skullcaps while the women were covered from head to foot in black shawls which they clutched tightly under the chin. Suddenly, three Australian soldiers appeared in front of us, in high spirits, quite obviously drunk. They bowed to us in mock gallantry, sweeping the pavement in front of us with their broad-brimmed hats. Once they realized that we were Poles, they grabbed us by the arm and insisted that we join them in their revelry. As my English was less than rudimentary and they spoke with an unfamiliar Australian accent, all I could make out from their prattle was, "Tobruk, Tobruk." Józek managed somehow to extricate us from their oppressive attention and we bolted without further ado. We turned into a side street followed by the shouts and giggles of our would-be Australian friends until we came across a barrier closing off the street and carrying a notice "Out of bounds for HM personnel." "We are not His Majesty personnel," said Józek quickly. "Come on!" and before I realized it, we were on the other side of the barrier, in a red light district—a forbidden territory. I did not follow him any further; our interests were obviously not the same.

Now, in the Agami camp, I found another companion whom I had met before in Sidi Bishr and with whom I had more in common. He was Staś Badeni, scion of an old aristocratic family. He spoke good French, so did I; and we could spend time in cafés and chat with educated Alexandrian girls.

Café Monseigneur on Ramlah Square was very much a European establishment, where all the waiters spoke French, and all ranks were welcome. The clientele was well behaved; as at the slightest sign of drunkenness, the culprit would be politely though firmly persuaded to leave. Once I witnessed such an incident, when two New Zealanders, a bit the worse for drink, were asked to leave, having started giving vent to their feelings about three sailors of the French naval squadron, also patrons of the establishment. The squadron was part of the French navy in the Eastern Mediterranean, which had sided with Pétain's Vichy government. In consequence, the French ships in the port of Alexandria were blockaded by the British navy, and their crews were rarely seen in town. No wonder, as treated by the Allied troops as traitors, they were often subject to rather explicit expressions about the morals of their mothers and thus their own dubious parentage.

One day, as we arrived for the five o'clock dance, the few tables close to the bar were already occupied by some pretty young women. I noticed a particularly attractive girl on the dance floor, but she was dancing with a British major. I could not keep my eyes off her. But how could I, the lowest of the low in the Allied forces, compete with a British major, my few piastres pitted against his stacks of pounds?

But suddenly—I held my breath—she finished dancing with the major and, instead of going back to her own table, she came over to where I was standing by the bar. "My name is Mia," she said simply. She told me she was Italian. She engaged me in meaningless chitchat, and then she was gone before I even had a chance to compose myself. I would learn later that she belonged to the affluent Jewish community living in Alexandria since biblical times. I met with her several times and told her the story of my escape to Romania, resulting, finally, in my arrival in Palestine. She listened attentively.

In exchange, I was told about the complex and explosive conditions existing in the Middle East. In Egypt, remaining under a de facto British occupation, I learned of the deep resentment of some Egyptians against the "oppressors." My Middle Eastern education had begun.

Back in the camp, one morning, my platoon was ordered to get ready for transport. After the initial confusion and the usual silly jokes of the gallows humor variety, we stood to attention for inspection by our captain. Following it, we had to wait for an unconscionable time in full kit—woolen battle-dress, steel helmet and the backpack with the oil cloth coat, as a protection against mustard gas attack, rolled on top—until trucks arrived and took us, surprise, surprise, back to Sidi Bishr.

But what next? Happily relieved of the tedious and mostly uneventful guard duty at the docks, we were looking forward to some excitement, some real danger. After all we were, at least in our own opinion, well trained, well rested and an excellent unit, straining at the leash. Yet nothing happened for a few days. And then we were ordered into parade dress: shirts with rolled up sleeves, shorts, webbing belts, gaiters. General Sikorski was coming to visit the camp. His visit had been kept secret until the last moment; General Sikorski was commander-in-chief of the Polish Armed

Forces and head of the Polish government in exile in London. The troops were electrified. This promised to be a very emotional experience for us all.

In fact, General Sikorski's visit moved us to tears. After all, we were a homeless army, "wandering soldiers," as a patriotic song would have it. We stood in tight formation in two rows along an invisible line, officers in one and everyone else in the other, ranging from the tallest to the shortest. It was not long before General Sikorski's party, which included high-ranking Polish and British officers, arrived in several staff cars. The general addressed us briefly, repeating what in our minds we already knew. We were, he said, the conscience of our enslaved country, and that back there, in Poland, all hearts and eyes would follow our struggles in the service of freedom and honor. Poland, he went on, was the only country in all of Europe that refused to yield to the Nazi occupant. He went on to stress that the purpose of his trip was to affirm our solidarity with Great Britain. He averred that our stand in Egypt and Tobruk was only the beginning of the inevitable defeat of German and Italian fascism. In our ignorance of international Realpolitik, we cheered his pep talk enthusiastically.

Gen. W.Sikorski visit

Two weeks later, six of us were comfortably seated in the back of a Citroën truck, under a tightly stretched, sand-colored tarpaulin. A lieutenant, whom we did not know, sat next to the driver. He had been introduced to us by Major Jankowski as our commander for the duration of the trip. A British offensive codenamed Operation Crusader had been launched from Egypt in the direction of Tobruk on November 18.

At the guardhouse, we were given our orders: we were to escort a convoy to Tobruk and ensure its safe passage. It was assumed that by the time we get there, the siege of the town would have been already lifted. We would receive further orders on arrival. The cargo included several metal coffers locked and secured with lead seals, their contents unknown to us. We started on our way through a labyrinth of dingy side streets of the southern outskirts of Alexandria. On our left stretched the real country: green fields, fellahin's mud huts, swarms of children trying to chase the truck, but soon disappearing in clouds of dust.

I had just turned nineteen, barely mature; but like my companions, I was jubilant at the prospect of going to Libya, of facing the enemy.

4

To Libya and Back

Continuing west, we entered the segment of the highway that ran through the desert parallel to the north shore of Maryut, a large lake—a remnant of the vast, primeval marshes of the Nile Delta. In the heat of the morning sun, the water shimmered, a golden mist blunting the sharpness of the horizon. At the intersection with the Alexandria-Cairo desert highway, we turned right and hit the coastal road near Agami. Soon we were in the desert proper. We were part of an endless convoy of supplies and equipment rushing to the Eighth Army, now entering Libya. At times, the paved road became so crowded that tank transporters and other heavy equipment would force other vehicles off the main road onto the wide, rough desert tracks running parallel—the traffic being directed by MPs.

At dusk, we arrived at a group of low buildings, a flag limp atop a pole. We realized we were in Mersa Matruh, where the Polish brigade has been stationed for several months, training and reinforcing the defenses of the town.

Our driver parked the truck between two concrete pillboxes, and a guard roster was established. As the bunker was overrun by fleas, we spread our blankets outside on the ground with the small haversacks for pillows and greatcoats for cover. By dawn, we were ready to board our truck again; but our departure was being repeatedly postponed. The sun rose quickly as we were sitting, leaning against a concrete wall, enjoying its warmth after the cold of the night. But where was the heavily reinforced fortress that we had come to expect? Moreover, to our great disappointment, there were neither any anti-tank obstacles nor antitank guns to be seen anywhere. As we shared our disenchantment, a wail of sirens rose in the distance, soon followed by others close to us. A British sergeant, yanking his helmet onto his head, ran toward us screaming, "Into the bunker with you! On the double!" As we slid through the narrow entrance into the semi-darkness, explosions and the staccato sputter of antiaircraft guns reverberated all around us. "Can you hear those ack-ack guns?" said someone. "We didn't even notice them before." "Damn fleas!" shouted another. "I'm getting out of here." We all scrambled out and ran in different directions, hitting the ground. The drone of bombers on the way out could be faintly heard from the direction of the coast. The sirens, however, were silent; the alarm has not been called off. As we raised our heads, the roar of engines grew louder again. Flying low from the south over the desert, four Italian fighters swooped just above the palm trees near our truck. They opened fire in long bursts, bullets hitting the bunker wall. Soon the sirens announced the all clear. Their monotonous whine continued for a while, only to disappear in the distance.

Our lieutenant strutted toward us, accompanied by a British officer. He smiled. "Well, what was it like? Now, that you had your baptism of fire? All pants clean?" he laughed. "Not scared I hope?" "No, sir!" we shouted in unison as we jumped to our feet, expecting further orders. But instead, he sauntered back to our truck, pointing something out to the British officer. Then he came back to us. "We leave in half an hour," he said. "We ought to reach Sidi Barrani later today, barring surprises like this latest one." Sidi Barrani was away only half the distance that we covered the day before, so making it by nightfall should not have been a problem. After a quick lunch, we loaded extra jerry cans of gasoline, strapped them to the sides of the Citroën, and we were off.

By now, we were part of a parade of imperial might rolling westward—heavy transporters painted in desert camouflage colors, laden with all kinds of equipment covered with tarpaulin, the shape of which often gave away its contents. Here was the arsenal of a modern army proceeding in the wake of advancing troops: tanks on long, low platforms; guns with capped muzzles; crates of ammunition, mortars in wooden cases. Here were English drivers and their escorts, there black soldiers from colonial regiments, there again New Zealanders and Australians. The South Africans stood out in their different uniforms and tropical helmets with narrow brims. The Indian drivers always smiled and nodded as we overtook their heavily loaded vehicles. Near Sidi Barrani the terrain became hilly, the road cutting through weathered rock formations. We crossed railway tracks outlined by piles of litter on both sides. At the first checkpoint, we were directed to the town itself, to a whitewashed, one-story school building with a large playground at the back. The classroom walls and wooden shutters were marked with bullet holes. Having established the sequence of our guard duty, we settled in for the night. As I was second in line for duty, I went for a walk. At the back of the yard, there was a school latrine with doors to three cubicles and squat toilets. The walls were covered with elaborate, colorful drawings depicting soldiers carrying out various functions, including the most intimate ones, with signatures, captions, and ditties—all in Polish! As it was getting dark and I had run out of matches, I rushed to our billets to get some more, the better to illuminate my archaeological discovery.

At the classroom door, I bumped into the lieutenant, "What's the rush? Slowly does it," he said. "I have important news. Is everybody here? "All present, except for one on guard duty, sir." "Good. So that's the situation: couple of days ago, Japan attacked the American naval base at Pearl Harbor in Hawaii; and it is believed that America will join the war on our side. As to the situation at hand, this morning the enemy withdrew its forces and the Eighth Army is marching on Tobruk." "Hurrah!" we whooped jubilantly and peppered him with questions about the future. "Would we be ordered back to Egypt?" "Would we be stationed in Tobruk?" "Will the Americans come to help us?" "Wait, wait," he said. "We'll proceed tomorrow as planned, but with a slightly changed itinerary. Bardia and Sollum, two towns straddling the Libyan border, have yet to surrender. So we shall have to bypass them in a wide arc through the desert. This will make our route harder and longer, but we ought to reach Tobruk in a couple of days. We leave at dawn."

It was my turn to stand guard now; and on my return an hour later, everyone else was asleep on the floor. In the morning, among the confusion of getting ready, I forgot about my artistic discovery. I did not remember it until we were well on the way. But when I told them the story, they just looked at each other and said nothing, I took umbrage, particularly as they started calling me "our shithouse explorer."

During the siege of Tobruk, the Polish brigade was responsible for nearly half of its defense perimeter, from its western extremity to the middle of the southern sector, while the British held the rest. The monotony of daily life was relieved by skirmishes with the Italians, but coming across and engaging the Germans was much more difficult. All the same, our troops itched for battle with the Germans, our historical enemy.

Yet preparations to lift the siege have been underway as part of Operation Crusader. A top-secret decision was made for a heavy concentration of tanks and infantry to sortie from Tobruk on a mile-wide front. At the appointed signal, the Polish brigade was to create a distraction in the Western sector by opening fire with all guns. On November 18, radio operators kept hearing the word "jam" time and time again. The Eighth Army was signaling that in forty-eight hours, it would be close enough to support the sortie from the other side.

In late November, after an all-night tireless effort by the engineers to clear the minefields and build bridges for tanks across the deep antitank ditch, the attack force moved in.

From the outset, the battle was fierce; the Germans were well armed and shrewdly positioned. As was later discovered to everyone's surprise, Rommel had been simultaneously planning an assault on practically the same segment. Ensconced in six powerfully defended forts, the Germans were intent on protecting all approaches to the vital, purpose-built bypass road circumscribing

Tobruk. The struggle for these forts lasted for over a week, even as fighting raged at a ridge called El Duda, near the bypass road where the bloody attacks and counterattacks never stopped for six days.

On December 6, after nearly a week of ceaseless fighting and shelling, the Poles attacked only to find that the Germans had quietly abandoned their positions the night before. The defenders of El Duda reached Sidi Rezegh, where they established contact with the Eighth Army. The Achsenstrasse, the Axis Road around Tobruk, so savagely fought for, was renamed Democracy Lane. By December 10, Tobruk was free.

That same day at dawn, our small unit left the school compound at Sidi Barrani. After about two hours, we turned off the highway and were making slow headway through the desert crisscrossed by ruts left in the wet soil by heavy vehicles. This was the season of sudden torrential rains, turning the desert into an expanse of yellow-brownish mud and the dry wadis into gushing rivers. Though our driver was carefully avoiding the bumpier tracks, it was nonetheless a rather rough ride. The lieutenant was busy with his compass, plotting the new course on his field map, superseding the one drawn previously, marking it with a green wax pencil on the cellophane cover. "We would be better off with a naval officer in charge," he joked during one of the short breaks. "As things stand, we might end up on Lake Chad in sub-Saharan Africa." We have concluded by now that our leader was a fine, well-intentioned man. An electrical engineer in civilian life, he served in the Signal Corps. Though not too eloquent, he exuded the kind of confidence that convinced us not to take his anxiety too seriously.

At around noon, according to our lieutenant, we crossed the Libyan border. Some road signs nailed to crooked wooden poles were scattered here and there along our way. Once we stopped near three of them stuck together in the ground and propped up with a pile of rocks, they bore only the names of regimental command posts, which have by then become history. When we stopped for a rest, it was pouring with rain and wind was howling all around us. It was getting dark and our commander decided that it was safer to stop here for the night, lest we risk losing our way. We settled on the ground and awoke the next morning cold and wet through and through.

But as we proceeded in daylight, the panorama changed dramatically. As far as the eye could see, right across the horizon, the desert was covered with the litter of blown-up and burnt-out carcasses of German and British tanks, abandoned infantry trucks, broken gun carriages, artillery rounds scattered on the sand. The stench of burning oil and paint, not yet dispersed by the wind, was pervasive. As we would later learn, we were in the environs of Belhamed village where a grim battle between New Zealanders advancing on Tobruk and a German armored column had been fought several days before. As we moved along, Bedouins from nearby villages and encampments, their donkeys loaded with loot, were scouring the killing fields for more plunder.

At Democracy Lane, we turned left and skirting El Duda, arrived in the vicinity of an airfield strewn with charred skeletons of airplanes and numerous containers of army supplies, now reduced to rubbish. British soldiers were busy moving about, taking stock of the captured material. It was a striking panorama of defeat, which made us wonder whether the war might be coming to an end.

At a crossroads, there was a cluster of small mud brick huts with broken fences and a pickup truck with MPs directing traffic. We were told that to get to Tobruk, we had first to turn right and then continue straight until we hit the town; we ought to be able to make it in over an hour. We must have failed to notice the Italian positions before spotting the British and Polish machine gun emplacements marked by piles of rock raising their frontal defenses. Debris lay thick on the ground; some old rags fluttered in the wind. The empty concrete bunkers and caves with shallow ditches were filled with piles of litter. Beyond a low ridge, there were artillery positions protected by boulders and sandbag walls. But the guns were gone. Heaps of spent shells glittered in the rays of sun breaking through the dark clouds. There was an eerie stillness.

We drove by a large field hemmed in by a double barbed-wire fence. German and Italian prisoners sat huddled on the ground, the collars of their coats turned up. Seen from a distance, they formed a bizarre, bluish-khaki mass, difficult to identify as a group of people. The road now led down an escarpment through hairpin bends until we came down and drove round the harbor. Finally, we stopped in front of a half demolished brick building. The lieutenant went inside, as we stretched our legs and chatted with the driver, exhausted by the difficult drive through the desert. "I'm pooped out," he repeated again and again.

We put up for the night in a cluster of tents, some already occupied by other Polish soldiers, many recently discharged from hospital. No sooner had we arrived than the lieutenant disappeared with his baggage in a jeep that arrived to pick him up. We reported to a sergeant lording it over us from behind a table with a field telephone, into which he kept screaming complaints about the connection, generously peppered with choice obscenities. He must have received new orders, as I was separated from my companions and assigned to a group of strangers. As the evening wore on, I understood from the snatches of the sergeant's screams and expletives that the brigade was on the move, but nobody had bothered to inform him of the destination.

Early next morning, we woke to an air raid on the port. Rumor soon spread that one of the ships bearing prisoners of war to Alexandria had been hit at sea. The presiding sergeant had vanished and another one, tall and thin, covered with dust and in need of a shave, arrived in a massive truck, looking for men to do some heavy lifting elsewhere. As there was no one in command, he paced nervously about. Suddenly, he homed in on our group standing idly by and yelled at the top of his voice, "You, you, and you, get your gear and into the truck with you! On the double! I have no time to waste. We'll tell your sergeant later." I never had the chance to return to that camp to explain my disappearance. We drove off, joining other able-bodied men in pickup trucks on the way, up an embankment onto a rocky plateau. Hidden in one of the many ravines were stores of all kinds of war material: weapons and equipment, clothing, food, water, gasoline.

We worked like mules well into the night, loading crates of canned food and blankets on to the trucks without a clue as to their destination. At last, a field kitchen arrived; and we were given some food and a container of **horribly tasting, brackish** water to **drink and** to wash in. We spent the night in concrete bunkers. I found an additional blanket and, snugly tucked in, immediately fell asleep. Only rats running up and down our exhausted bodies kept waking us up from time to time. From dawn to dusk the following day, we loaded more stuff on arriving vehicles. By evening my palms were covered in blisters, my back ached and I was thirsty beyond belief. I couldn't stop licking my parched lips and reluctantly gulped the salty, foul and tepid water from my canteen. We did not know one another and we worked practically in silence. Nonstop, from the stores to the trucks, and back. In the end, curiosity got the better of us and someone asked a driver where he was taking these supplies to.

"Oh, about twenty or thirty miles west," he replied, puffing on the butt of his cigarette.

"And what's there?"

"More fucking desert! That's what!" he screamed in answer. This news stopped us in our tracks; we stared at each other, and suddenly burst out laughing. I did not quite get the joke, so was first to stop laughing, though the others continued until tears trickled down their cheeks.

"What's up? What's so funny?" I asked one of them who really seemed to be crying.

"You've only just arrived," he said, "but we've been stuck in this hellhole for nearly four months, four fucking months! Now, instead of getting the fuck out of here and going east, they're busy fixing something else for us further west. West, of all the lousy directions! That's what up! For Christ's sake!"

The few words loosened our tongues, the overall mood seemed to have changed, and from that moment, we chatted and joked while helping one another to haul the heavy boxes and crates.

The tall, thin sergeant reappeared toward the evening and ordered six of us to get on to the last two trucks for "they need help at the other end," as he put it.

It was a long, slow drive through the pitch black, moonless or perhaps very cloudy night. Our driver seemed to be following a rather winding trail, and I wondered how on earth he knew where he was going. When we arrived at our destination, wherever that might have been, I had the distinct impression of having arrived nowhere.

Loud voices woke me up at dawn. I was up in a trice. A group of men under the command of a young officer was milling around me. We donned our helmets and reported for duty. I tried to explain our status, but he waved his hand dismissively.

"Later, later. Now join the others and get to work. They'll tell you what to do. I'll be back soon."

We were ready in no time, having arranged our belongings according to regulations, ran to a field latrine on the way back, grabbed some hard tack with marmalade, and joined the workers.

"Hey, you there!" I heard someone call out. I turned round, and who was there but the man from the French Foreign Legion who had befriended me in the camp in Palestine six months ago. A corporal now, he was in command of the unit which we were now part of. We used to call him Piotrek, but now he chose to be called Pierrot, as before, among the French. We exchanged a few words, and he told us what to do. Our job was to break open the crates and to sort out their contents company by company, according to the list provided. Soon men from various units started arriving in pairs pushing small two-wheeled carts. Trying to explain that one hundred tins of bully beef on the list meant one hundred just led to verbal abuse. Tempers flared. We were repeatedly told where we could stuff our list. The barren stillness of the desert eerily menacing in its desolation; the heaviness of the cloudy sky above, all probably added to the already frayed nerves. All at once, we heard heavy gunfire coming from the west, from behind a distant low ridge. The fire, at first sporadic, soon turned into a constant barrage; and the explosions lit the western rugged horizon of the ridge, yellowish-brown plumes ascending to the sky, rapidly followed by crashing sounds. These were soon followed by other, flatter sounds. What were those? We looked at one another.

"Our men must be on the move," said Pierrot. "Those are mortars you're hearing. They must have seen them coming."

"Who?" I asked naïvely.

"The Italians. Who else? Their artillery stopped us last night. They must have decided to make a stand here."

"But where exactly are we?" I inquired further, as my heart raced. "Who knows," somebody else answered.

On December 13, 1941, the Allies stopped for breath on the Ain El Gazala—Carmuset line, some thirty miles west of Tobruk. Italian fortifications began at the narrow Gazala bay, overlooked by a steep crag, accessible by a winding road defended by reinforced bunkers carved into the solid rock. The defenses continued for some fifteen miles into the desert. The CO of the corps, Gen. Goodwin Austen, asked General Kopański to move his brigade to the back of the Italians and thus cut off their retreat and deny them any supplies coming along the Tobruk-Derna road. This maneuver was designed to facilitate the frontal attack by the New Zealanders and Indians. However, their attack was repulsed by heavy Italian artillery fire. Having reconnoitered the situation, General Kopański decided to go on the offensive and, after regrouping on December 14, and having secured the support of Polish and New Zealand artillery, ordered the brigade to attack. The Polish right wing reached the enemy's position on the same day while the left wing, where I was and of which I had a good view, had to sink in and spend the night in the open desert.

Suddenly, the artillery barrage stopped; and at that time, our young officer, drove up with two Morris pickup trucks without their tarpaulin covers, and ordered us to load them with all the available cases of corned beef and all blankets. The pickups took off at speed, with us standing on the running boards and holding on for dear life.

We drove for about a mile up the same ridge that had been under fire a short time ago. Darkness quickly descended, broken now and then by flashes of fire on the horizon as enemy guns continued to shell some target to our left. Our vehicle came to a halt while the other proceeded for another half a mile. A soldier with a Tommy gun waved us to a stop and showed us where to park, but not before shouting, "Get the bully beef down quick . . . got any coats?"

"Only blankets. Can you use them?" "Bloody hell, yes! We're freezing!" One by one, bent figures of men came out of the darkness, their faces worn, streaked with dirt. They grabbed what was available, wrapped the blankets round their shoulders, and disappeared into the night. As the shelling stopped, we managed to talk to some of them. A lieutenant sauntered by with a sergeant and, while collecting their rations, commented on the sudden incomprehensible end of the artillery support. "What the hell has happened?" they wondered while stuffing their faces with chunks of cold beef. No one knew the answer. It was only later that we found out that the Polish artillery stopped its barrage because they ran out of ammunition that had been delivered by mistake to the different place.

This was confirmed in the next hour when we drove to the frontline with more provisions and equipment. As we bumped along a new trail, companies were regrouping into defensive formations and digging temporary trenches, anticipating a counterattack by the enemy. The short-handled spades that we brought were yanked from our hands. Tension was in the air. In the regrouping of companies, we were told to stay with the vehicles of the third battalion headquarters. It was here that I first saw Col. Józef Sokal, a heavyset, vigorous, square-jawed man of medium height. He wore a warm battledress and a soft field cap held in place by a pair of goggles; his trousers were held at the ankle by canvas gaiters. A canvas belt with his holstered revolver and field glasses round his neck completed the picture. He was surrounded by a group of his officers. As they stopped not far from our trucks, a junior officer came running from the front with a report. Sokal looked at his watch and issued orders. One of his officers dashed to the staff cars, where signalmen were manning field telephones. Whistles blared. The companies began to move forward, advancing behind the reconnaissance patrols approaching the ridge. The brigade went again into action on December 16, at the time of the afternoon siesta. The secured and fortified Italian positions were being run over and fell in continuous attacks, while the swift pursuit units followed the retreating enemy.

Even as the charge on the Italian positions was in progress, prisoners were being taken and led down to our lines. An MP sergeant quickly marched over to us, growling, "And what are these men doing here?"

Pierrot jumped to attention, saluted smartly and reported, "Five privates and one corporal, sergeant. Sir. Awaiting orders. Sir." "Good. Take your boys, run up the ridge, gather as many captives as you can and escort them over there," he pointed to a cloud of dust trailing a gray crowd of men. Pierrot yelled to our driver to stay with the truck and motioned to us to follow him up the long slope. By the time we reached the top, the firing somewhat subsided and groups of our soldiers were wandering from one abandoned enemy position to the next, using their rifles to poke into bundles of blankets and clothing left in disarray. Here and there, an Italian soldier prostrate on the sandy ground, his arms raised, would try to look around and beg for mercy. We spoke to them roughly and, with our rifles, gestured them to stand up before leading them to the assembly spot chosen by Pierrot.

Colonel Sokal happened upon the scene and seeing the columns of prisoners, he began to stomp his feet excitedly and shout repeatedly in his raspy voice, "Look, look, what my boys have achieved, my dear, dear boys. They've done it, and without artillery support to boot. They've charged five miles uphill and won!"

We were all gripped by euphoria, though subdued by the sight of three ambulances moving slowly, parallel to the captured enemy lines, medics running with stretchers, collecting the wounded and covering the dead.

I reached a group of Italian prisoners wearing long coats and tropical helmets, escorted by the crew of a Bren carrier. I was about to wave them to follow me but their escort asked me to wait, jumped off the carrier, mustered the Italians on one side, stood on the other, and, handing me a camera, asked me to take the group picture. Some time later, I received the photograph showing our smiling boys with their grimy faces and bottles of Chianti in their hands.

By the morning of December 17, all enemy positions along the entire line were overrun. The victory was complete and the enemy was retreating to the borders of Tripolitania, west of Benghazi. General Austen caught up with General Kopański and congratulated him. His special report of the victory was sent to all allied units. The exhausted Poles were there and then relieved from the pursuit of the enemy by the British.

However, the relief of Tobruk by the advancing Eighth Army did not end the brigade's service on the Libyan front. On the contrary, having already served twice as long as any other Allied unit, the brigade was incorporated into the Thirteenth Army Corps and ordered to pursue the retreating enemy.

Great quantities of military equipment fell into our hands but, most significantly, fifty-nine officers and one thousand six hundred soldiers were taken prisoner. We had accepted the surrender of a crack battalion of the Bersaglieri with its commanding officer. Our losses were twenty-five dead, ninety-four wounded, and six missing.

My group was posted to reinforce a depleted battalion in Cyrenaica, but Pierrot managed to fix an assignment for the two of us to a small unit at the direct disposal of the commander in chief. A beat-up truck picked us up in Tobruk and retraced its way, through El Adem and Gazala, to a highway leading to Derna and beyond. It took us two days to cover a distance of roughly two hundred kilometers. The surrounding landscape was covered with the debris of war. Many charred vehicles still carried the white emblem of the Afrika Korps: a palm tree with a swastika on its trunk. On the steep roads of the coastal cliffs with their serpentine bends, our truck repeatedly broke down; but on each occasion, our driver performed true magic with his toolbox. The sun had already set when we arrived in Giovanni Berta.

The colonization of Libya was one of the prime objectives of Mussolini's imperial scheme, and the district was studded with white, cubical buildings designed for the settlers. We were billeted in one of these farmhouses.

The present population of the region was very mixed. There were Italian colonists who occupied a few of the farmhouses; local Arabs of the Senussi tribe, forced off their land by colonization and reduced to living in mud brick villages and in squat, black tents on the edge of the desert; and bands of marauding Italian soldiers who, as insurgents, secretly assisted by the Italian farmers, would sometimes wait in ambush for our patrols. The result was that the farmers looked askance at us, conquering troops, with unsmiling faces; the Arabs despised the colonist farmers and tried to rob them at every opportunity, the rule of law, as they saw it, having collapsed; and the insurgents sought to kill us at every turn. Writing these words today, I cannot escape seeing that situation as a prelude to the war in Afghanistan and Iraq so many years later.

The British, in those days still champions of colonialism, ordered the Brigade to protect the Italian colonialists from the hostile Senussis, a policy that did not sit well with us. For my part, I sympathized with the Arabs for having been turned into refugees in their own country and vainly waiting for justice.

Yet we ourselves were in a dicey situation. It was vaguely assumed that the British had pushed, or perhaps, only followed the retreating German and Italian armies past Benghazi to El Agheila, wherever that was. Apparently, the Germans made a stand there, but the British lacked the strength or resources to attack them. A stalemate ensued. Toward the end of January, there was commotion in our units. Pierrot and I with several other lads were posted to the fourth company of the second battalion stationed in Cyrene. However, we never made it there. The following evening of January 25, events started moving very fast. This was the beginning of the retreat from Libya. We were ordered to pack and, because of a shortage of transport, we had to squeeze into trucks already piled high with gear and ammunition. It was getting dark when we were ready to leave. On the highway, we had to stop frequently as disabled vehicles were being deliberately set on fire, their cargo, human and otherwise, jammed into passing vehicles. A retreat was a new experience for most us; the feeling was sickening.

"Looks like we did the cut and run maneuver, doesn't it?" a derisive question broke the silence. The night dragged on. At sunrise, when the drawn-out columns slowly came into view, the gravity of our situation began to sink in. Would the Germans resume their air raids? If Rommel was indeed on the move, the Luftwaffe could not be very far away. On our narrow highway, we would be sitting ducks.

"I only hope the Germans won't attack us on those bloody hairpins near Derna," somebody said.

But fortunately, after the next break, all vehicles were waved off the highway southward, into the desert. We drove now at snail's pace, the vehicle shaking on bumpy ruts. The weather was atrocious, freezing cold, with stormy winds and frequent downpours. At one point, toward the evening, we changed direction to the southwest. One of the men checked his compass and groaned in desperation: we seemed to be on course for a head-on collision with Rommel's advancing tanks.

It must have been well after midnight when we stopped near El Mechili, the location of a nineteenth century Turkish fort, and were able to leave the vehicles and stretch our legs. When we fanned out in the flat empty desert, we felt somewhat safer and more determined to face the enemy. Even the dreamers and slackers among us, always talking about what they were going to do once they returned to Alexandria, picked up their spades and began to dig foxholes for the night.

Throughout the next two or three days, we were constantly regrouping to reinforce our defense positions. At the time, rumors started percolating, seemingly from the very top, right down to the foxholes. Apparently, faced with the dire straits his troops had been in, General Kopański had flown to Cairo, presumably to negotiate the brigade's withdrawal to Egypt. Another more sobering rumor had it that we were indeed the retreating Eighth Army's rearguard; the notion though that we could stop Rommel or even just slow him down was, at best, questionable. "Good god, what with?" a voice from some foxhole summed up the general opinion. As if in response to that question, antitank guns started moving into position in well-camouflaged emplacements. Before long, we were joined by the most unexpected allies—Les Français Libres! The Free French Forces had crossed the desert from Chad. Their brigade was comprised of two Foreign Legion and two black colonial battalions. And though a quip was spreading from trench to trench that they were only *plus ou moins Français, plus ou moins libres* (more or less French, more or less free), we were more than delighted to have them in our ranks.

While we were thus anticipating the inevitable confrontation with the Germans and worrying about what it might bring, the worst khamsin, or sandstorm, in recent memory blasted us at El Mechili. One might be able to fight Rommel's tanks, but how does one defend oneself against sand? It penetrated everything, our mouth, eyes, ears, nose; our underwear; our socks; our tightly closed water bottle; and our mess tin. And then, as we were sitting in our foxholes, buried in sand, utterly despondent, reluctant even to grumble, our heads swathed, our eyes and noses clogged with dust, somebody suddenly called out, his voice full of joy,

"Do you know what, gentlemen? I think it's blowing sand!"

We all burst out laughing and could not stop for a good while. But the situation was serious. The visibility was less than ten paces. The sensation of imminent danger perceptibly increased when we heard the approaching sound of motors. The rumble of engines came, first at short intervals, now from the left, now from the right. Suddenly, as if from nowhere, out of the cloud of dust, a black mass, a tank, was moving toward us. We grabbed our hand grenades, ready to attack, when the tank stopped, presumably because its driver noticed us. It turned left, its caterpillars clattering. The turret hatch opened and a red-haired British soldier popped out his head, his eyes squinting at the dying moments of the sandstorm. He kept shouting in what sounded like panic, asking for directions to Tobruk. One of our soldiers emerged from his foxhole and slowly approached the tank. He cupped his ear, as if he was having difficulty hearing. The crewman looked incredulously at him and continued to shout, "Tobruk, Tobruk, Tobruk!" The soldier turned around, scratched his head, and pointed toward the whirling storm. The tank rolled away. But how the hell had it managed to get through our newly laid minefield?

After nine days at El Mechili, the second phase of our retreat commenced. More than a thousand vehicles moved in several parallel columns, shrouded in billowing clouds of dust. In our wake, we left whirls of dark smoke as, once again, disabled vehicles and stores that we were unable to take with us were being set on fire. We drove all night over a forbidding rocky terrain, stopping only to refuel and to fortify ourselves with cold rations. Water was by now in short supply. By morning, we arrived at our destination. It was reassuringly familiar: we were back at Ain El Gazala, the Spring of the Gazelle. It was like coming home. The date was February 4, 1942.

We were entrenched in a range called Carmuset er-Regem, captured by our forces two months ago. What is more, we seized the positions formerly held by the Italians, but had to reconstruct them for the assault expected from a diametrically opposite direction. Having taken no part in the assault on the Bersaglieri in December, the second battalion, then held in reserve, was now ordered to the front line, with the two other Brigade battalions deployed a few miles behind us. Our left and right flanks were reinforced and protected by artillery batteries and antitank guns. To the north, in Bir Chesceua, we had the First South African division under General Brink in overall charge of the frontline forces; and to the south and west, the Free French who had followed us all the way from El Mechili.

The first days of our watch were unnervingly quiet. At night, we patrolled the no-man's land, the ten to fifteen mile wide stretch of desert between the enemy's lines and ours. I had a feeling that our command had no clear idea as to where the Germans actually were. Small units of three to six men on foot, without any personal armour, would go into the foreground, armed only with one automatic gun, hand grenades and rifles. We wore our wool battle dresses and leather jerkins; on our heads, vintage World War I, flat British helmets with netting and on our feet rubber soled desert boots.

There was a distinct possibility that Rommel was running a mobile campaign and might unleash his armored units to harass us anywhere. He also had the Luftwaffe and the Italian air force at his disposal, while our antiaircraft defenses were far from adequate. At that time, the Royal Air Force had no substantial presence because, as rumor had it, the British had moved some squadrons from Libya to the Far East, where they were engaged in a desperate fight with the Japanese.

The enemy air raids began in earnest in mid-February. The Germans must have reconnoitered our positions with great precision, for they kept attacking us twice a day. Early one afternoon, three Italian Macchi fighters appeared in the sky on a strafing mission. I had been looking for Pierrot who had a way of mysteriously disappearing in the open desert. I was running back to our position when I saw three black dots at low altitude beyond the barbed-wire fence separating the mine field.I heard nothing at first; but before long, the high-pitched roar of engines grew deafening. I could see the Macchi fighters looming and spraying bullets. I hit the ground, fully exposed, certain that one plane in particular was aiming at me. A burst of cannon fire with tracer bullets churned up the desert, approaching the ground where I lay. And then, as suddenly as they came, low over my head, the planes were gone. I raised my head and looked around. Their volley had stopped only six feet short of me. Then it continued some distance further on. Was this the pilot's deliberate action or my lucky day?

From a shelter, someone called out to see whether I was all right. I got up and shook the dust from my uniform. Other soldiers emerged from their hiding places.

"You are a lucky bastard," said one. "We gave you up for dead."

Another patted me on the shoulder and insisted that this was cause for celebration. It was Pierrot who had pressed through the small crowd around me. With him was a stranger who wore the Croix de Lorraine badge on his sleeve. Pierrot invited a couple of soldiers into our dugout, and produced a bottle of cognac, insisting I took "a sip . . . to calm your nerves."

But my nerves were in an excellent condition; and when I started thinking of similar situations of the last few weeks, I came to the only logical conclusion, namely that I was fearless and untouchable. The newcomer from the French Legion declared that he wanted to serve with us and had no intention of returning to the frog eaters.

It transpired that he had served with the Foreign Legion in the 1930s and had met Pierrot way back in Algiers. "Many legionnaires had moved over to the Polish Brigade still in Mechili," he said. And so he too stayed with us. The following night he came with us on patrol and the lieutenant didn't say a word.

He squeezed into our tight dugout sharing the bedding with Pierrot. During the long, boring hours between patrols or guard duty on the forward posts I learned about some aspects of their lonely and surprisingly dull life in the Legion. The talk was mostly about their old companions but not about women, as was our custom. There were endless jocks about certain German Legionaire. Without understanding the circumstances, I laughed with them. But before long I felt uneasy and started avoiding their company and distance myself from the topic. But then the soldier was moved elsewhere. The jock was that our lieutenant wanted to have him near his dugout. In similar vain, persistent rumors were spread about soda being added to our tea in order to keep our manly urges down. I can not vouch whether there was any truth in them.

The enemy air raids continued. One day we managed to shoot down a Messerschmidt 109 as it veered toward our positions. Its stalled engine spewed a trail of black smoke. Its pilot let it glide over our heads and ended somewhere in the third battalion's territory. With no workable undercarriage, the pilot belly-landed the aircraft, destroying a kitchen compound on the way. We were told that he came out unharmed and, apparently, on finding out that he had fallen into Polish hands, pleaded with his captors not to shoot him. It was German propaganda, of course, which made him believe that Poles tortured and murdered all prisoners. He was taken to the South African command post. The following night he managed to escape on foot toward the German lines. Gossip had it that he was let go by a sentry, a pro-German Afrikaner. Soon after, a German plane started dropping leaflets written in poor Polish, assuring us of a more than friendly welcome on switching sides and promising us prompt repatriation to our families so desperately worried by our wanderings in the desert. Whose idea could that had been, for goodness sake?

It's a minor story, one of the many popping up from the depth of my memory. And as so often, I ask myself: is it true? Yes, it is. As it turned out, a book of wartime reminiscences was published in Germany entitled *Jagdgeschwader 27 Stuttgart 1972*. There is a story there of a German fighter pilot shot down in Libya in 1942; but as he did not survive the war, it was related in the book by someone else. All the same, he comes across as an arrogant Nazi who took offence at being captured by Poles, whom he describes in a derogatory way, "They jumped and screamed around me like some monkeys." A different version of the same event, as described by two authors on opposite sides. His name was, appropriately, Heinz-Arnold Stahlschmidt.

As the days dragged on, our losses mounted, decimating our ranks. In addition to the killed and wounded, men continued to succumb to scurvy, jaundice, malaria and a number of other serious diseases. It was said already in Mechili that the brigade's losses amounted to one thousand five hundred men, i.e., 30 percent of its original strength. The personnel losses were matched by those of vehicles and other equipment. Our gunners complained that after roughly eight thousand discharges, the barrels were practically smooth, all rifling gone. Some of the personnel carriers and armored vehicles were fit only for the scrap yard.

At the beginning of March, the enemy air raids and patrolling activity intensified. It was also the time when spring came and with it torrential rains, making the desert bloom in spite of the war, in a variety of colors. Each downpour flooded our dugouts again and again, adding to our misery. The brigade had been on the frontline for over seven months; longer than any other Allied unit. Voices were increasingly heard that enough was enough. We learned at a later date that, finally, it was Churchill's decision but, apparently, General Sikorski had brought the matter to his attention, arguing that, as fighting men, his troops in the Libyan desert had to be counted as part of the Polish national treasure and could not be allowed to be brought to the verge of extinction either in the physical or the political sense. When these rumors reached us, we found it hard to understand why the British High Command was dragging its heels in replacing us. The Australians had been replaced after an only two-month stint.

Finally, on March 16, 1942, we received orders to pack our belongings and clean the dugouts and bunkers. We didn't need to be told twice. This time we really did it on the double, just glancing now and then at the western horizon to make sure that the Germans would not find a way of disrupting our departure. The following day we handed our positions over to a South African battalion. I flogged my booty, the captured bottle of brandy, to a beefy soldier with a thick Afrikaner accent. With thirteen pounds in my wallet at last, I felt rich.

We loaded our gear into our clapped out, rickety trucks and drove east toward Tobruk, the Libyan campaign behind us.

5

New York, Here We Come!

After five days' travel, we found ourselves on leave, cooling our heels at El Amriya, an old transit camp west of Alexandria. No sooner had passes been issued than the impatient among us vanished with their knapsacks and duffel bags full of war booty. Plans galore for rest and recreation were being discussed with great excitement. With thirteen pounds—a significant sum—in my pocket and having heard by then that my stepfather, Witold, whose whereabouts I had not known for the last nine months, was stationed at the military hospital in a town called Rasheed or Rosetta in the Nile Delta, I went in search of him at the beginning of my leave.

The bus stop was packed with waiting felaheen returning from market to their villages: men in skull caps and cotton galabiyas, some in rust-colored cloaks with embroidered edges, women in black shawls held close under their chins; as they gesticulated, rows of silver bracelets kept jangling on their wrists. I was the only passenger in uniform and a foreigner to boot. But on this, my first solo foray into the heartland of Egypt, I was in high spirits, full of wonder, and euphoria. Out of the corner of my eye, I caught a glimpse of a young peasant woman in a red robe in the window seat next to mine. Gold filigree pendants flickered on her forehead. She clutched the shawl under her chin with long narrow fingers, her palm died orange-red with henna. Her profile was exquisite, her neck long and slender, such as one might see on ancient Egyptian frescoes and bas-reliefs.

In Rosetta, I walked about a mile and came to a wall with a sentry gate and a sign announcing the ROSETTA FIELD HOSPITAL. Inside, I saluted an obese Polish sergeant sitting behind a desk and stated the purpose of my visit.

He looked me over and barked, "Family?"

"Yes sir." He told me to wait outside.

After at least half an hour, the door opened and Witold appeared. We ran toward each other and hugged tenderly for a long while, as I struggled to hold back my tears.

"Let's get out of here," Witold whispered. "I have a pass for the rest of the day, Yallah!" We walked back to the town. On the way, he told me that he'd had no news from home. A dapper man regardless of circumstances, he could have passed for a dashing young officer. But at the age of forty-one, he was still a lowly private. He asked me about my service on the Libyan front and plans for the future. I admitted that I had none, save for the trip to Upper Egypt. He brooded on my answer for a while. "I'm ashamed to say this," he said, "but I'm hardly in a position to advise you, much less to be of any help. I simply don't know what options might be open to you. For my part, I'm stuck here in this godforsaken place with funds that won't even stretch to a visit to Alexandria."

He confessed how much he hated serving in the army. On the way back, Witold explained to me the complicated history of nineteenth-century Egypt and the related aspects of imperialist crises involving the French, the British and the Egyptians—though now things were changing rapidly. The presence of the British army in wartime Egypt was aggravating the political situation. Who knows what the Middle East will look like after the war? He then pointed a finger at me and concluded, "Learn English, boy, learn English! We all may become emigrants one day, and English will become the international language."

Witold in Rosetta

I stayed in Rosetta for a few more hours. Later, we walked back to the bus stop. He waved me good-bye at dusk as the bus was leaving for Alexandria and his elegant tall figure rapidly grew smaller and smaller, until it eventually disappeared in the distance.

On my return to El Amriya, I found the camp virtually deserted. I yielded to sweet indolence and slept so profoundly in the quiet, empty tent as to even miss breakfast. I woke up to a wonderful feeling, such as I had never known before. I felt in total harmony with the world around me. I decided to visit Alexandria.

At the transport depot, trucks were coming and going, shuttling soldiers between the camp and the Mohammad Ali Square in Alexandria. I ran into two buddies from my company, also on their way to the city.

They suggested visiting a new Turkish baths, which they had sampled before, but, first, tradition demanded that we fortify ourselves with a few shots of Lappas's mum and dad. The baths were a complete revelation: the establishment featured a high atrium decorated with large palms and shrubs in bloom; its floor was tiled in a Greek pattern. Large rooms led from it in all directions, featuring wooden benches and blue pools glistening between columns supporting intricate stained glass roofs. I felt pampered as never before: a haircut, a manicure, pedicure, and, finally, a massage. I felt lucky to be alive; whatever hardships I had endured in the last eight months seemed washed away and massaged out of my body.

Later, sober and reinvigorated, I decided to indulge my mood by wandering alone along the Corniche and breathing the salty sea air, while my companions went to the Sharia Saba Banat (Street of

Seven Sisters) in search of further carnal satisfactions in official establishments manned by the British Military. I strolled toward the waterfront to the Corniche, where I stopped at the wide stone parapet and admired the breathtaking view over the crescent-shaped Eastern Harbor, the smaller of the two Alexandrian ports. From my vantage point, the city stretched on a curve into the distance, disappearing in a golden mist at the sea's horizon.

Suddenly, I remembered Mia, the girl I had met four or five months before; I knew she lived on the Corniche. I thought that I might recognize the entrance to the building from my previous visits. I did not. Neither did I know her surname, so I inquired of the *boabs* (the doormen) all in turn. "Mamzel Mia sakna hena? Eya min Italiya."

A tall Nubian in a white turban pointed meaningfully at me, raised his head, in a jesture of negation clicking his tongue, and replied, "La . . . Mamzel Mia mish Italia eya Yehudia." (No, she is not Italian. She is Jewish. And she lives here.)

Jewish? She told me she was Italian.

"Which floor? Heya sekhna fi eydor?" I tried to do my best in Arabic.

"Third floor," said the Nubian, pointing to the lift and losing interest in me.

I rang the bell. A servant girl with a white kerchief on her head opened the door and, without asking the purpose of my visit, ushered me into a small salon. I heard men's voices, and two New Zealanders appeared briefly in the hall on their way out. A few moments later Mia stood in the doorway with arms outstretched, inviting me to embrace her. "Ah! Quelle surprise! Bonjour, bonjour, comment vas tu?" And then, as if suddenly remembering something, she grabbed my hand and led me quickly to her bedroom. She asked me to sit on the bed while she frantically searched through a large wardrobe with a full-length mirror in the middle door. Presently, she produced a green-grey pullover, my last remaining piece of clothing from Poland, which I thought I had parted company with somewhere in Libya. The servant girl walked in, bringing me a tray with a cup of Turkish coffee and a glass of water, and left, shutting the door behind her.

As I was leaving, I was, to my horror, asked to pay two pounds, a private's entire monthly pay! Nervously, I counted my money and, to my shame, discovered that I was ten piastres short. Very embarrassed, I could only apologize profoundly and, with my pullover tucked under my arm, ran back to the parking lot behind Mohammed Ali's statue, where I hopped on a truck, joining a group of our boys rather the worse for drink and singing a popular Polish drinking song totally out of tune. My beautiful day in Alexandria came to a less than glorious end.

At the end of May 1942, the makeshift Polish Officer's School that I was now attending was moved from El Amriya to a permanent camp at Beit Jirdja in the Gaza Strip in Palestine. The camp was a complete village of tents, big and small, on an expanse of gentle dunes along the Mediterranean coast, merging on its perimeter into the desert. The only flat stretch of sandy terrain in the middle of the camp served as the assembly and parade ground. A two-mile dirt road connected our far-flung encampment to a narrow, two-lane, blacktop highway—a lifeline extending from the Suez Canal first to small Palestinian towns then on to Tel-Aviv and Jerusalem.

out of Egypt

Late one morning, in early June, a month into our basic training, and returning from the firing range, we noticed an unusual commotion near the camp commander's tents; parked there were some camouflaged staff cars, their drivers milling around. At high noon, as we were in our tents after lunch, dodging the intense summer sun, an unexpected order came for us to assemble in the parade ground. All three platoons finally stood in a U-shaped formation, facing a pole with the Polish and British flags fluttering in the gentle breeze. Accompanied by six officers and a man in a white civilian suit, our CO reported the companies' readiness. As soon as the lieutenant on duty shouted "at ease!" we were all ears.

The major introduced the civilian as a representative of the Polish government in exile in London who had come from the Polish Consulate in Jerusalem. Speaking loudly and clearly, the man brought us greetings from our commander in chief, General Sikorski. He then proceeded to tell us what he hoped we already knew.

"A historical change," continued the man, "had taken place in the relations with the Soviet Union. A year ago, as you all know, the Germans, turning against their former ally, had invaded their country. The Soviets were now on the run, unable to defend themselves against the Nazis. Believing that Hitler was worse than Stalin, the Allies intended to come to the aid of the Soviets. "And," the delegate continued, "our government recently concluded an agreement with the Soviets in Moscow, providing for the amnesty of all Polish citizens, whether interned in Soviet POW camps, kept in Soviet prisons, or deported to labor camps in Siberia, and for the formation of a Polish Army in the USSR. Those men are now being released and moved to the Middle East. They will be stationed and undergo training in Polish Army camps in Iran, Iraq, and Palestine; and soon some of you will be joining the newly formed units of the Polish Army in the Middle East." Silence reigned for a while as we were waiting for what was to follow, until our CO took over.

"Now for something else that may directly affect your future. The decision is yours, and you must give it some thought. Now, after the significant expansion of our forces here in the Middle East, our general staff in London has decided to offer you the opportunity to join our units operating out of England." The CO stopped, his remarks greeted by more silence. The unexpected prospects evidently needed time to sink in.

After a while, seemingly undeterred, he proceeded, "Prospective volunteers for the air force, navy, or paratroopers' brigade will have to report for a preliminary medical examination. The medical board will sit in the mess hall as from this afternoon. Any questions?"

After some shuffling of feet and subdued mutterings of many voices, two men raised their hands.

"Sir, how would we get to England?"

"Sir, what about our training here? We still have a full month to go."

Our CO conferred for few moments with the delegate from London and then turned back to us.

"Let me answer the second question first. Unfortunately, there will be no time for prospective volunteers to finish the course here. You have to make up your minds straight away. As to the first question, that's not your problem. If you decide to go to England, we'll get you there. I've nothing more to say. Captain, dismiss!"

In the oppressive heat of the early afternoon, stripped to the underwear, we sat in our tents with their sides raised, weighing the pros and cons of the new proposition, in fact, pondering what to do with our lives. It seemed to many of us the most difficult decision that we had ever had to make. So far, life in the military has been a matter of obeying orders, of being told at every step where to go and what to do. The instant decisions we had to make in the last three years were those of life and death, with no other choice. Now we had to chart our respective courses, without guidance, uncertain of the consequences. For few moments, I was racked with indecision, in an agony of uncertainty, when, suddenly, I had a clear vision of my future. I put on my uniform and, on the double, joined the queue marked Air Force. Flying was after all a passion of my schoolboy's life.

And so on the sweltering morning of July 21, 1942, after a voyage of almost half round the globe, via Cape Town and Rio de Janeiro, the MS *Queen Mary* approached New York Harbor. As the thin coastline appeared through the morning mist, the large group of Polish soldiers stood anxiously at the railing on the promenade deck, trying to divine the future. Passing the Statue of Liberty, somebody shouted, "Good-bye desert, New York, here we come!" We were all ready and packed since the preceding evening, but we still had the job of delivering our human cargo—one housand four hundred German POWs—into other hands. At 1:30 p.m., barges pulled up alongside the ship and started taking prisoners ashore. On the way, both our charges and we were in an excellent mood, all smiles and exchanging mementos. The Germans, it would appear, have, at last, found a temporary home. We handed them over to the Canadians who—careful to avoid overcrowding—placed them in elegant passenger Pullman cars on their way to the camps in either Canada or the United States. Subsequently, the same barges took us to the other side of the port to the U.S. Army camp in Fort Hamilton, Brooklyn; we were the first ever Polish Army unit to visit the United States.

So here I was in America. One of the three hundred men under the command of that familiar figure, Colonel Sokal. For days now, I have been wondering what kind of the country it would be: the funny one I knew from Laurel and Hardy movies, or the brutal one as described to me by Mr. Grabowski in Turkey? At least now, Americans were our allies in this war. But I had no idea where they were actually fighting, though we found out soon that their main effort would be directed against Japan. "Well, gentlemen," observed one of our soldiers, "we shall have to take care of Europe ourselves. That is why they are sending us there."

A group of us who had kept together since Egypt threw ourselves now headlong into the social life of the city, coming to know both its generosity and its dangers born of our naïveté.

On our first night at Fort Hamilton, after dinner in the camp's gleaming cafeteria, a group of American GIs came over to our table and invited us to a dance at the USO—the organization in charge of entertainment for U.S. Armed Forces. As we arrived, the canteen was full of pretty girls in pleated skirts and white bobby socks. A kaleidoscopic jukebox blasted out the hot tunes of the day; a dispenser offered iced Coke at five cents a bottle. As soon as we entered, the GIs silenced the dancing crowd and introduced us as "the desert rats of Tobruk." In the midst of the loud welcome, we were overcome by uncommon shyness and stood there like so many wallflowers, fidgeting, until several girls wandered over and unceremoniously dragged us onto the dance floor. In the hot canteen, still wearing our heavy woolen uniforms issued to us in

Suez, we were by the end of the evening drenched in sweat. Even with the temperature in the 80s, typical New York summer weather, our sergeant had forbidden us to wear tropical uniform in the city. "No shorts in America," he declared.

The next morning, five of us, including me, were chosen to represent our unit in meetings with some local politicians. Dressed with care, wearing ties and freshly shined boots, we were taken to Manhattan, seated at the top table and, though not entirely sure of what the local worthies were speechifying about us in English, we collected tumultuous applause. But oh, how boring it was! On another day, we attended a gala reception and dance at the Polish Club on St. Mark's Place, where at least we could enjoy our own language and breathe our own, albeit Polish-American folk culture. On Friday, July 24, we visited Manhattan again but, this time, in the company of courteous, young Americans acting as our guides; we drove in convertibles along Broadway, had an excellent Chinese meal, a novelty for us, and took in the Ice Show. At Radio City Music Hall, we watched a revue with a huge Cadillac car on the stage, flag-waving American soldiers, and the high-kicking Rockettes, followed by the feature film *Mrs. Miniver,* with Greer Garson and Walter Pidgeon, a love story set in the early days of the war in England; we laughed quite a lot and kept telling our guides that this kind of war was very different from the one that we had experienced.

in Brooklyn, NY

Save for an occasional little flag with a star in a window, indicating a soldier in the family, and posters featuring caricatures of the Japanese emperor being kicked in the arse with a boot inscribed USA, New York showed few signs of the war raging on other continents. During my fortnight's leave there, I experienced the

in American uniforms—Irvington, NJ

shock of the new, and yet I was also discovering the city and its history as the traditional gateway for new immigrants. Even the clichés and the hyperboles I had come across in the past seemed quite inadequate to describe its reality: the daring skyscrapers, the canyons, and the hubbub of the streets below, the frantic traffic. At the same time, I could sense the place being a magnet for dreamers of every kind and from everywhere—all those in search of a better life, full of ambition to succeed.

We were struck by the immense diversity of the place; but one night, we had a less than pleasant experience. Three of us went to a bar in Harlem to listen to jazz music as a result of a chance encounter on a public bus with a nice, older black man who struck up a conversation with us in . . . Polish. Apparently, as a young man, he had worked with Poles in Chicago and still remembered a bit of the language. The show at Small's Paradise was great fun and everything went well until we left the establishment. Outside, a smiling rogue in a zoot suit—an odd attire fashionable at the time in Harlem—approached us and, with a wink, promised us an even better time, this time with girls. We followed him to an apartment where some black men met us with hostile stares. An ugly situation was brewing, a scuffle was about to begin, we saw the flash of a knife. One of our group shouted, "Lets get out!" And we fled down the street as fast as our legs would carry us until we bumped into two policemen who took us to the nearest subway station, leaving us with a warning to stay away from the neighborhood. I am still not sure who and why provoked the incident.

Repercussions of our American visit were reported in the Polish press on both sides of the Atlantic. To our great amusement, we read,

"A unit of Polish defenders of Tobruk, straight from the battlefield, arrived in New York. Their unit commander received hundreds of invitations for a group of at least fifty soldiers to visit every venue, on every available evening. Fifteen thousand men would not have been enough to satisfy the demand."

There were over seven hundred telephone calls each day, and the switchboard had asked the colonel not to talk for more than five minutes per call to give others a chance. An event in Prospect Hall assembled eight thousand people. At midnight, when the commanding officer wanted to end the party and leave, beautiful ladies protested and formed a colorful barrier.

The chief medical officer at the camp enquired whether, in view of the fatigue and recent experiences of the troops, it would be advisable to supply each soldier with ten bottles of beer a day. When Colonel Sokal replied that he would rather see his soldiers in an upright position, the doctor prescribed some unbelievable quantities of milk . . .

Commenting on these events with hindsight one wonders why such a hullabaloo was created by our small group of fifty "veterans" of the Libyan campaign while the arrival of 250 Polish former prisoners of the Soviet gulag was met with a total silence, and why did it not raise a single question or comment in the press.

Our commander was summoned to the Polish embassy in Washington DC. In his memoirs, he reported that he met with high-ranking U.S. officials including the head of U.S. Military Intelligence-East. I wonder now whether he had been asked about the experience of his soldiers in Soviet Russia. Or was it the beginning of the U.S. policy to look the other way and not antagonize Stalin, which finally led to the Yalta agreement, which ceded Eastern Europe to Soviet domination?

The New York interlude ended on Wednesday, August 5, when, after lengthy farewells and a series of parades, buses took us from the Fort Hamilton camp to New York's port. It was crawling with American soldiers; while everywhere, huge road convoys were unloading men and equipment. Obviously, American troops were on their way to Europe too. That was reassuring.

We marched along the waterfront under the heavy creaking cranes. We passed by the wreck of the sunken French luxury liner *Normandie*, destroyed by a blaze. Passing the Polish liner *Batory*, now painted grey like all the other ships, quickened our hearts for a while. Were we going to board her? But no, we were marching past her, shouting and waving at the crew who, because of the general noise, did not hear our nostalgic calls. At long last we reached the *Andes*, a capacious British ship, which before the war used to ply the South American routes. We boarded her, finding her already full of GIs. We found our assigned places and discovered that this time we were to sleep in hammocks. But being unaccustomed to such accommodation, many of our boys spent the first night on deck. At dawn the following day, we sailed out of New York harbor; and as we passed the Statue of Liberty, many Americans on deck were in tears, taking leave of their country, some, no doubt, for good. The GIs, having discovered that we had already served on the frontline, kept asking us unending questions. But how do you describe the misery, the fear, the occasional fury of a real fight? Most of us would just say, "Oh well, it was all right."

We were part of a convoy of eleven troopships carrying mostly American soldiers and escorted by several Navy warships. Two days later, in the morning, we skirted Nova Scotia. We entered Halifax harbor at 11:00 a.m. still in the dark about our final destination. Soon though, we were at sea again, our convoy augmented by several Canadian troop ships.

The sea was rough, and it continued to be cold and foggy for the rest of our voyage, so we avoided the decks and spent most of our time in the various common rooms. By then, our Polish group enjoyed great popularity among our new American friends, quite a few of whom had Polish roots and started recalling some Polish words vaguely remembered from childhood. And to my great surprise, I suddenly discovered that my English has become fairly fluent, enough for an informal conversation.

August 15, celebrated in our country as the Soldier's Day in memory of the defeat of the Red Army in 1920, would have been the day of our graduation from the officer's school had we stayed in Palestine. Yet now, we were shivering with cold somewhere off Greenland, on an angry, menacing ocean.

At last, on Monday, August 17, the Irish coast appeared on starboard, with Scotland on the other side. The weather rapidly improved. The convoy headed for the port of Liverpool, where we, the Polish unit, descended the gangway to the loud cheers of our American Allies. In high spirits, with other volunteers for the Polish Air Force, I boarded the train for Scotland half an hour past midnight,.

6

There Will Be Heavy Casualties, You Know

Cowdenbeath was a transit camp, not far from Dunfermline in Fife. Here, we were given some ten days respite after our sea voyage. Photographs taken at the time show our unit in khaki battle dress and field caps, relaxing in the hilly countryside and attending a soccer match. It was also here that we first met local people—the ones we were interested in, being, of course, girls. These new encounters came easily and quickly, and we were amazed by the good will of the Scots and the ingenuous idea of dances organized by parishes in church halls.

first day in Scotland

At the same time, and without our knowledge, Polish intelligence officers were still busy screening the former Soviet prisoners among us for possible NKVD (Soviet Secret Police) infiltrators. Soon all air force volunteers were shipped off to Blackpool, a holiday resort on the west coast of

England. On September 4, 1942, aged nearly twenty, having passed another medical, I was accepted into the Polish Air Force and about to start a two-year fighter pilot training course.

The holiday season in Blackpool was still in full swing. Save for the large numbers of uniformed servicemen, there was no sign of the country being at war. Large family groups of holidaymakers, children, parents, grandparents were sitting on their small folding chairs, playing in the grayish sand, wading in the water at low tide, searching for half-buried winkles also available from stalls scattered along the seaside promenade. Between the beach and the town itself, one could also find such entertainment as jugglers, mini-theatres, curiosity shops, flea circuses, and chambers of horrors; there were kiosks and tents selling a variety of trinkets and snacks, the most popular of the latter being fish and chips served with salt and vinegar in newspaper cones. To the servicemen stationed in and around the town the main point of interest was the Tower Dance Hall, an establishment with a high steel tower on its roof, seemingly a scaled-down version of the Parisian Eiffel Tower. This Tower Dance Hall was to me the epitome of luxury and excitement. I was no less bewitched by the crowds of local girls milling round the dance floor, obviously here for a knees-up. When male partners were not available, the girls would dance with each other, now and then casting shy looks to see if by any chance a serviceman might emerge from the crowd to cut in; to refuse a dance was simply not done.

in Air Force uniform

However, even among all the partying, dancing, and other pleasures of Blackpool, we were not allowed to forget about the reality of war. Shortly after our arrival, we exchanged our khaki uniforms for brand-new air force blues. Every morning, after roll call, we drilled in some wide street or square, marching back and forth, and singing, ad nauseam, Polish army songs whose origins went back as far as the Napoleonic wars to the enjoyment of holidaymakers who must have regarded us as figures of fun.

The Polish Air Force training schools were organized along the lines established by the Royal Air Force. In the flight training schools, all instructors were Polish pilots. Following the initial ground courses, the same for all volunteers, the budding aircrews were divided into three specialties: pilots, navigators and bombardiers; gunners could be accepted without the first two long stages. Eleven months would pass before my first solo flight.

Sometime in the latter half of September, we were transferred to Hucknall in Nottinghamshire for the first stage of ACTC (Air Crew Training Course). We lived in one-story barracks, partly occupied by a senior group already attending a flying course. Our commander was an acquaintance of my family. I reminded him one day that in 1937 we had met on a country estate where a group of us children crawled all over the small sports plane in which he had flown in with Major Stanisław Skarżyński. He nodded then went serious and asked whether I'd heard that Skarżyński had been killed. Skarżyński used to be called the Polish Lindbergh; in 1933, he made the seventeen-hour nonstop transatlantic flight in a small sports plane of Polish design and construction. He flew from Warsaw to Dakar and over the south Atlantic to Brazil and then to Buenos Aires.

I was dumbstruck; I was actually intending to ask him how to get in touch with the major, with whom we parted in Bucharest three years ago. Nor did I know that his widow, who for me would always be Aunt Julia, and their son had made their way to England and were living not far from here, in Radcliff-on-Trent. I was eager to see them and quickly dashed off a note. I received a warm reply from Aunt Julia, asking me to consider her house as my "home away from home."

I also placed an ad in the paper *Soldiers' Daily*, searching for my fellow refugees from Poland. In response, I soon learned that the Leppert family were now living in Swansea, South Wales. Zygmunt, a chemical engineer, was working in the munitions industry; their son Władek had joined the air force and was about to be shipped to Canada. As for Zygmunt's wife, Marynka, and their daughter Lala, who had been left in France in 1940 and now smuggled out through clandestine channels via Lisbon, they have recently joined their menfolk in Great Britain. As soon as I got in touch, the Lepperts asked me to visit them.

In mid-January 1943, I completed the first stage of my training and passed all the exams, and there was no doubt where I would be spending my coming week's leave. But I also went to London and saw the devastation wrought by the German air offensive in the Battle of Britain. Underground stations were jammed with people camping out, sprawled all over the place, lying on mattresses that had seen better days, sitting on dilapidated folding chairs, huddled in blankets. The fear was pervasive and palpable. This picture of total war carried to the civilian population became symbolic of London at the time.

A family friend invited me to a cinema in Leicester Square. The film, in Technicolor, was *The Four Feathers*, depicting Lord Kitchener's nineteenth century expedition to quell a radical Muslim insurrection in Sudan—a true imperial theme. Memories of the desert war came back to me as I was leaving London, lost in a thick yellowish-gray fog—understandably called a peasouper by the locals—with visibility reduced to several paces.

I spent the next five months in Brighton, another holiday resort, but this time on the Channel. Our tiresome technical courses and particularly the drilling experience came in useful one day when, unexpectedly, we were ordered to prepare for a military parade to take place in London. No one seemed to know what the occasion

was supposed to be or who would be reviewing the parade. From Victoria station, we marched in our natty uniforms, white belts, spit-shined boots toward Trafalgar Square. Other air force units have already gathered in a wide side street. We took our place next to the Americans. We still had no clue as to what all this was about. The Polish Daily and other papers reported the event:

> The culminating event of the "Wings for Victory" week was the parade of the Allied Air Forces in Trafalgar Square on March 11, 1943 . . . This was a splendid demonstration by the fighting nations of Europe, nations defeated but not vanquished.

This parade was the last such event of the time in which Poles would participate. As a result of the later pro-Soviet, and thus anti-Polish, sentiments in Great Britain, the Polish Armed Services were not invited to take part in the Great Victory Parade of June 1946 in London. We, in the ranks, were slow in comprehending the reasons for such a change of attitude toward the most loyal of Allies. But soon we understood. In the spring of 1943, we were suddenly faced with several external crises of major proportions affecting us all.

In March, the German army had discovered in the forest near the village of Katyń in Soviet Byelorussia mass graves of more than four thousand Polish officers captured by the Soviets in 1939. The mysterious disappearance of most of the officer's corps has already been known for two years. After the signing of the Polish-Soviet pact in 1941, the Polish government made their first inquiries about more than fifteen thousand of its officers who had been taken prisoner by the Soviets. Now, in the absence of any plausible explanation, the Polish government requested the International Red Cross in Switzerland to investigate the Katyń tragedy. Following this, events developed very quickly. In a note dated April 23, 1943, the Soviet Union broke off diplomatic relations with Poland, denouncing the Polish government in London and its armed forces as fascists. No one could have predicted such a turn of events. Great Britain and the United States were caught off guard. As Stalin was at the time too important an ally for the Western Allies to antagonize while Poles were expendable, the Polish government in exile was sidelined. Poland had lost its standing as an important political force while we, men in uniform, were oblivious to the vicious anti-Polish campaign gathering strength in the press, fuelled in part by the slavish British Communist Party and rabidly pro-Soviet trade unions. In the long run, the Katyń case continued to be presented as proof of the fascist tendencies prevalent among Poles, both in the government in exile and in her armed forces. It was only in 1991, after the collapse of the Soviet Union that the new Russian government admitted to the murder of over twenty-five thousand Polish prisoners of war on Stalin's orders in 1940.

May brought news of another tragedy: the Jewish uprising in the Warsaw Ghetto, followed by the slaughter of all its inhabitants and the razing of the whole Jewish quarter to the ground. Somehow, my companion, Ludwik Gutnajer, new already for some time about this tragedy. His entire family perished there. The *Polish Daily* published a letter by Szmul Zygelboim, the leader of the Jewish Socialist Party and a member of the Polish National Council in London, addressed to the president of Poland and the prime minister, General Sikorski. This was written prior to his suicide, which was a gesture of despair and protest:

> With the latest news from our country, it appears incontrovertible that the Germans are murdering the remaining Jewish population of Poland with unspeakable savagery; the responsibility for this monstrous crime falls first of all on the perpetrators, but indirectly also on the whole of humanity, the peoples and the governments of the allied countries which so far failed to act to stop this.

In the second half of May, during one of the weekends I was spending in London with my WRNS (Women's Royal Naval Service) girlfriend Anne, I noticed the big bold headline in a newspaper held by a man sitting next to me on a bus. It said, THE POLES GOT THEIR CHANCE AND THEY TOOK IT!

with Anne in Brighton

The article was protesting against all the indignities and humiliations we had suffered in the recent times. Seeing my interest and evidently having noticed the POLAND tabs on my shoulders, the man passed the paper to me with a smile. It was there that I read for the first time of the Polish Army's assault on Monte Cassino, a fortified Benedictine monastery on top of a steep mountain. The monastery, part of the formidable German Gustav Line stretching across the Italian Peninsula and denying the Allies access to Rome, was taken by the Second Polish Corps after a three-day-long battle, suffering the loss of close to three thousand—more than total Allied loses during the D-day invasion in Normandy one year later.

By the end of June, I completed the tiresome three-month stint in Brighton and with other would-be pilots returned to Hucknall to be admitted at last to the EFTS (Elementary Flying Training School). My new companions came from different backgrounds; whereas, the majority of trainees were now evacuees from the Soviet Union, the school also included volunteers from the Polish army units stationed in Scotland and Polish emigrants from as far away as Latin America and the Far East. It was an unparalleled recruiting scheme reaching the Polish diaspora on all continents, in many countries. Large groups of Poles from the Middle East were also coming, some retracing our voyage via Halifax and also taking German POWs to Canada, some sailing more directly to Great Britain along the western coast of Africa. One of these transport ships was torpedoed by a German U-boat, resulting in many casualties in that shark-infested waters. The Germans had been operating in this area from Dakar, the former French base in Senegal, which was surrendered to them by Vichy France in 1940.

after first solo flight

Our training in Hucknall was taking place in lovely summer weather. On my very first day, my instructor flipped the plane and let it dive, as exhilarating an experience as any I'd ever had.

"How do you feel?" asked the lieutenant as he pulled out of the dive.

"Fine!" I shouted back.

He then turned the plane abruptly at low altitude and called out, "Look down to the left . . . see the cemetery? That's where those who don't learn to fly properly end up! Got it?"

"This is not my intention!" I shouted back. I was in seventh heaven.

And then we were hit by our third national tragedy. On July 4, the sky was overcast; a storm was in the offing. As we sat in the dispersal hut listening to the radio, the regular program was suddenly interrupted by shocking news: General Władysław Sikorski, the prime minister and commander in chief of the Polish Armed Forces, died in a tragic air accident in Gibraltar, returning from his second trip to the Middle East. There were no survivors save the Czech pilot of the *Liberator*. An investigative committee was appointed and was already flying to Gibraltar to begin its grim task.

We sat there, numb with grief, wondering how this calamity would affect our future.

"This was not an accident," said someone grimly. "It has 'Soviets' written large all over it."

"Well, maybe," agreed somebody else. "After the discovery of the Katyń massacre, Sikorski became even more of a thorn in Stalin's side. But gentlemen, on the other hand, his stand on postwar Polish-Soviet relations must have become inconvenient for Churchill and Roosevelt who wanted to appease the Soviets. And what about some elements of the Polish intelligence services and their leaders who opposed the Sikorski—Stalin agreement in the first place." All heads turned in the direction of the voice. We were gripped by paranoia, haunted by thoughts of all the betrayals we had suffered by the Soviets in 1939, the French in 1940—and now what? With friends like these, who needed enemies? The suspicion cast a long shadow on our continuing participation in the war.

(The mystery of Sikorski's death failed to go away. Even fifty years after the accident, British archives which were supposed to be made accessible after that period, did not become available and their classified status was extended for a further fifty years. Recently a researcher at The Hoover Institute at Stanford University reported that there is some evidence that there was an attempt on Churchill's life, only two days before the Gibraltar crash. If this were proved to be true it would add another layer of mystery to other unexplained secrets of that time).

I completed the EFTS course on 23 August 1943, with 785 out of the possible 800 points. While entering this result into the flights record, Major Czerny, our CO training, smiled and said, "Carry on like this and you will make a decent pilot."

Toward the end of August 1943, after a short leave in London, I reported to the 16 (P) SFTS (Secondary Flying Training School) in Newton near Nottingham to begin the final phase of my pilot training.

Newton was a large Polish Air Force base, where pilots were trained for service in either bomber or fighter squadrons. There were forty-one of us, candidates for pilot's wings. My first flight was on September 1, the fourth anniversary of the beginning of the war; the significance of the date not lost on any of us. While going with me over the cockpit drill in the Master, my instructor remarked,

flight of Masters

"Had we had even such planes in Poland then, the Germans might have paid a higher price than the two hundred plus of theirs we shot down in 1939."

I knew from the beginning that I wanted to be a fighter pilot. As a fighter pilot is his own navigator, this involved intensive navigational training, which one would need in daylight hours; while at night, one had to rely on instruments. But all this was child's play compared to the aerobatics that we had to master. A typical routine was like this: the lead plane would shoot up and proceed to a tight starboard turn, gain more height and make a port flip; on its back, it would go into a steep dive, pulling up a couple of thousand feet below. Then it would ascend again, rolling and flipping, dive once more, and pull up again, having described a full circle, and so on and on. To be the leader in these exercises was fairly easy and great fun, but to be the pursuer was altogether another matter. In either case, one would return from these flights drenched in sweat, adrenaline pumping furiously as in no other situation in which I had ever found myself. Feeling neither fear—we were beyond fear at that stage—nor anger, nor sense of rivalry, only euphoria issuing from the absolute freedom of movement in the big sky, away from the restrictions of two-dimensional motion on the earth below.

We were waiting impatiently for the end of the course. I achieved my dream on February 9, 1944, my performance at the school having been judged "above average." Somewhat disappointed, I brooded on my grade, only to learn that it was the standard satisfactory evaluation.

One of us, a smart aleck, cheekily asked our sergeant, "Are 'excellent' marks not in the CO's vocabulary?" "You'll give yourself an 'excellent' if you survive the war," he answered brusquely. "There will be heavy casualties, you know."

After the passing-out ceremony, I packed my belongings and left together with three of my buddies for our next posting at the Air Gunnery School (3AGS) at Castle Kennedy, an airfield near the town of Stranraer, in Scotland, for the final stage of our flying practice. There, good boys that we were, we flew regularly, twice a day for three months, in the Martinets, the working horse of the school, to gather the required flying hours. One plane would tow a long canvass sleeve, which served as target for air gunners flying alongside in another plane, a twin-engine Anson.

On June 6, the day which would be called D-day, we woke up to the news that at long last the Western Allies had set foot on the continent of Europe. On that epoch-making day, Castle Kennedy and its environs were shrouded in fog, and no flights were scheduled. We sat all day in the sergeant's mess, listening to the BBC's up-to-the-minute reports. We had no idea whether any Polish units were taking part in the invasion. We did know that some months before, the First Polish Armored Division was moved from Scotland to the south of England, and that most of Polish fighter squadrons too were stationed in the south since 1940. But that was all the information we had and, naturally, there was no end to speculation. We heard that American troops had landed near Cherbourg.

On June 14, I completed three hour-long flights. One of my friends was waiting for me in the dispersal hut and shouted as soon as he saw me, "We are leaving tomorrow! You and I, to 61 OUT (Operational Training Unit) in Rednall!"

Later that day, I boarded the train for London where I broke my journey for two days. Here, I sadly learned that Władek, Lala's brother, serving in bombers, had been killed in action. Last time I saw him was during my first visit to Swansea.

Bomber crews were in constant action and suffered heavy losses. RAF Command had devised a plan for mass-bombing raids on German cities, with something like a thousand planes at a time. Polish Air Force mobilized all their active and operational training units and flew over a hundred bombers. In one year, their bomber squadrons made 2,450 combat missions—significant contribution to the overall Allied effort. As we learned later, Polish fighter squadrons had been active on and after D-day. They flew three times over the landing beaches and, in the first two days of the operation, clocked up the top score of thirty German planes shot down, as well as bombing and strafing positions and columns in the enemy rear.

In Rednall, of the forty-one members of our training unit, twenty-one were Poles while the other half comprised English, Scots, Welsh, Irish, Canadians and New Zealanders. On June 23, I took a Spitfire up on my first flying hour in this plane. My joy was indescribable. I was in seventh, no, tenth heaven. The famous plane was a technological marvel. At three thousand feet, I accelerated and tried a barrel roll to the left—no problem; to the right—just as easy. I increased my altitude to above the heaped rounded mass of cumulus clouds, cut off the gas, and pulled the joystick toward me. The plane lost speed; and when it started to stall and began coming down, I pushed my left foot. The plane turned gently over the left wing and entered into a spin. After three or four turns, I pushed the right pedal and the joystick forward. Immediately, the plane came out of the spin and went into a steep dive. Accelerating, I got it out of the dive. Looking up, I waited to see the horizon, upside down, behind me. On my back, I executed a half-roll, and the plane went straight on. I could not stop marveling. Wonderful, miraculous, I kept saying to myself, ready to give credit to the plane alone.

Rednal-sergeant's mess

From time to time, we would sneak out to the nearby town of Shrewsbury to a dance hall. As pilots, we enjoyed great popularity. Other units, such as the Royal Engineers or the Signals Corps could not compete

American pilots

with us. But nobody could compete with the Americans who had seemingly unlimited supplies of money, cigarettes, oranges, and nylon stockings. We used to meet them in the air, on the airfields, and in the Shrewsbury bars. On the ground, each one of them seemed to have two girls at his side at all times. But maybe this was just my imagination or jealousy. Still, I wondered whether they boasted of their conquests in their letters home. Unfortunately, my home was inaccessible; and I had no one to show off to.

Some time during this period, we learned that one of our pilots shot down the one thousandth enemy plane brought down by Polish airmen since the beginning of the war. We were itching to add to this score.

At last, in July, nearly five years after Hitler's invasion of Poland, four of us received the posting we had been impatiently waiting for. We were being sent to 308 (P) squadron stationed in France.

For the second time in three years, I was leaving for the frontline.

7

Snap to It, Gentlemen! The 308 Goes First

In the summer 1944, our first airfield in France worthy of its name, following the previously used mere grassy landing strips, was B51 Lille-Vandeville. The Polish Fighter Wing 131(P) was a self-sufficient unit with its own technical and maintenance personnel. It was part of Eighty-fourth Fighter Group. It comprised three squadrons, altogether more than three score Spitfire IXs and auxiliary planes.

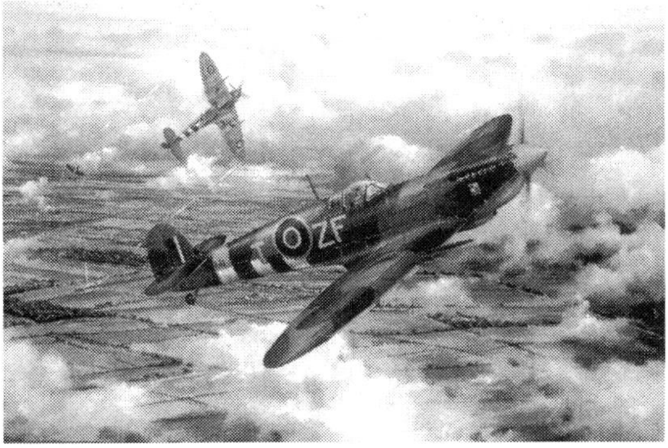

ZF—T (by P. Górka)—combat action in Holand

In April 1944, a new air force agreement was signed by the British and Polish governments, which gave the Polish Air Force (PAF) complete autonomy under overall Allied command.

My reporting to frontline duty coincided with the heart-wrenching news of the insurrection in Warsaw, organized by the Home Army—the underground Polish fighting force. The uprising against the Germans had started on August 1, 1944, and, in my opinion, largely due to the fatal miscalculation by the Polish leadership in London and in Poland, was doomed from the start. It seemed to me then that all it achieved was a massacre of the lightly armed fighters and civilians alike and the near-total destruction of the city. Huge Soviet army was already camped on the opposite bank of the Vistula River, the Polish leadership believing that it would come to the aid of the insurgents. But it suited Stalin's plans to have the best of the Polish nation massacred by the Nazis. Still, the leadership ought to have known that the geopolitical climate was hardly conducive to playing a power game with the Soviets, using innocent people as pawns.

On October 2, after two months of this uneven struggle, we heard the news: the fight between several crack German divisions, commanding tanks, heavy artillery, air power on one side and young insurgents was over. Warsaw had capitulated. Historians would determine later that twenty thousand insurgents, half of the fighting force and two hundred thousand civilians, had died during sixty-three days of house-to-house fighting. It averaged over three thousand a day or equal to combined Allied losses during the D-day invasion and the total of 9/11 victims.

I was at first torn between the impotent rage of a combatant denied the chance to avenge, to punish, to come to the aid of the fighters, and the anxiety for my mother and the rest of the family, from whom I have had no news for nearly five years. Sometimes, the homesickness, the remoteness, and separation were unbearable. Taking active part in the war was a blessing and attenuated the bitterness of the last few years.

Meanwhile, the air war was gaining momentum. We flew two or tree combat missions each day, which took its toll of the pilots.

On October 11, after bombing and strafing a fortified stronghold on the Dutch coast near Bergen op Zoom, we landed on the B-61 airfield at St. Denijs-Westrem near Ghent, meant to become our next base for a while. We arrived all together, the entire wing of thirty-six Spitfires IX and several spare machines. We got out of our planes in a drizzle, with yellow mud splashing underfoot. The airfield's only starting strip consisted of metal mash laid directly on the muddy ground, covered here and there with clumps of brownish grass. The field was surrounded on three sides by yellowing poplars and, on the fourth, by an unsightly assortment of blackened huts and barracks, including our dispersal hut, which stretched along a two-lane highway. One of the maintenance crew helped me to unhitch my parachute and pointed east to a cluster of dark brick buildings faintly silhouetted against the cloudy sky. "We're all billeted there, at Don Bosco, a Salesian fathers' monastery. Pilots stay in those villas over there." He pointed to some two—and three-story buildings on the other side of the highway. They were decent buildings with front and back gardens. Not bad, I thought.

It was only a few weeks ago that the First Polish Armored Division had liberated the city. Our boys had managed to empty several well-stocked beer cellars, to break a few dozen hearts, and then to drive their tanks on to Holland. So now it was our turn. So far, encounters with German warplanes had been few and far between so that our deeply felt anger and passionate wish to avenge Warsaw was frustrated. Destroying an enemy position here, few armored vehicles there did not give us enough satisfaction. Sometimes, this war seemed infuriatingly dull or is this rather an exaggeration in view of our multiple daily sorties, evading enemy fire, and the rest? Whatever it was, boredom or impatience, it was sharpening our awareness of loss and, in my case, brought to the fore the long repressed worry: what fate had befallen my family.

One day, as we were in readiness, sprawled idly on wooden bunks and chairs of our dispersal hut, in full gear, talking about nothing, waiting for the "scramble" signal, I started wondering what I was really doing here, in Ghent of all places. Ghent, the name sounded familiar, particularly in its Polish version, Gandawa. Why, of course, why hadn't it occurred to me before? It was in this very city that aeons ago my paternal uncle Józef had studied architecture!

"Boys! Do you realize?" I called out. "There is a famous school of architecture here in Ghent."

"Yes? So what?" answered a blasé voice.

"My paternal uncle was a student here."

"Don't say! Is that why it's so famous?"

"Oh, shut up! No point talking to you. You don't understand a thing. After the war, when the world is back to normal, I may even try to enroll here myself."

"I am sure they can't wait."

"You'll see!" My patience was at its end.

"Careful, Jerzy!" someone else remarked. "Don't bomb the university by mistake the way you did yesterday with the Dordrecht railway station."

"What do you mean?"

"Your job was to take care of the ack-ack, and the station was to be left to us. That's what!"

"So?"

"But you didn't, did you? And when we got to the station we were just sitting ducks for their guns! I felt like a duck with a backside full of shot."

At that point the telephone rang. The duty officer took the call. "Yes, right. Roger, out."

"OK, Flight B, north of Bergen op Zoom, a resort on the seacoast. Five hundred pounds of bombs and then strafing."

"What's there? Antiaircraft batteries?"

"Yes . . . among other things. Thanks." Lieutenant Lipkowski, formerly of the Polish cavalry, grabbed his mascot, a fox's tail, and rushed out. Three of us followed hot on his trail. Ten minutes later we were in the air. I had a good look on Ghent, I must come back here in better times, I thought.

Suddenly, there was Lieutenant Lipkowski's voice in my headphone. "Bloody hell!" he shouted. "I am going down!" I stretched my neck this way and that, up and down, there was no sign of him. A short while ago, in the heat of battle, we were joking that Bergen op Zoom was going to be a piece of cake. Just some bloody resort . . . And what about his lucky foxtail? One hour later, having got through furious antiaircraft fire, we were returning to Ghent, my close buddy Andy leading, our hearts racing.

Two bits of good news came through in the evening. First, a radio message: Lipkowski was OK. He baled out and was picked up by the Dutch resistance. And second, after four years of uncertainty, Andy received, out of the blue, a letter from his mother. She was now working at the recently opened Polish embassy in Paris. Andy managed to wangle a few days' leave, and one of our boys flew him to Paris in a small Auster plane. Four days later, I was ordered to fetch him back. Within half an hour, I was taxiing in the small plane to the starting line. I cruised at low altitude and, having myself plotted the course over Lille, Saint-Quentin, Compiègne, and on to Le Bourget, an airfield in the northern outskirts of Paris, I had a chance to admire the views. I flew past Lille, past various small towns—all sites of recent fighting—their centers reduced to rubble, their church steeples tumbled to the ground, farms burnt to ashes. The dense forest of Compiègne, changing to autumn colors, spread below me like a sumptuous red and gold carpet. Somewhere here, in a railway carriage in these woods, the armistice ending the Great World War had been signed on November 11, 1918. Here too in 1940, in the same railway car, a representative of France, a world power then, signed the shameful surrender document.

The first thing I saw of Paris was the Eiffel Tower, majestically rising above the horizon. At Le Bourget I hitched a ride in an army truck which dropped me off close to Les Invalides, in the historic center of the city, where the Polish embassy was located.

Andy's mother was surprised to see me. "Welcome, welcome, I am delighted to meet you. Andy talked a lot about you. But he left this morning for Belgium." Andy, apparently uncertain about arrangements for his return to Ghent and anxious not to be away too long, hitched a lift back in a transport plane and arrived in Ghent about the same time as I was taking off for Paris. Seeing that I was taken aback by this unexpected development, she tried to comfort me. "But don't worry; your trip wasn't actually a waste of time. Do you know that an uncle of yours is here in Paris? He's been writing to London to get some information about you . . . Hold on a second, I'll give him a call."

War does separate and bring people together in most mysterious ways.

It was my uncle Antoni or Antek as he was called at home, who was also my godfather. Both of my mother's younger brothers were French citizens and have been living in France since the mid-1930s and thus I hardly knew them.

Soon after, obviously arrived in a hurry, huffing and puffing, Antek burst through the embassy door. Our first embrace was somewhat awkward, but we warmed to each other after a short session of breathless questions and answers. We got into his car; and as he started it, I asked where he was taking me. "Home, of course; Aunt Irka is expecting us, and she's not one to be kept waiting." Not far from Versailles, in Vaucresson, we drove through narrow cobbled streets and arrived at Place de l'Église; Antek's house was next to the church. Aunt Irka, a small young, plump blonde, ran out and fell into my arms, laughing and crying all at once. I had met this charming girl very briefly before: first at their wedding in Warsaw and then before their departure for France.

Their home was an imposing residence, a former vicarage next to the fifteenth century church. Its interior was most impressive; it was furnished with antique furniture, candelabras, paintings by Polish masters, luxurious rugs; and it boasted a neat, if rather intricate garden. Was all of this acquired during the war? As I stood there on the fancy terrace, I wondered how Antek, in such dire straits in the 1930s, had come by his fortune.

We gathered in the salon, Antek brought a bottle of champagne in a silver bucket; the maid came in with a selection of snacks on a tray. As usual in such moments, we talked for a while at cross purposes and all at the same time, until we finally got to family matters. Unfortunately, Antek and Irka had no information about the fate of my mother and brother in Warsaw. My story was a revelation for them. They did not know that Witold and I had made our way to the Middle East. They had met the Lepperts, but lost track of them after the collapse of France. I had one more day at my disposal before having to fly back to Ghent, so Antek and Irka drove me to Paris in the morning. They insisted on buying me some warm clothes at the famous Hermès shop on rue du Faubourg Saint Honoré, stressing that winter was round the corner. I wondered what my mates at Ghent would make of it. We stopped for lunch in a crowded, black market restaurant, French haute cuisine at its best. In France, even under occupation, anything and everything was available. The Germans did not interfere with business; they even profited from it themselves. All manner of enterprises, theatres, cinemas, concert halls, restaurants thrived; turnover had never been better.

Parisian women at the Ritz Hotel, Oct. 1944

So that's how it is here, I thought to myself. Business is business. One buys, one sells. One makes a fortune. And what about taxes? But, of course, there was no state to pay taxes to, and you could not be expected to pay taxes to the enemy.

Et voilá!

In the evening, we went to the Lido, a nightspot on the Champs-Elysées, where, to sensual music, a line of long-legged girls in ruffles and ostrich feathers and not much else cavorted on the stage. "They are mainly English and Scandinavian girls," Antek told me. "The Germans had loved these shows." "English girls here, during the war?" I found it difficult to believe. Even though the place seemed to be full, a generous tip instantly produced a choice table near the stage. There were many Allied officers at the Lido, chiefly American, swilling champagne by the bottle, whistling and hooting at the performers—as no doubt had the Germans before them. Two months after the liberation of Paris, on my

American officers in Paris

first visit to the city, I found the place weirdly disconcerting yet bizarrely seductive.

Next day, on the way to the airport, Antek stopped the car on the corner of Place de la Concorde and rue de Rivoli. The stonewall of the Tuilleries Gardens showed some bullet marks and a hastily erected temporary board commemorating the death of several people killed here by a German sniper at the time of the liberation. "Mort sur le champ d'honneur [Fallen on the field of Glory]," I read with a dose of sarcasm as I could not help comparing this with the fate of Warsaw. At Le Bourget, I had to promise Antek and Irka to visit them again on my next leave, a promise I was quite happy to make. As they were waving their handkerchiefs, I taxied the Auster to the starting line. I made a round low over their heads and turned north. An hour into the flight, the small plane became enveloped by fog; visibility was atrocious. Flying low and keeping the highway under my wing, I managed to reach Saint-Quentin, an airfield under American control, where I was told that, because of the fog, all flights to Belgium had been grounded. I got a voucher to spend the night at a shabby little hotel, the bar of which was packed with Canadian soldiers, American GIs, and local girls.

GIs at the Sacre Coeur

shy Canadians

That night, in the bar, a tipsy American sergeant started telling me about his complicated amorous problems, particularly in communicating with one or two local girls. As I offered to help, he got up a bit unsteadily and brought round a shapely brunette, sat her next to me, and yelled in her ear "Tell him!" She burst out laughing and started telling me some involved story about another girl and another sergeant. Soon I lost track of her tale. Then our sergeant brought another girl by the hand, shoving away one of his mates. The two girls, rather scared, were perched on one chair and watched the two men across the table arguing and almost coming to blows. At that point, two Frenchmen in berets and with tricolored armbands bearing the letters *FFI* for Force Francaise d'Interieur swaggered into the bar. These "heroes of the French Resistance" began loudly to berate all French girls who befriended and, God forbid, slept with the Americans. The bar grew silent. Suddenly, a girl, hitherto snugly ensconced in the lap of a GI, shouted at the top of her voice, "So what? And where were you, you cowards, before the Americans arrived? And who do you think are you anyway?" In the next minute, all three girls stood up, facing the alleged "heroes," and, arms akimbo, let go a steady stream of abuse. Not to be outdone, the men shouted back, "You filthy whores, German whores then, American ones now. My two drunken sergeants stopped arguing. "What's all this about?" they asked me. I briefly summed up the situation for their benefit. "Oh yah," the first sergeant drew himself up and turned to his erstwhile enemy. "Jack, the girls got it right, don't you think? Who'd ever heard of those two shits? Some partisans! Commies, I bet. You know," he said turning to me, "when we were close to Paris, Ike stopped us in order to let the Leclerc division, those so called Free French, enter Paris first, liberate their capital, you know. What a joke, eh? For Christ sake! Come on Jack! Let's liberate those two scroungers! Kick them out!"

Without further ado, the two, suddenly, more or less sobered up, went up to the frightened "partisans," grabbed them by the collar, and threw them out to much cheering and applause. Jubilation spread like wildfire through the bar; and our table with the two girls, two sergeants, and myself became the center of attention. The party was just getting started.

The next day, I found out without regret that flights to Belgium were still grounded. I dutifully wired my commanding officer in Ghent that willy-nilly I had to return to Paris to wait for the weather to clear. After four more enjoyable days with my kin, I returned to my unit on October 26. But nothing much was happening there. The entire wing was still grounded. I had to describe my adventures in Paris in minute detail again and again, while the rest of my companions listened with mock disbelief and good-natured envy.

From late October to Christmas, our sorties, in support of advancing ground troops, became routine, breeding complacency, disturbed only by the death of two of our pilots shot down by antiaircraft fire. From time to time, we escorted American Flying Fortresses on their daylight raids on targets like the Ruhr basin—a task we were particularly keen on because the Americans, having acknowledged Polish expertise at providing airborne protection, would specifically request our services. In exchange, they called us their "little friends." Many Americans of Polish descent wrote to their families about our encounters in the air and on the ground; and in turn, we would get words of gratitude from the Polish Immigrant Organizations in USA and from their local authorities.

in the spitfire cockpit

Christmas Eve came, my fifth in exile. By now, at twenty-two, nearly a quarter of my life has been spent away from family and home. The cooks at the base did their best to keep up all our traditions; and as was the custom, we had a meatless supper on Christmas Eve, the most important night of Polish Christmas. A bottle of Aquavit contributed to the holiday spirit, aided further by the champagne. Soon the walls of our room were spinning.

"Let's go to midnight mass," suggested someone. "Yes, let's!" we responded in unison.

"Wait, I am coming with you," shouted Kazik Becher. He had just joined the 317, and we got to like him from the start. He was younger than most of us and of such short stature that straight away he earned the nickname "Junior." He was Jewish. He apparently had a beautiful sister who lived in London with their parents; and he painted her name, Roma, on his Spitfire. Kazik liked to play the violin, but we kept teasing him that he was always out of tune.

Kazik Becher

We were still rather tipsy as we ran to the Salesian fathers' compound. The chapel was tightly packed with Polish airmen in blue uniforms standing shoulder to shoulder with local inhabitants.

"Wait a minute, boys," stammered our Junior, trying to get his breath as we were pushing through the crowd. "You go ahead and pray, while I'll see to the collection."

"Off with your cap, Junior."

"OK."

We sang Polish carols and hymns loud, clear, and, for a change, in tune. The crowded, candlelit church, the familiar melodies, not to mention the alcohol circulating in our blood, plunged us into sentimentality, even elation. We all felt close to one another—Poles and Belgians, for the first time together in their liberated country. Later, in the sacristy, we found Junior, his collection tray piled high with banknotes. Our chaplain was delighted. "How the hell did you get all that loot?" he asked Junior with a smile. Junior smiled in return, giving us a naughty wink. "I have a foolproof method; let me show you." He picked up the tray with his outstretched left hand which partly covered the gun in his right hand. "You know,

Junior," said the chaplain, laughing heartily while removing his chasuble, the blood of those Jews Jesus chased out of the temple must be running in your veins." We returned to our barracks in high spirits, and Junior played carols on his violin late into the night.

On December 25, we escorted the Americans in a raid on Cologne. From the altitude of twenty-two thousand feet, in sunlight and clear air, I saw the city underneath us reduced to rubble. A silver ribbon of the Rhine ran through it, and the great mass of the cathedral stood in the middle. Warsaw is divided by the Vistula River in the same way. "And does it look like that now too?" I wondered, trying to recall the familiar city's sight in my mind's eye.

Les Ambassadeurs in Ghent

It was December 31, 1944. "Hey, you, stop daydreaming and let's get going or we'll be late. We mustn't keep the girls waiting." We were going to celebrate New Year's Eve at Les Ambassadeurs; our girls might be there already. I took one last glance in the shard of mirror on the wall to make sure that I've achieved the desired effect: tight fitting tunic, upper button undone—the privilege of a fighter pilot—the left breast proudly sporting my Gapa, the Polish pilot's badge, with other minor decorations and my squadron badge; the wings of the Royal Air Force just above the right breast pocket.

All three of us, slipping and sliding on the icy road, heady with joy, laughing, singing, and shouting at each other, ran to catch the departing yellow tram. Pulling one another up by the collar, we managed to scramble on to the platform and finally reached the city center. It was the first New Year's Eve since the liberation, the first year of freedom. We joined in wholeheartedly, basking in the honors normally reserved for true heroes. With champagne corks popping and among toasts *á nos liberateurs Polonais* (to our Polish liberators), crowds of people in funny hats and fancy masks rhythmically gyrated, their colors changing in the constantly varying lights. At one point, with two lovely bare arms round my neck and my two holding a luscious nubile body in a taffeta dress, a thought crossed my mind that I'd rather die than miss a night like this. We left the dance hall about five in the morning with the girls clinging to us as for sheer life. Such a difficult decision! The press of female hips was compelling us one way while duty called us the other. Not without turmoil, the latter option won. The squadron was, after all, at action stations. At the terminal, an abandoned tram was stalled. A Canadian soldier, a pink balloon tied to his greatcoat, stood on the front platform, banging the steering box.

"Stop hitting it and go home!" we shouted.

"I wish I could," came the slurred reply . . . there ain't no fucking steering wheel." "OK, come with us."

We'd slept, at the most, two hours when the orderly came in, making a terrible din and screaming at the top of his voice, "The 308 and the 317 . . . ready in fifteen minutes!"

Christ! As the room spun around me, I grabbed my bomber jacket, jumped into my fur-lined boots, and, almost tripping over our Canadian friend spread-eagled on the floor, ran across the road to the dispersal hut. Burning my lips, I slurped some tea as Karol Pniak, our squadron leader—his pajama pants showing under his coat—gave instructions. Shivering like a bunch of wet dogs, we were setting out to bomb the ferry on the River Maas—hardly our idea of curing the New Year's Eve hangover.

"Snap to it, gentlemen! The 308 goes first. The sooner you get back, the sooner you'll be able to hit the sack again."

I was shaking from head to foot when the mechanic, helping me to fasten the straps in the cockpit, dramatically turned his face away. "Jesus Christ! You do reek like a distillery." He jumped off the plane, grabbed an oxygen dispenser, climbed back on to the wing, pushed the rubber tip of the hose into my mouth, and hissed, "Breathe," as he opened the valve.

Soon the shakes were gone, the universe came back sharp into focus. In few minutes we were airborne. The weather was miraculous, the sky light blue, the sun shining bright on the snow-covered landscape. The world seemed empty and serene but for the roar of our Spitfire engines. One of us switched on his mike and gave a mighty yawn, resulting in mock improvisations all round. "Shut your traps," ordered Igo, our commander. "The barges are right ahead; chop down, fellows!"

Our squadron, followed by the 317, dived to five hundred feet and unleashed its bombs, each plane swiftly zooming up in turn. Strangely, we encountered no antiaircraft fire. We made another run, this time all guns blazing, spraying the water and nearby woods with bullets. Still, no response; nobody home? The radio silence was exemplary, everyone dreaming of his unmade bed. I smiled to myself as New Year's Eve's unfinished business came to mind.

The airwaves were silent for most of the trip until the quiet but clear voice of ground control disturbed the peace. The controller called our two squadrons in code, "Einsworth, Peacock, Einsworth, Peacock. About sixty enemy fighters, FWs, flying low, have crossed the front line, direction Brussels. Your course two hundred-twenty degrees; you'll spot them in about ten minutes. Over."

We change direction. Automatically, the left hand switches on the gyroscopic target finder, setting the type of the plane. The red beads form a little ring on the screen. The right hand presses the button of the fuel gauge. And, not surprisingly, we have only sufficient fuel to return to base. Igo reports the fact to ground control. Over the next few minutes, the voice from ground control grows increasingly agitated, calling us again and again, reporting more German planes flying from all directions. Bloody hell! Are we the only ones in the air to stop them?

By now, we were only ten, as two Spitfires had problems with the bomb release mechanism and returned to base.

Nearing Antwerp we received a signal: our airfield was under attack. As the Ghent suburbs slipped beneath me, a giant column of dark smoke became visible, rising in the still air ahead of me, its top spreading as if to form a massive anvil above our airfield.

Stan, who had gone ahead of us, radioed unexpectedly saying with chilling nonchalance, "Gentlemen, a mob of Huns is attacking us. I have just shot down two Huns . . . out of fuel; I'll try to belly land in a nearby field . . ."

The smoke enveloped the entire airfield. Reserve planes on the ground were in flames, barrels of fuel exploding. Above it all, the silver green streaks of Focke-Wulfs crisscrossed the sky, their black crosses clearly visible. The enemy had the advantage of speed, but we of maneuverability and altitude. As we learned later, seen from the ground it was an unusually spectacular "cauldron," the more fascinating as it was taking place just overhead. It was probably one of the last classic dogfights in which survival depended on the acrobatic skill and lightning reflexes of the pilot. Then, suddenly, the green back of an FW flashed about two thousand feet below me, along the axis of my right wing. "Attack right and down!" I yelled. Excited, I flipped my plane too fast, so it swayed now to the right, now to the left. I stuck the throttle to full power. Now I had him in my sight. The black cross pulsing toward the luminous circle on the screen. I had to correct for the pilot's cabin. I was closing in at great speed as we both plunged into the black cloud of smoke. Barely avoiding treetops, the German suddenly shot up, my Spitfire hot on its trail. I pressed the trigger; pieces of the enemy plane flew away. Trailing smoke portside, it rolled up in a tight turn. I followed, lost him, then saw him again on my screen and fired a burst. By now smoking profusely, the German plane flipped and disappeared under the belly of my Spitfire. Another long burst hit home: a flash and a boom; a slow, forceful attempt to ascend. As I looked over my shoulder, the Focke-Wolf was a crumbling crucifix against the bright, morning sky. Another

dogfight on Jan1.1945

cockpit instrument panel

explosion, it tumbled down. I fired a celebratory salvo in the air and headed back to base. The black cloud over the airfield was to the south. Where the hell was I? I was flying on empty now; emergency fuel must have kicked in, allowing me to drift to the base. Flaps down and undercarriage down. Twenty feet above ground, my engine went dead. I landed with a heavy thud, which made my teeth shake and kicked the rudder right. The plane whirled and came to a stop between an unrecognizable wreck—black swastika on its undamaged tail—and a group of our ground crew hiding behind a burned-out maintenance truck. They helped me out, took my parachute, slapped me on the back, and passed me a bottle of whisky. I too was suddenly excited. My mechanic tugged at my sleeve and, with tears in his eyes, whispered in my ear, "Brother, this was for Warsaw! Serves them right, the bastards!" We walked past the wreck of another FW, its wings sheared off, its cockpit open. The pilot, still strapped in, was headless. Somebody was checking his pockets for documents.

"Look," I heard a voice, "he must have hit the ground so hard that his head just came off." One of the FW wings was later exhibited in front of our dispersal hut.

The wing commander's hut was a beehive of activity, pilots and ground staff all talking excitedly. Every pilot in turn was making his report. Our intelligence officer prepared the preliminary analysis. It seemed that the German

High Command, counting on our poor vigilance on New Year's Day, ordered the Luftwaffe to destroy allied aircraft on the ground along a 250-mile stretch from Rotterdam in Holland to Metz in France. Operation Bodenplatte was a massive, highly ambitious, early morning attack. They threw at us practically everything they had. Eight hundred and seventy-five German planes took part in the attack, flying low to avoid our radar. Among them was the fabled fighter wing Jagdgeschwader 1 *Oesau*, forty-five of its Focke-Wulf 190s raided our airfield at Ghent, destroying everything in sight. Fortunately, our two squadrons arrived within ten minutes, in attack formation.

intelligence report

Some individual stories are worth noting. When Tad Szlenkier had fired at a FW, his engine stalled for lack of fuel. He crash-landed on a field close to the very spot where the German pilot had grounded his badly damaged plane. When they got out of their respective cockpits, the German surrendered, and an army transport took them both back to base.

Stan, who alerted us to the assault on our base and landed his Spitfire in the mud on the other side of town, took a city tram back to the airfield. He arrived, pushing his way through the dense crowd, which gathered on the far side of the highway skirting the airfield, escorted by two young boys carrying his parachute and staring at him in admiration. He had shot down two enemy planes, one of them over the center of Ghent; it smashed into a florist shop, and in the evening, he was handed a huge basket of flowers—all that remained of the wrecked premises. Rumor had it that the pretty brunette he was later seen with was actually the owner of the flower shop.

Our casualties were few. We lost two pilots and three men of the ground staff were killed by enemy fire, many were wounded.

author in his U-ZF taxing off

Jagdgeschwader No 1 lost forty two planes, twenty one reportedly shot down by our pilots, though the command of the 84 Fighter Group later revised the number to eighteen, plus one half-destroyed, one probably destroyed and five damaged; this in an effort to give some credit to our anti-aircraft batteries. Through the broken glass of a window in the Wing Commander's hut, I stared at the black smoke still rising from the fuel depots. An acrid stench hung in the air. I looked at my watch; it was exactly one hour and forty minutes since we had taken off for Maas. After filing my report, dead tired, I left the hut an hour later.

The New Year 1945, destined to become the last year of the war, has thus begun with the sublime feeling of being victorious. Eventually, in mid-January, the entire 131 Wing left Ghent for nearby B60 airfield in Grimbergen, just outside Brussels. I had flown fifty combat missions by then, had dropped twenty-three thousand pounds of bombs, and completed my tour of duty. I was due for leave and, as aircrews were allowed to travel to England, I seized the chance and hopped on a DC-3 transport shuttle.

At the time, German V-1 flying bombs and V-2 rockets were wreaking havoc in London. The fear of sudden death was almost palpable and brought out the best and the worst in people. For me personally, it was not a pleasant visit, particularly as an anti-Polish bias was becoming more widespread, affecting particularly those of us easily recognizable in our uniforms. I was struck by a graffiti I noticed passing the Earls' Court Underground station; sporting a large swastika, it likened the Polish government to the Nazis. It was obviously sheer stupidity, but I could not understand who would want to spread such calumnies.

The resulting deep personal hurt was augmented by the fact that it was only a day or two before I saw for the first time photographs of the total destruction of Warsaw. This was the result of the Germans razing the city to the ground following the surrender of the insurgents in September 1944. Brokenhearted, hurt, and disgusted by the insensitivity of Londoners who not so long ago cheered us on practically every street corner, I fled in despair to Radcliff, to Aunt Julia's "home away from home," seeking her warmth, calm, and reassurance.

After several days, on February 12, 1945, I hitched a lift in a transport plane from Newton to Paris. I planned to spend the rest of my leave, as promised, in Vaucresson. In the last three months, faced with the daily grind of war, with the death of so many friends, I had hardly given Uncle Antek's house a thought. Now it felt as if years had passed since my previous visit. The peace, the quiet, the general ambience of this largely empty house was indeed the medicine I needed. I stopped thinking of Warsaw, of my family, of my postwar plans, at least for the time being. I rather regretted not coming here sooner and spending all of my leave in this lovely, peaceful house.

As I sat alone at the long table in the dining room, sipping coffee and waiting for breakfast to be served, the telephone in the hall rang.

It was Antek, calling from his office in Paris, "Jerzy? I'm glad it's you. Listen, I have bad news; it's all over for Poland. We've been sold down the river! All is lost. The Americans and the English have reached an understanding with Stalin. It's in today's papers." He broke off for a while. I felt a tightening in my chest. "Listen, not a word to Aunt Irka! I'll come home early for lunch. See you soon."

I could not believe my ears. To my mind, the war was far from over and I was still fighting for my country. Antek must have got the wrong end of the stick! I dressed in a hurry, ran over to the Tabac-kiosk opposite the church, and grabbed the nearest available newspaper.

In bold letters, the heading across the front page announced, "Le grand succès de la conference a Yalta." The name Yalta was

Greek to me. And what conference? This was the first I heard of it. I looked at the page: The summit meeting between Churchill, Roosevelt, and Stalin has just ended in the old tsarist resort town of Yalta in the Crimea. The meeting was a great success, and the allies unanimously approved the strategy for defeating Nazi Germany; West and East now see eye to eye, and a vision of postwar Europe has been agreed upon.

And apart from an editorial lament that France had not been invited to the conference, that was it. No mention of how the agreement would affect any other nation in the war apart from Germany.

When Antek arrived, I showed him the newspaper. He crumpled it, "A communist rag," he said with disdain and dropped it into the wastepaper basket. We went up to the wall-mounted map on which Antek and Irka have been plotting the moving frontlines in the East, West, and Italy. Looking at Poland's position on the map, we realized that Stalin would in essence control all of postwar Poland, and our government in exile in London was in no position to do anything about it. This was betrayal—there was no other word for it! I was seething with rage, appalled by the twists of international Realpolitik. My thoughts turned to my friends and comrades. What will they say about all this; how will those with homes in areas either designated or already annexed by the Soviets feel? I seemed to have lost my country and my home in one fell swoop, still unaware whether my family and friends were dead or alive. Would the conscientious service of so many Polish soldiers, sailors, and airmen count for nothing? I decided to cut my leave short and return to duty. Perhaps just to escape, to break the vicious circle of my thoughts.

"Quite frankly," said Antek, hugging me as I was saying good-bye, "if you feel like settling in France when the war is over . . . this will be your home."

But I had no idea what I was going to do. Would our armies in Italy and Holland refuse to fight now? Would the Polish Air Force be grounded? And what about our honor as soldiers? I concluded that in all likelihood life—and death—would go on as usual on the frontline. The Polish government was obviously facing a dilemma, but I couldn't believe that it was about to pull its armed forces out of the frontlines as an act of protest. Anyway, where would the men go? We no longer had a country to claim as our own. At base camp in Grimbergen, everybody, the pilots and the ground staff alike, were subdued, upset by the news. Yet we had no choice but to go on fighting this war, going about our business, even though feeling that it was all in vain. Toward the end of March, some older pilots in the squadron had finished their tours of operational duty and left.

The replacement pilots newly arrived from England kept telling us of the increasing hostility of the British toward servicemen in Polish uniforms. Not surprisingly, in these circumstances, some of us lost interest in the war, particularly, as we felt that our efforts and our casualties no longer served any purpose as far as Poland's cause was concerned. By April 1945, my comrades and I were still embarking on bombing missions but, to say the least, without enthusiasm. As far as we were concerned, we were fighting for a hopeless cause; our war was lost.

By then, the Red Army had occupied all of prewar Poland and was now extending its frontline further west to the Oder River, pushing deeper and deeper into the Third Reich's territory. We had no idea what the map of postwar Europe would look like. In my mind, Poland under Stalin was already becoming the sixteenth republic of the Soviet Union. Had we known that two Polish Army divisions and armored corps were advancing with the Red Army on Germany as part of the Soviet offensive and would take part in the April assault on Berlin, our morale might have improved. My old dream of a victory parade in Warsaw, where once I saw myself marching in tropical shorts, in desert boots, maybe a tropical helmet on my head or perhaps flying in close formation wing to wing with other Polish squadrons in the cockpit of my ZF, came to an end. On April 13, we were ordered to bomb a village called Garell in Germany. As usual, we carried one thousand pounds bomb load each. Why Garrell, what was there? I had no idea.

dive bombing

Looking behind me after the raid, I saw that practically nothing was left standing; there was no point even in strafing. We gained altitude and landed in B101 airfield in Nordhorn. We were now on German soil. Soon after, a memory of an incident from the war in the Libyan Desert came back to me. This happened during one of the intensive missions pursuing the retreating German units in the Papenburg area. After we dispersed, looking for mobile targets, I came down pretty low and noticed two vehicles partly hidden in the shade of roadside trees. I gave them a short burst of fire. There was an explosion, and black smoke was rising above the trees. A German soldier in *feldgrau* was running away from the burning car into an open field. I turned sharply back and gained a little more altitude so as not to lose him. Back on a straight course, I saw him dropping to the ground in the middle of the field. It all took only a few seconds. I had him in the bull's eye on my fluorescent sight screen. I made the Spitfire go lower still and then, suddenly, my engine roaring, I zoomed straight up. At the same moment, I burst out laughing, joyously, uncontrollably, shouting to myself, "I didn't, I didn't shoot him!" I made another run over the field. It seemed to me that the German soldier was standing up and waving something white or was it just an illusion? And only then did I

strafing

remember a similar situation in the desert at El Gazala. The roar of an engine overhead, I spread-eagled on the sand, and the Italian pilot who did not shoot me.

Not long after, on April 26, with a bombing raid on enemy positions east of Oldenburg, I completed my one hundredth combat flight. My second tour of duty, and my war, was over. Only the farewell party remained.

victory flyby

While signing the totals for April 1945 in my flight book, our squadron leader told me that he had recommended me to the officer's school in Scotland. "You ought to get your commission," he coaxed me, "who knows what the future holds for us? Being an officer will do you no harm, it may even prove useful."

An officer of the Polish Armored Division visiting the airfield told us that their units have fought their way to the German navy base in Wilhelmshaven; they were regrouping, poised for final assault. On the airfields, preparations were made for more intense activity in support of the drive forward; more bombs were delivered. But I was already detached. I suddenly lost all interest in matters military. I packed my bags and left.

leaving the squadron—
May 4, 1945

Some time later, in London, I heard the story of the surrender of this main German naval base to the Polish Armored Division. It holds a tremendous symbolic meaning because, in this way, the circle of the brutal, armed Polish-German conflict came to an end. It was started on September 1, 1939, by a salvo from the battleship *Schleswig-Holstein* aimed at the Polish naval fortifications at Westerplatte in Gdańsk harbor and ended with Polish tanks entering Wilhelmshaven. By a strange coincidence, the names of both naval strongholds begin with a *W*.

8

We Lost the War—So What's Next?

Paris. May 6, 1945. Great excitement reigns in the city; the atmosphere is electrically charged. Everyone is expecting the war to come to an end in a matter of days, at least in Europe, while the butchery still going on in the Pacific is very far away. I am passing through the French capital on my way to report to the Polish Air Command in London and, with luck, to the officer training school in Scotland.

It was hard not to be charmed by the streets teeming with people, many just wandering about, stopping strangers, waving Allied flags, incapable of restraining their joy. The French *tricouleurs* were fluttering everywhere. Big posters announced to the world, "Nous avons vaincu les Boches [We have defeated the Krauts]." Who did? The French? A bit irritating at first, but the beauty of Paris in May overcame these musings and made one forget the war and its consequences.

But that was the least of it; the real joy awaited me at my uncle's office at 15 rue Pigalle. As soon as I came through the door, he opened his arms, embraced me warmly, and, looking me in the eyes, exclaimed with great emotion, "Good news from Warsaw! Did you get my letter?" I didn't, I left my unit before it could have reached me.

The news had come from my mother via Sweden, and good news it certainly was: all the members of our family have survived the war. My brother was now presumably in a POW camp in Germany, following the debacle of the Warsaw Rising. Aunt Maria, with a group of curators and art historians, was working at the National Museum to retrieve and restore our looted historic heritage. Our apartment in Warsaw and the lithographic works were unbelievably intact, and Mother had already taken steps to restart the plant.

Struck dumb by these revelations, I stood for a good while rooted to the spot, my duffel bag slung over my shoulder. At first, emotionally drained, I did not feel anything at all. Just an emptiness in my head.

I had been out of touch with my family for over five years—my entire adult life—and for most of that time, I managed to suppress my anxiety and keep a lid on my memories. Now, thoughts of my mother flooded my mind like a cinema screen showing unedited sequences from my previous life. Only a while later, sitting in my uncle's salon, I regained my composure and was overcome with pure relief and joy, eager to share it with my kith and kin.

I decided to stay a few more days with them; and it was there, in Paris, that the news of the end of the war reached me. A day later, on May 9, Antek took us to the Trocadero to watch the fireworks at the Eiffel Tower, celebrating the arrival of peace.

How glad I was to be in Paris and not in England at that time. The French had played a distasteful role in this war; but at least, they did not betray us Poles. They just did not want to fight, but that was their problem.

In contrast to Paris, I found Polish London restless and glum. People expected or perhaps just wished for some fortuitous event to alter the outcome of the war. The undeserved and humiliating spectacle of the United Nations' convention in San Francisco without a Polish delegation was the last straw. The host nation, the United States, had not seen fit to invite representatives of Poland, the first country to reject Hitler's demands. This was obviously done so as not to antagonize the Soviets. It was left to the great

Polish pianist, Arthur Rubinstein, to defend his nation's honor by starting his recital at the conference with a dramatic rendition of Poland's national anthem. The power of his artistry compelled all the delegates, including the Soviet delegation, to rise to their feet.

The officer's school I was posted to was housed in an imposing building with turrets on each corner and two yards, one opposite the main entrance and the other, larger one, to the side—perfectly suited to infantry drill. I ran into some companions from my stint in the Middle East and in my early days of air force training. I also found, in the graduates book, the name of somebody I knew way back in Tel Aviv and was told that he was now studying at the Polish school of architecture in Liverpool.

A Polish school of architecture? This was the first I heard of it. I recalled now how long ago, still a schoolboy in Romania, I dreamt of becoming an architect. And it was at that very moment, in Scotland, that I decided to turn my dream into reality. I wrote immediately to Liverpool University. The reply was laconic: there were no vacancies for the present academic year 1945-1946; inquiries regarding possible admission for the following year had to be submitted in the spring of next year. But that was months away! And what was I going to do in the intervening period?

Unexpectedly, the curriculum at the officer's school was enriched by the introduction of weekly seminars on the postwar world, conducted by our captain. Their aim was to quell our anxieties. One day a student stood up. "Now that the war has ended and in view of the fact that it ended so disastrously for our country, what is the purpose of training even more officers?"

Perplexed, embarrassed, perhaps both, the captain rearranged some papers on his table, went up to the first row of desks, and pronounced with conspiratorial gravity, "What I am about to tell you, well, it's rather confidential. Please keep our little chat within these four walls."

A dramatic pause followed. "For all intents and purposes," the lecturer continued, "the war appears to be over, but is it? An armistice is in force, but some of the players are bound to redefine their priorities. I'm, of course, talking about the United States, where, following Roosevelt's death, the arrival of a new team in Washington promises fresh thinking on international affairs. The most important issue for them appears to be the armed incursion of Soviet Russia into the heart of Europe. Remember that, thank God, Roosevelt's advisers are history now. General Patton is ready to move against the Soviets. Remember how they prevented him from taking Berlin? He won't allow Washington politicians to stand in his way again. Do I hear murmurs of disagreement? But indeed, you've heard me right! I can't go into details, but there are powerful circles, mainly in America, that recognize the ignominy of the Yalta agreement; see it for the disaster it really was and want to do away with it. The USSR must be pushed out of Central Europe and back to the east where it belongs. It's that simple! Trying to persuade us of the merits of a diplomatic surrender is hopeless. We shall never concede. Look at it this way . . . we stopped the Red Army from invading and occupying Europe in 1920, so let us repeat this feat.

The captain paused to assess the effect of his words. With hands clasped behind his back, he stared us down and raised his voice, almost as if he were trying to convince himself. "Don't kid yourselves; the war in the Far East isn't over either. Who knows what surprises the Japanese have in store? And the Chinese and the Koreans, are they not able to stage a strike against the Soviets? There is a good chance that we might be called upon to assist the Americans. General MacArthur, the U.S. commander in the region, is a farsighted man. We thus have to be strong; we have to be prepared for any eventuality. For us," he stressed the word us, "the war is far from over."

We, the future officer corps, sat there dumbstruck. We left the seminar in total silence. The prospect of having to fight another war was unexciting, to say the least. I, for one, decided that more fighting was not in my schedule; what came next was university.

One day, I had a talk with a girl whom I had known since my first visit to Scotland in 1942. She was a university student now. I questioned her at length about all the formalities of applying to university and about student life in general. As she was telling me about it, I began to realize that the world she was describing was totally alien to me: necessary qualifications, entrance examinations, semesters, admission fees, grants, lecturers, tutors, rectors, deans, vice-chancellors—all these were terms significance of which I could only guess. At times, she lost me altogether, as if she were speaking a foreign tongue. A chasm was opening between me and the studies I have been dreaming of. The Polish schools in Bucharest and in Tel-Aviv could not fill that great gap in my education from the beginning of the war in 1939 till the present time.

On July 5, 1945, our commanding officer announced to the gathered cadet officer, "Today the governments of Great Britain and of the United States revoked their recognition of the Polish government in exile in London. They've chosen to acknowledge the so-called Temporary Polish Government of National Unity, which is but a cabal of Polish Communists, hand-picked by Stalin, some of whom are still Soviet citizens."

"And what about that Third World War?" called out someone as we were leaving the hall.

Toward the end of July, I received an unexpected letter from Karol Pniak, CO squadron 308. "Our annual festivities will be held on June 24 in the present field conditions," Karol wrote, "they will have to be rather scaled down, but we hope nevertheless that you will accept our sincere invitation." Dear man, I thought. This invitation, coming as it did a month late, nevertheless gave me the idea of what to do next. The words "field conditions" suggested to me that the squadron was still in Germany, where I had left it two and a half months ago. I replied that I was about to finish the course to which he recommended me, that I could do with some quiet time to think over my future, and that the field conditions would be ideal for the purpose. The graduation ceremonies over, I took my leave, planning to go to Paris. However, that same afternoon, before I had a chance to get on the train to the Calais ferry, the world changed forever.

I was sitting in a crowded pub with a couple of friends from a squadron flying American Mustangs. We were joking, talking about old times, when, rather unexpectedly, they brought up the subject of possibly enlisting in the American air force for action in the Far East; apart from the war with Japan, they too have heard rumors of a likely conflict between the United States and the USSR. With a ticket to Paris in my pocket and my dream of becoming an architect, I was barely listening to them when I was distracted by a sudden commotion. Several men barged into the noisy pub, brandishing the latest edition of a newspaper. "Silence, silence!" they shouted excitedly. "Atom bomb, atom bomb!" they repeated over and over again until the noise died down.

"Listen!" one of them shouted at the top of his voice, "the Americans dropped an atom bomb on Japan, on a town called Hiroshima!"

The statement was met by a dead silence. Atom bomb—what did they mean? An avalanche of questions followed, with few answers making any sense. It was not till the next day, when on my way to Paris, that I gathered some information about the mysterious new weapon and the unprecedented slaughter and destruction which it had left behind. All conversations on the way to Calais were focused on the subject, on the destruction of Hiroshima, on the likelihood of an early end to the war with Japan. And what it meant to me was that there certainly was not going to be any more fighting now.

On the personal front, the pace of events suddenly accelerated. In Vaucresson, I met my brother who, upon release from a POW camp in Bavaria, hitchhiked his way to France. From him I heard, for the first time, about the horrors of the German occupation and about our mother's courage.

Next, I received a posting to a flight instructor's course back in old Hucknall. And my English girlfriend sent me some disturbing news, which she had learnt from her uncle, the foreign secretary, Ernest Bevin. The British government was about to distribute to the Polish armed forces a leaflet, signed by Ernest Bevin. In it, Britain graciously acknowledged Poland's contribution to the war effort, advising at the same time Polish fighting men to return to "liberated

Poland" to assist in her rebuilding. Furthermore, while promising to be sensitive, it could offer no guarantees that Polish soldiers would be allowed to stay in Great Britain.

Furious with indignation, I felt ashamed for the Brits. And any thought of settling in England vanished from my mind.

Not long before my twenty-third birthday, I received a letter from Uncle Antek, with postscripts by Grandmother Bernhard and Aunt Maria who, both being French citizens, at the urging of my mother, had recently arrived in Paris aboard a Red Cross train from Warsaw. They hoped to see me soon and had lots to tell. I managed to wangle a special leave from my commander and left Hucknall at once, having hitched a lift on an American transport plane, which happened to be in Hucknall in transit to Paris.

reunion at Vaucresson with grand mother, aunt, brother and Oltek—Bernhards' cousin

What my grandmother and aunt had to tell me in Vaucresson focused my mind, as nothing else had, on the tragedy of Warsaw. Both women had lost everything. "The whole city will have to be rebuilt," they told me. During my stay, I came across one of my old companions, Ludwik Gutnajer, before the war a student of history of art in Paris, who had now come to revisit his prewar haunts. I moved in with him for several days, and we planned to make the most of Paris's flourishing nightlife. Near Place Pigalle, the center of the Montmartre district where we stayed, dozens of little hotels were used almost exclusively by American GIs on leave. Their howls and screams and the noise of breaking glass reached the sedate family houses at the other end of rue Pigalle, causing frequent complaints. The red-light district's bars were busy through the night, packed with crowds of disheveled soldiers and half-dressed giggling girls, and overflowing into the streets. Sometimes, a local inhabitant, maybe a housewife returning early in the morning from the market, shocked by the goings-on, would give vent to her outrage, "All you Americans! You are like wild animals, even worse than the Germans!" and shake her fist in our faces.

Back at Hucknall, speculation was rife among my comrades as to whether it would be best to emigrate to the United States, to Australia, Canada, or perhaps even to Brazil or Argentina. The consensus seemed to exclude staying in England or in Europe in general. But now, heaving heard about my mother and increasingly identifying with the family, I was getting even more resolved to return to Warsaw. After all, that was what we had been fighting for. The practicalities of such a move, however, would have to await further developments.

As if ordained by fate, or perhaps as a result of my letter to my old wing commander, a helpful hand reached out from the past to pull me back to familiar surroundings. Out of the blue, I received a posting to my old 131(P) Fighter Wing still stationed in Germany as part of the Allied occupation forces.

There, in one of the camps for refugees, I came across a girl whom I had known as a child before the war. "What were you doing in Warsaw before you came here?" I asked with interest. "Oh, don't you know? I was in the first year of the Warsaw school of architecture." School of architecture? I pricked up my ears. What was it like? I kept showering her with questions while thinking of the difficulties I would have run into in the British academic establishments.

She told me how, as soon as the Germans retreated in January 1945, small family groups of survivors, expelled from the ruins of Warsaw, began trickling back to the deserted city. Soon the trickle became an avalanche. The returning inhabitants were settling in bombed and half-burnt buildings, in rubble-strewn ground floors and basements of apartment buildings, which had lost their upper floors. In response, the new authorities of the temporary government entertained a notion of leveling the ruins of Warsaw and building a new capital elsewhere. The so-called progressive town planners nurtured a dream of an ideal socialist city built from scratch, untainted by history, bearing no scars of previous epochs—those of "injustice and exploitation by the capitalist ruling class." This utopia was thwarted by reality: the return of Warsaw's survivors was so spontaneous and massive that any thought of building the capital elsewhere had to be abandoned. Exuding optimism, the people were determined to rebuild their city. The first students of architecture were enrolled in the autumn of 1945, and lectures started in the winter in unheated classrooms with glassless windows. In February 1946, shortly before she and her mother left Poland through clandestine means, the students held their traditional Young Architects' ball: the corridors were brightly decorated, the auditorium turned into dance hall, all dominated by the youthful spirit of optimism and determination to rebuild Warsaw again as a capital of Poland.

Hearing all this became a huge incentive in formulating my future plans. In addition, in August, I received the eagerly anticipated word from my mother that at long last she managed to obtain a passport and would be arriving in Paris by the end of the month. I arranged to be there at the same time.

At the appointed time, we all gathered at the Gare de l'Est, pacing back and forward on the platform, looking into the distance where the shiny tracks disappeared in the mist. We did not realize at the time how difficult it was in Poland to get a passport entitling one to foreign travel. The iron curtain, which would eventually put a stop to all such private travel, was already descending. At last the train rolled slowly into the station, and as Mother's car reached us and as her unforgettable radiant face appeared in the window, her white-gloved hand waving to us, we broke into loud cheers and laughter.

Mother stepped off the train and tenderly greeted me and my brother, pressing our faces to her cheeks, tears streaming down her face. Tears of joy, she insisted; and with a swift motion of her thumb, she made the sign of cross on our foreheads. Mother, in her beige Burberry trench coat, which I remembered from before the war, and a narrow brimmed navy blue hat looked as elegant as always. She might have just come from London rather than from a devastated city on the wrong side of the iron curtain. Then I noticed a ladder in one of her stockings and made a mental note to buy her a pair of the sought-after nylons from one of the black-marketeering Americans.

with uncle Antek and Witold

Over the next few days, I kept relating in great detail all my wanderings and adventures right from the day when Witold and I left Warsaw in September 1939. I had to retell bits of the story time and time again. On these warm August afternoons, when not visiting Paris, we would spend long hours on the large terrace of Antek's house, talking nonstop. From time to time, Mother would laugh, repeating with wonderment, "My god, what am I doing here? Boys, pinch my arm, I have to make sure this is not a dream." The two of us would also spend long hours wandering about Paris. She shone with happiness. At the age of forty-six, she still captivated our friends by her youthfulness, energy, and sense of humor. She always insisted that I wear my uniform for our outings. She would stroke my decorations—the silver air force badge on my breast, the RAF wings, the medal ribbons and the shiny buttons embossed with the

with mother and brother

Polish eagle—saying, "My god, look at this! That's what I've been living for through all those dark years! Now I can really see them on my own son's uniform. Nobody can take this kind of victory away from me!" Witold came from Italy, where he served in the Second Polish Army Corps. When he decided to remain in exile, they decided to divorce.

Toward the end of September, Mother went on her own to Lens, in Pas-de-Calais, to visit Felix, her younger brother, who had lived there since before the war. Then it was time for her to return to Poland. It was agreed that my brother would join her in Warsaw in the near future while I still had to attend to the unfinished business of my demobilization.

I returned to our base in Ahlhorn, which was in the process of closing down. On October 6, the pilots were briefed on the protocol for handing over our Spitfires to the British. The entire wing of thirty-six fighter planes, with several reserve machines, took off one by one, circled the base, and, in close formation, flew over Belgium to the southeast of England. After one refueling, we landed on the airfield in Hethel. There, we surrendered our Spitfires to the local maintenance crews. With a lump in my throat, I asked one of them, "What will become of the planes?" "Oh, I've no idea," he replied. "They'll go for scrap metal, I guess."

The process of the discharge from active service was far from simple, and I had to wait in England; though following the family decision taken in Vaucresson, I asked to be demobilized in France. Toward the end of November, I received a document specifying the demobilization pay for my service from 1941 to 1947: the sum of eighty-three pounds and eight shillings. In addition, I was due a pound sterling for each month of service, a further princely sum of sixty-one pounds. All told, I would collect one hundred forty-four pounds as well as a couple of complete civilian outfits. This, with my old bomber jacket and a Burberry gabardine coat with camel-wool lining made to measure in London on one of my previous visits, made me feel well equipped for civilian life. I kept my Smith & Wesson six-shooter revolver as a souvenir and added to it a hunting gun, which I had bought in Germany.

I was now ready to start a new life. And I had no doubt in my mind that my decision to return to Poland was leading to just that, a new life at home, not as an émigré somewhere in America, Canada, or Argentina.

On December 17, I caught the morning train from London's Victoria Station to Paris and reached Vaucresson in the evening. But this was only the first stage of my journey home.

Part Two

Incurable Optimist
1947-1967

9

The New Beginning

The train, which for some reason carried the grandiloquent name of the Orient Express, proceeded rather leisurely, often slowing down to a crawl. Every few miles, the monotonous landscape in the window, dissolving in the mist of a March morning, was broken by the ruins of warehouses, of broken deserted buildings, and of small stations with no one waiting for the train.

"Funny, I was thinking of you yesterday," said Colin, joining me for breakfast at the table of the restaurant car. "I thought that you had made the right choice not to emigrate but to return home."

It was mid-March 1947, the beginning of the second day of our journey.

Urged by my mother, who had survived the war in Warsaw, I was now going home. Before I made that decision, I had sought reassurance that my long service in the Polish Armed Forces in the West, with their allegiance to the Polish government in exile in London, would not expose me to persecution by the new Communist regime in Poland. Colin, a short, slim man with salt-and-pepper hair, was on his way to Warsaw to take on the deputy directorship of the British Council, an organization promoting British culture. Colin and I occupied adjacent single sleeping compartments and had chatted a bit soon after leaving Paris. He was full of enthusiasm for his new post. Having received some introductory training in

London, he was keen to demonstrate his newly acquired knowledge of basic Polish. His enthusiasm was infectious and fell on a highly receptive soil.

To tell the truth, though, my enthusiasm was marred by doubts arising from the bits of information reaching the West in the previous three months. On the one hand, the Warsaw press, the postcards from my brother, who returned to Warsaw, and Mother's letters kept invariably and exuberantly stressing the enormous improvements taking place in Poland almost from one day to the next. On the other, the free elections supposed to take place after the war had not materialized. And then, there was Churchill's widely reported speech delivered in the presence of the new American president, Harry Truman, in which the British war leader censured the expansionist, aggressive policy of the Soviet Union. Europe was being divided by "An iron curtain stretching from Trieste on the Adriatic to Stettin on the Baltic," he declared. And here was I, voluntarily travelling to the other side of this iron curtain, with some misgivings, to be sure, which I tried, however, to lull with my incurable optimism.

When I shared my misgivings about returning to Poland with Colin, he dismissed them out of hand. "You are doing the right thing," he was adamant. "Pay no attention to the twaddle of conservative politicians. There are other methods to influence the Communists, and our new labor government is sure to use them. My job is but one example. An iron curtain indeed! What nonsense! We shall reach out directly, people to people. Build bridges between nations. Exchange information. Shake hands."

"Anyway," he added after a moment's hesitation. "A true democracy deviates now to the right, now to the left. That is its very nature."

Soon enough, I would come across another aspect of events developing in Poland. After breakfast, as I followed Colin back to our sleeping compartments, we met a portly gentleman in a pinstripe suit, making his way to the dining car. "Buenas dias, séñor, mucho gusto en verle," the man squeezed Colin's elbow. "El gusto es mio . . . Hasta la vista," replied my companion. "An interesting man," said Colin as we stopped outside our compartments. "He is going to Poland. All the way from Argentina. He has a lot to tell. You'll find him fascinating too. We must talk to him some time."

The man, the third passenger of our sleeping car, was a Pole named Kowalewski, who had settled in Argentina many years ago. He cut an imposing figure, emanating strength, vigor, and an unbending faith in his own opinions. We had several talks on the way to Warsaw, and I gathered that he was going there at the invitation of the new authorities and with a mission to carry out. His ideas inclined to the far left, though his whole bearing and his overpowering behavior would seem to place him at the opposite end of the political spectrum. Our conversations focused primarily on the situation in Poland and the consolidation of the new government. He countered Colin's conciliatory views with a severe criticism of the Polish public—in his opinion, obstreperous and unruly, which obstinately refused to accept the benefits of the new and just system. Unable to contribute to these discussions, I kept mum. However, I listened and learned that in Poland, in this second postwar year, there still existed an anti-Communist underground, and that political assassinations, arrests, demonstrations, students' strikes, and disturbances at universities were commonplace. This amazed me, while Colin's face remained absolutely expressionless. Kowalewski also informed us that a show trial of the leaders of the wartime underground resistance had been taking place. It was difficult to imagine, but it would appear that the leaders and officers of the biggest anti-Nazi resistance movement in Europe were being accused of collaboration with the German occupier!

I looked out of the window. We were nearing Prague. So we had already crossed the notorious iron curtain. Painlessly! We had supper together, all three of us. No political subjects were raised, and Mr. Kowalewski treated us to a bottle of red burgundy while extolling the merits of Argentinian wines from the Mendoza district.

At about 10:00 a.m., we reached the outskirts of Warsaw. For some time already, I had been watching the murky early spring morning. Dilapidated, blackish walls, broken crooked fences, heaps of brick-colored rubble partly covered with the remains of dirty snow, railway lines and ditches on both sides overgrown with last year's yellowing weeds. The landscape did not differ much from that of Germany and Czechoslovakia. But the same desolation seen in one's own country was so much more painful, almost heartbreaking.

Huffing and puffing, the train was laboriously drawing alongside the open platform of Warsaw's Central railway station. Leaning out of the window, I saw from a fair distance, in the middle of an almost empty platform, my mother and a small group of welcomers. A few minutes later, we were on our way in an open droshky, a horse-driven hackney carriage, with Mother holding on tight to one of my arms while my other hand clutched the enormous bouquet of roses handed to me on arrival.

At the entrance to our apartment block, I was welcomed by the wife of our prewar concierge. Her husband, Stefan, was there as well, though it was a different Stefan. The man I had known had perished on the barricades in Warsaw in 1939. The new Stefan helped me with my cases, while his wife, wiping her tears with a scarf, pointed to a baby in her arms and said, "I named him Jerzy, after you."

New emotions stirred in me as soon as I entered our flat.

"My god! Our young master is back!" exclaimed our old housekeeper, bringing in a freshly baked cake, the aroma of which brought back old memories. I went wandering around the flat, touching the furniture and walls. I was delighted that my fingers found the light switches without fail. I found my way without difficulty to all the nooks and crannies. Solemnly and with feeling, I kept turning the familiar brass doorknobs.

After a while, Mother held out her hand. "Let's greet the men in the workshop." We had to leave through the kitchen exit onto the service staircase, which provided the only entrance to the lithography workshop occupying all five stories of the side wing of the building; the lithography offices, in the back wing of the quadrangular house built around the courtyard, had been destroyed.

"It's almost a miracle," said Mother, pointing through the staircase's window to the yard. "When I came back to Warsaw in December 1944, well after the Rising, but when the Germans were still setting fire to houses, I could not believe my eyes when I found that the conflagration had stopped at these ruins here. The front and the wing with the workshop survived. Vandals and looters left their trail in the flat, of course. Do you remember the Dresden china dinner service, the one with the black meander border? It was all over the floor, smashed to bits . . . all premeditated vandalism . . . but let's go, they are waiting for us. Oh, one more thing!" She smiled. "Do you remember the near life-size portraits of your father in tails, and mine in the plum-colored silk dress? Painted by Stefan Norblin? My head had been cut out . . . someone must have taken a fancy to me," she laughed.

On the door, half a story up, a red board announced

ARTISTIC LITHOGRAPHY W. GŁÓWCZEWSKI
UNDER STATE CONTROL

An old family friend, Karol Whitehead, came to see us that evening. He greeted me in English, laughing heartily. His family had its distant roots in England. He sported Scottish tweeds and an Eden-like moustache. After a brief consultation with Mother, he decided to show me Warsaw by night. Our street has not yet been quite cleared of rubble, heaps of which, on both its sides, covered with dirty snow, the night sky clearly seen through the windowless walls.

Our destination was a building which had been literally decapitated, having lost all its upper floors, the ground floor and basement alone having survived. The large sign above the entrance announced, NIGHT CLUB PARADIS. Inside it was a different world, almost from a Fred Astaire film though minus the evening gowns and tails. We descended the wide semicircular stairs. The night was still young. A dozen tables were occupied by groups of men, some sporting riding boots. Several couples gyrated on the round dance floor to the rhythm the of latest hits, played by a septet whose red-and-silver music stands flickered in the light of rotating floodlights.

During a break, the band leader came over to our table. "Is there any particular tune the gentlemen would like to hear?" Karol told him a bit about me. The band leader was very impressed; there were lots of questions and handshakings all around. He told me that he too had returned home only one year ago from Russia. As a Jew, he was lucky to escape the Nazis and, at the same time, survive Soviet camps. As soon as he returned to his bandstand the sound of *"Sentimental Journey Home"* filled the room. On the first Sunday after my arrival, we went to the fashionable prewar garden city named Horseshoe Woods,[1] some forty kilometers outside Warsaw. During the war, Mother had taken care of an elderly man as well as his house and garden. The gentleman was in his seventies, of short stature, with a long gray beard, and a hat with the brim turned down all around, which never seemed to leave his head—he looked rather like a garden gnome. Rather lonely, he had become a kind of honorary member of the family. I soon found out that he too was an architect. He too? Wasn't I rather premature in identifying myself with the profession, which so far I was only aspiring to? He took me aside and seriously asserted that he was a true communist, and that what was happening in Poland now was far removed from real Communism. Even the flag was wrong. A proper Communist flag ought to be red and black. He then invited me to have a look at his house. I was far from an expert in building matters at the time, but I was greatly impressed

first day in Warsaw with Mother

1. Original name in Polish: Podkowa Leśna.

by what I saw; and my admiration intensified after he told me that he himself had designed the house and had built it entirely with his own hands.

It was a timber house with a shingle roof. Inside, it had paneled walls and all the furniture: glazed cabinets, folding beds, and collapsible chairs was built into the paneling. But most interesting of all was the garden gate, also constructed of timber, with a rather steep two-tiered gable roof resting on two richly decorated gateposts over a sculpted wicket-gate and a mail box. The two gable ends of the roof carried wooden bas-reliefs: on the right was the Virgin Mary; and on the left, a hammer and sickle in an odd combination with Masonic symbols.

Toward the end of March, all three of us, Mother, Andrzej, and I, went to Sopot, a Baltic seaside resort, to visit my paternal uncle Józef. "It's going to be the most important visit for both of you since your return," Mother said. "He is in charge of the reconstruction of Gdańsk," she added. The Warsaw Airport, with its two temporary structures, was already back in operation. We flew in a DC-3 Dakota; previously, the workhorse of all the allied armies.

Józef Główczewski, an architect, was a prewar official of the building section of the Ministry of Foreign Affairs. He congratulated me on returning home and took us round Gdańsk, showing us the sights. Tall and slim, in an elegant black homburg known in Poland as the "Eden" hat, he looked exactly as I remembered him from September 1939. He was telling me now about the enormous effort being put into salvaging architectural treasures in the lands recovered from Germany, where cities such as Wrocław, Szczecin, and Gdańsk had suffered damage as bad as Warsaw's. The shortage of architects and civil and structural engineers was a great impediment. The immediate aim was to safeguard damaged buildings from further deterioration. The Mariacki Church (Marienkirche) was a particularly difficult proposition. We stood in the central nave of this monumental gothic church, the walls of which, left bare and blackened by the conflagration that had spread from the side altars, were now covered with timber scaffolding. We looked at the sky above us, framed by the jagged, thornlike remains of the collapsed vault; and only gulls cruising within this nightmarish frame brought one back to reality.

As Mother had predicted, visiting Uncle Józef proved to be an important event for me. I had hardly known him until September 1939, when he left Warsaw with us to seek those illusory Polish Army units somewhere in the east of the country. Now my firm resolve to study architecture has brought us much closer.

Practically every week since my return from the West abounded in new experiences while significant events were almost too many to keep up with. One day a friend suggested that I accompany him to one of the main streets of Warsaw to see an interesting funeral.

"Whose funeral?" I asked.

"Come and you'll find out."

We found a good place on top of a heap of rubble. The funeral cortege was headed by troops, followed by a bishop, the clergy in two rows, and more soldiers bearing cushions with military decorations. Then came four horses drawing a gun-carriage with the coffin draped with the Polish flag. This was the funeral of Gen. Karol Świerczewski, shot several days earlier in the Eastern mountains by Ukrainian insurgents. The general, under his pseudonym of Walter, had commanded the International Brigade in the Spanish civil war of the 1930s. I had coincidentally just finished reading *For Whom The Bell Tolls* by Ernest Hemingway. I thought that the character of General Goltz was actually based on Walter. Following the coffin was Bolesław Bierut, the newly "elected" president, as well as the entire government headed by the prime minister, Józef Cyrankiewicz. So these were our new masters.

After the initial period of making new friends and getting used to life in radically changed postwar Warsaw, the time came to seriously consider what to do about my future. Again, it was my ever-dependable Aunt Maria, who came to the rescue. One day, she invited me to her flat in the national museum. The flat was actually one large basement room, which she shared with two other art historians; nothing unusual in the largely devastated and overcrowded city. The three women were engaged in the retrieval of works of art stolen by the Germans in the recent past. It was there that I met Piotr Biegański, professor of the History of Modern Architecture at the faculty of architecture of the Warsaw Institute of Technology.

Professor Biegański welcomed me warmly and confirmed that he already knew of my wish to study architecture. I reiterated my intention and began to tell him of my difficulties: the loss of schooling in the war years, my futile attempts in England . . . "Just a minute," the professor stopped me, "many are in your position now, and we are starting a special course—classes preparing students for the entry examination will last throughout the summer vacation, you ought to enroll straight away." He handed me the application form. He then invited me to visit the design department of BOS where he was the head of historic buildings reconstruction office.

One day, I took a walk with Colin along one of the prewar arteries, looking at the newly rebuilt classical townhouses on both sides of the street. "I wonder," asked Colin with an expansive gesture, "who manages this titanic work? Who draws up the plans? Where does the money come from?"

"Do you know what BOS stands for?" I asked.

"No," said Colin.

"The Capital Reconstruction Bureau. I have an invitation to visit their design studios. Would you like to come along?" Eventually, the time came for the long-delayed visit to the BOS offices. Colin came with his secretary, Mary Wardropper, in tow. Professor Biegański's office was too small to accommodate us all, so he led us to a bigger room, the walls of which were covered with photographs of prewar Warsaw, each flanked by a picture of the same area in 1945 plus drawings and sketches of the proposed reconstruction work.

"Quite a lot of tentative planning work on the capital's reconstruction had been done secretly already under the German occupation," mentioned the professor, "but the scale of destruction visited on the city following the Uprising could not have been foretold even with the most pessimistic assumptions, so the whole planning program had to be started afresh while rubble clearance was in progress."

Design work in the BOS started soon after the liberation of Warsaw in early February 1945. Technical teams visited the individual sites, assessed the damage to buildings, and reported on local needs. Collection of preliminary data on destroyed monuments, historical buildings, etc., took about a month.

I was interpreting as fast as I could. At some stage, Colin asked for a break and went up to a long drawing of the eastern side of the entire historic street. He had a good look at the meticulously executed Indian ink drawing. Shaking his head in disbelief, he tried to express his thoughts in halting Polish, "Professor, sir . . . such enormous work . . . what an enterprise . . . so many buildings . . . entire complexes . . . with a new team of town planners . . . is that so?"

Biegański sprang from his chair and with a gleam in his eye, joined Colin, telling him emphatically with joy in his voice, "Yes! You've hit the nail on the head! We are reconstructing entire individual urban complexes of inestimable historic and cultural value. This approach was recognized even before the war, in Italy and in France. But the cities in Europe have no problems comparable to our cities like Warsaw, Wrocław, or Gdańsk, What we are doing is actually entirely novel."

"But how do you define a historical monument?" asked Colin.

"In our current thinking, a monument is not just a particular outstanding work of architecture, a turning point in the history of the art of building, but also any edifice from the past, however modest, yet possessing some artistic merit or historical importance."

Mary whispered something into Colin's ear. He nodded and turned back to the professor. "So many buildings have been turned into heaps of rubble, sir. So how do you know? . . . Sorry . . . do you have documents showing what kind of building that ruin was before? I am not sure that I am asking the right question . . . but do you get my meaning?"

"No, no, this is an excellent question!" exclaimed the professor. Our work would be well nigh impossible without the inventory of the faculty of architecture of the Warsaw Institute of Technology. Fortunately, these documents have been saved, and we used them extensively."

Our visit was coming to an end. We got up but could not get our eyes off the photographs and drawings on the walls. Colin kept shaking his head and repeating, as if to himself. "Money . . . money . . . such enormous sums of money . . . This must be costing the earth . . . where is it coming from?"

* * *

Now, reminiscing about those times and having since had opportunities to be involved in a great variety of building projects in many countries all over the world, I can honestly say that the reconstruction of Polish towns and cities, with Warsaw at its head, in such unfavorable conditions, was an undertaking of such heroic proportions that nothing comparable anywhere else comes to my mind.

Nowadays, the most striking and the most delightful are the faithfully reconstructed and now already mellowed with age old towns with their palaces, churches, fortifications. However, the raising from the ashes of Warsaw's Old Town, the labor of love that it was, constituted only a small part of the gigantic work involved in the complete re-planning of many quarters of the city and their speedy rebuilding work, which involved tens of thousands of workers, hundreds of young architects, surveyors, civil engineers, and other professions.

* * *

The relative comfort and peace of our homey existence was unexpectedly broken by disquieting rumors. My brother, a student of the SGH (Central School of Business Studies) and a helping hand in the administration of our house, heard about some upcoming and unspecified changes, definitely for the worse, supposed to affect private house owners in Warsaw.

As far back as November 1945, a decree had been signed by Bierut, then chairman of the National People's Council, beginning the process of nationalization of all the land and properties in

Warsaw. Mother had then managed to get a judicial decision returning the house to us as its rightful heirs and owners. It appeared now though that the land on which the house stood could neither be returned to us as our property nor even be leased to us. Our lawyer quoted to us recent cases of houses rebuilt by their rightful owners, which were now about to be appropriated by the state.

One day, without any arrangement or warning, a team from some city department descended on us in order to inspect the building and the land. "Why," I asked, "do you waste time on inspecting a property, which has rightful owners and is obviously cared for? Wouldn't you be better employed looking at the derelict ruins which are not claimed by anyone?"

A rather obnoxious, sweaty virago in knee-high boots despite the hot summer weather, replied through clenched teeth, "The citizen would be well advised not to teach the authorities what to do."

Furious, I determinedly required that my objections be included in the form they were filling in. Reluctantly, one of them handed

Warsaw 1945

me the property inspection form. I made a note in the right lower corner stating our objection, in my own and my brother's name, to any change in our title to the property.

Fifty years later, this hastily scribbled angry protest became one of the main trump cards in our application for the restitution of our property. It proved that we had appealed against the decision to nationalize it well within the stipulated period. This was just a stroke of luck, as hardly anybody knew that only two weeks were allowed for an appeal; obviously, the authorities did not broadcast the information.

However, toward the end of July, a lucky break took my mind off the cloud hanging over our house and business. Upon my satisfactory completion of the preparatory course, I was allowed to apply to the school of architecture. In the end, though, recognized as a war veteran, I was exempted from the entry examination and thus, without further ado, found myself a student of the first year of the faculty. I accepted the fact as my due and went to the Baltic coast for a brief vacation.

Warsaw 1965

On my return, I found Warsaw stagnating in the August heat. The still air was saturated with dust, raised by the hundreds or thousands of people clearing the rubble. Long lines of men and women, even troops of Boy and Girl Scouts, were passing, hand to hand, the old bricks salvaged from the ruins. The bricks were stacked in neat piles, whence columns of horse-drawn carts were taking them to new building sites. The devastated capital was thus recycling and regenerating itself. In the Old Town Square, I found my aunt clearing rubble with some employees of the Warsaw University. Having unearthed a fragment of the old gothic walls, they stopped and went in search of one of the antiquity conservation experts. Aunt Maria, sweaty and covered with dust, her hands protected with some torn man-sized gloves, looked happy; and her eyes sparkled with excitement.

center—author's future mother-in-law

"Congratulations on your university admission!" she shouted to me. I was wondering whether she has had a hand in this. "Thanks for your support," I said uncertainly. "Rubbish," she said as if annoyed. All combatants are exempt from entry exams." Well, it wasn't actually as simple as that; officially, exemptions applied only to those who had served with the Polish Army under Soviet command.

10

That's Your Building Baptism

I was already twenty-five years old when the academic year began. There were about a hundred of us of both sexes in my class, and most were five or six years my juniors. I attached no importance to it, while they did not treat me as some older, more experienced person. The war years were never talked about; and though each of us had, no doubt, his or her own kind of history, there was no reason for us not to feel equal. All of us took study very seriously; but when it came to partying and play—for which we always managed to find time—we were all equally reckless.

Most of our professors and lecturers were excellent teachers, architects of renown with a considerable and recognized body of work from before the war and, last but not least, totally dedicated to the reconstruction of the country. The pace of our training, imposed by the magnitude of the work awaiting us, precluded the emergence of plans other than those based on the present government's socialist premises. At least, I had never heard of any other ideas for the reconstruction of Warsaw. In fact, what we were witnessing around us seemed to represent a perfectly logical and popular program, which was being carried out without misgivings and, most importantly, enjoyed the full financial support of the treasury. Perhaps, I was simply happy at being home again or else it was my political naïveté; but, be that as it may, I could find nothing to criticize in the setup of which I was increasingly becoming part. In the circumstances, the socialist ethos of the reborn country seemed perfectly natural with no place for doubts. Though some doubts were sown after our hopes were first raised in July 1947 by the USA's offer of the Marshall Plan, and just as quickly dashed when the government announced that Poland, together with the entire "progressive" camp, decisively rejected the plan as an attempt by foreign capital to interfere in our affairs. And that was that—there was no room for discussion.

Having begun my studies, I now had to look for work in order to earn my keep. Again, I learned from Aunt Maria that Professor Biegański was enlarging his studio, which was located in our faculty's building. I managed to get an interview, and he took me round his domain.

"As you see, the Institute is in the process of being organized," he explained. "We are acquiring new equipment; we are rebuilding the library, which had been partly destroyed. Here," he said as we entered an adjoining room, "we have set up our architecture studio and are already working on several interesting projects. All these buildings were completely burnt-out inside with only the sooty walls left standing. There is a huge amount of work to be done, and I thought that you might join us here. How would you feel about it?" And so I became a draughtsman in an architecture studio. Suddenly, my days were filled with all kinds of duties done according to a strict protocol and timetable. And I was earning real money for the first time.

In the afternoon, I worked in the studio. My job was to transfer to scale on to a clean sheet of tracing paper the cross section of the dome and upper storey of the Staszic Palace. It was a difficult job, and older colleagues in the studio tried to help me with advice and by checking my calculations. One day, Eva, the professor's sister-in-law as I learned later, noticed an error in the originally recorded dimensions. She advised me to check them personally on the building site.

The Staszic Palace, designed by the famous Italian-Polish architect Antonio Corazzi to house the Warsaw Scientific Society, was built in the early nineteenth century and named after the prominent Polish scientist and educationalist. After the 1863 rising against the Russians, the tsarist authorities converted the neoclassical building into a Byzantine orthodox church. It was restored to its original appearance after the First World War only to be destroyed in the Warsaw Rising of 1944.

I went to the building site and made my way beneath the scaffolding. I found the foreman on the second floor. "Good morning, sir; we haven't seen you here before, have we? You are a new architect, right? OK, Stevie, take Mister Architect round and give him all the help he needs . . . on the double."

An hour later, we returned to the foreman. Someone was helping me to brush the plaster dust off my clothes. As I was making my way out again under the scaffolding, a sudden downpour of mortar descended on me from above. I stood there like a statue, my legs astride, clasping the sheet of my recorded dimensions with one hand and trying to scrape the wet mortar from my head with the other. The sticky stuff was dripping off my shoulders and back. Everyone around me was laughing and clapping their hands. "That's your building baptism!" someone called out, "as befits a new architect . . . you'll be safe from now on." Laughter and friendly shouts saw me out.

After supper, I usually looked for company. I had kept my wartime habit of visiting bars, be they English pubs or Paris and Brussels bistros; and I tried to continue this routine in Warsaw. The new Warsaw nightclubs were dangerous places—vodka was consumed there in vast amounts. I wasn't used to this kind of drinking for drinking's sake. In the air force, we used to drink only moderate amounts of whisky, though our customs did begin to change a bit in Germany after we captured large supplies of spirits. So these days, I would sit occasionally on a bar stool with a glass of brandy in my hand and observe my countrymen, eavesdropping on their vehement discussions and quarrels. One day, sitting in the bar, I heard someone call me from the back of the room.

"Come over, Jerzy . . . come and join us."

To my amazement, I recognized Tadek Schiele, a colleague from my old squadron. He had company and, as usual on such occasions, was already tipsy. As his right arm rested round the neck of a pretty brunette with big expressive eyes, he could only spare his left hand to wave to me.

"Do you like her?" he asked me in English, "it's Jeanny . . . my wife . . . my wife, you understand . . ." he stressed. The girl extended both her arms to me and smiled, showing a row of beautiful white teeth. A short, slender man with carefully parted dark hair and black-framed glasses, sitting at their table, gave me a searching look.

"You're from the air force too?" he asked with a gleam in his eyes.

"Sure . . . a mate . . . but he is hiding . . . doesn't want to visit me in Zakopane . . ." Tadek was going on as tipsy men do, still waving his hand at me and knocking down a glass in the process. "We are setting up a first jam session . . . Understand? Jazz," he corrected himself. "Jean will be the singer."

"Where?" I asked. "Here, in this bar?"

"Nooo . . . Leopold," he pointed to his pal, "thought of doing it in some room he found in the ruins, in the center . . . to make it more interesting."

"Correct," his friend chipped in. "Feel invited to the rehearsal . . . Charles Bovery will play . . . a great talent . . . from Czechoslovakia . . . By the way, my name is Tyrmand, Leopold Tyrmand."

As I was leaving, Tadek invited me to visit him in January in Zakopane, where he now lived. Still in the door, holding on to my neck, he added "Yes, come to Zakopane, you'll be able to ski . . . though don't count on my company . . . skiing is not my thing . . . but you will have a lot of fun with the highlanders. A BBC team will be there . . . you will feel like an angel in heaven," he finished in the highlanders' dialect.

Tyrmand caught up with me in the street. "I try to avoid meetings in bars, but my idea is to produce something different, a whiff of fresh air from the West. We need it here, badly," he said, all in one breath. "You know, I heard Jean sing. She is sensational, a revelation.

He told me he'd met her in England. I don't know how she can stand this sentimental, patriotic, tearful Polish overindulgence." We said good-bye, and I promised to come to the rehearsal.

Not all pilots, however, had been as lucky as Schiele and I. One day, I answered a knock; and there, on my doorstep, was Karol Pniak, commander of our 308 squadron and one of the legendary Polish pilots from the Battle of Britain. Ours was an emotional greeting; we stood with arms entwined for quite a long while. Karol was dressed in his uniform, though he had removed the British insignia. After a few words, he asked whether I could offer him a bed for the night. When I showed him into a small bedroom next to our dining room, he seemed to sigh with relief.

"I don't know how or where to start . . . what have they done with this country . . . it's such a tragedy." I was not sure whom he meant, the Germans or the Soviets, and just waved my hand hesitantly.

"May I talk to you candidly? As in the old days . . . well?" "Yes, of course," I explained that my settled position was simply due to a happy coincidence. He wondered whether returning to Poland had been such a good idea. But he hoped that he would manage. Today I know that he fell on very hard times and eventually died in poverty. He, the ace of our air force.

* * *

In the meantime, we learned that the Lithography Works would remain a property under state administration with Mother remaining as manager—for the time being. Having listened to the review of procedures of a truly Byzantine abstruseness, I simply could not understand why the relatively uncomplicated affairs of our property had to be so obstructed by these relentless bureaucratic procedures laid down by our own state. What a contrast with the ease of dealing with the infinitely more complex problems of the reconstruction of the devastated city. The thought that I was completely useless in this situation and had to leave it to my mother, my brother, and their advisers was truly painful. And there must have been thousands, perhaps hundreds of thousands of people, trying to save what remained of their property from the rapacious hands of the new Communist authorities. Perhaps, I ought not to complain. No doubt, many had it much worse.

* * *

The first semester concluded with a period of meetings, conferences, and discussions so that I had great difficulty in keeping up with my tasks in the studio. Other jobs also had to wait. Why? We were busy organizing a lucky-draw ball, traditional for first-year students, in celebration of credits received and colloquia passed.

A dais was built in our large lecture hall, stage sets with somewhat rickety supports were erected. One of my colleagues, nicknamed "Anoda," had wrote a cabaret script with antique Greek theme. The performance was followed by dancing to the records of Louis Armstrong, Harry James, Tommy Dorsey, Benny Goodman, Arty Shaw, and Cab Calloway. They were all part of my collection of two hundred U.S. Army's long-playing records, which were still quite a novelty in those days. They were a present from my uncle in Paris, who must have bought them on the black market from American soldiers. The vocal numbers of Dinah Shore, Ella Fitzgerald, and the Mills Brothers carried right through the neighborhood; and frozen pedestrians with bent shoulders and lowered heads, hurrying through the dark and

School of architecture lucky-draw ball 1947, MC Jan "Anoda" Rodowicz

muddy streets, would stop and look with amazement at the large, brightly lit windows of our lecture hall and listen to the cheerful, if rather unfamiliar, music.

After Christmas, our first spent as a family since 1938, I went to Zakopane in the Tatra Mountains to visit Schiele. Ski boots not being available in Warsaw for love or money, I bought a pair of second-hand, heavy army boots in a street market. After an eight-hour train journey, leaving the railway station in a horse-drawn sleigh with harness bells ringing, I went to my friend's house. The Schieles owned a well-known ski workshop, so I soon found a suitable pair of hickory skis of their own manufacture. All of Zakopane was under a thick blanket of snow, particularly abundant that year. Timber houses with steep shingle-covered roofs were hidden under vast mounds of snow, also often reaching halfway up their walls. The Schieles' house was also in this local style, built of thick logs with intricately plaited ropes of straw inserted between the logs, inside and out. The rooms were kept warm by tall tiled stoves in the corners while highland kilims and sheepskin rugs were scattered on the wooden floors. A green-shaded old-fashioned lamp, converted from an oil lamp, lit the long wooden table. Tadek introduced me to his parents and his younger sister, Danka. We drank *krupnik*, a fiery liquid made of strong spirit with burnt sugar and spices, served hot in small, decorated earthenware beakers. We felt wonderful. Minutes later, Jean came downstairs to join us. Her warm welcome moved me to such degree that I dropped my beaker with the remains of the krupnik to the floor. As we both bent down to pick it up, our heads collided, to great general merriment.

We spent New Year's Eve in a popular nightspot called Gong, half hidden in a snowdrift. Fortified as I was by several stirrup cups drunk before departure, the exhilarating sleigh drive accompanied by the jingling of the harness bells, and our highlander driver shouting encouragingly at his horses, propelled me suddenly into a mysterious fairytale world. Sitting in the back seat, tightly squeezed in between Danka and Jean, all three of us covered with a sheepskin rug, we kept screaming and shouting for the sheer joy of being alive.

The New Year's Eve party lasted well into the morning. The place was, by that time, a scene of messy disorder. The attendants were shifting the sleeping and the comatose revelers to one side to get them out of the way of the more tenacious dancers. The musicians were replaced by a highlanders' band, three fiddlers and a double-bass player. The space vacated by those who had fallen by the wayside was now taken by the sleigh drivers. I was quite unfamiliar with the local folk music, so I stopped near the entrance to listen for a while. The new music seemed to have a sobering effect on the two BBC crew in our group, who were slowly coming back to their senses. It wasn't easy to persuade two of the drivers to take us home, but, eventually, they relented. It had stopped snowing by that time, and Giewont, the picture-postcard peak of Zakopane's view, was already lit by the rising sun. The year 1948 has just begun, and I felt happy as never before.

It was difficult to get back to the grindstone after the holidays, and only bit by bit did I get back to work in the new semester. I was not the only one; the lecture rooms looked half deserted. And to balance my finances, I needed to spend more time in the studio.

My work on the reconstruction of the seventeenth century royal residence, in which the chancellor's office and the administration of Warsaw University were now located, allowed me to skip lectures on surveying. The principal portico of this building, as well as its main three-story body, had already been reconstructed. Now, we were starting on designs for the interior. It was quite a task to recreate the rich baroque decorations of the walls and ceilings, not to mention coming up with an appropriate design for the parquet floors. I do not recall whether any prewar documents or photographs had been discovered. I rather doubt it, or we would not have needed to prepare endless drafts for each session of the Conservation Commission. We kept going back to the huge photo albums of French and Italian examples of interior decoration. And we never lost our sense of humor. I remember the fun when one of us working on the design for the ceiling of the chancellor's office suddenly shouted, "Where the hell is that photograph with Napoleon's bed? There was a detail there which would be absolutely perfect here." And thus, while reconstructing Warsaw, and in spite of the steadily growing influence of a foreign ideology coming from the East, we endeavored to return the city to the traditions of Western European art and culture. It was an experience and a lesson, which, later in my professional work, I would follow to save the diversity of other cultures and traditions against the imposition of foreign models. But it will be twenty year later that I will realize that these sentiments were imbedded very deeply in my mind

last Architects' Ball 1948

with Jeanny Schile

However, neither my work on increasingly interesting projects nor the need to study, succeeded in reducing my participation in the unending string of parties.

After the success of our Ball of Young Architects, the carnival period of 1948 could not be wasted, and not a week passed without some function to attend. The Academy of Arts revived the prewar tradition of the Ragamuffin Ball. Young men and girls, happy to rid themselves even for a few hours of their dull daily handouts from UNRRA—a relief organization—or their second-hand clothes bought in a flea market, were full of joie de vivre, their faces framed by Elizabethan ruffs or hidden by small colorful masks. There were also the Medics' ball, the Journalists' ball, the ball at the Academy of Physical Education.

I wrote to my friends, who had stayed in England, describing those balls and parties. They wrote in turn about their problems in finding a university place or suitable work through the specially created British service for the preparation of Polish servicemen for civilian life. Some decided to seek better luck overseas. I wonder now what they thought of my impressions of life in Poland. They were accurate, as far as I was concerned, though perhaps a little too enthusiastic for more sober-minded people. Or perhaps they thought that I was forced to spout propaganda as a condition of my letter reaching them. I don't know. On one occasion, an ex-pilot colleague wrote to me that he had decided to go to America, to brave the unknown, and ended his rather sad letter with the couplet:

> Alas for us who fled in times of pest,
> And, timid souls, took refuge in the west!

It took me a while to realize that this was a quotation from the "Epilogue" to *Pan Tadeusz.*[2]

Summer came; and we were all busy, preparing working drawings for several projects executed by senior members of the studio. With people away on vacations, the school was pretty empty; and for once, we were able to work quietly and steadily.

Later in the summer, I took a short vacation trip to the "Regained Lands," Western territories that, before the war, were within German borders. While in Szczecin (formerly German Stettin), I came upon long lines of lorries and horse-drawn carts loaded with the belongings of people relocated from the Soviet-annexed eastern parts of Poland and now taking over flats and houses vacated by the expelled ethnic Germans. Bowls, sacks, chests, baskets, washtubs, and stacks of mattresses tied with string were heaped on the pavements, in the shade of beautiful old trees, in front of the façades of imposing building.

---

2. An epic poem by Adam Mickiewicz, as translated by Kenneth Mackenzie.

I noticed that the wide streets, the star-shaped squares, the character of buildings in Szczecin, were, in spite of the war damage, reminiscent of Paris; and that all bore witness to the prosperity of its prewar population. I kept looking round, hoping to see some of the departing Germans; but there were none. They had disappeared some while ago, like actors after a performance, leaving behind them a stage where their old lives, their joys and sorrows, their comedies and tragedies, had been played out. New actors had now taken their place: women, their heads wrapped in colored headscarves, and flaxen-haired children perched on top of the family's belongings in loaded vehicles. Men in short gray overcoats and dusty knee-length boots kept asking for directions in their soft eastern accents. Organizers with armbands checked their lists and issued directions. The faces of the new arrivals, dusty, gray with fatigue, showed obvious relief that, at last, they were at the end of their long journey. As I passed a group of people, someone grabbed me gently by the elbow. "Please join us in our celebration," and a bottle of vodka and several thick glasses appeared from a basket. We drank a toast, splashing the last few drops on the ground—for good luck.

A huge migration was in progress, involving millions of people driven from their ancestral lands in the East.

Toward the end of September, just before the start of the academic year, Mother and I took a trip to Lower Silesia. Our main aim was to see the Regained Lands Exhibition in Wrocław (formerly German Breslau). Mother did not want me to miss the new architecture and the graphics so widely reported in the press. I was rather taken by the large nongovernmental production exhibition hall and the neat, colorful, modern pavilions with varied wall and roof structures that I had never come across before. I made sketches of most of them. I ran into a senior colleague who had a hand in planning the exhibition. He told me about the general congress of the SARP (Association of Polish Architects), which had taken place in there just before the opening of the exhibition. One of the topics discussed was a reform of the way Polish architects worked. This would involve the creation of new State Architectural Offices, each offering the whole range of design and planning services from urban studies to architectural and structural design, including water, sewage, and electrical engineering. At present, the structure of such multifunctional offices, their running costs, salaries, etc., were being analyzed. Uncertain whether this was good news or bad, I did not comment.

"Don't you understand what this means?" he continued. "This is the end of private design studios. We shall be like soldiers mobilized into large organizations, ruled by ministerial decrees or by directives from some other bureaucratic body. I heard at the Congress that the proposed system would be an exact copy of the one being introduced in Moscow. What else are they going to ape?"

Before leaving Wrocław, we went for a stroll in the Old Town. Though war damage was extensive, many old buildings were being reconstructed. Some of the scaffolding bore huge graphic propaganda billboards showing the different stages of reconstruction in various parts of the Regained Lands, and announcing that their population had already grown to five and a half million resettled people. Groups of tourists and flocks of children, clearly school excursions, thronged the streets. But suddenly, as soon as we turned off the old Market Square into one of the side streets, the picture changed. The pavements in front of the dwellings were teeming with poorly dressed people carrying suitcases or big bundles, resting on their boxes, pushing carts and prams, some carrying babies, others laden with personal belongings. There were dark-clad older men and women; there were little girls with dolls under their arms. As we progressed along the street, more and more people were leaving the houses. Silence reigned; nobody spoke, nobody cried, nobody called. All of a sudden, the crowd began to move, everyone going in the same direction. We followed them to a wider road leading to the railway station.

"All said and done, this is a pitiful sight," said Mother. "I never expected that after all the horrors of the occupation, I might one day be sorry to see Germans being thus driven from their homes."

The following day, back in Warsaw, I went with my fellow students, all of us having volunteered to help with rubble clearing.

It was a gray, windy morning. We gathered on the square in front of the main building of the Institute of Technology and were divided into groups. My group was directed to Muranów, several kilometers north of our square. There, a notice on a large board announced that this was the site of a projected new workers' housing estate and a shining example of . . . and that the aid extended by the Soviet Union would guarantee its success . . . and general peace—or words to that effect. The caption under one aerial photo informed us that in 1939, this district had one hundred fifty thousand inhabitants. The second photo I recognized straight away—it was one of the Jewish ghetto areas, first walled off by the Germans then razed to the ground in 1943 in retaliation for the armed resistance by Jewish fighters. Not one building, not even one wall, remained.

Ghetto area (author' photo)

The third photograph showed the master plan for the new quarter covering 430 acres, and planned to house approximately forty thousand people

We were directed to the team searching through heaps of rubble for remaining whole bricks, which, thus recovered, were passed from hand to hand to be neatly stacked in an already cleared street. We were exhausted. Finally, someone standing at the top of the heap of rubble shouted to a construction worker passing below,

"Hey, boss, are you sure that the Soviet Union, with their aid and support, would not send us some spare hands? We could do with a few new ones, as ours are dropping off!"

The general laughter and more ribaldry in the same vein relaxed us and thus helped us to survive the backbreaking job until the welcome break. We were invited to one of the barracks, a kind of workers' clubroom, for tea and biscuits. We sat round the tables, quite pleased with ourselves. President Bierut and Generalissimus Stalin watched us from their portraits on the walls, accompanied by the kind of ubiquitous slogan-bearing red banner. A slight man in a beret came in carrying a new board with the town plan for Muranów, slightly different from the one near the entrance. He suggested that as students of architecture, we might be interested in what kind of final scheme we were now contributing to. What he started telling us sounded really interesting, and we listened to him in silence. He had introduced himself as an employee of the town planning department of BOS and gave us a brief rundown of the history of town planning for Warsaw's reconstruction. Several teams of town planners and architects were involved. Each quarter of the city would have specific functions assigned to it, coordinated with the existing transport network. Thus, the former concentric growth would be replaced, by a degree of decentralization, with the specialized town sections: residential, commercial, and industrial separated by green strips arranged on either a radial or a cross-shaped pattern of urban spread.

I suddenly realized that what was going on in Warsaw now was by no means accidental, but that a lot of preliminary thought and work had gone into directing the reconstruction of the enormous areas of the devastated city.

"Let us consider Warsaw," concluded the lecturer, "as our greatest opportunity to build a new socialist city, a city of social justice, of homes full of light, of attractive green areas. Let us forget the tragedy of its destruction and concentrate on the benefits coming in its wake. Prewar theoreticians dreamt of a chance like that, of starting to plan from scratch, from what they called a tabula rasa; and as you can see, we have now been given this open space to be converted into a city of the future."

On my return home, I could not stop thinking about this "tabula rasa" and the "city of the future." Thus, at the nearest opportunity, I questioned Professor Biegański; instead of an answer, he gave me a little square booklet.

"This is the modern town planners' bible," he said

The booklet, published in Paris in April 1943, was entitled *Congres Internationaux D'Architecture Moderne, CIAM—La Chartre d'Athenes.* (International Congress of Modern Architecture—Athen's Charter. By Le Corbusier—footnote) I read the first sentence. "The Charter provides an answer to the chaos dominating our cities. With its descriptions, comments, and its true understanding of the subject, it could, in the hands of appropriate authorities, become a tool for securing the destiny of future cities. "Le destin des villes sera redressé." And further on, "This is not the work of one person, it sums up the thoughts of top architects devoted to the new art of building."

Problems of this type were not Professor Biegański`s particular field of expertise, but he appreciated the fact that one of the Charter's stipulations was the preservation of monuments of the past. However, he was against the concept of tabula rasa, considering it an obnoxious, totalitarian idea.

"For instance, Le Corbusier suggested demolishing all of nineteenth century Paris except for the Louvre and had a similar plan for Moscow. It could not really be taken seriously, but it has muddled many heads. And I don't know what the outcome in Poland and in other countries will be now—the devastation of war has presented the planners with something very much like the stipulated tabula rasa."

In the second year, a great number of new students were admitted to the school; the total must have reached about a thousand. Crowds were going to and fro the corridors, which are made even narrower by the tables and drawing boards set up along their walls. Compared with that, the Institute of the History of Modern Architecture, together with our studio, was an oasis of calm. Quite often, I stayed behind in the evening to work on my homework in peace. Both the working and the living conditions of the majority of students were very difficult. It was well nigh impossible to find a room to rent. The only consolation was the fact that it was easy to find work either in a private architect's studio or on one of the innumerable building sites growing all over the capital like proverbial mushrooms. It became virtually the norm for students to combine their studies with quasi-professional work. This was, actually, to everyone's advantage, as the lack of qualified technical personnel would otherwise seriously hamper the reconstruction of Warsaw and of other devastated cities.

At the beginning of December, construction work around the main building of the institute visibly intensified. Laboring teams worked day and night resurfacing the square in front of it. All round its boundaries, rows of flag posts were erected. Fresh green fir trees in large planters were brought in to line both sides of the main entrance. We were frequent visitors to this building, as lectures in land surveying were held there; and we were puzzled by this sudden frantic activity. The reconstructed and freshly decorated building now stood out clearly among the burnt-out apartment houses of the area.

One morning, someone brought to the studio *Trybuna Ludu* (the Voice of the People), a Communist party newspaper, and read to us aloud during tea break the announcement that the Congress of the Polish Socialist Party had unanimously passed a resolution to unite with the Polish Workers' Party, previously known as the Polish Communist Party.

Organized mass demonstrations in favor of the resolution took place. Columns of workers marched, carrying the standards of their factories as well as red banners stating that "The Unification of the Workers' Parties will hasten our march to Socialism—Long Live the Congress of Unity of the Working Class." They kept coming from different directions, all making their way to the square in front of our main building, which was obviously the site chosen for the congress. Now we understood the haste with which it had been reconstructed.

Though at the time we did not quite grasp its significance, this move was the beginning of the Communist takeover of the state. It would bring serious consequences, affecting most lives. I got the first taste of it soon after.

After Christmas, I was again traveling to Zakopane with a group of students for the students' sports association camp. That year, I took to skiing in a more professional manner. I had been training on an artificial slope all autumn, and now just huffing and puffing up a steep slope only to scramble down it in clouds of snow was not acceptable anymore. And the association promised to provide further training in the Tatra Mountains after these trials.

On the eve of my departure, I unexpectedly ran into one of my fellow students. He grasped my sleeve and pulled me to the shelter of a burnt-out house.

"Listen," he whispered. "They arrested Anoda on Christmas Eve."

"Christ! Anoda? The best student in our class? How come? Where?"

"Psss . . . Not so loud. In their home. They say it was in the middle of their Christmas Eve celebration." "But why . . . why . . . what has he done?" I asked naïvely.

He did not answer my question. He looked left then right, raised the collar of his coat, and, as he was leaving, he just put his finger on his lips.

11

Lenta

"My name is Jerzy, and what's yours?" I asked the slender girl standing on the other side of the long table, wearing a simple navy blue dress and lace-up army boots. She smiled, shook her head, tossing back her chestnut-colored mane, and playfully wrinkled her shapely nose. "Lenta," she answered simply.

"And what kind of a name is that?" I asked, amused.

Leaning over the table, trying to be heard above the rising noise, she explained, "It's actually Irena; but as a toddler, I could not pronounce it, it kept coming out as Lenta instead, and so I got stuck with it."

We were all standing in the dining room of the White Trail pension, around a table laden with plates of hors d'oeuvres and a big pot of steaming *bigos*—a hunters' dish of cabbage cooked with sausage and various kinds of meats—not to mention the carefully concealed bottles of vodka and some Hungarian plonk. Our whole group, some twenty strong of the winter sports training course, were waiting for the New Year's Eve party to begin.

By the tenth day of our training, we were already skiing from the top of Kasprowy Wierch, one of the higher mountains of the resort and the only one accessible by cable car. We even mastered an infallible method of quickly getting into a departing car, for which ordinary mortals had to queue for hours.

One day, packed like sardines in an open truck standing in for the local bus on our way to the ski slopes, I came face to face with a Warsaw acquaintance. This young man had a small shop there next door to the British Council, which specialized in imported men's wear. He complained that a new state policy was designed to squeeze out all private commerce. The term "private initiative," as used in the press, had lately become a term of abuse. He leant now close to my ear and whispered that he'd heard on the grapevine that our training course would be the last one of its kind. All prewar students' organizations were going to be replaced by one national Communist association (though the term "Communist" was being carefully avoided in Poland) to be called the Union of Polish Youth. "I have good reason to believe that life in this country will become impossible," he ended. Some time later, I learned that both he and his fiancée had tried to clandestinely cross to the West. They failed and were given long prison sentences. Seeing how other people's luck ran out so frequently made me count my blessings.

Suntanned, rested, and having had a good time, we were returning to Warsaw as a well-knit group. Someone brought in a bundle of Warsaw newspapers; and having been cut off from all news for two weeks, we listened with interest as he started reading aloud:

"We are entering the new year of 1949 . . . a year of intense work and great coming achievements . . . we no longer fear anyone's threats . . .

"What are they talking about?" shouted the reader. "Listen! Listen to that. 'The Polish nation has now gained a better understanding of the struggle taking place in the world . . .'

"What struggle, for goodness' sake? Or listen to this, 'The Workers' Housing Projects has already had a good beginning . . . are we going to win the housing battle?'

"So . . . it's up to you, gentlemen," said the reader, turning to the budding architects, "are you ready to gird your loins for the coming battle? According to the papers, it seems that we are constantly engaged in one battle or another; but from what they are saying, the situation is no better in the West. Now listen to this, 'Truman has approved the Marshall Plan, which will be disastrous for Europe . . . The situation in Western Europe is already critical as a consequence of American aid.' Or look at the 'Letters from America,' they quote a saying that to kill a Negro is not a sin."

Night was descending fast, and we were starting to fall asleep, lulled by the stupefying rhythm of the wheels.

Back in Warsaw, I stepped into a hive of activity. The great project of the reconstruction and simultaneous enlargement of the Warsaw Opera House was thrown open to competition. Designed by Antonio Corrazi and built in 1823, the great theater fronted the entire elongated Theater Square. One afternoon, as we stood in front of this building with its terrace surmounting the portico colonnade, I could see the sky through the gaps of the former windows. We stood there silent, fascinated by the enormity of this ruin, almost discovering anew the sight so well known to us in the past. The sudden thought that I was now a small part of the project became a moment of revelation; I stood there thunderstruck by the confirmation of my true vocation.

Even while working on the first drafts, we realized the enormous complexity of the undertaking. A colleague and I were given the job of drawing some basic plans. I put up a drawing board at home and spent all my time on the project, neglecting the school's plans for a residential apartment block. Our entire team spent the last two weeks before the due date transferring the plans onto large sheets of white cardboard, anxious to work as cleanly as possible. Unfortunately, we did not win the first prize. We were, however, rewarded with a commission for another project of a similar scale and importance.

After the frantic period of the competition was over, I took some time off playing truant. There was no point going to the studio, as the countrywide reorganization of architectural services, predicted by the guy I had met in Wrocław a while ago, was now taking place. Biegański had managed to secure for us the status of a semi-independent office, and we moved to the site designated as our next project—our own grand prize—the restoration of a devastated complex of three imposing buildings, also designed and built by Antonio Corazzi, on the west side of Bank Square.

The studio's move took a number of days, which gave me time for a few meetings with the Zakopane ski-training group. At one of them, I ran into Lenta, who was a first year history of art student at Warsaw University. With the baptism of fire of the project competition behind me, I felt almost like a full-fledged architect. Thus, when she asked whether I could help her with the description of some architectural details of one of the recently reconstructed historic town houses, I replied nonchalantly, "Of course, no problem."

The March thaw had set in, and we had to wade through a mixture of melting snow and the yellow clay of unfinished pavements. We stood there in the mud for quite a while, looking at one another, not saying a word. She was wearing a coat with a molting fur collar and the same army boots she'd had in Zakopane. I wore my London Burberry trench coat, its collar turned fashionably up. Lenta was the first to come down to earth.

"Where do we start?"

"From the bottom up," I said authoritatively and began my lecture. "A classical building is usually constructed in three layers . . . This building has eleven windows on each floor. At the very top of the façade, you can see the cornice, the coping, and above it the pitched roof, sometimes with mansard windows. Ah! Just one more detail . . ." Lenta, who had stopped taking notes a while before, just kept looking at me. In her characteristic gesture, she threw her head back, wrinkled her nose, and shook her head in negation.

"You were going too fast," she said, laughing.

I repeated it again much more slowly and added, "This street, having been completely destroyed, is now being reconstructed in its original style. It will, in time, be one of the most attractive streets in town," I completed my exposé.

I accompanied her as far as the gate of the university and watched her walk away with a spring in her step, not looking back even once. I went home slowly, shuffling through the mud, halting now and then as if held back by some unknown force. I stopped in front of our house. This one had nine windows in a row, and the stucco and cornices above the windows of our flat were badly chipped. The balcony was gone, and only forlorn stumps of its supporting consoles remained. It was not a pretty sight, its war history writ large. But unlike the majority of Warsaw buildings, it had survived. Back in our flat, I was still subdued and just sat there looking into space. Mother came in.

"What's the matter? Why are you so still?" she asked anxiously.

I didn't answer. A minute later, I got up and followed her. We met in the little corridor.

"So what is it all about? Why this strange expression?" she smiled at me.

"Hm," I cleared my throat. "There was this girl from the university, I was telling her about styles of buildings."

"And what happened?"

I had to clear my throat again. I kept looking at the ceiling.

"Nothing."

"So what has she done to you? Do I know her?"

"I don't think so. I am not even sure of her surname, something like Henisz, I think."

Mother took my face in both her hands and turned it toward herself, her eyes all smiling. "Don't tell me that you've met little Lenta? It's incredible. After all those years . . . Do you remember that big photograph on the wall of grandmother's flat? It was a group picture of young people at a fancy dress ball during the carnival of 1911. Do you recall it now? There were two little girls in identical white dresses and big white wigs—the two marquises—sitting right in the middle, next to one another. Well, I was one of them; and the other was my friend, Zosia Rossmann, Lenta's mother. Amazing, isn't it!"

My eyes were still focused on the ceiling. "I've heard little Lenta is quite a beauty now, is that right?"

The awareness of it suddenly hit me.

"Yes, she must be," I answered in a whisper.

Mother gave me a searching look and called out, "I'm so happy; what luck, my son has fallen in love at last! And how! A *coup de foudre*, as the French say." Suddenly, something gave way in me; the ice began to melt. Weak at the knees, I put my arms round Mother and felt my eyes fill with tears.

Mother and I were sitting after dinner on our wide Turkish ottoman talking about what happened. I was still in shock, and Mother's words "he fell in love" kept coming back to me. Was it true? I had never felt like this before, so how would I know? Ought I just wait and see? I was left alone with my thoughts.

Soon after, Mother left, I heard the doorbell ring. One of my friends burst in, out of breath. Looking rather grim, without any preamble, he said, "Anoda is dead."

"How do you know?"

"I went to see his mother. Several days ago, she received an official letter from the Army Prosecutor's Office saying that he had jumped from a corridor window while being escorted to an interrogation at the Ministry of Public Security."

"But does anyone know why he'd been arrested?"

"I have no idea. All I know is that he died in January, two months ago, and that the UB[3] buried him straightaway in an unmarked grave in a public cemetery without informing anyone."

It was only many years later that it came to light that he died when one of his torturers during interrogation crushed his chest by jumping from a table onto his prostrate body. The official autopsy report did not mention any injuries.

In the next few days, I heard whispers that soon after the war, Anoda had joined the so-called second conspiracy led by his old commanders of the wartime Underground Home Army. Apparently, some weapons had been secreted for possible future use, and he had been involved in hiding them. A newspaper reported that "some diversionist and terrorist groups, financed by dollars received from abroad, had been formed . . . there is no doubt that the strings of the conspiracy are being pulled by foreign secret services."

3. *Urząd Bezpieczeństwa*, State Security Office, or secret police.

So the man from Argentina traveling with me on the train from Paris was right. There was an insurgency in action. When I mentioned it to our close friend who had a room in our flat, he took me aside.

"Quite a lot of weapons is hidden in this apartment too, dating back to the German occupation. We have to get rid of them as soon as possible," he added very softly. "Possessing firearms is strictly forbidden."

"Good god! Where?"

"Under the floor of the small bedroom, where your brother sleeps now."

"Does he know?"

"Probably not."

Of necessity, we had to confide in one of our neighbors. He lived in a small flat, entered from the courtyard. A tailor by trade, during the war, he used to make clothes from the available German cloth to be used by couriers from England, dropped here by parachute. They had sheltered in our apartment until equipped and ready to go into action. The neighbor had to be included in our dangerous undertaking as he owned a small prewar car, which he was constantly repairing in our courtyard. Without hesitation, he agreed to help but needed time to think how best to carry out the clandestine operation. A week later, having recovered the arms cache from under the floor and loaded it in the trunk of the car, we drove over the bridge and then turned south along the Vistula. After some twenty-five kilometers, we turned into a country lane and stopped under a willow tree. He had it all ready. There was a freshly dug trench under a clump of shrubs, and a spade appeared from the trunk. Our job done, we drove toward the river and came upon a bunch of anglers gathered over a bottle of vodka. Seemingly interested, we chatted with them about fishing, wondering whether this was a good stretch of the river. We shared some of their refreshment and merrily started on our way back, when my friend suddenly turned to our driver.

"Have you heard the latest news? Jerzy has fallen in love!"

The swine! It was supposed to be a secret.

In April, I celebrated my name day by giving a traditional party. It was the first time that Lenta had come to a party of mine. Leopold Tyrmand, by then a well-known writer and bon-viveur, was also there. He was inspecting my jazz records with great interest, though keeping a beady eye on Lenta, so far not noted in Warsaw society. At one stage, Lenta and I found ourselves sitting on the ottoman and, rather lost for words, I started telling her some amusing—or so I thought—wartime stories. It somehow misfired, the circumstances were wrong and my stories less amusing than I thought. Lenta kept a frozen smile on her face, but her eyes were on the dancers in the next room. Suddenly, Leopold appeared from nowhere and asked her to dance. She got up without giving me another look. I sat there rather disconcerted, when he returned with his arm round Lenta's waist. "You know," he said, "this girl is a revelation. She ought to change her name though to Pamela or Gladys; that's what beautiful girls are called in good English novels." I'd learned a lesson: that was the last time that I ever talked about my wartime adventures; it took half a century before I started writing these reminiscences.

The latest propaganda posters assured us that bricklayers, working in teams of three, had increased their productivity in celebration of the July anniversary of the Communist rule and were setting an example to others. The press was praising a team, which apparently managed to lay sixteen thousand bricks in one day. The papers were full of pictures and names of these workers, their achievements, and the prizes they received. A certain outstanding foreman bricklayer was now rewarded with a desk job as a building inspector. The local wits maintained that he was so sickened by his efforts that was no longer fit for work. I noticed that there were also women's bricklaying teams. When they interrupted work for a while, I could see their swollen hands tremble.

At one of the frequent Party congresses, Roman Piotrowski, an architect and prewar member of CIAM (Congres Internationaux D'Architecture Moderne) and coauthor of the Athens Charter, was appointed director of reconstruction. Bolesław Bierut, president of the Polish Peoples' Republic, used every occasion to talk about the future of Warsaw as a "workers' city," which would grow in six years from 144 to 400 square kilometers and have over eight hundred thousand inhabitants; he kept repeatedly stressing that "Warsaw would never again be the capitalist medley of private businesses."

These words, ideologically foreign to myself and to my colleagues, would, however, convince some people. I wondered what a Warsaw reconstructed as "a medley of private businesses" might have looked like? Would it actually be a problem? Meanwhile, the greatest headache was the shortage of bricks and other building materials. The pace of reconstruction was ahead of all the laid-down schedules. Thus, in order to keep up the effort, over twenty towns, with Wrocław and Szczecin leading, began sending their salvaged bricks to Warsaw. All the usable bricks from Warsaw's ruined buildings were also being recovered. Apart from building the twelve residential quarters, the cultural needs of the city were being catered for too. The reconstruction of the Grand Theatre of Opera and Ballet and of the National Philharmonic Hall has begun. Children's and young people's theatres were being erected; cinemas, film studios, a broadcasting station, sports facilities, and open green spaces were all moving ahead. Over thirty-five thousand building workers, architects, town planners, engineers, and artists were employed; but manpower shortages were a constant problem.

One day, I was invited to attend a slide-illustrated lecture by Edmund Goldzamt, one of the architects who had recently returned from Moscow. He was introduced to us with a stress on his Russian doctoral degree, and the purpose of his presentation was to acquaint us with the new style and achievements of Soviet architecture.

The lecturer began his talk with a statement that the world was divided into two camps: the camp of democracy, socialism, and peace under the leadership of the Soviet Union and, on the opposite side, the camp of warmongers and imperialists under the American flag. The struggle between those two camps extended even to the field of architecture. Polish architecture had to join the socialist camp. According to him, Polish architecture had so far not arrived at a clear definition of its aims and direction.

I kept one eye on the man, watching simultaneously the images on the screen. I wondered where all of this was leading. I found everything he said quite shocking, as I had never before heard anyone describe architecture as a fight or a battle. Several questions followed. A well-known architect, struck the floor with his stick—he was lame—and asked what the difference was there between the Soviet buildings we had just seen with their towers, huge arches, and rows of gigantic columns, and those of the Third Reich with its very similar structures. The lecturer gave his reply without the slightest hesitation,

"That's very simple. In socialist architecture, the columns represent rows of equal men and women in close ranks, ready to fight for peace; the columns in German buildings, on the other hand, represented people oppressed by fascism."

So simple indeed!

My respite from ideological lectures was the growing closeness between Lenta and me. After the original enchantment, I became rather embarrassed. How did it actually happen? How could I have allowed myself to be caught unawares by this kind of emotion, never experienced before, and over which I had no control? Though just short of her twentieth birthday, Lenta was exceptionally self-contained and thoughtful in her speech and manner. If she was fond of someone, she would express it without undue emphasis while always seeking mitigating circumstances for those who did not meet with her total approval. She liked literature, poetry in particular, and was sensitive to many other aspects of culture.

Lenta lived with her mother in one room of the large prewar apartment, which had belonged to her maternal grandfather, Kazimierz Rossmann. It was now a typical postwar Warsaw "kolkhoz." The only difference between it and the original Soviet invention being the fact that it was urban, and that the inhabitants were, in this case, members of the old Polish intelligentsia; thus, courtesy and circumspection were the norm.

The roots of the Rossmann family were in Saxony; its members emigrated to Poland at the end of the eighteenth century. Lenta was the daughter of Tadeusz Henisz, a career soldier, captain in the elite

Regiment of Mountain Fusiliers. He died prematurely in 1935. The Henisz family were, far back, also of foreign extraction, originally from Berlin and Brandenburg.

In August 1944, Lenta and her mother, like most of the civilian population of the capital, were caught unawares by the Rising. Having lost all their personal belongings, they were given shelter by strangers. Eventually, Ukrainian units in German service began to expel all residents from that particular part of the city. They were driven in a crowd of civilians into the yard of an abandoned factory. Lenta spent the night hidden under a wooden chest, older women sitting on top of it, while drunken Ukrainian soldiers were dragging young women away from their families and raping them in full view of the terrified crowd. The next day, Lenta pretending to be seriously ill, a Red Cross nurse helped her and her mother to get to a hospital outside the gates and, from there, to freedom. They stayed until Warsaw's liberation on a small suburban country estate managed by a cousin. When they returned to the city, they found their apartment looted and devastated; not even family mementos, letters, or photographs remained.

In July, Lenta, a couple of friends, and I went for a week's holiday at the seaside. We took a boat to the tip of the Hel Peninsula. Of the former magnificent beach, only a small section was open to public. The rest of it was closed off by barbed-wire entanglements. After sunset, even that part of the beach was out of bounds, the sand was harrowed; and anybody trying to escape to Sweden by swimming across the Baltic or any spies trying to land from an American submarine, could be observed from the guard towers. Seeing this paranoia at first hand, I now fully realized that we were indeed living behind an iron curtain.

with Lenta on Hel trip

In Warsaw too, strange things began to happen. The atmosphere in the school changed. Large numbers of students, both boys and girls, were now sporting the khaki shirts and red ties of ZMP (the Union of Polish Youth). Meetings, large and small, were the order of the day. Often, in these meetings, all those present would suddenly stand up and clap, not really having listened to what the whole thing was about. The hall would be decorated with red banners bearing slogans and calling students to join the struggle to establish lasting peace and maintain eternal vigilance.

The resolution of the Party's National Council of Architects, published in June 1949, clearly declared formalism, nihilism, and constructivism to be symptoms of bourgeois cosmopolitanism. The greatest menace in town planning was, according to the resolution, the pessimistic Anglo-Saxon concept of not placing the urban center as the nucleus of social life. So what remained? The resolution left no doubt, what the requirements were "The need to disseminate Soviet ideas of architecture and town planning . . . to denounce any influences of the imperialist camp in the field of architecture."

There was no doubt: we had been put into a straitjacket. One of the architects, irate on having read the resolution, said to a more easily converted colleague, "You'll see, one day you'll curse your profession."

The atmosphere in our studio, not affected by the new stereotypes forced on all state offices because of its nature, remained cheerful and calm. We did not have to sign in at work at 6:00 a.m., neither did we have a party secretary to keep a watchful eye on our activities nor his Soviet "technical adviser" to check most projects for their political correctness.

Unfortunately, the world outside our working milieu was not quite as carefree. In August, our Lithography Works were placed on the list of "establishments to be nationalized with compensation," as published in the official gazette. The piece ended with a statement to the effect that "the decision was final and could not be appealed against at the High Administrative Appeals Court." We never received any compensation, of any kind, whatsoever.

This was my first personal encounter with Stalinism, which was rapidly engulfing the country, though the word had not yet entered our vocabulary; the process being referred to as "the democratic introduction of the one and only equitable system of social legislation under the leadership of the father and teacher of all progressive mankind."

It was slowly dawning on me that I wished to spend all my time with Lenta, though I had no idea how to achieve it. Until one day, I had a revelation—there was such a thing as marriage! Why had it not occurred to me before? Well, yes, but the other person had to agree to the proposition as well. I started dropping hints, mentioning through various circumlocutions of friends and acquaintances who had just got married. I was wasting my breath. Lenta did not respond. At best, she would smile, wrinkle her nose, and that was the end of it. To make matters worse, one day, I dropped a hefty brick. Walking along a dug-up street, jumping over puddles, I reached for the ultimate argument:

"You know, I feel that I ought to settle down at last, turn a new leaf. All those dalliances, all that riotous living . . . I think I am ripe for marriage, for the next stable stage of my life . . ." Lenta turned toward me, a big question mark in her eyes, as if she was saying, "Well, what about me?" It got through to me just as I was saying my last word, but it was too late. She burst out laughing and ran ahead on to a plank thrown over a trench.

One night, during the 1950 carnival season, Lenta and I went to a party in a friend's suburban residence, which he had inherited from his parents. Lenta and I were having a very good time. As we stopped dancing, I turned to her and asked her more simply to marry me. Out of breath, we dropped on a sofa in a dark adjacent room. Lenta got hold of my hand and said one word, "Yes!"

12

The One and Only Correct Way

There were big excavations in progress at the corner of two main streets: the holes were filled with brown, stagnant, dirty water, from which old bits of scaffolding and iron rods protruded. The entire crossroads was, in fact, one big heap of rubble with the outlines of old cellars showing their muddy insides here and there. The two streets were being widened and underground pipes, conduits, and cables were laid. Grey figures of workers in rubber boots and quilted jackets shuffled about this muddy confusion. Some carried lengthy boards; others pushed metal barrows full of cement along planks laid over the mud. Still others, standing on top of horse-drawn platforms, were flinging bricks, one by one, on to a heap, breaking and knocking bits of them off in the process. I watched this goings-on every morning, on my way to the studio in Bank Square. Colorful posters, stuck to the remains of a wobbly wooden fence, broke the monotony of the general grayness. One of the posters showed a black anvil against a blue background; big black tongs held a large digit, a six, glowing red; from the white edge of the numeral resting against the anvil, letters, like white sparks, formed the words "present" and "plan"—the meaning of the poster stressing the six-year plan. In the upper corner of the poster, a caption in bold black letters read, "We are forging the foundations of Socialism." On another day, I noticed a second poster, its bottom partly torn off, with captions exhorting workers to fight absenteeism, work shirking, and lead swinging. “Socialist work discipline is mandatory! Down with the bricklayers’ Mondays!” Indeed, drink—on most days and weekends in particular—was the great public enemy. As early as the breakfast break, workmen were eating bread with slices of pork fat and washing them down with a quarter liter of vodka. The problem was said to be even worse on the building sites of new large housing estates where unskilled labor, men newly recruited from country villages and given little or no training, were being employed. Their quarters, though given the proud name of “workers’ hotels,” were no more than primitive timber barracks thrown together in the middle of nowhere with nothing but rows of bunk beds inside. The workers thus existed in virtual isolation, cut off from their homes as well as from the town they were building. The enormous scope of the six-year plan and the great investment involved, forced the management to keep bringing in new labor from increasingly distant parts of the country. Deprived of contact with their families, spurred into long hours of heavy physical work by the never-ending calls for increased productivity, they looked, almost without exception, for solace in the bottle. They were not alone, of course, in drowning their sorrows in lakes of alcohol—the traditional Polish way. Both joys and tribulations were dealt with in the same way. Even in periods of the worst shortages of essential products, I cannot remember vodka ever being in short supply.

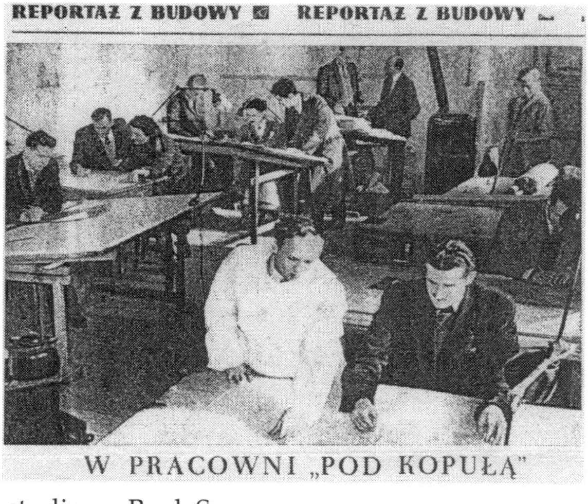

studio on Bank Square

The winter was particularly severe that year, which did not help our work on the Bank Square site. The room we used for our design work was not even finished. The floor was naked concrete, and the walls had been provisionally plastered. The upper parts of the walls and the barrel vault were still showing sooty old bricks. The two windows, tall, wide, with semicircular upper parts, were ill fitting; and wind blew directly on to our drawing boards. The only, insufficient, heating came from two coal-fired cylindrical iron stoves, one at each end of the room, each with a long tin pipe leading to a hole in the wall. The coal had been delivered by cart, tons of it having simply been thrown onto a pile outside the still-unfinished stairs leading to our story. At first, we were bringing it ourselves upstairs in buckets, until somebody remarked that getting our hands numb and covered with coal dust was not conducive to the production of precise, clean drawings. Thus, we acquired a peasant granny, complete with her quilted jacket, her floral headscarf, a long fustian skirt, and felt boots. She swept our floor, carried the coal, and brewed our tea in an enamel teapot on top of the iron stove.

At the beginning of April, a law on "Socialist Discipline" was passed; special labor camps for "shirkers, profiteers, racketeers, wreckers, and enemies of progress" were set up. One of these camps, surrounded with barbed wire, with watchtowers and floodlights throughout the night, was located in our neighborhood and became known as Goose Street Spa. One could find oneself there even for a minor offence.

One way to avoid being accused of breaking any of the new labor laws was to commit oneself to some production target at one's place of work. The press was flooded with descriptions of such commitments entered by workers in celebration of the May 1, Labor Day. A miner's brigade thus vowed to increase their production by 460 percent. Some railway men received a prize for covering ninety thousand kilometers on their locomotive without a single boiler rinse; they immediately undertook to run it for one hundred forty thousand kilometers without any repairs.

The Labor Day parade was planned, with the main review stand to be erected in front of the large building of the Central Committee of the Party, popularly called the White House, which was under construction. Frenzied preparations were taking place in all the workplaces, from factories to offices. Party members were checking lists of names, organizing people into marching units, and establishing their place in the parade. Many joined the parade without compulsion, as there is actually something quite thrilling in hundreds of thousands marching in step, flags fluttering in the wind, music blaring from big loudspeakers, all throats singing the song. "Thousands of hands, millions of hands, yet one heart beats for all" reverberated through the city with the radio broadcasting the celebrations throughout the country. As a rather isolated studio, we seemed to have been forgotten in the general fever of preparations for the Party-inspired raptures. Not that we complained.

In the newsreel, Konstanty Rokossowski, the newly appointed marshal of Poland, astride a fine black stallion, approached to the sound of the "March of the Generals" the stand full of dignitaries and reported to the president that the army and the workers of the capital were ready to begin the parade. Later, some artist painted a huge kitsch picture of the start of the parade, to be preserved for posterity as a great masterpiece of Socialist Realism, or Soc-Realist, art. Rokossowski had, in 1944, commanded the units of the Soviet Army, which had first reached the eastern bank of the Vistula, with Warsaw just across the river, and who, on Stalin's orders, stopped there; thus, depriving the Warsaw Rising, still in full swing, of any help whatsoever. He became the most hated man in the country, and a symbol of Soviet domination. Rokossowski, as seen in all his pictures, had a characteristically raised left eyebrow. Local wits quickly came up with an explanation: it was a result of his utter amazement on receiving Stalin's order to become a Pole.

For a considerable time now, both the press and the radio had been mounting increasingly virulent attacks on the United States—denouncing the recently concluded North Atlantic Pact as an American capitalist plot aimed at wrecking Europe. Though busy on the reconstruction work, concentrating on my studies, and preoccupied with my private life—mostly my relationship with Lenta—I still found enough time to follow the political developments in the world and the victorious, so far, progress of the Communist revolution. Following the events in China, there begun the "liberation" of the entire Korean Peninsula. I became concerned about the irreversibility of changes taking place in Poland. Now that the power of the Communist system has reached the far extremes of Asia, could one expect any change taking place in our country without some unimaginable new events abroad? And suddenly, as if to order, that was what happened. At the end of June, President Truman announced that, sponsored by the United Nations, American troops were coming to the aid of Korea. This coincided with the "liberation" of Seoul by the Korean People's Army.

Relieved that at last somebody was taking steps to halt the so far unchecked march of Communism and having passed my end-of-year exams, I turned my mind to plans for the summer vacation. Thus, in the summer of 1950, with a group of friends, we decided to go to Mazury, a region of a thousand lakes and of virgin forests.

Toward the end of this enjoyable vacation, Lenta and I went to a seaside resort to see Lenta's mother, who was resting there, and to tell her that we had decided to get married in September.

The civil marriage ceremony was performed at the Warsaw Registry Office in the old Branicki Palace, the prewar seat of the British embassy. The church wedding was celebrated in the brightly lit baroque church of the Visitation Sisters. We left the following day for our ten-day honeymoon in Zakopane, the place where we first met, enjoying the views and walks in the mountains.

We started our married life in our—by now overcrowded—family apartment. Because of its layout, some doors had to be kept permanently closed. Thus, I hung a Turkish tapestry over the door between our bedroom, which used to be my parents' bedroom in the old days and my brother's room, and placed my drawing board against it. The kind of open house we had kept, with friends regularly dropping in for meals, had to come to an end now. After our honeymoon, Lenta went back to university while I had to deal with all the backlog of work; hence, the drawing board in our bedroom.

The Korean intervention provided the Communists with new material for attacking the USA. Our propaganda machine kept bemoaning the fate of Korean mothers and children, apparently the main victims of American aggression. Another favorite topic was that of the American air raids, which were being equated with those of the German Luftwaffe. I saw a caption under a picture of flying American planes, which read, "First over Warsaw—now over Korea!" As if Americans had ever flown over our capital with hostile intent! I was particularly incensed, as I still remembered my sojourn in New York in 1942 and the cooperation with the Americans in the air during the war. I remembered the long-legged, scantily clad pinup girls, which they used to paint on the fuselages of their bombers. And now, some ignorant cartoonist was comparing those spontaneous flights of male fantasy with the Nazi skulls and crossbones.

The country was now strictly following "the one and only correct way." Socialist Realism had become a dogma. Soviet experts were now installed in all the design studios, and their opinion was holy writ. The same rigid standards were imposed on all the arts—music, literature, sculpture, and painting. The opening phrases of press articles frequently read "Inspired by the genius of Stalin the Great, we shall stand united in our struggle."

By the beginning of 1952, virtually all the members of our studio were qualified architects with master's degrees. Somebody suggested that we celebrate the occasion by throwing a New Year Eve's costume ball in the newly reconstructed Blank's Palace, where our offices were now located. The idea met with general approval. We were certainly no exception. The whole of Warsaw, as if attempting for a brief moment to forget the monstrous reality and

the ghastly boredom of Communism, ignoring the grim appeals to fight American imperialism, was dancing and reveling with unrestrained passion.

Soon after, we began to gear up for one of the most ambitious projects of the whole postwar period—the reconstruction of the Old City district, strictly based on available historical data.

One night, toward the end of the summer, I was woken by loud voices and noisy footsteps in my brother's room. Suddenly, the closed door between our rooms, crash opened, violently kicked from the other side, overturning my table. Three men with electric flashlights burst into our room. All I could see were their dark silhouettes. Lenta, startled, sat up in bed, covering herself with the sheet. I too was naked, which was rather embarrassing. In spite of that, a blind fury I had hardly experienced before, made me jump out of bed and scream at the top of my voice, "Bloody hell, you dirty swine! About turn! Face the wall! This minute!" It worked. I reached for my dressing gown lying on the floor and got Lenta's wrap from the wardrobe. We stood there facing the intruders. One of them passed me a piece of paper, mumbling something about a search order. With a sweeping arm gesture, I indicated our room and said through clenched teeth, "Now, carry out your orders." Having searched the whole apartment, they left after dawn. When I tried to call Mother in Horseshoe Woods, I learned that they had also experienced a search during the night; she was arrested, and her bedroom had been sealed.

Then came weeks and months of waiting, asking questions here, there, and everywhere; seeking possible contacts to get any shred of information—all to no avail. The only thing we managed to dig up was that Mother was incarcerated in the Mokotów prison. But on what charge? We could not get any answers. Our only consolation was that at least prison was probably better than a labor camp. But under the legal system in force, you were guilty until you could prove your innocence. There was no point in hiring lawyers as they would not be able to find out anything either. After a while, the prison authorities allowed us to take some parcels of food and clothing to her. We were also permitted to visit the military prosecutor's office once a month to seek information. It did not augur well that Mother's case was in the hands of the military prosecutor; it meant that the case was serious and of a political nature. Each visit was truly a humiliating experience. Citizen prosecutor was Julia Brystygier, who was dreaded by the prisoners and their families alike.

The anti-West and especially the anti-American propaganda campaign intensified from one day to the next. We interpreted it as a sign that the Americans were winning in Korea; they were also being accused of using poison gas and bacteriological weapons.

In the spring, a small beetle was discovered attacking the potato crop in the fields. A mad campaign began: American submarines were accused of depositing the Colorado beetle at night on Baltic beaches. Masses of schoolchildren were taken to the countryside to comb potato fields to destroy the pest. Members of youth organizations were patrolling beaches in search of the enemy. An exhibition entitled This Is America was opened, showing a great range of American trash products offered for sale to tourists in places like New York's Times Square: ghastly mugs used for advertisements, T-shirts with pictures of nude girls, covers of pornographic periodicals, examples of vulgar lingerie, stills from film comedies of the Marx brothers, photographs of black jazz musicians, and other well-known personalities caught in ridiculous postures. There were garishly colored ties for men and crinoline-like petticoats made of foamy nylon for girls. Above the entrance, a big red banner with white lettering warned one: "The enemy is tempting you with Coca-Cola." Loudspeakers flooded the hall with bebop and swing music. The exhibition, contrary to intention, became an overnight success. Crowds of people were leaving the hall, laughing and cheering, happy to have got a glimpse of another world where apparently there were no limitations, where anything went. One day, a group of American diplomats parked their big, shiny Chevrolets and Fords and left the exhibition on foot, leaving the cars behind. The throng of curious onlookers, keen to see such cars with their own eyes, was so dense that no one else could get through. The show of real American achievements proved very effective; no wonder that the exhibition was quickly closed down.

Mother's case was still unresolved, and there was nothing we could do about it. Worried though we were, Lenta and I went to the mountains toward the end of winter 1953, having booked a room in a mountain hostel well in advance. The morning of March 5 greeted us with blue skies and warm sunshine. Along with a large group, we decided to go to the top of Kasprowy Peak cable car terminal. There were no ski lifts then, so one had to struggle uphill to a height some two thousand feet above our lodge. After several hours, we reached the terrace of the building. A soldier of the frontier guards, unsteady on his feet and smelling strongly of alcohol, bumped into me in the entrance door. Inside the station, the men building the cable lift could hardly stand upright.

up hill to Kasprowy Peak

What's happening here? Why is everyone drunk? There were only a few tourists in the restaurant. Yet empty bottles with labels of a dreadful fruit wine were scattered all over the tables and floor.

"What's the occasion?" we asked the barmaid serving us hot sausages. Timidly, she pointed out the manager. He thought for a while, scratched his head, and then, composing his voice into somber tones, said, "Well . . . yes, citizens . . . well, I mean . . . the nation is in mourning . . . It was in this morning's bulletin that we heard that . . . Comrade Stalin had died . . . God rest his soul. But sorry, all the wine has gone, not a drop is left."

Was this the end of an epoch? We skied down back to the lodge with an amazingly light feeling in our hearts.

Back in Warsaw, it was my turn to visit the prosecutor's office. This time, I was escorted to a different office; a gray-haired man in a colonel's uniform sat behind the desk and, unbelievably, he actually smiled at me. "I see you've been skiing. Good, very good. You've had a lot of sun, did you?" I looked at him, full of suspicion, and didn't say a word. "Well, it won't be long now before I'll be able to give you some news about your mother." This could mean either the end of the investigation and the beginning of a trial or, difficult to believe, a forthcoming release. Several weeks passed without any news. It was a lovely spring day when a few friends came to see us. We did not even hear the doorbell. And suddenly, the door opened; and there stood Mother, a headscarf tied under her chin, a bundle of belongings in her hand. We all ran toward her, embracing, kissing, laughing. But Mother, radiant, pushed us away. "Don't touch me yet," she explained. "I stink of prison. First of all run me a bath and get me lots and lots of soap!"

13

Gradual Departure from the Only Way

"Old man river, that old man river . . ." the powerful voice of Paul Robeson resounded over the Old City Market Square. I was standing, amazed, among oblivious road workers laying a basalt block pavement, while the famous last lines reached me above the clatter of jackhammers: "He just keeps rolling a . . . looong . . ." Huge loudspeakers had recently been installed in the Market Square; and inspirational music, such as military marches, folk songs, and mass choirs was now blaring from them day and night. The incongruous combination of red banners with their Labor Day slogans and tunes of the Mississippi Delta created a truly surreal effect. Though at the time Paul Robeson was considered a "good American"; and a couple of years before, I had attended his concert at the central tennis court of the Legia sports club. He had then stopped in Warsaw on his way to Moscow, where he was to receive the Stalin Prize; and for several days, his songs were being broadcast from loudspeakers all over the town. Then a long pause followed, when neither Robeson's nor any other American music was to be heard. And now, suddenly . . . had the censorship rules changed?

When the national holiday of July 22, 1953—anniversary of the communist take-over—was about to be celebrated, there were frenzied preparations for the opening of the first Old City tourist route to show the public what progress in its reconstruction had been made in two years. All the decisions regarding the design of individual buildings were based on painstaking studies of old documents and drawings, which had been removed by the Germans during the war and only recently recovered. Even though they had destroyed it without mercy during the Warsaw Rising, the Germans intended to rebuild the Old City as Deutsche Stadt Warschau. I consider the reconstruction of the Old City, the work on which our team had already been engaged for over a year, as a milestone in my professional life.

By the end of 1953, twelve thousand five hundred dwellings in Warsaw had been completed, including two thousand five hundred in the Old City. Meanwhile, Lenta got her history of art master's degree at Warsaw University and started work at the National Museum as assistant to its director, Prof. Stanisław Lorenz. She also reported on the progress of reconstruction in the Old City.

About that time, a foreign periodical found its way to our studio; and in it, I came across a photograph of a recently erected glass tower block, the Lever House in New York City. The building was the first example of a curtain wall: a smooth glass surface superimposed on the building's skeleton as its external elevation. It revolutionized our perceptions. This was modern architecture par excellence. What a contrast with our Palace of Culture and Science, the gift of Comrade Stalin! All at once, I knew that I needed a change. I was aware, though, that there was no room for deviation. Within the precepts of Soviet Socialist Realism, "change" was a dirty word.

At the end of April, my former professor, Jerzy Hryniewiecki, came to see me in the office and invited me to his home. He would not tell me what this was about, but just smiled mysteriously. When

I got to his apartment, Marek Leykam was already there. Both these architects belonged to a small and, perhaps the only, group of independent lecturers at the school of architecture who enjoyed the opinion of being steadfast in their stand, not yet tamed by the Establishment, and who, swimming against the current, continued to express their frank opinions on the dictates of Socialist Realism. They invited me to join them in the competition for the design of a new Warsaw stadium. It related to the government's decision to hold the International Festival of Youth in Warsaw. These festivals or world congresses of leftist youth were part and parcel of the enormous Moscow-directed Communist propaganda apparatus, which wanted us to believe that everything good and progressive was here on our side while the other consisted of Nazi criminals, warmongers, Americans, and their European puppets.

The site chosen for the stadium was just across the river from the center of the city. The panorama of the center was now quite striking due to the enormous silhouette of the Palace of Culture and Science. The date of the festival was fixed for July 1955. We had one year to go. As the soil conditions at the site, used earlier as the city's garbage dump, were poor, the only way of dealing with the problem at the time was to build an earthen stadium with a thick layer of soil fill. The material should be easily available. The bottom of the nearby river would provide the sand, and the ruins of Warsaw the rest. The vast amount of rubble to be cleared—millions of cubic meters—has been a serious problem in the rebuilding of Warsaw. Very few trucks were available to the builders, and transport depended largely on horse carts recruited with their drivers from surrounding villages. Hundreds, even thousands, of such carts crowded the still-unmade, manure-covered approach roads and streets of the capital. So no wonder that, as soon as the news spread that rubble was in demand, we were overwhelmed with offers of hundreds of thousands cubic meters of broken bricks—for free! Soon a design of a large bowl to accommodate close to eighty thousand spectators with a sports field surrounded by an athletics track at its bottom was taking shape, all conforming to Olympic standards. We were totally engrossed in working out different versions of that bowl, the graceful geometry

stadium design team

of the large shapes of the embankments and ramps emerging from the surrounding grounds and gently descending toward the river. In late spring, we presented our design to the highest state authorities. Our design won the competition!

At this stage, I realized that I had to review the direction of my professional life. I decided to leave Piotr Biegański's studio and to say good-bye to historic monuments. The last eight years spent on the reconstruction of the most beautiful buildings of the capital had given me excellent training in architecture, right from its historical roots. I had greatly appreciated the friendly, cultured atmosphere of the studio, something that ought to be the norm for people devoted to our noble profession. And this I never forgot. In the same way, I always remembered our professor's reply to the journalist who visited our studio.

"I surrender to my troops. I have no wish to restrain their enthusiasm, the speed of their work, and their evident enjoyment."

Thus, it was with embarrassment that I went to tell him of my decision. "I do understand and cannot disagree," he said. "I am happy that you are going to be under Jerzy Hryniewiecki's wing." But I was not the only one leaving the studio. Four others followed me. Again, we were lucky in being able to stay outside the enormous bureaucratic network of the state planning establishments. We had a large barrack built for us on the riverside, next to the stadium site, where construction work was already starting. The fact that we, a group without party affiliation, had landed such a responsible commission was, by itself, a sign of change. By autumn, almost sixty general and specialist designers were engaged on our project.

By that time, I had an additional job at home, as our one-month-old Klara now reigned supreme in her beautiful "Moses basket" placed on a tall stand under a little frilly canopy. A nanny was helping us to look after her. My brother got married and moved to a bigger apartment, close to the Opera House in construction, where he worked in the construction's management. It was a lucky stroke for us, as we could now claim his room for the baby.

In early July, shrubs were planted and flowerbeds laid out around the stadium to complement about a thousand trees planted the previous autumn. Seating was being installed. There was no doubt now that the stadium—now dubbed the Stadium of the Decade—would be finished on time for the celebrations of July 22, the national holiday. In the meantime, participants began arriving for the Fifth Youth Festival. If one ignored the official, the purely propaganda side, the festival gave us a welcome glimpse into a different world, many-hued and definitely less authoritarian than ours. It seemed that our government had agreed to this confrontation and wanted the Polish side to prove equally attractive to the guests. For myself, for my colleagues, and probably for all the Varsovians, the stadium became a symbol, which could successfully compete with the Palace of Culture and Science, which was completed at the same time and named after Joseph Stalin.

In the autumn, our stadium group of five was offered a chance to work for the Industrial Building Bureau, which promised the chance of designing, for a change, large industrial projects, with good opportunities for experimental design work. As the alternative was to be employed in the studios designing grim housing projects, we all almost instantly agreed.

In February, we went once again with a group of colleagues and their wives to Zakopane. There was plenty of snow and skiing conditions were perfect. In the evenings, we would tune the big radio in the dining room to the American station in Germany, which was broadcasting music for the GIs. We also listened to news on the Voice of America, surprisingly not jammed. We suddenly realized that while we were away something important must have happened in Moscow, at the Twentieth Congress of the Communist Party of USSR. On the train, I met the bandleader who greeted me on my first night in Warsaw, nine years earlier. He confided in me, that a true revolution is underway in Russia. He said that now, perhaps, he will be free to immigrate to Israel. Back in Warsaw, I got a newspaper, which carried Nikita Khrushchev's amazing speech, seven closely printed pages of it. I quickly turned the pages. Stalin's name wasn't mentioned even once. Things were changing indeed. Suddenly, we were all reading newspapers. Each day brought some sensational admissions of great errors of the past, of distortions of Communist ideology. "We will not shrink from rejecting the dead wood of dogma . . . . Let creativity, released from ideological constraints, be the hallmark of the new era." Whatever the reason, this was an epoch-making change for our profession; and we could see that something had irreversibly shifted, that another barrier had been lifted. And we were quite proud that it was in Poland that the attempt to change the Communist system had started. There was a kind of thrilling anxiety in the air. I even began to follow events in the Middle East. King Faruk of Egypt had been removed, power passed into the hands of Colonel Gamal Abdel Nasser who, to the great dismay of France and Great Britain, nationalized the Suez Canal. My wartime trips across the canal came to mind, and I even reminisced about them at home and at work. I got to know the Egyptian chargé d'affaires in Warsaw at the time. This handsome, dapper man became a good source of information. He told me that after the British and French pilots who used to take ships through the canal were withdrawn, the Egyptian government signed a contract for Polish and Yugoslav sea captains to take their place.

But my interest in the Middle Eastern conflict quickly gave way to the growing conflict in our own country. The brakes controlling our responses to the grim rhetoric of our leaders suddenly gave way. October was the time particularly rich in events, some occurring practically at the same time. One day, the press reported that Soviet armored divisions stationed in Western Poland had left their bases and were moving in the direction of Warsaw. Poland seemed to be facing a bloody intervention. The city trembled with news and rumors. Rumor had it that the workers' self-defense units, mysteriously armed, were prepared to fight. The specter of yet another suicidal uprising and of our just rebuilt city being devastated once again would not go away. The Plenum of the Party's Central Committee was in emergency session to elect new leadership. All the omens indicated that a radical change in the power structure was in the offing.

In December, an architect friend of mine and I put our heads together and decided to try our luck and apply for foreign passports to go to France for several months of professional practice. In those days, it was still more than impudent, it was defiant, hubristic, simply not done. We received an introduction to a high-ranking official. He received us most cordially in his Central Committee office, stressing that it was of the utmost importance for architects to visit other countries. We could not believe our ears. The wind of change was definitely blowing. We left the hitherto impenetrable fortress in very high spirits.

14

The Taste of Success

The speed of events made me keep asking Lenta whether it was just a dream that I was going again to the West or was this political "thaw" for real? Will it last? As soon as I get organized—I kept reassuring her—and as soon as I find a paid job, I'll do my best to get her over there, even if only for a week.

In January 1957, I arrived in Brussels, where I stopped for several days. I was in a state of shock. After ten years of absence, I found the West profoundly changed. It wasn't so much a question of the condition of the buildings, they were the same as before, though no longer showing any signs of war. It was the general appearance of the streets, the lifestyle of the inhabitants. My impressions were pouring out of my pen as I was writing my first postcard to Lenta: the brightly lit shop windows, the unending columns of shiny cars, the exquisite restaurants, the streets teeming with people well into the night. I made a thought-provoking discovery: in the West, the towns were slowly aging, the roofs of churches stood out green with the patina of oxidized copper. The life of people in those streets had grown meanwhile more intense, varied, and colorful. The reverse was true of Warsaw; we had more and more bright new buildings, churches, and palaces shone with their golden roofs while the shops, increasingly few and far between, were looking more and more grey, monotonous, and shabby, and queues of people, hungry for goods, kept growing in front of them.

My personal history had again turned full circle. In Ghent, I fell into the arms of the Tydgadt family, my wartime friends, with whom I had spent many an hour when my squadron was stationed close to the town, and who now greeted me like a long-lost member of the clan.

After several days, I flew to Paris and found my Uncle Antek and his wife living in their prewar flat at 15 rue Pigalle. Their splendid residence in Vaucresson, where our scattered family had met after the war, was rented to a young Vietnamese prince, member of Emperor Bao Dai's family. I stopped in a small local hotel.

My finances did not look too healthy. I had enough money to last me about ten days, and I urgently needed a job. I met a group of young French architects, several of whom had been to Poland the previous summer. And so, a week later, I was sitting at a drawing board next to a large window giving on to the cascade gardens of the Saint Cloud Palace. The chief of the atelier was Maître Felix Bruneau, distinguished architect with many official titles: Architecte de Batiments de France et des Palais Nationaux, Conservateur du Domaine Saint Cloud, Conservateur de Mont Valerien. This very distinguished gentleman, wearing his well-cut suit with the red rosette of the Legion d'Honeur in his lapel and his invariable white silk shirt with a well-chosen sober tie, carried about him a discrete whiff of eau de cologne. As he bent over a drawing board to run his delicate, manicured finger over some detail, his hand would emerge from a pristine white cuff with its gold cufflink.

Thus, I began my architectural practice in an entirely new environment of established traditions, old customs and, uninterrupted by wars, social connections. I became friends with Yves Chauvin. Yves was planning to leave Paris and to return home to Lyons, where he would open his own atelier and start a new practice, hoping to land some small commissions to start with. I did not even envy him this risky move; as in my case, it was just out of question—there were no private architect's practices in Peoples' Poland, though jobs were waiting for the architects everywhere.

Yves intended to vacate his flat in April and promised to let us have it once Lenta came to Paris. Toward the end of March, Lenta told me that she had managed to get a passport too. Yves threw a farewell party in his flat and handed me his keys. I met Lenta at Orly airport in early April.

Our intention was for me to finish work at the end of April, and, before returning to Warsaw, spend all of May traveling, in my uncle's second car, all over France. I invited Andrew, a friend with whom I planned this foreign trip, to accompany us.

One memorable incident happened on the road in the Pyrenees. We stopped for a picnic, admiring the panorama of snow-covered peaks. A fast stream ran below us, sweeping melting lumps of ice from its frozen banks. Another car stopped after a while and spewed out a bunch of Germans.

They asked us where we came from. "Aus Warschau," replied Andrew briefly. They seemed surprised. Having first gone into a huddle, they produced their sandwiches, proceeded to eat them; but instead of admiring the view, they kept looking us up and down. At last, one of them could not contain himself any longer. "Is that your car?" "Yes. We rented it in Paris," I lied.

They shook their heads in approval. We offered them some of our lettuce and cheese. They in turn opened a bottle of wine that loosened all our tongues. Were we really such a curiosity; we, travelers from behind the iron curtain? I stepped down to the stream to wash my hands. A German woman followed, squatting next to me.

"There is quite a gale blowing, bringing a thaw to your neck of the woods," she said, pointing to the east. "It must have blown you all the way here, to the Pyrenees . . . where the ice is melting too."

In Marseille, we came upon marches and demonstrations by members of some trade union. There were groups of people carrying red flags and banners as in Poland, but they were condemning the French government of various misdeeds on the labor front. This was interesting. We had never witnessed an antigovernment demonstration or heard protests expressed so spontaneously and so freely.

We traveled back to Poland in two cars, together with my uncle, while Andrew decided to remain in France and seek immigrant status. I was a bit shocked by his decision.

Back in Warsaw, our reunion with Klara was full of joy, while Lenta and I were both happy to return to work. A pleasant surprise awaited us: our trip had been confirmed, retrospectively, as "educational"; we were thus entitled to paid leave and were expecting quite a bit of money to come our way.

There were many changes at work. New studios had been created. Our Soviet adviser left at the end of the previous year, as indeed had happened in all the workshops, factories, and other work places throughout the country. Thirty-two Soviet generals, with Marshal Rokossowski at the top, were discharged from the Polish armed forces and sent packing back to the USSR; as mementos, they were given the highest decorations of the Polish People's Republic.

Our work in Poland, compared with that of architects in France, differed in many respects. We were easily drawn into large, interesting projects. I agreed with my French colleagues that from this point of view, our situation might appear enviable, but that was ignoring the fact that we were deprived of the chance of finding our own pace for professional development and for determining our own interests and directions. And we had no contact whatsoever with the client or final user. Basically, we were tiny clogs in a huge state machinery.

Nevertheless, in the next three years, I benefited from my experience in the West. Several large industrial projects came my way. One of the results of the political "thaw" was the emphasis on the economy and on technological advancement, with a watchful eye to the advances made in other parts of the world. We were in the forefront of that movement. In the event, I enjoyed many important awards and had to give press and media interviews. With all this attention, with more business trips to the West and to the East, I felt quite content.

In the meantime, considerable changes were taking place in our family. After several disquieting incidents suggesting that she was still under observation by the secret police, Mother decided to move to France. After many turbulent years, at the age of fifty-eight, she was saying her farewells. She whispered in my ear that she was not planning to return to Poland; she would not feel safe in the country unless her French citizenship, which she had lost on marrying my father, was restored. From today's vantage point, it was as if she were sowing the seeds of emigration for us all. My brother was already planning to move to France with his family.

Unexpectedly, the Ford Foundation offered me a study grant in the USA. The firm offer of a five-months-long visit arrived by post in the spring. I decided to accept it and began to prepare my program for the study. But then, my passport request was refused. This was a shock. After all, not everything had changed; the old police state was still in operation.

My appeals to the ministry went unanswered. The American Institute of International Education (IIE) had by then opened an office in Warsaw, and they were dealing with the formalities for grant recipients who were to travel to America. I kept reminding them of my existence and apologizing for constantly postponing my departure date.

Our deputy prime minister had recently returned from a visit to the USA, and the papers kept quoting his opinion about the need for contacts between the people of both countries on all levels; there was a lot of waffle about old examples of cooperation, and the repetition the old platitudes going back to Kościuszko, Pułaski, etc. Pages were written about the new president of the USA, John F. Kennedy; about his wife Jacqueline, and about her sister Lee, married to the Polish aristocrat Stanisław Radziwiłł. Suddenly, we all thought of America as less distant, more approachable. Thus, I was not too surprised when one day the phone rang in the office and a polite voice asked whether I'd like a meeting arranged in connection with my passport application. He suggested a café in the center of town.

"How will I recognize you?" I asked. "What's your name?"

"It doesn't matter. We know you."

There were two of them, young, handsome gentlemen in navy blue suits, white shirts, good quality ties, with short, fashionably cut hair. Our conversation or, more precisely, their duologue ran approximately as follows:

"We'd like to congratulate you on gaining the American grant. We have been following your professional success; we realize that you wish to develop your talents fully, to hoist your sails, so to say. We are convinced that you, perhaps more than anybody else, deserve our help in furthering your career. You and your wife run an open house, and you count many foreigners among your visitors. We are all for such contacts, except that there is a bit of misunderstanding between us."

What were they talking about? What misunderstanding? I was trying to read their thoughts while they went on with their discourse. "The gist of the misunderstanding is that we get nothing in return for the support we are offering you. Just give it some thought. We do understand that hospitality is expensive, and we are prepared to offer you financial help. We also have well-stocked stores of wines and other alcoholic drinks. We could help you with service staff, waiters, for example. All we would like in return is to learn something about the people who visit you or—"

"Just a moment," I broke in, my blood beginning to boil. "You want me to spy on my guests, on my friends? I am not another Judas! And here you are, offering me pieces of silver while for a year you have been refusing to grant me a passport for a journey which wouldn't cost you anything!" I was just about managing to control my voice. "How dare you ask me to spy for you? What connection can there be between dinner party talk and my journey to America?"

"But no . . . no . . ." protested one of them, smiling ingratiatingly. "That's not what we are talking about, let's leave it for some other time. Now, that you are going to the States—"

"Am I going?" I interrupted, startled.

"Well, yes, that's what we wanted to tell you; you will get your passport within the next few days. But what we mean is that there, abroad, you might meet lots of people, some of them may be unfriendly to our People's Republic. All we want of you is a list of your contacts in USA. That's all. We shall be very grateful."

I stopped listening to their claptrap. The relevant news was about my passport. I obviously had no intention of drawing up lists of "enemies of the People's Republic"—I would have to add my own name to it. Another thought suddenly struck me. What would I do if they started exerting more pressure on my return? Earlier on, when asking the Association of Polish Architects for a letter of support, I had promised to give them the names and addresses of American architects, for the purpose of correspondence in organizational and professional matters. I smiled to myself at the thought of what would these guardian angels of mine do with the addresses of Mies van der Rohe or Eero Saarinen?

The parting with Lenta and Klara was the most difficult bit of my venture. Not that I doubted that they would manage. Our home was well organized, we had adequate home help and care for our daughter, who was already attending kindergarten.

In early April, I flew to Paris; and from there, via Amsterdam, to New York. In my boldest dreams, I could not have foreseen that this flight would be the beginning of an entirely new life for me and my family.

15

Hoisting My Sails

After almost nineteen years, I was approaching New York again. Last time we sailed slowly toward the Statue of Liberty, outlined against the skyscrapers of Manhattan emerging from the morning mist. Then, as the ship was dropping anchor in the port roads, I stood at the stern of the *Queen Mary* surrounded by my comrades-in-arms, full of a great, almost childish, curiosity; the city was offering a sharp contrast to my recent experience of front-line service in Libya. There was nothing then to compete with the trinity of images: the unforgettable infinity of the desert, the voyage on board the huge ship, and the tallest buildings in the world.

This time, my field of vision was limited to the cabin window of the KLM Boeing 707. I was more taken by the air brake devices and movements of the flaps slowly emerging from the wing than by the bird's-eye view of America. Past Boston, the white frozen spaces began to be broken up by thin ribbons of highways connecting the scattered gray townships. Viewed from our great height, with no details discernible, the effect was similar to bomb craters observed during the war. Their scattered pattern differed greatly from towns in Europe, still planned concentrically at the time. Approaching New York, the towns grew increasingly closer to one another and, eventually, merged into one massive creamy-gray conurbation. As we gradually descended, thousands of small dots stood out of the mass and became houses joined by a dense, irregular network of roads. Then the roads merged into wider arteries, eventually to become wide expressways, the many lanes thick with traffic.

Next day, I took the subway to the center of Manhattan and, after a noisy ride, got out at Madison Avenue. I was looking for the Polish Institute of Art and Science on East Sixty-Sixth Street, where a guestroom was waiting for me. The subway stations and their surroundings were ugly, the purely utilitarian platforms built with not a spark of imagination, witnesses to the rapid development of the town. The Fifty-Third Street station is very deep underground and, with the two suitcases in my hands, I stood on the escalator running between high and ugly iron screens, separating different parts of the station. Finally, after one more iron staircase, I emerged into daylight. Several more steps and I put my cases down on the sidewalk. What a relief!

The Polish institute, situated in one of the tree-lined streets running between Madison and Park avenues, proved to be an oasis of calm. It occupied an attractive, narrow, six-story townhouse, typical of midtown New York.

In the office of my American sponsors, I met an elegant lady of around fifty, who was to be my guide in the city. Louise Woods lived with her husband in an old high-rise building on Fifth Avenue. Their apartment occupied an entire floor. Her husband, George, at the time president of the World Bank, was spending a lot of time in Washington DC. Louise decided to show me New York "from the best angle," as she put it. She made a point of trying to convince me that New York was in reality "A charming little town where people all knew one another. We are talking of those worth knowing, of course," she added. In the first few days, she did not let me go anywhere on my own. I escorted her therefore

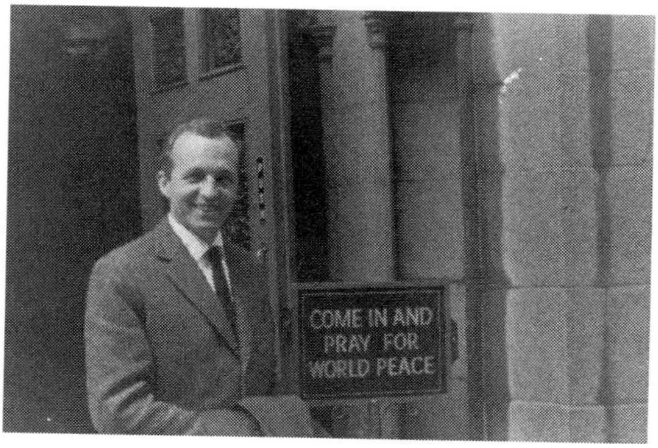

to midday luncheons in Le Pavillon, the French restaurant and get-together of her lady friends. She introduced me to dozens of jewel-bedecked ladies who assured me unanimously that they were thrilled indeed to meet me. "From where? Poland? Really? All you Hungarians are so interesting."

One day, Louise came to fetch me in a big black cabriolet with the top down and offered me the driving wheel. As I drove up Park Avenue, Louise, relaxed on the wide, red leather front seat, kept laughing as if she had just heard a really good joke. When, suddenly serious, she bent toward me and stated that I definitely need to buy myself a car for my forthcoming journey. "You cannot really see America without a car. Come to the Institute tomorrow, and I shall introduce you to someone who may help."

I thought this was an excellent idea; and the following day, I became the owner of a big black 1952 Oldsmobile. Louise's protégé with his bargaining skills got it for me for $200. He even volunteered to have the car registered and insured in New Jersey without any need for me to be present.

My days were filled with visits to various architectural offices. I received an invitation to the Annual Congress of the AIA, the American Institute of Architects, to be held at the end of April in Philadelphia. I still had to work out the timetable and itinerary for my intended journey around the USA. I planned to time it so that at the end of the academic year, in late May, I would reach Raleigh, North Carolina, to visit its famous School of Design. The first postwar director of its Department of Architecture was Matthew Nowicki, an architect from Warsaw.

First I decided to go to Philadelphia by bus. To begin with, I was introduced to Edward Bacon, the head of Philadelphia's development planning department, who was particularly interested in certain technical aspects of the rebuilding of Warsaw; of special importance to him were the financial aspects and the role of architects. I sensed that he was worried about some related problem. He told me that American architects were interested exclusively in their immediate assignment, usually the single building to be erected on the site bought by the client, and nothing beyond their current commission, for which they were paid, was of any interest to them. This was the culture he was trying to change, deploring the fact that here nobody was interested in the larger concept of urban planning.

Toward the end of our conversation, Ed Bacon added, "We could use people with your experience."

This single sentence preyed on my mind ever since, but I could not foresee that fate would soon propel me in this very direction, which some twenty years later would prove to be . . . a blind alley.

Ed Bacon had invited Wilhelm (Wilo) von Moltke from Harvard to take over the project of the revitalization—as it was termed at the time—of the town center. At the reception following the spectacular presentation of his team's work, I had a chat with Wilo. In his opinion, American towns, old as they were, and in the European sense of the word unplanned, and now in need of enlargement, even if just to allow for the ever expanding suburban sprawl, were on the verge of a very thrilling phase of reconstruction.

On the last day of the AIA Congress, I was telling someone about my planned journey; and when I mentioned my desire to visit the School of Design in Raleigh, my interlocutor advised me to talk straight away to the dean and fix the date of my visit. Within minutes, I was shaking the hand of Henry L. Kamphoefner. He suggested I visited the school in August. Consequently, I decided to drive first through Pennsylvania to Detroit and Chicago, and then west to San Francisco. My intention was to return via Los Angeles and the southern states.

But first I had to return to New York. The driver of the express bus drove into the huge, many-storied bus terminal and, opening the door, called out, "New York City! Watch your step!" I decided to take the warning both literally and metaphorically.

Three month later, having driven a total of almost ten thousand miles, I went via New Orleans, Alabama, and Tennessee to North Carolina. In the course of the whole journey, I only had to change a wheel once, and even that happened in a most beautiful spot, on the edge of the precipitous shore of the Pacific, near Santa Barbara.

I lost my way also only once and had to phone my hosts to come and rescue me. This happened in Los Angeles when I took a wrong turning off the four-level expressway. When toward the end of my journey in Raleigh I was describing the incident, Henry Kamphoefner shook his head. "Only once? You must have been born under a lucky star." Perhaps he was right, as after two days of meetings, talks, and evening receptions, on the eve of my departure, the dean invited me to lunch in the Students' Union cafeteria. We were joined at the table by Duncan Stewart, a thickset man with a crew cut, one of the tenured staff whom I had already met before. As I learned later, he was a close adviser to the dean. Without many preambles, the dean offered me a post, the top one in the school of architecture, where I would be in charge of the fifth-year students. I could begin at the start of the next semester, in February 1962. Would I be interested?

The sudden offer left me stunned. I didn't know what to say; my head full of thoughts and calculations. After a short break, the dean continued as if wanting to cover all the aspects of the proposal at once: yes, I could bring over my wife and daughter, the school would cover the cost of our flight from Warsaw; yes, they knew they would have to apply to the State Department for a special visa. He supposed that I might need the agreement of the Polish authorities to my transfer, and they would try to smooth my way there too.

At long last I recovered my powers of speech. "You do understand that I have never taught before?"

Duncan smilingly assured me that most of my predecessors had no teaching experience either. "That what's so good about it," he said. "We want new faces, new people with fresh and different experience, ready to experiment, to shake up the school. What we don't want is routine, any routine. We are seeking new trends, new approaches," he ended while pointing to a picture of one of my buildings.

textile plant at Kalisz

The offer was utterly unexpected, and I had to give it some thought, as it would mean a radical change in all my plans. I needed time. We agreed that I would give them a definite reply within a month. I drove next to Cambridge, Massachusetts, where a Polish architect was already teaching and sharing his time between Warsaw's Academy of Fine Arts and Harvard. We talked late into the night about various aspects of my plans; but somehow, this conversation proved of no practical value to me. What I needed was advice on how to tackle the problem of leaving Poland again. How had he managed it? Would he help me? Only at the last minute, when, disappointed, I already sat behind the steering wheel, did he mumble something, half to himself,

"What can I say, my dear man . . . these are such difficult subjects. Perhaps for some outstanding individual . . . with academic experience . . . I really don't know. Maybe a letter from the Polish Academy of Sciences? Something of the kind . . . I really don't know." It was pointless to continue this conversation.

I left New York in the middle of a very hot September. In Warsaw, I received from Henry Kamphoefner copies of letters he had mailed both to the American authorities and to the Polish embassy in Washington. This international bureaucratic commotion around me was a bit embarrassing, but such were the times and I could not possibly help it. Then a letter arrived from the passport office, informing me that I was granted permission to travel to America.

Soon after, the award of annual prizes was announced; and our triumph of a couple of years before was repeated. Together with my team, I received the first prize for our projects. Once again, architects from all over the country, together with their families, assembled in the beautiful columned hall of the old Radziwiłł Palace. It was a solemn occasion, and I felt that another chapter of my life was coming to an end in propitious circumstances. The distribution of prizes completed, with their recipients standing round a long table, the presiding official turned to me and, glass of white wine in hand, wished me further successes and hoped that I would eminently represent Polish architecture abroad.

Had I been laboring under an illusion that my official contact with the People's Republic was about to be severed, a telephone call I received before my departure brought me back to earth. It was the same honeyed voice that I had heard ten months earlier. "Oh no, no, Professor! We are making no demands whatsoever, why would we? We just wish to congratulate you on your successes and wish you bon voyage." That was all. I never mentioned it to Lenta, nor to my colleagues at work. But it got under my skin. I decided to deal with the problem in person and at a time of my choice. But this wasn't yet the end of the story. When I went to collect my passport, I was surprised to see that its cover was green, and not navy blue as usual, and to my amazement was labeled On Official Business. What did that mean?

"It means, Professor, that you are leaving the People's Republic of Poland on official business."

And so, back in the USA, the Eastern Airlines turbojet serving the East Coast took off from La Guardia airport after dusk on the last day of January 1962. The flight to Raleigh-Durham was to take about four hours. Through the scattered clouds below us, one could see, as if through gauze, towns, ablaze with lights, their sharp outlines softened. Once again, I was fascinated by the view of American urban landscape, this time seen at night. The intensity of lights below us was so much greater than that over towns in Western Europe, not to mention the dark towns of Poland, hardly visible from that height.

The new semester was to start in two days' time. The school of architecture in Raleigh was at the time one of the best known in the USA. Its first postwar director, Mathew Nowicki, was a visionary architect as well as a superb teacher. In 1950, in cooperation with a large New York firm, he became involved with the conceptual work on the design of the new capital of Punjab, in the then newly independent India. The plane in which he was returning from India crashed in Egypt; there were no survivors.

Horatio Caminos, my predecessor in my new position, was an Argentinean whose passion was to design the thinnest possible spatial structures to span the largest possible area. The studio next to the drawing room I inherited was full of partly broken models of such constructions. Some were flat and of uniform thickness. Others were either bossed in the center or thicker on the supported four corners and thinner in the center. Their rigidity was to be achieved by a tridimensional, honeycombed, internal web of rods. All those otherwise interesting but highly specialized engineering studies seemed to me slightly out of place in a school of architecture.

The students were obviously curious of what I would suggest to them as their final prediploma project. Brian Shawcroft, an Englishman, lecturer of the third year, told me frankly that my students had been fed up with assisting their previous lecturer on projects of interest to him alone. This was enough for me to know.

I suggested that they present me within two weeks with a proposed design of their choice and on the actual site selected for its realization; this would constitute the final design of their course of studies. They responded like colts released from a cramped paddock on to a lush meadow. One month into the semester, I felt at ease with my class, although I noticed some racial tensions emerging here and there in the freewheeling discussions.

This came to a head when one afternoon a call for a demonstration against recent Ku Klux Klan racist excesses in Alabama spread round the university. Large numbers of teachers and students gathered in the street outside the university. With Brian, my neighbor, I joined the crowd. I told him that this was the first time I had ever taken part in a protest march. We proceeded through the center of town and never before had I witnessed such xenophobia and such intense hatred. We passed between rows of enraged people, screaming obscenities, and spitting at the marchers. Afterward, as we sat in a bar across the road from the university over a cold beer, we talked about the afternoon's shameful events. I had the impression that I've heard about this problem long time before, but I could not remember when. What would have happened, I wondered, had Hitler won the war, occupied America, and ordered the extermination of Jews and blacks? Would he have found many willing executioners here?

It was in May when Henry suggested that I bring my family over and accept the school's invitation to stay in my position longer than originally envisaged. I agreed without hesitation and informed the Polish ambassador about my decision. Since I had visited them in their home back in February, he and his wife had shown a great interest in my progress at the university. It was by sheer accident that I had met them. Their daughter used to work in one of our studios in Warsaw and, when I was leaving, gave me a parcel and letters to take to her parents. The ambassador confided in me during after-dinner drinks, that he was a totally different kind of diplomat than his predecessor. "After all, I used to be the president of the National Bank of Poland," he said. "Now, we ought to give more thought to international cooperation. President Kennedy shares this opinion. There ought to be more contacts such as yours; we are glad indeed that you have made such a good start." We talked quite frankly, and I did not feel there was any duplicity either on his or on his wife's part. I did not, of course, mention the mysterious phone calls I had had in Warsaw and was waiting to see whether anyone on the embassy staff would approach me in a similar vein. Luckily, nothing like that happened. I was introduced to the cultural attaché and obtained access to the embassy's shop offering alcoholic drinks at ridiculously low prices. And that was all.

Soon after, I left Raleigh on the first stage of my journey to Warsaw, this time with the intention of returning with Lenta and Klara. I crossed the Atlantic on the French liner *Liberté*. As we were casting off from the New York pier, I stood in a crowd of passengers waving good-byes, watching the famous skyline. I noticed a young blonde standing next to me, her cheeks streaming with tears. As the ship was rounding the tip of Manhattan, she shook her fist at it and shouted, "New York . . . New York . . . you damned city . . . I hate you! I hate you!" I looked at her in amazement. Being an optimist by nature and happy at the present turn of events, I did not allow myself to think that other people might feel so very different. I thus took the scene I witnessed as a kind of warning. I suddenly realized that I was choosing a new way of life, leaving behind not only the security of a settled professional position, but also all my relations and old friends. I was taking with me, moreover, Lenta and Klara, who, from that moment, would be totally dependent on me. It was a sobering thought, not easy to forget.

After a short spell in Paris, I took a train to Warsaw. In Berlin, I noticed the train proceeding very slowly on a temporary viaduct over a building site—it was the Berlin wall rising and dividing the world into two increasingly hostile parts. I suddenly imagined myself standing on top of the wall, keeping one leg on each side. Not a comfortable position—would I be able to maintain it for much longer?

The three weeks in Warsaw passed in a whirl of visits, meetings, and preparations for our—as we thought—yearlong absence. I left for Paris by train a couple of days before Lenta and Klara, who were going to travel by air. All my Paris relations watched from the Orly airport balcony as the Air France caravel came to a stop in front of the building. The sky was dark and it was drizzling as the passengers ran down the steps, holding umbrellas or newspapers above their heads. I noticed Klara's raspberry red coat and Lenta's white-gloved hand holding on firmly to that of our daughter's. The girl stumbled on the steps, but Lenta picked her up and they ran quickly to the building. My mother put her arm

family's first day in Paris

round me. "Now that we are all together on this side, I can die in peace." I held her tight, "Oh, stop this nonsense," I said, and we went down to the arrivals hall.

I had my passage booked on MS *United States*, while my family traveled later by air, courtesy the Raleigh's School of Design. Brian, my colleague from Raleigh, was in New York; and we went to meet Lenta and Klara at Idlewild airport in Brian's open MG sports car. On the way back, we were packed like sardines, my two girls next to the driver, and me, on the tiny back seat, with the suitcases fastened to the trunk.

Entering Manhattan for the first time by Queensboro Bridge is an unforgettable experience. It seems that the car is plunging straight into a wall of tens of skyscrapers of the Fifty-Ninth Street area. Above are the ornate tops of the bridge's steel support towers and huge cables on each side. Underneath, in the canyons of the streets, framed by the skyscraper buildings, the cars look like so many crawling ants. We booked at the Great Western Hotel on Fifty-Seventh Street for nine dollars a day.

My old friend, Louise, invited us to tea. On seeing Lenta, she exclaimed, "Oh, but you are so lovely!" and looked now at me, now at Lenta, and held her hand as if she needed to reassure herself that what she was seeing was real. Later, she took Lenta aside and told her that there were wonderful bargains in ladies' clothes to be had presently in New York. "For a mere $100 you can get a really good two-piece suit or a little black dress," she whispered in Lenta's ear.

So while the ladies were thinking of clothes, I'd invested $250 in a magnificent black Buick limousine with seats like sofas and plenty of legroom. On the day of our departure for Raleigh, I drove first to the mansion of the Polish representative to the United Nations to pick up the Polish journalist, whom I had met on the ship and had promised to give a ride to Washington. He was telling me with great excitement about his visit to Hyannis Port on Cape Cod, President Kennedy's summer residence, where he had the promised talk with him. The journalist was quite obviously pleased with his first few days in America. On the way, he asked me to let him have a go at driving a car with its new automatic transmission. "Is that the Americanization of the Polish Communist system?" I quipped. But in fact, I was in an optimistic mood and sincerely believed that changes for the better were already taking place in Poland.

In Raleigh, it did not take us long to find, with Mabel Kamphoefner's help, a decent semidetached house surrounded by magnolias and other southern flowering shrubs in an area of mixed woods of oak and pine. Next door lived a widow with a daughter, Cynthia, two years older than Klara; needless to say, the two became friends from the word go. After three months, Klara could already speak English, while Lenta enrolled on a course at the university's Department of English.

In January 1963, I received a letter from Zenon Zieliński, a structural engineer I used to work with in Warsaw. He happened to be in USA on a State Department grant and wanted to visit us in Raleigh. I invited him to come and give a talk in our school. He arrived in Raleigh in February and gave a lecture on the engineering and construction aspects of the design of industrial halls, on which we had so successfully collaborated. His talk was very well received.

During his stay, the four of us made a trip to Kitty Hawk, the site of the Wright brothers' first controlled, powered flight in 1903. It was then that it occurred to me to find a temporary job for Zenon at the Raleigh school. Academic work apart, we could get involved in serious projects. The dean was all for it. Charlie Kahn, who was teaching structural design, behaved in a most generous manner: he took unpaid leave at the school, creating thus

with Zenon in Raleigh

a vacancy for my newly arrived friend. In June, we drove to New York to pick up his family at the airport. His wife was a onetime colleague of mine at the school of architecture in Warsaw. Their two kids, a boy and his younger sister, walked off the plane dressed as if for a children's fashion parade. When I commented on it, she replied, "Let the Americans see what good taste we Poles have. So there!" We returned to Raleigh in two cars.

The 1960s have been described by the United Nations as the decade of developing nations. This was a euphemism. The countries in question were not so much developing as backward and needed all the aid the industrialized nations could provide. In many parts of the world, more or less, bloody revolutions and power struggles were erupting all the time. The world was manifestly splitting into pro-Western and pro-Soviet camps. Each side fought for influence; and the simplest and quickest way was to offer them development programs in agriculture, industry, housing construction, the protection of environment, health, and education. The competition in all those fields had been going on since the middle 1950s; now arms trade joined the race. Only later would we appreciate that the cold war was, in reality, fought out not in Europe but in Africa, Asia, Latin America, and in the Middle East, where the West was slowly losing it.

President Kennedy created the widely acclaimed Peace Corps of young people, mostly students of American universities, whose task was to help the disadvantaged in those countries in their villages, schools, clinics, and settlements. Some of my students had been to Central America and the Caribbean Islands and were appalled by the living standards of the people. Then, I had an idea, derived I suppose from my work in Poland. During the reconstruction of cities and buildings, we were then actually trying to save our national heritage against foreign, Soviet models. I was worried that now, with such massive help from outside, local traditions and customs might be swept away, creating maybe, a backlash against the Western culture. It would be interesting to see what we would be able to come with. I suggested that we work out a project, for instance for inexpensive housing, for a selected country. We would have to begin by studying the country's history, cultural traditions, climatic conditions, and other aspects of foreign cultures of which young Americans knew next to nothing. The students accepted my suggestion with enthusiasm. It gave them a chance to rise above the limitations of their own narrow experience and engage in problems other than those they were familiar with at home. Letters I sent to a number of embassies in West and North African countries with description of our intended studies, appending lists of pertinent questions, and requests for information concerning the country in question, did arouse interest. My subsequent visits to the embassies and talks with their cultural attachés produced even better results when reported to their governments. In the beginning of the academic year 1963-1964, in addition to the material we had gathered in libraries, we had maps, photographs, and precise suggestions from a number of countries. Nigeria sent us specifications for a university project in one of the provincial capitals; Ghana expressed interest in housing and in the design of a school for a medium sized town; Egypt would like to see a project for a small port and housing development in Safaga, on the Red Sea coast.

In the first semester, we concentrated on collating the collected material and preparing large sheets of a colored graphic and photographic presentation of climatic, topographic, and demographic data preparatory to subsequent town planning and architectural studies. All three topics were so well developed that I decided to set up a public exhibition of the material and was offered a large hall in the school's main building.

In early January, before the beginning of the new semester, the dean's secretary phoned me to say that some outside visitors had come to see the exhibition and would like to have a word with me. In the hall, I found Henry and three gentlemen examining the exhibits. They began to question me on how I managed to obtain all the material as well as gain access to the data from the governments in question. Our study of the Safaga town and port attracted their particular attention. They scrupulously read our legends and were interested in our working methods.

I got a bit worried. "Do these men represent some government agency?" I asked Henry sotto voce. He smiled and whispered back, "No, they are from the Ford Foundation." After they finished viewing the exhibition, we went to the dean's office. I now learned that our guests worked for the Cairo office of the foundation and that their job was to visit American universities and other institutions involved in studies of third world development, to get acquainted with their methods of work, and the techniques employed. As they were leaving, one of the men thanked me for mounting such an interesting exhibition and gave me his business card. His name was Jim Lipscomb, and he was the representative of the Ford Foundation for Egypt and director of its Cairo office.

Soon after, I received an invitation to visit the New York office of the Ford Foundation. On arrival, I was warmly received by the foundation's director of international development programs. He told me that his office, in cooperation with the Egyptian government, was organizing an international conference on the development of the Aswan region in Upper Egypt to discuss essential problems arising from the pending completion of the High Dam on the river Nile. The conference, he said, was to convene in mid-March; and he was delighted to inform me that I was invited to take part in it. "Would you accept our invitation? And have you any suggestions to make?"

My first thought was about Zenon. "We are a team," I said, "so that he ought to be included in the group of experts going to Egypt." I remembered that Zenon had previous experience from Libya and Tunisia, where he had organized on-site production of concrete elements for speedy erection of, among other things, dwelling houses.

From then on, events began to proceed at a fast pace. We had a ten-day spring break in mid-March, but I needed at least a month to prepare for the journey and the conference. In order to get visas, the university gave me letters to the consulates of Egypt and countries where I would be in transit, but the main problem was that the kind of passport I had last been issued in Warsaw—the one On Official Business—meant that I had to obtain Polish embassy's permission to apply for any new visa. Our ambassador was helpful, but advised me to stop in Warsaw on the way back from Egypt and exchange the "official" passport for an ordinary one. It did not even occur to me what trouble this was to cause.

Having secured substitute teachers for our students, Zenon and I took off for Cairo, leaving our wives and children in the care of friends. The journey brought back old memories. I had been to Egypt twenty-two years before, in an officer's school following the Libyan campaign. I still had in my mind the views of Aswan, where I went on leave, keen to visit everything there was to be seen. Aswan is situated at the first cataract of the Nile, with islands and granite boulders breaking the flow of the water and eroded into fantastic shapes. For thousands of years, people had been trading with the area and had been attracted to it by the fascinating views and, with its dry climate, found it a good place for rest and relaxation. Legend had it that Cleopatra had brought Caesar there for their honeymoon. In Cleopatra's time, the Nile went over the cataract, forming a huge waterfall. In the early 1900s, the British used the rocks to build a dam that partly controlled the annual flooding. In

work on The High Dam

the 1950s, Egypt's new ruler, Colonel Nasser, took up the old project discussed over many years, of a much bigger dam and a massive hydroelectric power station to provide electricity for the development of industry, land reclamation, and construction of new towns. By this time, the cold war rivalry between East and West had reached Egypt, and both America and the Soviet Union presented their projects for the Aswan dam. The Soviets won the "competition"; and by 1964, the work on the dam was well advanced.

In accordance with the prevailing theory, the region was designated for rapid economic development, expected to follow the construction of the dam. This theory had been tested in the USA, where President Roosevelt created the Tennessee Valley Authority (TVA) specifically to lift an enormous area, covering five states, out of the Great Depression. Toward the end of the 1950s, the American government was rapidly losing friends in Egypt, as the Soviets were penetrating the country in all possible ways. Soon the Egyptian army and air force were being rearmed with Soviet equipment, while Egyptian offices employed thousands of Soviet experts and advisers. I believe that the creation, with American help, of the Regional Aswan Project was an attempt to put the American boot in the door before it was shut for good. It is possible also that the Egyptian government tried to preserve a semblance of balance between the East and the West. Be it as it may, the Regional Planning of Aswan has been created and funded by the Egyptian government. At its head stood Dr. Abdel Rezzak Abdel Meguid, an Egyptian economist educated in Britain and America and married to a British woman, whose idea was to create a modern decentralized territorial unit. He wanted Aswan to demonstrate that the ossified, bureaucratic method of state governance dating back to the Ottoman Empire could be reformed. But how? It was decided to consult an international body of scientists and experts in many fields of knowledge. This was the background of the Aswan conference, planned to last a number of days, to which the Ford Foundation invited several dozen specialists from America and from Western Europe and an appropriate number of Egyptians.

The initial government presentations made it obvious that from the economic point of view, apart from the construction of the High Dam, an artificial fertilizer factory, the wretched town of Aswan itself, and several places of tourist interest in its immediate surroundings, the region had nothing else to offer.

When the conference split into a dozen or so discussion groups, Zenon and I formed one of our own. I decided to explore the town and its potential for modernization and development. I told Abdel Meguid that any local development in the region would have to start with changes in the town of Aswan itself. The possible directions of its modernization would have to be explored and included in an overall plan. His face lit up. He took me by the arm, and we joined Jim Lipscomb. Jim asked me to prepare a short report of our findings and to present a plan of action. After several hours of hard work, we produced an outline of the future office in charge of town and regional planning and housing. We also offered to return in early June to take on the overall management of the work.

Assured that our proposals aroused great interest, we returned to Cairo and took a flight to Warsaw.

As soon as we changed for the Polish Airline plane in Zurich, we found ourselves in a different world. We were still, no doubt, under the influence of the atmosphere and the events of the last month. Having left behind sunny Cairo, the magnificent views of Egypt, the company of well-mannered, smiling people, we knew that we could not avoid unfavorable comparisons with ordinary everyday life, yet it was the sudden confrontation with the communist reality that was such a shock for us. The Warsaw airport greeted us with its yellowish flicker of low wattage bulbs and a shortage of taxis. We boarded an old, rickety bus, which took us to Constitution Square, where Zenon and I parted company. In our apartment, I was greeted by our faithful housekeeper, whom I had forewarned about my arrival, and a vase of flowers with a welcoming note from my mother-in-law.

The next morning, going from one office to another, I sensed that I wasn't wanted here anymore and that I had nothing in common with the huge bureaucratic machine of the Communist system.

In my old place of work, I was told, "But you don't work for us anymore; you have taken unpaid leave. You will have to return your official passport in the Town Planning and Architecture Committee, where it was issued." But there I was told, "It is not our business to issue you with an ordinary passport, you will have to apply to the passport bureau." In the bureau, the woman behind the counter was truly perplexed. "What do you mean? You have just returned from abroad and you want to leave again? What kind of invitation have you got? What? From a university? Have you got it in writing? So where do you actually want to go, citizen? To Egypt or to America? And what for?"

I spent all day going from office to office, and none would accept the papers justifying my journey. In the evening, I had a call from Henry Kamphoefner telling me that Lenta and Klara were well, but he would like to know when I would be back. He wished me luck, though I did not tell him about my disastrous day. I still had four days to present myself back in Raleigh. I met a friend, whose wife I had at one time helped to get a job in Ghana by convincing their state delegation visiting Warsaw that a woman could in fact be a hydrologist and land reclamation expert even in Africa, though I myself was quite surprised by the fact. He, with their five-year-old son, was now trying to join her, and his papers were being processed. He advised me not to say anything about the past, but to fill the necessary application forms and apply for a passport from scratch. "You ought to have your answer in about a month's time," he concluded. "I am due in Raleigh in four days!" I yelled at him in despair.

The following day, I picked up an application form and deposited all the necessary documents in the passport bureau. Two days later, the telephone rang. A muffled male voice was saying something I could not follow. In the end, I caught on that he wanted to meet me. "What is it about? Where? You mean the coffee bar opposite the Atlantic cinema?" So after all, I thought, they haven't forgotten me.

The diminutive bar was furnished with several shaky tables covered with poor quality orange plastic. I sat down near the wall, on a stool at what passed for a counter but was, in reality, just a narrow shelf. It offered no legroom, the place was airless, full of tobacco smoke; I felt quite uncomfortable. A short man in a gray overcoat placed himself on the stool next to me. "So you want to go to USA again, Professor?" he began softly while placing an attaché case in his lap. This was just the beginning of a long conversation.

"Why do you want to go to America again?" he repeated his question.

"Not again," I corrected him, "I have to continue my course of lectures."

"What was it like in Egypt?" he wanted to know.

"My attendance at the international conference in Egypt was part of my university job in Raleigh; and now, I have to report at the university the day after tomorrow at the latest. Don't your people understand that my being late would be a great loss of face for Poland?" I was using powerful arguments and began to worry whether I have overplayed my hand. He nodded, adjusted the attaché case in his lap, and said, "You know, Professor, we are very interested in your journeys to Egypt. A number of our Soviet comrades are there, and they would like to get to know you better. What do you say?"

My right hand involuntarily clenched into a fist, and my immediate reflex was to knock him off his stool, but I managed to restrain myself. It would not have solved anything. I replied calmly and emphatically, "Your people know very well that I have a responsible post in a large American university. My wife, my daughter, and my students expect me back in two days. What you are suggesting has nothing to do with either my job or my profession. Will you let your superiors know that I have to leave Poland tomorrow or, at the latest, the day after. Our ambassador in Washington is also aware of the dates in question. And as to your suggestion regarding your Soviet comrades, I don't know how you ever arrived at the idea, but my answer is a most definite no!"

On the way home, I decided to call Zenon, but I did not want to use our own phone, which was probably bugged. The nearest public phone, at the department store, had been vandalized. I ran up the broken-down escalator to the next floor. The same. Unusable. I went to a small private wireless and electrical appliances repair shop. They had a working telephone.

"Please, may I use your phone for an urgent call?" "Help yourself. But do make it short." Zenon answered the phone; but before I could say anything, he actually declared that he was very ill. I wanted to tell him about my problems but he interrupted me, saying that his passport has been extended and that he had to leave that very afternoon. The people in the shop kept looking at me, eavesdropping. So I changed into English and started telling him about my meeting with the secret policeman. This was a mistake. Someone pulled the receiver out of my hand and showed me the door. "We don't want spies here. Out! Or I'll call the police." I knew I was in trouble. I decided to go home and call Lenta from there. Let them bloody well listen! But the phone was dead. Somehow, I got through the night and woke to the phone ringing.

"Good morning, Professor," said the familiar voice. "So what are you up to? Your passport is waiting for you, and you haven't come to pick it up. Has something happened?"

Bastards, I thought and waited.

"Do come to the passport office. Straight to the counter, please."

In the passport office, I was told to wait. Another official appeared and asked me to follow him upstairs. A balding man sat behind the desk in a large, brightly lit room. There was no chair on my side of the desk, so I had to stand and was furious at being treated this way. I reached for my pocket and took out the two passport photographs I had had taken the day before. He put them in front of him and kept pushing them around on his desk.

"But that isn't you, Professor. Come here, round the desk, next to me."

"Choose whichever one you like best."

I looked inside the drawer. It was full of photographs of me, on my own, with other people, taken in the country, on a train, in the mountains.

I did not say another word and neither did he. Suddenly, I was very, very tired. I turned toward the door. As I was leaving, I heard the voice of the man had who had led me upstairs. "Go downstairs and wait for your passport."

Having dealt with all kinds of formalities, having got my visas, and having packed some of our things and mementos we had previously left behind, I took a coughing and spluttering taxi to the airport. At the corner of the two main thoroughfares, at the hub of the capital, I noticed a man in a creased, open raincoat, standing by the curb, unsteady on his feet, with a tattered attaché case in one hand, while the other was trying, unsuccessfully, to find a lamppost for support. The view of this wretched drunk, with the Palace of Culture for background, remained engraved on my memory, together with a feeling that I was leaving everything that had been dear and close to me, which yet, from that moment, was becoming increasingly remote and almost foreign.

16

Back in Egypt

North Carolina greeted me with an orgy of colors: many-hued azaleas and pink and white dogwood in bloom. Red cardinal birds flitted from one tree to another. Blue-crested jays chased flocks of tits away from the feeding trays. By the kitchen window, tiny humming birds, fluttering their wings and shimmering colorfully in the sun, were inserting their long beaks right into the depth of the hibiscus flowers. Through the shrubs, I saw Klara on the swing, gently moving to and fro, telling Cynthia about some event of the day, the latter listening with rapt attention. Lenta was sitting next to me at the kitchen table, reading the letters I brought from Warsaw. It was a warm, sunny afternoon, and I felt as if I had just slipped out of a trap.

However, I soon forgot about these happenings. Since my return, I had worked out a timetable and adhered strictly to it. The mornings, I spent in my study, which I had partly converted into a town-planning studio by adding a big table where I could spread large maps and sheets of tracing paper. The afternoons were spent with my students, while the evenings, often well into the night, at the drawing board placed in the living room at home.

In mid-1960s European architects and town planners were constantly discussing the planning problems of new towns. Great Britain was the leading light, with her tradition of nineteenth century garden cities and with her prewar vanguard of town planners, who, as yet, had had no chance to go beyond theory. But now, a dozen or so towns were either being built or were in the final stages of planning. In France, Paris was being surrounded by a ring of satellite towns. However, this work was largely subsidized by the state and supported by private capital and, consequently, could provide no model for Aswan. Outside Europe, I could not find many satisfactory town planning models either. I began to sketch preliminary designs of houses adapted to the specific climatic conditions of Aswan and taking into account the local building traditions. More and more students, attracted by the unusual subject, kept dropping into my studio. The layout of every town depends on its topographic position and its main lines of communication. In the case of Aswan, the essential features were the shipping on the Nile and the old caravan routes, only recently converted into roads. Next, one needs to study the people who had been living in the area for generations and assess the likely population growth under favorable conditions. One also has to define the type of dwelling, which is to be financed by the state, leaving enough space for privately funded housing. And as trade has been the soul of this town for fifty centuries, market places have to be provided as an essential element of the overall design—a central market as well as peripheral markets in the dormitory quarters.

For my work, I used photographs and a selection of maps. Aswan is situated on a triangular plain on the eastern shore of the Nile, bordered on the south and east by rocky crags and desert hills. The only highway and a railway line connect the town with the fertile valley of the Nile that extends from there to the north. The road forks as it enters the town, one branch running some five miles south to the site of the High Dam, the other crossing the river by the old dam and leading to the airport on the western shore of the Nile. This western side of the steep, rocky bank of the river shows entrances to ancient stone tombs surmounted by miniature buildings, not unlike our wayside shrines, dedicated to long-dead sheikhs. In Egypt, the side of the setting sun is where tombs are placed. It was also there that the mausoleum of the Aga Khan, one of the richest

men in the world, was built. South of Aswan, between the dividing roads, lay the quarries of that famous pink granite used since the times of the Pharaohs for carving obelisks, statues, and temple columns. The high terrace of the Old Cataract Hotel gives a fabulous view of various rocky islands and the ruins of an old temple on the biggest one, called Elephantine.

In my attempts to design new towns and settlements, I searched for help wherever I could. In the Raleigh library, I found Mathew Nowicki's photographic records, taken in connection with the planning of the town of Chandigarh, the new provincial capital of Punjab in India. I was sadly disappointed. These were architectural sketches for public buildings erected along a monstrous, miles-long promenade, inclining upward at one end. The town's plan was based on the design of a leaf, in which the midrib, the central artery, led to the capitol, the seat of power. This was a design of a town for rulers, not for people. His mind seemed to have been set, perhaps on the subconscious level, on the prewar giganto-mania, the form favored at the time by many ambitious architects dreaming of new cities. The construction of the new capital of Brazil followed this "autocratic" design tendency.

When I eventually asked for the opinions of my colleagues, I received an amazing range of ideas. One of them advised me to follow the designs of American pioneers for new American towns: a regular grid of equidistant streets meeting at right angles, with some spaces destined for parks or communal buildings. Raleigh, for instance, had four such square parks and a town hall in the fifth. Another one suggested a town shaped like a gigantic, hollow airconditioned pyramid. Still another—bewitched, in his own words, by the cult of the sun god Ra—would have liked to see

Aswan designed in the shape of a huge circle enclosing both banks of the Nile, which would symbolize the reflection of the sun on earth. Thus, I decided to take the bull by the horns myself.

When some eighteen months later I was, together with Lenta and Klara, going to Egypt, I could not help feeling that I was finally on top of the problem. It may have been wishful thinking, but all the signs led me believe in its eventual success.

In the meantime I was entering, as it later transpired, a very fruitful period of exhilarating creative work. Zenon and I spent the two summer months of 1964 in Cairo and Aswan. Lenta was with me for part of that time, while Klara was on holiday in France, learning French in preparation for a possible transfer to a French school in Cairo.

One day, in July, Medhat Shaheen, an architect born in Cairo, educated in Britain, and presently living in Canada, took me for a walk in Cairo's Old City. We stood at the ramparts of the Citadel with its mosque.

"Why do you say that Islamic Cairo ends with Mohammed Ali's Turkish style mosque?" I asked.

"Good question," said Medhat. "This building is the last major expression of the local cultures and styles which left their stamp on Cairo. Subsequently, Egypt opened up to French and British influences and became a typical cosmopolitan metropolis, especially in its mercantile center and in many residential districts. But believe me," he continued, "there are many here who are fiercely opposed to this Europeanization of our towns. They would like to see a return to the idealized Islamic architecture of arcades, domes, galleries, and fountains. This can, of course, be truly beautiful, but how do you marry these forms with a modern culture? I do know something about that. You have met our famous architect Hasan Fathy, haven't

with Hasan Fathy

you? He is a dedicated advocate of the return to the ancient forms of buildings and to the native building materials best suited for the purpose."

We came down to the citadel's terrace. Below us rose the gray mass of Sultan Hasan's fourteenth-century mosque, a fortresslike quadrangular building with a magnificent inner courtyard surrounded by a structure several stories high with deep and wide recesses ending in pointed arches. The mosque was a madrassa or seminary for students of the Koran and of the Shariah law, one of the centers of the Sunni Islamic religion and culture at the time.

To the north rose the gray, crowded mass of the city with a forest of minarets and domes soaring above it and with a mighty old wall separating it from the large Muqattam necropolis and the Mameluk cemetery with its monumental tombs in the form of domed and richly sculpted stone buildings slowly crumbling into ruin.

"On the city side of the wall," continued Medhat, "is the old part of Cairo that gave the city its name. Al-Qahirah means 'the Conqueror.' It was founded in the eleventh century by the Fatimid caliphs who introduced the religious cult of Fatima, the youngest daughter of the prophet Muhammad. They also built the great Al-Azhar mosque and the Islamic university which, modernized and enlarged, is now the principal Arab center of Islamic learning, competing with the secular University of Cairo."

Later, I often wandered the streets and alleys of the Old City, invariably finding myself in another world, almost untouched by Western influence. The overhanging bay windows of the many-storied houses were screened with an intricate wooden latticework, the mushrabiya, from behind which, the women of the household could watch the people and the traffic in the street below, remaining, themselves, out of sight. From the high stone south gate of Bab Zuweila, a busy, two-kilometer-long road leads to the two north gates, Bab el-Futuh and Bab al-Nasr, with the Sultan El Hakem's mosque situated in between. The road crosses the famous Khan el-Khalili bazaar, which I remembered visiting as a soldier during the Second World War. There is no space for cars in the Old City. Some streets are so narrow that there is only room for pedestrians; some can accommodate a small donkey-drawn cart. But for the voice of Um Kalsum, the famous Egyptian chanteuse, reverberating from loudspeakers, one could be in a different epoch, remote from the modern world.

For me, these surroundings were a rich source of ideas to be incorporated into modern building techniques for the homes of people who, for centuries, had been living and building in this way. I am absolutely convinced that the contemporary rulers, or rather dictators or modern day emirs of Egypt, did not understand the need for making use of the country's own traditions and culture. Nasser's form of socialism and pan-Arabism imposed foreign patterns of society on the Egyptians and blurred the ancient political boundaries. Eventually, the socialist system collapsed, having managed to introduce only limited changes into the lifestyle or working practices of the millions of the Egyptian population.

Whenever the subject of the country's modernization came up in those days, it was more as an expression of a longing to change the general attitude to life and to work, for which there were, as yet, no concrete proposals. Following the long periods of foreign domination and influence throughout the entire Arab world, Islamic traditions and practices remained clinging to its roots laid down in the Middle Ages as a bulwark against the "infidels." That caused the polarization of

Government—built village

the Islamic society, leading in turn to religious fanaticism whose objective is to block the spread of Western culture.

I was working at the time with Kamal Abu Hamda, an Egyptian architect with a doctorate in town planning from Washington's Catholic University, employed by the Aswan Regional Planning Bureau. His assignment to the Aswan team was of great benefit to us. In the spring and summer of 1964, helped by a group of young architects, he prepared a detailed inventory of the entire town—an enormous work by any standard. With this information available, I would be able to begin in the autumn, back in Raleigh, to work out the concepts of historic preservation and further development of Aswan. We knew by then that the Egyptian government had given us the green light and that we could now concentrate on details and finalize the program of work outlined in March. Zenon prepared the complete technical documentation for many variants of dwellings. I designed them rather like children's building blocks, which could be assembled in various architectural shapes and forms, creating buildings reminiscent of old towns in the Middle East. They would not lead to the erection of rows of monotonous housing blocks favored by the contemporary socialist-type housing architecture of the third world.

Old Aswan

This was an attempt to create a town of a novel, unique appearance, which combined designs originating in traditional social housing with the time-honored practice of private construction, giving scope to the inventiveness of individual builders.

The graphic presentation of the design and a large three-part model were prepared by two of my old students. The lot, packed in cases for its journey to Cairo, filled almost an entire truck.

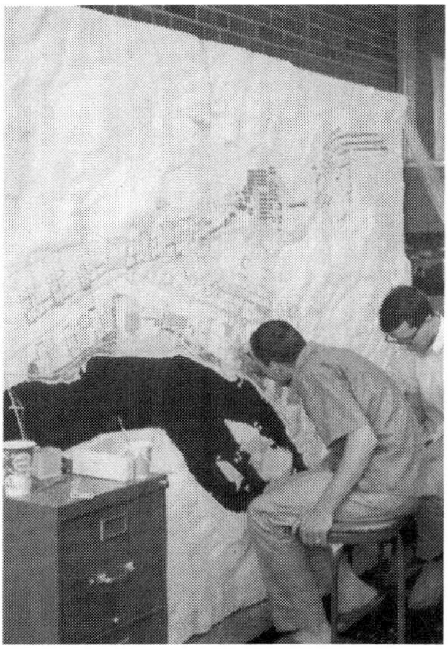
the model

In June 1965, our two families said good-bye to our friends in Raleigh. Zenon with his wife and children was going to Egypt in a roundabout way via the Far East and India, and we were to meet in Cairo at the end of July. We left New York aboard the luxury liner *France*. These were happy moments. Our departure from Raleigh was recorded in the local newspaper in the town events column; and we were seen off by a group of friends with whom, in our ample first class cabin, we drank champagne, raising toasts to a good voyage and successful future.

Our intention was to drive, in our new car shipped with us, from Cherbourg, across France, Switzerland, and Italy to Naples and then travel by boat to Alexandria, where we were to be met by a representative of the Ford Foundation who was to help us with our further journey to Cairo.

in Milan

In Cairo, we returned to the same ninth floor apartment on the island of Zamalek, which Lenta and I had occupied the summer before.

I was anxiously waiting for the opening of our office in Aswan. My staff included three Egyptian architects who had previously worked with us. Abdel Meguid, the director of the regional planning office, told me that for quite a while he had been fighting the government bureaucracy to have his office transferred to Aswan. The move was supposed to take place immediately after the official presentation of all the material brought from Raleigh: the models, diagrams, maps, and illustrations. The presentation was to take place in the exhibition halls of the Ministry of Housing in the center of the capital. The description of the project, the captions to the photographs, and the explanatory texts had to be translated into Arabic. Consultations were needed to find the correct translation for certain terms and expressions, and the Arabic script had to be presented in an elegant, calligraphic form. Zenon supervised the making of large collapsible models of dwelling houses that would be used to demonstrate how a number of different types of housing could be built using just five basic prefabricated light concrete units.

arrival of Zenon's family,
back—Kamal Abu Hamda,
author, Georgia Lee Kangas, Zenon

On December 25, 1965, the exhibition was opened by Zakaria Mohy-El Din, the prime minister of Egypt, in the presence of a number of ministers and heads of departments. The occasion was widely reported in the press. The festive mood filled our home too: it was Christmas and my mother had come over from Paris to celebrate both the occasions with us. Our New Year's party was attended by many Egyptian, American, and Polish friends.

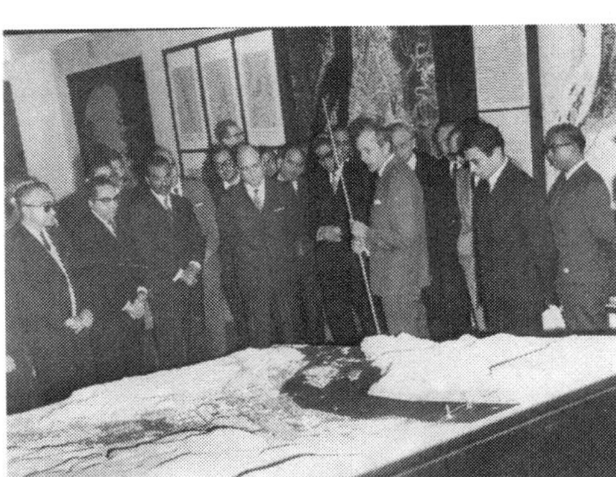

presentation of Aswan project

New Year's party: Neshi Shaheen, Lenta, Leia and Boutros Boutros—Ghali

Our Aswan office was opened in the New Year. From then on I was spending four days of every week in Aswan, as we had already started work on the first stage of my project: the widening of the riverside boulevard, roughly by one hundred feet, on a stretch two miles long. This was a gigantic undertaking, authorized by Madkur Abu El Izz, the governor of the Aswan Province. He was a handsome, swarthy man of average height; a former fighter pilot and one-time chief of the Egyptian Air Force. He was now about to assume the management of the entire Aswan project. Unfortunately, this marked the beginning of a power struggle between him and Abdel Meguid. The governor, brought up in the old school of centralized authority, was incapable of adjusting to the changes we were proposing for modern Egypt. However, for the time being, he was passionately involved in supervising the day-to-day progress of the work. Over a period of six months, the work continued by day and by night. Thousands of laborers

on the waterfront with governor

were unloading truckloads of rocks, carrying them on their heads and backs, and dropping them into the river while the sand for the filling was pumped up from the riverbed. It was the same method we had used in Warsaw while building the stadium. The water was twenty feet deep by the shore, and the latter needed to be built up by another twenty feet above the water's level. Someone calculated that the volume of stone used in this enterprise equaled that which was needed to build the pyramid of Cheops.

on construction site

I accompanied the governor on his daily inspections and got his approval to start the pilot project of six housing complexes of my design to be build on the reclaimed riverside plots in the northern part of town. Construction was to begin in the summer of 1967. I had by now a well-functioning office in Aswan as well as an apartment I could use while there. From time to time, I would visit the construction site of the High Dam; this was by far the largest building site I have ever come across, spanning both banks of a particularly wide part of the river. In town, one would come across Soviet engineers supervising the unloading of enormous turbines, glimmering with their new brass, brought to Aswan on barges, still in their packing, from the seaports.

viewing reclaimed land:
Abdel-Meguid, author, governor

Lenta and the press

The three free days a week I was spending in Cairo were filled with social events, tennis tournaments, and galloping on horseback in the desert around the pyramids. Boutros Boutros-Ghali, at the time professor of Cairo University and later secretary of the UN, and his beautiful Alexandria-born wife Leia tried to explain to me the still-medieval mentality of Egyptian officialdom; any progress in that area was additionally impeded by the not yet much in evidence though increasingly spreading Islamic fundamentalism. One day, three heavily bearded men in traditional dress came to visit the exhibition in the Aswan Cultural Center, showing the future town and its buildings. They talked to me about my concept of housing settlements and how it related to Islamic tradition. As my thinking has been taking those traditions into consideration, I felt that they had left quite satisfied. One of my helpers, a Coptic Christian, whispered to me that the three men were almost certainly members of the Muslim Brotherhood, a radical grouping aiming to overthrow the government and banned by Nasser.

housing unit

Occasional visitors from Poland were telling us about the dominance of the Communist Party back home, now once more on the rise after the thaw and of the mounting discontent in the country. I had a feeling for some time that in Egypt we were living in a fool's paradise. What with Polish passports, on temporary leave from an American university, employed by the Ford Foundation, working for an Egyptian government, leaning more and more toward Socialism in the presence of a rising number of Soviet advisers, we were indeed on very shaky ground. The Polish authorities were not inclined to offer us any kind of help either. It was indeed time to extend the validity of our passports, issued, as a rule, for only one year. I thus made an appointment with our Cairo embassy and was received by the first secretary. He flipped through a thick file of papers, pushed them aside, calmly looked me in the eye, and said,

"Well, I have here a telex from Warsaw, telling me that you refused to cooperate with our Soviet comrades . . . do not try to deny it, the conversation has been recorded. The tape is as good as a document." I recalled the bulging attaché case on the lap of my interlocutor in the Warsaw café. I remained silent. The secretary went on enumerating all the difficulties he would encounter in extending our passports. He finally remarked, "You might wish to have a word with Ambassador Moskwa[4] . . . the final decision is in his hands." "Moskwa?" I asked incredulously.

"Well, yes, that is the ambassador's surname," said the secretary with a shadow of a smile. As I entered the ambassador's office, he moved from his desk to the informal part of the room, motioned me to an armchair, and ordered Turkish coffee. He repeated what his underling had already told me. Then, putting the little cup daintily down, he added, "I do understand that most people welcome the opportunity to earn some extra money. Our pilots and officers of the merchant marine, who, for some time, have been taking ships through the nationalized Suez Canal, spend a year here, and then return home. They manage to save enough to buy a car and few other mementos of their stay in Egypt. I am sure that by now you too could afford to have a new car. I know how such a luxury makes

4. *Moskwa* is the Polish word for Moscow.

life easier in our country, which is in the early stages of building socialism. Whereas you—"

"I am sorry, sir," I interrupted him vehemently, feeling the pulse beating in my temples. "I regret the misunderstanding. I am not working here to buy a car. For your information, I have three of them at present: my own, which I brought over from America and which my wife is using, one placed at my disposal by the authorities in Cairo, and another one in Aswan. I am afraid, Ambassador, that I have no time to play at spies, collecting information for the Soviet comrades. I am in the process of realizing an important architectural and planning project, which had already been acclaimed in international professional circles. I am working in tandem with a Polish colleague, and I have never made any secret of being a Polish citizen. I cannot predict how long I shall remain here; there are all sorts of difficulties. But I certainly would not like to tell the representatives of the Egyptian government that I am leaving everything unfinished simply because the Polish authorities prevent me from staying in Egypt on the assumption that I had saved enough to buy a car. This would really be a disgrace."

Moskwa did not say a word. He kept looking out of the window at trees covered with clusters of red flowers. Minutes later, he got up and called the first secretary, telling him to extend our passports for six months.

The latter, on seeing me out, said softly, "I am very sorry, but I am only a small cog here. I do apologize." We shook hands.

In April, during our vacation, we had a disastrous car accident on the desert road to Safaga on the Red Sea. There were, apart from me, four passengers in the car, Lenta, Klara, our guest, Marylka, the hydrologist visiting us from Ghana, and her young son. Due to a mechanical fault, the car hit a stony outcrop and overturned. Marylka was killed on the spot, the two children and I were unscathed, while Lenta suffered a concussion. After two days in coma, she recovered, except for a patchy loss of memory, which stopped her attending the university. A rest in a moderate climate was recommended; so all of us, including Lenta's mother, who had come from Warsaw to help us, flew to Athens. The ladies went on to France,

where they spent the rest of the summer in Normandy. I stayed longer in Athens to attend an international conference on the construction and development of urban settlements.

At the end of October, after a month-long lecture tour of American universities, we were back in Cairo. I was spending more time in Aswan now, supervising the final stages of the new riverside. In winter, life in Aswan proceeded at a very different pace. Boats were bringing hundreds of tourists from all over the world. Buses were plying to and from the airport. Hovercrafts with dozens of passengers were going from the provisional harbor just upstream of the High Dam to the Abu Simbel temples further south.

By February, Abdel Meguid had been dismissed from his post as director of the bureau. Before he left, he wrote me a letter, which gave me much pleasure. "Dear Jerzy," it said, "I cannot leave without a final 'thank you' for all you have done for our project. Without you and your boundless Polish energy, your humor and your motivation, Aswan would still be that dusty old township we found three years ago. Mabruk, congratulations! . . . This was an achievement, both personal and professional, so much the greater for the number of reverses."

The Cairo bureau was transferred to the offices of the provincial administration. My talks with the governor had to be conducted in his huge audience hall, where, on gilded chairs lined along the two long walls, sat petitioners patiently waiting to be called before the imposing desk to present their requests or complaints. Everything was discussed in public. In my case, it was important to consult plans and drawings; and I kept stubbornly demanding that the governor visits my office, now staffed with a new team of newly qualified architects and draftsmen. But there was no more talk of opening the province to private investment, which could have been granted tax relief and offered special advantageous electricity rates. The whole idea of creating new employment in industry and allowing the population to increase was abandoned. As long as the number of inhabitants remained static, my concept of the new housing no longer made sense. When I mentioned it once to the governor, I could see that he had no inkling of what I was talking about. He answered that according to his calculations the number of tourists would considerably increase.

The memory of our car accident kept returning to me in waves of tension, on some days more powerful than on others. Our Egyptian friends kept advising me to detach myself for a while from the Aswan problems. There was nervous tension in the city. The Egyptian Army was moving troops and armor through the traffic-jammed streets. Zohair Farid, our friend as well as our doctor, wrote a letter to the Ford Foundation recommending a period of rest. I decided to go once more to the Red Sea to inspect in some detail the site of the tragedy. My new car, a Land Rover ordered quite a while before, had just arrived in Cairo. I intended, at some future date, to drive it from Aswan through the desert toward El Kharga, an oasis some one hundred miles to the northwest, to explore an idea of connecting the two areas by a road; thus, opening a new trade route. I decided to drive from Cairo to Aswan taking the Red Sea route. I stopped in Hurghada for a rest. In was the end of May, and Hurghada was much cooler than the sweltering Cairo. I took a room in a small hotel near the fishing port. The only other guest was a German student from Hamburg, who was traveling south on his own, down the east coast of Africa. I offered him a lift along the coast to at least Al Bernice, a town south of Safâga, where I had to turn west into the desert to reach the Nile valley.

One night, we were woken by the rumble of engines of low flying planes. In the morning, the hotel was full of Egyptian officers, pilots and crews, all in high spirits, joking and laughing. They all wore khaki air force overalls and carried only hand luggage. Rows of huge Soviet transport planes, Antonovs, were parked some way off at the airport. The pilots would not tell us what kind of exercise they were engaged in and when it was supposed to finish. The police commissioner I was acquainted with told me that the road to Cairo via Suez was now closed. As from that day, the entire Suez Canal zone was declared a military zone and thus out of bounds for civilians. After repeated attempts, I managed to get a call through to Lenta. She told me that Egyptian forces were still moving through Cairo; the atmosphere in the capital was very tense, and she wanted me to return home as soon as possible. My German companion and I packed our belongings and, wasting no time, started on our way.

Forty kilometers out of Hurghada, I stopped the car. Even now, over a year after the accident, one could see on the asphalt—a forty-meter-long black trail made by the blocked left wheel of my car. It led directly to the yellow wall of rocky rubble. Further on, I found the damaged road surface and the deep gash made by the overturned car. Small fragments of the shattered windscreen were still scattered on the ground. Lenta, sitting in the passenger seat without a seat belt, must have been projected through it, which no doubt saved her life, as the right side of the car had been completely crushed. I collected some rocks and erected a kind of cairn on the ill-fated bank, intending to visit it some time in the future.

As I was filling the car at Al Bernice, some local fishermen approached us, asking whether the war had already started. At that point, my companion decided he would stay with me. Feeling quite anxious, we drove at speed toward the desert track. What faced us was over one hundred kilometers of driving between dangerous rocks, through sandy wadis, dry old riverbeds dating back to prehistoric times when the present desert was a green savanna. We hit the Nile valley near Edfu, close to the most beautiful and best-preserved

at Al Bernice

temple dedicated to the Falcon God Horus. When we reached Aswan toward the evening, we learned that the Egyptians had occupied Sharm el-Sheikh, the demilitarized zone on the southern tip of the Sinai Peninsula, thus taking control of the strategic strait and blocking access to the Israeli port of Eilat. In the evening, I met the governor who told me that the Ford Foundation had been calling him to find out about my whereabouts. He offered me a place on his plane. He was leaving in order to take command of an air force unit. On the plane, we talked about the situation in Cairo. At one time, he said that he wished the air force could hit Jerusalem and Tel Aviv. Ten years later, in Cairo, someone told me that this was actually his proposal to President Nasser, which resulted in his dismissal from the command post. I have no way to confirm it.

At home, I found almost all our belongings packed. Lenta told me that all the employees and consultants of the Ford Foundation had been advised to leave. We were thus included in the evacuation of American families. For me, it was my third evacuation since the World War II, again, in completely different circumstances, boarding this time on surreal. As we moved through nearly empty rooms, unexpectedly a doorbell rung. It was our friend, Magdi Wahba, then a high official at the Ministry of Culture, bringing his guest Roberto Rosselini, the film director, whom he wanted to meet Lenta. We sat on packed crates and drank the last bottle of champagne. The following day, in the office, Jim Lipscombe gave me two large buff envelopes containing our immigration documents, one for me, the other for Lenta and Klara, which had arrived from the American embassy several days earlier. "This," he said, "will allow you to go back to the States once you decide what to do next."

He added that the foundation would pay for our return journey to the States and provide funds for a three months' vacation or time to organize our new life. Our belongings, meanwhile stored in Cairo, would be sent to our future address.

The first available plane was one of the Malév Hungarian Airlines. Suddenly, we found ourselves in a totally novel situation: we were refugees and possibly future immigrants, flying first class with considerable luggage and a dachshund to Budapest and then on to Paris. The following day, in Hungary, we learned about the sudden surprise counterattack by the Israeli army and air force. All those planes, which several days earlier had been brought by the Egyptian forces to Sharm el-Sheikh, were destroyed on the ground. Nasser's army was in retreat all along the line. During our brief stay in Budapest, the Israeli forces routed the armies of her three neighbors: Egypt, Syria, and Jordan. All this happened before we even managed to do our winter shopping, buying the smart sheepskin coats that were a local specialty.

In Klara Rothschild's stylish ladies' fashion shop in Vaci Street, we met Gloria Emerson, then a fashion correspondent of the *New York Times*. She was so fascinated by our story that she wrote an article about a Polish emigrant family, who after a flight from Egypt, were shopping in the smartest boutiques of Europe. The piece included a photograph of Lenta trying on a white coat.

Gloria gave us a copy of the paper when we met her several days later in Paris. Events had been developing so fast that it was only when we joined the family in Paris, that the full implications of the situation hit us. I suddenly realized that all my efforts over the last three years and all my associated hopes had been irreversibly turned to dust. The decision we faced now was what to do with the rest of our lives. The option of returning to Warsaw we rejected outright. I could no longer see myself as a state employee, hoping for an early pension, ministering to that precious car in the yard as suggested by Ambassador Moskwa in Cairo. Mother tried to persuade us to stay in France as all the family were there, and so were many of our Warsaw friends. The familiarity with the environment would no doubt make a new start easier. Yet America too was no longer foreign to us, and the advantage was that we no longer needed permits or visas or any other documents to settle there. True enough, we no longer had a home there and no job to begin with, but the same conditions applied in France. As we were parting with Mother, who was leaving for a cure in a spa in Poland, we told her that we were leaning toward immigrating to America. But it was a difficult decision. We decided to settle somewhere in the New York area, particularly as I had informed Henry Kamphoefner in Raleigh the year before that I was staying in Egypt longer than expected and that he should no longer keep my job open. Neither Lenta nor I were keen on settling in any of the southern states. In spite of the federal legislation acknowledging and promoting the equality of races, the South remained fiercely racist. In the previous two years, serious racial disorders kept breaking out in many towns. Entire quarters were on fire. Papers and magazines were calling for a mobilization of forces to help in the reconstruction of damaged quarters and for Congress to pass legislation similar to that which enabled Western Europe to rebuild her towns after the destruction of World War II. I felt that my experience in the rebuilding of Warsaw and my contribution to the development of Aswan ought to help me find a job with some large project in USA.

But first I had to identify such a project. I wrote a letter to the architect, John Johansen, whom I had met earlier. He lived in New Canaan, a small, attractive historic town in Connecticut, one hour's drive from New York. Lenta and I had visited him there in 1965, a day before leaving for Egypt. I showed him then my Aswan album that aroused his great interest. He mentioned that he himself would like to work on that kind of project. Coming back from that visit, we agreed that New Canaan was indeed a charming place and that perhaps some day we could live in such a picture-postcard place with such easy access to New York. Quite a number of well-known architects chose to settle there. Yet at that time, I was so preoccupied with the Egyptian project, that settling there or anywhere else could only have been treated as a dream.

We did not have to wait long for John's reply. There was an interesting project for the taking, he wrote. Not a town, but a large campus for the New York State University. With his team, he was in the process of organizing a large studio in New Canaan and would keep a job open for me. This was a great stroke of luck and, coming as it did just one month after our "exodus" from Egypt, it did indeed delight us. "We shall be with you towards the end of August," I assured John.

With a load off my chest, I booked a passage to New York on the *Queen Elizabeth* for the three of us, plus our dachshund Romulus and our car. It was the same British liner, which I came across in 1942 when, serving as a troop ship, it was taking British soldiers to Egypt while I was aboard the *Queen Mary* on my way to England to join the air force. Before embarking, we took a two-week holiday in Alsace to walk on its flower-strewn meadows, ride, and, last but not least, enjoy its exquisite cuisine.

In mid-August, we were to collect our new car, ordered when we were still back in Cairo, and finished to our specifications in the Mercedes-Benz workshop in Stuttgart. The color chosen by Lenta from the firm's brochure was called Havana brown, and the interior was to be upholstered in off-white leather. We kept joking that she had chosen the color to match our brown dachshund.

This summer, as during our previous visits to Paris, we met many of our old Warsaw acquaintances and friends. It was good to see Poles being still able to travel, yet we found that many of them had suddenly felt—as we had done—that they could no longer stand the conditions in their own country. And that was very sad. Lenta felt it more keenly than I. Her profound sensitivity, subtleness, her attachment to memories, to people, to certain situations and moods, made the severance of all ties with the past hard to cope with. In spite of all that, she has always been and, is to this day, a woman of strong personality, facing adversities with great courage, never complaining when facing real or potential difficulties or afflictions.

Before leaving, we invited an old friend of Lenta's to join us in Paris for a short break. She must have sensed that our carefree appearance covered some anxieties resulting from our, after all, rather uncertain situation. As we were saying good-bye, she complemented us on our ability to cope so well with an unknown future on the other side of the Atlantic.

"You must be an incurable optimist," she concluded, turning to me.

Klara, who was now almost twelve years old and fluent in three languages, tolerated all the changes with great equanimity. So to sum it all up, both my wife and daughter proved to be perfect companions in our unsettled life and gave me their moral support whenever I was in need of it.

We were preparing for our second journey to America systematically and starting it by doing some shopping. As we were going there by boat, there was no limit on the luggage we could take. We could not count on our belongings, left behind in Cairo to reach us any time soon, so we decided to take with us all the essentials for the first few months in the States.

The ocean was smooth as a pond throughout our four-day crossing. I could not wait for the voyage to end and our new life to begin. Lenta, on the other hand, suspended, as I believed, between two worlds, wished in her mind to delay the moment of having to face the unknown. Klara was busy visiting Romulus in the animal hotel with its run on the top deck, between the ship's two great chimney stacks.

We entered New York harbor very slowly, in advance of the scheduled time. The outlines of the recently opened great suspension bridge between Brooklyn and Staten Island appeared in the distance. Its only span, nearly a mile long, makes the ship passing underneath it appear much smaller than it really is. There was no wind, just the heat and humidity—typical of New York in this season. I pointed out to Lenta and Klara the former site of Fort Hamilton, the American army camp on the Brooklyn shore, where in August 1942 I, among three hundred other Polish soldiers, had stopped on our way from Egypt to England. On the left, there appeared through the mist the New Jersey coast, where we delivered to the Canadians the one thousand four hundred German prisoners of war our unit has been escorting all the way from Egypt. Two tugs took now their place at the sides of the *Queen Elizabeth*. We passed the Statue of Liberty and were approaching the tip of Manhattan with its forest of skyscrapers. I was trying to take a photograph of Lenta with that view in the background, but she refused to smile.

"No reason to jump for joy," she stated with a serious face.

Part Three

My America—An Uneasy Choice
1967-2007

17

No Reason to Jump for Joy

The hard-working tugs finally got the boat into the dock. Two hours later, unhurriedly, we went down to Immigration Control. We gave our provisional address in Providence, Rhode Island, where we were going to stop for several days with a friend of ours. We wanted to get there as quickly as possible but, meanwhile, had to wait by the large pile of our luggage for the unloading of our car. When it was our turn to go through the customs, the officer looked at us somewhat surprised.

"Where are you from?" he asked.

"From Poland."

He thought for a moment, then said quietly, as if to himself,

"I have seen many immigrants from Poland, but never the likes of you. I wish you a lot of luck . . . which, it seems to me, you already have."

New York was sweltering in an August heat wave with humidity close to 100 percent. The customs hall, where we had been waiting for over an hour for our new car to be brought ashore, was full of noise: loud mechanical clatter, some indefinable whistles, and wailing sirens. Finally, our car was unloaded. Some of our luggage went into the trunk while several small pieces were placed on the back seat, leaving just enough room for Klara and her Romulus.

I had to leave an address for the remainder of our luggage to be delivered. It seemed like a good time to call our Polish friends in Providence. And now followed this rather embarrassing conversation with Izabella. "No, Janek did not say anything about you coming. Never breathed a word. But that is Janek for you in a nutshell. He had these fantasies . . . as usual. But do come all the same. We shall manage . . . somehow . . . I'll expect you in the evening," she concluded.

Later, nearing Providence after a three hours' drive, we were struck by the sight of fires over part of the city. At the time, a wave of racial riots was spreading through the United States. Bigger and smaller towns on the East Coast, in the South, and in California, with their large black populations, were exploding, as desperate crowds, imbued with some elemental hate, went on a rampage, destroying and looting whatever came to hand. One could, in a way, understand it. The promises of racial equality and improved living standards embodied in a recent act of Congress had not materialized and would take many more years to bear fruit. In the mid-1960s, the despair could no longer be contained and led to the growth of black radical, militant, and armed organizations calling for the overthrow of the government.

But there was yet another undercurrent to the social unrest. The country was beginning to split into two opposing camps: those for and those against the Vietnam War. The costly and bloody U.S. intervention in Indochina was, like the invasion of Iraq some forty years later, based on a lie. In the same way as there proved to be no Iraqi weapons of mass destruction and no Baghdad's support for terrorist groups, so the claimed provocative attack on an American warship in the Gulf of Tonkin had never happened, and North Vietnam was no threat to the United States.

Mass student demonstrations began at colleges and universities and new organizations calling for a retreat from Vietnam sprang up all over the country. Lists of war casualties, dead, and wounded grew in length from one day to the next. President Lyndon Johnson and his administration in Washington felt besieged by the growing wave of protests around the country and by the dramatic news arriving daily from the theatre of war. But this was only the beginning.

As we arrived in Providence, we had to stop and give way to fire engines and to speeding ambulances with their sirens blasting. It was late, it was dark, and it all boded ill. "Oh, well," said Izabella rather reluctantly as she greeted us at the door with a screaming baby in her arms. "The house is still in disarray, but by all means, do come in. We'd only just moved here, and Janek went to Europe straight away . . . I don't even know where he is at present . . . I am alone here with my little boy . . . I didn't know what to do at first . . ." she continued in a shaky voice. The whole thing did not sound promising.

Tired and somewhat disconcerted, we took our belongings upstairs to the second floor of the timber house. As there were no beds in the bedroom yet, mattresses had been laid directly on the floor. It was only later that our host laughingly remembered the look on our faces when, just off a luxury liner, we had to make do with sleeping on the floor among heaps of unpacked luggage. Well, we were truly new immigrants now.

In spite of the initial difficulties, I hope that Izabella did eventually appreciate our help in organizing her new home. She has been going through a hard time, left alone in a new place, with no friends or acquaintances to turn to. But we did not stay long. My first objective was to find a suitable job. Without much delay, I went to see John Johansen in New Canaan, Connecticut, and visited the Ford Foundation offices in New York. I was pleased to hear from John that there was a place for me in his new partnership of three architects, created specifically to design a new campus for the rapidly expanding New York State University. The virtual new township in Old Waterbury, Long Island, was to include both housing and teaching facilities for several thousands students. It was all exactly as he promised me in the letter that I received still in Paris. The problem, which did not emerge till later, was that his partners had not been co-opted with a view to a fruitful creative cooperation but for their individual connections with the officialdom of the enormous state university administration. This was eventually to have unhappy consequences; but at the time, the job looked tailor-made for me. Our studio was being organized in Elm Street, in the center of New Canaan, a charming little colonial town. My next priority was to find accommodation.

There were few apartments for rent in New Canaan, and these were occupied mostly by temporary shop and office employees. I was advised to look for a house to buy. This was an entirely new kind of enterprise, and I had to consult with Lenta first. Following Izabella's advice, we also began looking for occasional small household bargains as well as for old-style American furniture, which could in those days be bought for next to nothing in roadside antique shops and at garage sales. In the second half of August, we went to New Canaan to look at houses for sale. We had no experience with the real estate market nor did we ask for anyone's advice, but we were very lucky to come across Elsa, an amiable broker at the Mabel Lamb Real Estate. Having looked over several small houses, we finally chose one in a short cul-de-sac bearing the rather charming name of Kimberly Place. It was situated only a ten-minutes walk from the center of town and from the train terminus. A direct railway link to New York is still a great asset of the town, and it was essential for us, as, following our road accident in Egypt, Lenta still felt insecure behind the driving wheel.

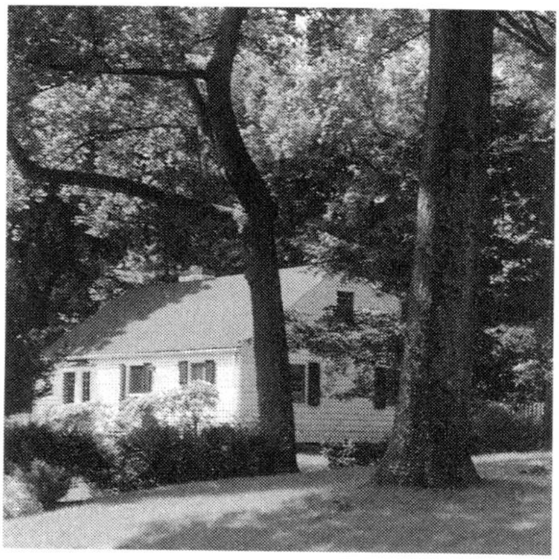

Kimberly Pl.

Our house had been built at the beginning of the war, when the development of New England townships within easy reach of New York began. A stone footpath led from the parking space to the front door across the large lawn, and a paved patio abutted the back of the house. By American standards, our plot was rather small, but the large number of big old maples, oaks, beech, elms, and tulip trees all around us and the absence of fences gave one an impression of living in a park.

"In buying a house, the monthly payments would be half of the cost of renting; and should you want to sell, you will have no difficulty in finding a buyer," Elsa explained. "Shall we go ahead with the transaction?" "Yes," we agreed unanimously and felt as if another new chapter in our life was to begin.

While waiting in the lawyer's office for the deeds of the house and all the necessary sale documents, I picked up a magazine, on the first page of which a truly fantastic photograph struck my eye—the earth as seen from the space probe *Orbiter 5*. "The *Orbiter* has been circling the moon for some two weeks now, taking photos of suitable places for the first astronauts to land," said Jack Silverman, our smiling and good-looking lawyer. "You know, my grandmother too came from Poland," he added. "From . . . now what was the place called? Oh, yes, I remember, Galicia . . . do you know it?" It was easy to confirm; indeed, most of southern Poland in the nineteenth century, while under Austro-Hungarian rule, went under the name of Galicia.

In the evening, returning to Providence, we ran into great traffic jams on the Boston expressway. Interstate I-95 was at the time still unfinished and in parts under construction, and we had to take many detours. As we were reaching New Haven, the home of Yale University, yet also the home of large black ghettos of tens of thousands of poor and desperate people, we noticed police cars and the flashing lights of emergency vehicles. We were told that new riots had broken out and some buildings near the expressway were on fire. This happened in spite of the police curfew and the ban on meetings. The riots and arson continued for three days.

We were getting ready to leave Izabella's hospitable home. The necessary preparations did not, however, reduce my interest in the daily news. The continuing war in Vietnam on the one hand and the burning American cities from Detroit in the north to Montgomery in the south and from coast to coast—from Los Angeles to Newark—were somehow creating the two markers into which we would have to fit our new life. I was subconsciously hoping that the burnt-out towns would have to be rebuilt in the near future, thus creating a demand for architects with suitable skills. After all, that had been my experience in Europe. But we never lived to see it.

Yet attempts were being made to help the affected cities and that by the highest levels of the administration. In August 1963, after the assassination of President Kennedy, his successor, L. B. Johnson, addressed the Congress with a fervent appeal, calling for an immediate start to preparatory work on the required legislation. Over twenty acts had been proposed, yet none had so far reached the House of Representatives. In contrast to postwar Europe, there was a great reluctance in America to involve the government in any direct investment bearing on peoples' welfare. That was supposed to be the domain of the self-governing towns and cities, of the private building industry and of individual developers. American capitalism and European socialism were two very different worlds; but at the time, I had not yet understood that. With my inborn optimism, it took me some ten more years to discover this simple truth. In addition, the problem of racial discrimination played its part. To the large segment of American people, the burnt-out cities were not the result of a war but by the lawlessness of the despised class of subhumans who had got what they deserved and could thus expect no taxpayer's help. As a result, the legislation was blocked in Congress by the powerful coalition of the southern conservative Democrats and the northern conservative Republicans. In their opinion, the Vietnam War took precedence over everything else; and they were supported in this by the Pentagon, who considered that bombing Vietnam was more important than rebuilding American cities. This bombing, ordered by the president some two years previously, continued with increasing intensity. Toward the end of the conflict, it transpired that more bombs had been dropped on little rural Vietnam than had been used in the Second World War by all the participants put together.

Twenty-eight years from the date, I left my family home at the outset of the World War II in Poland, we moved into our new family house in America. Klara joined the fifth grade of the local school, Lenta began organizing our life, and I started work in our atelier as one of several designers. The atmosphere at work was far from pleasant. We were a group of strangers, some aggressively trying to assert control. With clenched teeth, I did my best to avoid the arguments and disputes.

Organizing our new life was not easy, in spite of all the modern facilities. We had neither the time nor the extra money for a thorough renovation of the house. I decided to do all the work myself, sanding the floors and painting the walls late into the night. I quickly got rid of all the horrid blues, greens, and pinks, painting all the walls white. It made the rooms look much larger. I had no compunction in getting rid of the last traces of the house's previous owners and their three children. I was puzzled though by the use that had been made of the attic bedroom, where I discovered a woman's dirty footprints on the sloping ceiling above the bed.

We did not have to wait long for the fall. It has a particular charm in New England. Our property held five magnificent hickory trees arising originally from a single trunk, two tall tulip poplars and four umbrella-like elms. Magnificent azalea bushes spread widely in front and behind of the house. Initially enchanted by the amazing range of autumn colors, we soon discovered the drawback: great masses of falling leaves had to be raked up to the side of the street, whence once a week a special vehicle would vacuum them up for recycling.

The elms were next to cause problems. One of our neighbors, Mr. Kelly, the local police chief, pointed out to us that one of the trees was dying. "It's the Dutch elm disease," he declared. But cutting down a big old tree was an expensive proposition, more than we could afford at the time. Kelly was one of many of our new neighbors who, true to American custom, had been dropping in one after another to welcome us,

Klara in New Canaan

the newcomers, bringing small gifts: a home-baked cake, a cookery book, or just the offer of help or advice. Unexpectedly, Kelly soon returned with his son, bringing a ladder, saws, and some ropes and, in several hours, with professional skill, felled one of the elms growing near the street. All done in the spirit of good neighborliness. We began to discover the friendly side of America.

There were other visitors as well, representatives of local churches: Lutherans, Methodists, Mormons, and others, leaving brochures describing their social programs and times of services. The St. Aloysius Catholic Church sent us a form to enroll Klara for religious instruction classes. The local dairy proposed a daily delivery of half a gallon of milk. The laundry offered weekly collection and delivery. The automobile workshop called Foreign Cars of New Canaan suggested we use their professional expertise to service our Mercedes. Day in and day out, we were bombarded by unending offers of services and facilities, all designed to make life easier. By buying a house, we seemed to have dropped a proper anchor in America.

Before the holidays, we took delivery of our belongings, left behind in Cairo some six months earlier, on the eve of the outbreak of the Israeli-Arab war—our Exodus from Egypt, as we used to joke. On the appointed day, the movers gingerly backed their large trailer into our garage drive. All our belongings were there but, apart from Lenta's clothes placed on hangers in three tall cardboard boxes, all were, surprisingly, without containers and just loosely placed on the floor. Bit by bit, the porters patiently carried in our dinner service for twenty-four persons, dozens of glasses of all types and sizes, cups, saucers, boxes of cutlery, bronze candlesticks, assorted copper bowls and plates, rolled up Egyptian and Syrian kilims, Polish tapestry, engravings, pictures, my vast collection of Polish film posters, our stereo system, hundreds of books and long-playing records. All our goods and chattels from Poland and from Egypt, which had furnished our large apartment in Cairo, now found temporary quarters in our garage; only then did we come to realize how much we had acquired in the previous five years since leaving

Warsaw. In a way, these treasures were a kind of ball and chain, making even the thought of another move difficult.

In New Canaan, however, some problems soon appeared on the horizon. It all started with the question of buying a television set. It was, for the first time since we settled in what we considered a safe country, that we had a feeling that the USA was taking a wrong turning. The press, the radio, and, of course, television were full of daily reports from the frontlines: the brutal war in Vietnam, black riots in many cities, student protests at university campuses—all threatening to destabilize the country. Due to the efforts of teams of reporters with their television film cameras present at all these events, for the first time in the history, their reports could instantly reach TV screens in every home. Every evening one was bombarded, if that is the word, by vivid pictures of the war. One could not avoid them. And it wasn't just the war. Concerned how it might affect Klara, we hesitated to buy a television set. Also, the standard of television programs, especially the entertainment ones, was said to be dismal and a stupefying waste of time. Even now, forty years later, it has not changed much; or if anything, the programs have become even worse. We believed that our daughter, having in the last two years attended a French school in Cairo, ought now to spend more time reading in English and getting better acquainted with American literature. However, we had completely ignored the peer pressure in her American school. She felt excluded, sometimes even ridiculed. "So what is this language that you speak?" asked one nasty girl over and over again. Klara, ignorant of the popular television programs, often had no idea what her schoolmates were talking about, she felt like an outsider and was complaining bitterly about it. For instance, one of the subjects of conversation in her class was the satirical program, *Rowan & Martin 's Laugh-In*. It had been quite unique at the time in combining intelligent entertainment with the matchless professionalism of the participants. And there was the relatively new public television station the PBS. It is free of commercials and specializes in various forms of culture-based programs, the news and political commentaries unavailable, then and now, on any other station. We had to give in, join the mainstream, and acquire a television set.

In March, our studio was hit by a sudden crisis. There had been whispers and gossip for several days, and an almost palpable uneasiness was growing by the hour. By the end of the week, the studio ceased to exist.

When the partnership fell apart, the project was split up between the principals, and each worked on his part of the design independently in his own studio, while I and a few other architects were fired there and then without any notice—the usual practice in America.

For me this was, however, a new situation. I had no one to turn to for advice. So far, we had been able, more or less, to make ends meet. Now we have fallen on hard times and were not helped by feeling depressed and uncertain as to future developments in America. These were our personal feelings, largely shaped by the press and television; but we knew next to nothing about our neighbors' response to the current events. Even back in February, when television was full of reports and pictures of American casualties, victims of the new, bloody, countrywide offensive staged by North Vietnam, not a single word was uttered on the subject at work. And that was when the weekly deaths exceeded five hundred and the TV screen brought the tragic news to every home in the country. This would have been unthinkable in Poland, where one could not escape heated discussions in the streets, in trains, and at work. While here, in our new world, seemingly insulated from outside events by the splendid old trees, the manicured lawns, and a strange conspiracy of silence, nobody mentioned the riots in towns, disturbances in colleges, and dramatic events of the war.

At the beginning of March, astonishing news began to reach us from Europe. I was particularly bewildered by the riots of students of architecture in Rome. Why architecture? What iniquity in my profession could have led to such revolt and demands of reform? In Italy, the riots left several hundred people injured, streets blocked, widespread strikes, and calls for the sacking of the old and the appointment of new teachers. In France, not a day passed without rebellious students spilling out into the streets. In Czechoslovakia, a process of reforms was attempted, referred to later as attempts to produce "Communism with human face."

In Warsaw, the suppression of the performance of a patriotic nineteenth century drama led to a spontaneous demonstration initiated by students and promptly joined by crowds in the street. This, in turn, led to mass protests against Communist oppression. Arrests of student leaders, accused of "Zionist" conspiracy, followed. This particular twist of government propaganda, inspired by Nazi and Stalinist anti-Semitic slogans, tainted for years the already unfavorable image of Poland in America. It was with great concern that we read reports from Warsaw of a passive or even hostile attitude of workers toward the reforms demanded by students and representatives of the Polish's so-called working intelligentsia. This was followed by news of the persecution of Polish citizens of Jewish origin. No greater damage to the image of Poland abroad could have been done than the news of Holocaust survivors being deprived of Polish citizenship. These events, combined with the specter of prewar pogroms by members of the nationalist parties, were now adding to the poor opinion many Americans had of the behavior of some Poles during the German occupation.

Leopold Tyrmand, a well-known Polish journalist and writer and an old friend of ours, who had eventually found himself in New York, wrote a letter to the editor of the *New York Times* in which he ostentatiously renounced his Polish citizenship. The issue of that same paper of March 3 commented on a speech by Władysław Gomulka, the Communist leader of Poland, adding, "Let us find consolation in the hope that the students protesting now will find themselves leaders of a future Poland." The unwittingly prophetic words materialized twenty year later.

My mother's letters from Paris were full of comments on the students' revolt in France. She was alarmed, naturally, by the leftist rhetoric of the speeches delivered during street demonstrations. A more direct account was given to us by our recently arrived in New York artist friend, signing his paintings with the mysterious acronym Witold-K. According to him, the disturbances in France had the ominous marks of an impending second French revolution. We met him in the West Side apartment of a dark-haired beauty called Abigail and her Polish boyfriend. Abigail was a member of a wealthy American family in the coffee business. There was yet another Pole in the apartment, a dark-haired, slightly built young man with burning, penetrating eyes. His name was Jerzy Kosiński, already widely known in the media through his recent books, most of all *The Painted Bird*. He had recently lost his American wife, who had been instrumental in introducing him to the elite circles of art and money. It was through him that Witold met Abigail. Those Polish contacts of hers would one year later bring her to a tragic end.

Some less dramatic news was also reaching us through many of our old acquaintances, who were now quite frequently arriving from Poland. Thus, the constantly updated exchange of information coming from the two different parts of the divided world kept us really well informed. More than at any other time in the past, we felt that we were part and parcel of the historical changes taking place in our known world—even if that feeling was to prove purely illusory.

18

OK, Jerzy, So What Is Our Next Step?

My room was next to a large drafting space with scores of architects working at their boards. I was sitting at a long table, looking through a complete set of the most recent copies of drawings when my telephone rang.

"Hallo, Jerzy," I recognized the voice of the secretary. "Wes would like you to come to his office as soon as possible. He says it's urgent."

"OK, tell him I am on my way." Wesley Pipher was the partner in charge in the Perkins & Will Architects, a large planning and design office with its headquarters in Chicago. This was its branch in White Plains, half an hour's drive north of New York. I had been working for them since the breakup of the New Canaan partnership.

I had found the job very quickly with the help of an agency, specializing in talent spotting for design firms, notorious for their high staff turnover. In my initial meeting with the partners, I described my professional experience in design work in Poland and in Egypt; they were particularly interested in the plans for the development of Aswan and, of course, my part in the rebuilding of Warsaw. I realized later that they were mistakenly thinking only of the reconstruction of the relatively small area of the former

Jewish Ghetto, destroyed by Germans following the Ghetto Rising in 1943.[5]

Several men were already sitting round the conference table in Wesley's office. One of them, from outside the firm, smiled at me; and I thought that his face looked familiar. "This is Prof. Willo von Moltke," Wes introduced him, "from the Harvard School of Architecture and Planning. I understand that you two had met before." But of course, seven years earlier, during my first visit to the States, Willo was the town planner who presented his design for the regeneration of Philadelphia's old center at the annual convention of American Institute of Architects. He had been telling me then that the time was coming for a replanning of growing American cities. Now Willo joined our firm as an urban planning consultant. But what was to be our next job? A bombshell indeed. Our firm has been commissioned by the city council of Ottawa, Canada's capital, to present a conceptual design for the center of Ottawa. What a commission! And that was not all. By the board's decision, I was put in charge of the project. Would I be willing to undertake this task? I was to pick a team and start work in the near future. Willo would cooperate with me by commuting weekly from Boston to the White Plains airport, thus adding Harvard's prestige to the project. This was, of course, an offer I could not refuse, and I accepted with alacrity. To begin with, we celebrated the event by going to lunch in a nearby French restaurant.

Apart from landing an unusual plum commission, committing myself to such fascinating work in Canada was also giving me a chance to leave behind, if only for a while, the depressing atmosphere of America of the day. The spring and summer of 1968 saw a seemingly unending train of tragedies, belying, as it were, our quiet existence in New Canaan. I had recently come across

5. The history of the tragic Warsaw Rising of 1944 fought by the Underground Home Army and the subsequent destruction of most of the capital, and the epic reconstruction of the entire city from its ashes, was then and still is practically unknown in the USA.

an article saying that a wall of indifference had risen between the towns and the suburbia of America. John Lindsay, the Republican mayor of New York, had unexpectedly appealed to college students to organize a campaign of passive resistance to the Vietnam War. In April came the assassination of Martin Luther King Jr. The specter of J. F. Kennedy's assassination in 1963 once more haunted the land. Racism and the bigotry of certain social groups would not easily be laid to rest. Another tragedy struck in June. Robert F. Kennedy, the candidate in the presidential election, was shot dead at a meeting in Los Angeles. To make things even more complicated, the killer was an Arab immigrant.

In mid-August, during the Democratic Party's convention in Chicago, riots and battles with police reached a severity unprecedented in USA since the establishment of the country's political machine. The main bone of contention was, of course, the continuing Vietnam War, to which no end was in sight. The government's claim that it was meant to halt the world progress of communism was still believed, but it was the strategy that was in doubt. On the other side of the iron curtain, something was brewing too. On August 20, a large force of the Warsaw Pact countries, including two divisions of the Polish People's Army, invaded Czechoslovakia, brutally putting an end to the reforms initiated by Alexander Dubcek. In Great Britain, scuffles between the police and opponents of the Vietnam War became an almost daily occurrence.

The New York Poles, true to the old Polish habit, almost a knee jerk one, were in favor of fighting, as long as it included an element of "for our freedom and yours." They were favorably disposed toward the American military, even though this particular war was a bloody lesson in how not get involved in a conflict without a well-defined cause and without a strategy for its termination.

And then suddenly, on December 25, a unique event lifted the feeling of general gloom. The *Apollo VII* team of three Americans succeeded in circling the moon. We heard the captain of the team reading an excerpt from the Bible, "In the beginning God created heaven and earth . . ." There was no certainty whether the rocket's engine would provide enough power to ensure the astronauts' return to earth. We all held our breath through the minutes of radio silence, when the vehicle's command module went over to the dark side of the moon. But after several orbits, the ignition kicked in faultlessly, and the team was on its way home. The event generated a true avalanche of letters from all over the world. One in particular, from a woman, summed it all up admirably. She wrote simply, "You have saved the year 1968 for us."

Toward the end of the year, the Ottawa project team was complete. With a Washington DC firm of economic consultants in overall charge, the legal aspects of the area's development were entrusted to a Chicago group, while the road-planning engineering team and the team specializing in social aspects of the project were based in Toronto. As luck would have it, in our office, I ran into Jurek, a younger graduate of the school of architecture in Warsaw. Even though our specific task was far removed from the European town planning, anyone with that kind of experience was bound to be of great help.

in Ottawa

Our task was to work out a design for the center of Ottawa that would preserve the historic Parliament Hill with its great complex of neogothic buildings on the rocky escarpment overlooking the river and prevent it from being overwhelmed by high-rise buildings. But I had not yet hit on the right formula for combining the demands of a capitalist development of a city with the requirements of good taste and respect for its historical past. We were forever meeting and debating the main problem: would the owners of land in central Ottawa agree to building restrictions and, if so, at what price?

Severe winter weather set in. Flights were being delayed or cancelled. We had no direct flights to Ottawa, and I had to change planes in Montreal. Once a month we had to meet with the city council, and my job was to provide a progress report, limited so far to collecting information on the status quo. I began to suspect that the majority of our consultants were waiting for the architectural team to come up with ideas. One day, a Chicago lawyer told me that his team was in a position to propose a legal outline, which would secure the property and business rights of the owners. For that, they needed a new plan of the city clearly outlining the areas to be affected by restrictions. Phil Hammer, the chief Washington economist, turned to me, spreading his arms. "OK, Jerzy, so what is our next step?"

March was coming. We went again to Canada. The center of Ottawa, situated on the south bank of the Ottawa River, stretched in a semicircle from east to west, with the parliament buildings in its very middle. (ill.) Driving round its boundary, we had the idea of marking on the map those main access roads which provided the best view of the Parliament and which, we felt, ought to be preserved. We repeated the process in Hull, the town on the other side of the river in Ontario and thus not within the administrative boundaries of the capital. This gave us an interesting drawing, as if of five bunches of rays emanating from the historical buildings in different directions and demarcating the main areas requiring building restrictions. Next came the process of presenting the idea to the economists and lawyers and, in turn, of trying to secure the agreement of the city authorities. Back at work, my mind was full of ways of presenting our project. It wasn't easy to coordinate every aspect with the rest of the team as well as with the clients, and time was running out. Presenting spatial solutions of a future townscape to bureaucrats and, generally, to people not used to thinking in three-dimensional terms, is always difficult and demands great patience. It is a problem encountered by all architects and planners, whether of towns or of individual buildings. In this case, we also had to convey an appreciation of the fourth dimension—time. Another difficulty was getting hold of people—everyone was busy or traveling or otherwise engaged. This being the end of the academic year, Willo was very busy and stopped coming to White

Plains. Meetings with economists and lawyers were arranged in hired conference rooms at airports, where our paths happened to cross. Mobile phones were yet to be invented, so we had to spend hours on the phone day and night to find whomever we had to contact at his home or at work.

I had to come up with a publicity stunt which would appeal to everyone. I stumbled upon it entirely by accident. One day, as I was standing in line at a supermarket checkout, I noticed a large bunch of children's balloons. For nothing better to do, I began to play with one which, having lost some air, was quite pliable. As I pressed it, the balloon kept assuming various interesting shapes. I pushed it in the middle and suddenly saw in my mind's eye a three-dimensional image of Ottawa as it might look scores of years hence should my vision ever come to be realized. Having brought the balloon home, I kept pressing it this way and that and rehearsing my verbal presentation, which I could illustrate with the help of the balloon. For my meeting with the city council, I bought a large red balloon and picked a lovely piece of granite rock from the stone wall at the back of our property. I had made also a small clay model of the complex of Ottawa's parliament buildings. I was risking turning the important meeting into a farce.

My moment came when all the dry presentations by lawyers, statisticians and economists were over. I spoke in short sentences. When I put my model on the table, they all looked at it with interest. But when I started to blow up the balloon a deathly silence enveloped the conference hall. "Ladies and Gentlemen," I began, "American cities usually grow upwards, getting crowded in the centers. What we have in the middle of Ottawa is a complex of historical parliament buildings on a high rocky base. Our task is to protect this historical monument from obliteration by the mushrooming of high-rise buildings around it. And here is our scheme . . ." I put the flaccid balloon on the table and placed the rock with the clay model in the middle. All those present got up and surrounded the table. The balloon remained inflated at the edges with a flat section around the rock. "This is just the general idea," I continued. "We suggest that the highest buildings of the city center be erected at its present periphery, leaving five open parkland corridors offering unrestricted views of the central complex. My colleagues from other expert teams will present to you the administrative and legal aspects of the project."

Our presentation was a great success. We were given the green light to prepare a publication of the entire project. I was put in charge of its preparation and editing in French and English. Phil Hammer, the man in charge of the Ottawa Central Area Study, 1969, wrote to me, "Dear Jerzy, Your knowledge and enthusiasm have greatly contributed to the success of our joint undertaking . . . and it is you who deserves the recognition for having undertaken the major part of the enterprise." Did I recall similar words and sentiments? Could Phil have known the contents of the letter I had received from Abdel Meguid, the director of the Aswan Project, written when he was about to leave his post? Could someone on our board have shown it to him? "Not to worry," said a friend, "consider it another feather in your cap. Congratulations."

That summer we took a long holiday in Canada. Having first taken Klara to a horse-riding camp run by a retired Polish cavalry officer, we rented a fisherman's cottage in Peggy's Cove on the rocky Atlantic coast of Nova Scotia. On the way back, in Montreal, we watched with bated breath Neil Armstrong's first ever landing on the moon. It brought it home to us how the progress of science and technology was continuing, unstoppable and unabated. In spite of the enormous domestic problems and the Vietnam War, that particular summer, America seemed invincible.

Returning home, we heard on the radio a shocking piece of news. Los Angeles police had discovered a mass murder in the house of Roman Polanski, the well-known Polish film director; the victims were his pregnant wife Sharon and, among others, also Abigail and her Polish boyfriend. This case, due to Polanski's fame and the despicable cruelty of the murderers, was to stay on the front pages of newspapers for many weeks to come. We soon had a visit from Witold-K, who arrived in a sporty Jaguar X car borrowed from a wealthy friend in New Jersey. He told us that he had escaped the murder by sheer luck. He missed the party by being engaged elsewhere. Later, a similar story was told to us by Jerzy Kosiński. The plane he took to fly to California was delayed for several critical hours. So was it possible? Maybe both had a lot of luck.

In the autumn, we received a message from Ottawa. After their local elections, Ottawa had a new city council and the Ottawa Center Study was shelved.

19

All on My Own . . . Sort Of

The general disquiet and the alienation of a large section of university and college students began to acquire the traits of a mass social movement. Other factors were now being added to the frustrations of the Vietnam War and to new age groups being continuously added to the draft. The hitherto seemingly infallible authorities had now lost their credibility. First came the state authorities, soon to be followed by the administrative bodies of schools and colleges. Finally, parental authority was shaken as the new generation saw their parents unable to keep up with current events. The already widespread use of marijuana was now aggravated by the appearance of synthetic drugs like LSD and other hallucinogens. This was followed by the sexual revolution, wiping out in its wake many widely accepted taboos upheld by the age-sanctioned Puritan ethic and by the nineteenth-century standards of Victorian morality still in operation. Church teachings were also being questioned and rejected by some as antiquated.

Pop music and protest songs carried throughout the entire West and were also reaching Poland. All these growing trends suddenly reached a peak in an open-air concert in Woodstock, New York State. Nothing seemed to foretell its impact and magnitude. During three days of August, over half a million young people gathered in a farmer's field. All the currently admired, indeed idolized, celebrities were there. The music captivated all minds while speakers, who advanced the most radical social and political ideas, were wildly applauded. During the three days, there were two deaths and two births. The success of the concert provided inspiration for further resistance and calls for a completely new philosophy of life.

Soon after these events, I attended a meeting at the School of Architecture of the Pratt Institute in Brooklyn. This well-known private college founded in the nineteenth century as a technical school had since grown and included now the faculties of architecture and fine arts. The students' rebellion had led at the time to the resignation of the entire administration of the school of architecture. New lecturers were urgently sought. Only two teachers, Stanley Saltzman and Sidney Katz, both adored by the rebellious students, survived the purge. Those two greeted me by saying that their grandfathers had come to America from the old Polish territories. Two others, John Bell, a glib-tongued Englishman, and John Lobel with his wife Mimi gave me an impression that they were already maneuvering to place themselves at the most influential positions in the new team. I felt welcomed at the school and was interested to hear of new objectives, and proposed changes in the curriculum. Those changes still had to be tested as to their acceptability to the students. Because of my other work commitments, I was only able to take on just one course of lectures, namely macroplanning. This course was introduced in response to the students' demands for moving from the narrow field of designing for one private client to the consideration of the wider effects of design on the environment and on society's general welfare. This concept was alien to America and, as I soon discovered, resulted from the Marxist utopia and the yearning for a new kind of society. My experience of town planning proved practically unique and generated much interest. Willo von Moltke's words in Philadelphia about the need for rebuilding American towns came again to my mind. He too believed that architects would have to consider the general welfare and not just the wishes of a private client. And, good god, where else had I heard similar sentiments? Was the specter of Socialism invading America?

My first lecture was attended by over 160 students, greatly exceeding the capacity of the lecture hall. Facing the crowd, I had a funny feeling that I was on stage, surrounded by the cast of *The Gypsy Baron* operetta. The clothes of my students, in all colors of the rainbow, were an amazing collection. There were wide-sleeved shirts, flared trousers, embroidered Afghan waistcoats, black cowboy hats, not to mention bandanas on long hair, dangling earrings and Indian necklaces, colored spectacles, boots with high wedges, and feet placed on tables. Everyone was talking at once, moving about, while wafting around the hall was a blue smoke with the sweetish redolence of marijuana.

I had to attract their attention. I approached the blackboard and with a thick piece of colored chalk started drawing something of which they could not possibly make head or tail. When several drawings were completed, the noise died down, and they all looked at them with curiosity.

"Here you have," I said, "several examples of the development of towns and settlements in various civilizations. Each was determined by an overwhelming need to build in a particular place and by the exigencies of their natural environment. For instance, as our hovercraft approaches the huge rocks emerging from the foamy waters of the Nile, with the rocky wall of the first cataract in the distance, we can confidently expect a town or port on the left bank of the river. There is no other suitable place for it . . . When we look at old Peking, the main approach road must lead from here . . . And there is the island, the site of the city first built by the Gauls and then by Romans and known now as Paris . . . And this is Philadelphia, a mercantile city lying in the fork of two rivers."

This approach worked. The course became very popular. In the spring semester, John Lobell became my assistant. He helped me to supervise and mark the exercises, which I had been able to organize in spite of the lack of space in the school. John was at the time quite popular with the students. He and his wife Mimi had published a book describing in great detail their individual and group sexual escapades. Excerpts were being published in popular pornographic magazines mushrooming at the time and surreptitiously read in classrooms during lectures. Female students kept going to Mimi for all kinds of advice. Times have indeed changed. The here and now was colorful and, in some ways, amusing, but there was a whiff of menace in the air.

And disaster did strike eventually, though indirectly. The Indochina war had spread to Cambodia and Laos. And that despite the new president's (Richard Nixon) promise of an early end to the fighting and the coming of peace. In May, the news of the stealthy invasion of the two neighboring countries by American and South Vietnamese troops kindled new disturbances at a number of universities. At the beautiful, parklike Kent State University, Ohio a large crowd of young people attacked the ROTC (Reserve Officers' Training Corps), the military draft office, and burned the building down. The state governor sent a detachment of the National Guard to restore order. On May 4, the troops opened fire and four students died. The entire country almost audibly gasped.

And it wasn't even the end. Two days later, at the Jackson State campus in Mississippi, two more students were killed in scuffles with the police. At our school, all work stopped. Fortunately, the academic year soon ended. Many students refused to participate in the commencement, marking the beginning of an independent life.

In the course of the summer, we returned in New Canaan to a quiet life, insulated as we were from all of the world's hubbub. The circle of our friends increased, and we got to know our neighbors better.

On the left of our house lived an elderly retired couple who kept to themselves. As soon as we moved in, Mr. Sanford came to welcome us and to advise us that all the people in our street liked a quiet life and detested noisy parties. "We value our privacy," he stressed. After a year of neighborliness, I even found it possible, time permitting, to discuss the Vietnam situation with him. The two of them were deeply conservative and supported the government's policy. They were of the opinion that America had to fight the spread of Communism anywhere in the world. They believed in the popular domino theory: that once Communists come to power in one country, this inevitably led to their take-over of all its neighbors. Thirty-three years later, President George W. Bush would put this argument on its head, postulating that the introduction by force of democracy in Iraq would lead to the acceptance of this foreign system by all the Arab countries of the Middle East. In both cases, the theories proved to be dead wrong.

The Donaldsons, our neighbors on the right, were also an older couple, but they were still at work. Our contact was limited to good neighborly relations with few words lost. He usually complained of his health, "It's the cancer in my guts. They will be removing at least a yard of my gut . . . and that will be the end of me . . . ha, ha, ha . . ." And indeed, he did die quite soon after the operation. She lived into her eighties.

Across the street lived Charlotte Trumpy, a widow. Her small house, not unlike ours, was gracefully furnished with antiques, with landscapes by American artists on the walls and English china displayed in glass-fronted cabinets. Charlotte was a European snob and liked to pepper her conversation with French expressions. She kept inviting us to cocktails and social gatherings, which she held on the terrace at the back of her house. One day, she invited us, well in advance, to an afternoon tea that she described as "une réunion très importante." The guest of honor was Rudolph Chelminski, a handsome, middle-aged man, the scion of a family of major landowners in Podolia, once part of Poland, now of the Soviet Republic of Ukraine. He was, at present, head of the Moscow bureau of the weekly *Life* Magazine. He had recently published a report of his sentimental journey in search of traces of his family's grand past. He told us of the great problems he had encountered in trying to get permission to travel in the USSR outside the usual foreign tourist itinerary. He, with his young American wife and an aunt from Paris, with the help of letters and maps supplied by an uncle in Argentina, managed to find the family mansion and even came across people who remembered the family.

"This was a journey into the past," he said, "into a lost Polish world, almost out of a fairytale. Who else but Poles," he continued, "would have brought customs from the middle ages into the twentieth century? In the same way as who else but Poles would have used mounted cavalry to attack German tanks?"

These absurd romantic fantasies, I thought, would last forever. In his article, he described what his old aunt, who still remembered the pre-Revolutionary times, had been telling him about the way of life in their mansion home: about the children taught by foreign tutors, about the odd whimsies of her uncles and grandfather, about the racing stables of Arabian horses, about the multitude of servants, about the foreign travels. She reminisced about their old neighbors and their great estates; and one of them in particular, owned by Jan Ignacy Paderewski, the pianist of world fame. All of us listened with rapt attention in complete silence, when suddenly one lady, obviously not well versed in history, timidly asked a question, "It's all so very interesting, but I still don't understand how those dreadful Communists have allowed people to live a life of such luxury?"

Next to Charlotte Trumpy's property stood a two-story house, the style of which is called salt box. It had white window frames and black shutters, and cedar wood clapboard of a natural gray color. Its owner was the paralyzed and bed-bound Jack Piech, a stockbroker, who actually worked from his bed. We could clearly see him in his hospital-type bed placed close to a downstairs window. The bed-head was powered and was rhythmically moving up and down to help him with his breathing. At the foot of his bed, he had a large television screen on which he followed the movements of the stock exchange.

At the back of our property, past the remains of an old stonewall and a dense barrier of old trees and bushes, past the tennis court, one enters a large meadow of closely mowed grass. This was the way that for years, during our family sojourns, we had been taking our grandchildren to the swimming pool. In the distance, among very old and gone-wild apple trees with gnarled trunks, stands a large house with a stone facing and a steep roof of bluish-gray slate. A smiling black woman, the old housekeeper, with the unusual name of Saint, waves to us. This old house is the residence of Stanley Resor, a member of the American elite, the so-called old money.

These people, white Anglo-Saxon Protestants or WASPs as they are known, represented until recently the essence of American tradition, social order, morality, and work ethic. Stanley Resor had been appointed secretary for the army during the presidency of Gerard Ford. At present, WASPs are in retreat, giving way to new money, people lacking in manners, aggressive, and often of different ethnic origins. Stanley always kept an open house. One approached it through a tree-lined street along a stone wall, and one entered the drive between two massive stone granite posts without a gate. There was a copper plaque on the front door, saying, "You are welcome. Come in, relax, feel at home; let us talk. Our house does not always look like this—at times it is even worse."

Our compatriots managed to find their way to us too. One day, I heard a female voice on the telephone telling me unexpectedly, "The consul of the Polish Peoples' Republic would like to have a word with you." My first thought was, They have found us after all . . . The previous attempts of the security services to enlist my cooperation in Egypt came vividly to mind. I was already angry, prepared to give them a piece of my mind. But what I heard instead was the friendly voice of the man who had proved so helpful to us in Cairo by extending our Polish passports against the instructions from Warsaw. He reassured me straight away that his call had no connection at all with the Cairo episode. He had simply just been appointed the consul general in New York and was, at present, negotiating the purchase of a suitable building for the consulate in Madison Avenue. He was calling in order to reassure us, that as Poles domiciled in USA, we were entitled to be issued with new passports. It wasn't long before we took him up on it—we still had to wait a little longer before applying for American citizenship. After this call, we did not hear from the Polish consulate again. But what disturbed me was the question of who had given them our address?

The old Puritan traditions did not survive everywhere. Parties occasionally held in the houses of our other younger neighbors were often fuelled by large amounts of alcohol, and the company was not always congenial. Cocktails were still fashionable at the time. Sometimes, as the party progressed, couples would start disappearing from the crowd around the bar. Here was someone's wife with somebody else's husband slipping out of the living room and making their way to the bedroom or guest room, not even arousing much curiosity in the others. After one such party, Lenta decided that she was no longer interested in cocktail parties and that this was not the kind of experience she would be seeking. I was not surprised to hear it, having noticed how many glances had been directed toward her. I found, though, witnessing these loose morals in such a traditionally Puritan country quite fascinating, treating these parties as a kind of entertainment after a week of intensive work. It was from the novels of John Updike that I first found out about the morals of suburbia, apparently quite widespread and certainly not limited to our quiet Kimberly Place. He often described instances of wife swapping, though I could never understand the term. Why just wives? Desperate wives? After all, husbands had to be swapped as well.

Some time later, I talked about it to Leopold Tyrmand, the Polish writer. Leopold, with his new American wife, had recently bought a small house in New Canaan, on the rim of a ravine. He just laughed. It reminded him, he said, of our old times in Warsaw, except that our cramped living conditions made this kind of entertainment so much more difficult to organize. He gave me his novel *Social and Sentimental Lifestyle* to read.

There were also some unexpected encounters, quite pleasant to recall. These were our first contacts with a wider circle of Polish wartime immigrants. In fact, several Polish families lived in New Canaan and its environs.

One lady, Barbara, introduced us to members of her extended family and to their large circle of friends. Barbara's sister, Wanda, and her husband Hugo Jaeckiel had also recently moved to New Canaan having returned from Italy, where Hugo had been the cultural counselor in the American consulate. A tall, handsome man, he rather liked to boast of his familiarity with European culture, a feature not often encountered among Americans. He seemed to value the fact that through his marriage, he had entered the rather interesting group of Poles, i.e., Europeans. A lively, erudite conversationalist, he could turn quite caustic and sarcastic. We kept having heated though friendly discussions, rare in American company, where people are often bland in their effort to appear polite and agreeable. I enjoyed the sparks flying; it reminded me of the debates I used to have in Warsaw in the past. "So what next? When are you going to move?" asked Hugo as soon as we met. I looked at him with amazement. "I know," he continued, "that here in America, people never stay put. They are in constant motion. They find a better job, or their employer transfers them to another branch. Statisticians tell us that on average an American family moves every five years." "We don't intend to prove the statisticians right," I replied. And to confound the latter, both our families continued to live in New Canaan for many years.

Lenta's mother came to stay with us for a while that summer. Popularly known in the family as grandma Zofia, she was a modest, unobtrusive, rather diffident person. She stemmed from the well-known Warsaw family of Rossmanns, originally Lutheran, owners of the Bielawa estate near Warsaw, greatly reduced after the war. There is one amusing incident dating back to the times when we still lived in Poland, which clearly illustrates my mother-in-law's personality. She arrived after work to take our little Klara for a walk. She seemed quite upset, her face flushed. "What happened?" I asked anxiously.

"Oh, my dear, I had such an unpleasant incident at work. One of the coworkers behaved reprehensibly towards me and used such common, rude language."

"So what did you do?"

"Well, I am sorry to say, but I had to respond accordingly."

"What did you tell him?"

"I said, my dear sir, this is not the way . . ." She seemed to feel very guilty having given him such a sharp reprimand.

We had to go to Montreal to meet her, as she arrived on the Polish liner *Batory*, which since 1951 had not been allowed to berth in New York. This was as a result of the fact that Gerhard Eisler, a convicted East German spy of atomic secrets, was allowed by the

Poles to use the ship for his escape from America. This was one of the episodes of the mutual spite between the East and the West, so common during the cold war.

We witnessed the joyful reunion of grandmother Zofia and a friend's mother, in whose home we briefly stopped. The two ladies had been friends as children and through an amazing set of coincidences appeared together in a photograph taken at a fancy-dress ball in the house of my grandparents in 1911; the same picture which also included my own mother. How strange are such coincidences in time and space.

Back in New Canaan, Grandmother Zofia was repeatedly surprised by the courtesy of people and their ready smiles. After decades of traveling on Warsaw trams and buses, where both were conspicuously absent, she found this very welcome and, indeed, quite fascinating. She would look with interest at the typical low-stone walls and at the large houses built in the traditional New England style. In New Canaan, there are no sidewalks, as no one is expected to stroll in the roads. Every day, as she went for her walk, cars would stop and people would offer a lift to wherever she was heading. She would just thank them with a smile. Returning home, Grandma would pick an armful of wild flowers or collect bunches of autumn leaves. We would take her to New York to its splendid exhibitions, to the ballet, concerts, or other performances. One day, together with friends from Montreal, we went to explore Chinatown and ended the day with dinner in a Japanese restaurant, all sitting on mats on the floor—the latter was not considered my most brilliant idea. The performance of Tosca with Regine Crispin in the Metropolitan Opera was an unqualified success though. It seemed that the happy days of the golden Indian summer would go on, unspoiled.

in Manhattan

But it was not to be. Unexpected world news had their impact on us. The war in Vietnam was turning truly macabre. It was the court martial of Lieutenant Calley that reminded us of the terrible massacre of over a hundred peasants, mainly women, children, and old people in My Lai, which had hitherto gone unnoticed. My students put up posters that equated American soldiers with Nazi SS troops. They held protest meetings against the use of defoliating chemicals employed to denude the jungle through which the North Vietnamese supply routes could run. The number of American military in Indochina had by now exceeded half a million, and still one could see no proverbial light at the end of the tunnel.

In the summer, I took the risky decision of venturing out on my own, without the illusory security of a large office. I was forty-eight years old and felt it was time to become independent. Following the Ottawa job, I had become a project manager, and the jobs that came my way were mainly the administrative buildings of the various campuses of the New York State University. These were the times of a major reform and development of education at all levels, introduced by the liberal Republican state governor, Nelson Rockefeller. I must admit that my interest in that kind of project was beginning to wane. I might have been spoilt by my previous, more attractive jobs both in Poland and abroad. But the projects coming my way were a rather soulless routine; on top of which, I had to deal with far-from-exciting team, which included two Chinese and one Indian, who hated one another's guts. One of the Chinese men had placed a small poster above his desk. When I kept pressing him to translate the text for me, it transpired that it was a slogan taken from Mao Tse Tung's *Little Red Book*: The East is Red. I decided too seek my luck elsewhere.

The press had been frequently mentioning the governor's intention to introduce new legislation, which would enable new towns to be built with the help of public funds. New York State was supposed to be the leading light in these ventures—it all sounded interesting and promising, especially for an architect like myself establishing his own practice. I wrote an article on the subject, and sent it to the *New York Times*. To my surprise, it was conditionally accepted for publication. My school colleagues prophesized a rosy future for me, and I even received two partnership offers.

One of them was from Bob Schofield, a Princeton graduate. He was a partner in a family firm of architects in Nyack, a small town on the Hudson River, forty miles north of New York. His wife, Barbara, came from a wealthy family settled for generations in Shaker Slope, an exclusive millionaires' quarter of Cleveland, Ohio. The Schofields lived in Manhattan. One snowy Sunday, we were invited to visit them in their large weekend house in South Salem, not far from New Canaan. It was very cold, so we wore our new Hungarian sheepskin coats bought in Budapest after our flight from Egypt. "Now look at them, just look at them!" cried Barbara as we entered the house, "and tell me why they constantly invent these stupid stories?" Obviously, we did not fit the stereotype of the backward "Polacks," subjects of so many jokes. We quickly became friends.

The other offer came from Ed Bye, a landscape architect and professor at Cooper Union, a prestigious private school of architecture and fine arts, not unlike the Pratt Institute. He came from a Dutch Quaker family settled in Bucks County, Pennsylvania. He had many wealthy clients who owned vast stretches of land likely to be suitable for the development of new towns and settlements.

Bob's firm had an office in downtown Manhattan, in Fifty-Fifth Street, which provided a suitable home for our new partnership, CODA (Community Design Associates). I began my daily immersion in the crowds thronging the streets and the foyers of the nearby St. Regis Hotel where Salvador Dali used to stroll, attracting attention not only by his odd-pointed moustache but also by carrying a live young leopard draped, collarlike, around his shoulders, and where Jacqueline Kennedy-Onassis could be seen going with her friends to their favorite restaurant. We set ourselves the task of preparing development projects and detailed designs for new towns and settlements. I was put in charge, and I designed an illustrated brochure describing our past achievements and our future program. We ordered a batch of company stationery and engaged Karen, a lovely girl, as a secretary. Everything was ready, except for commissions. Yet our hope shone bright.

I went to Washington DC with Bob to get a clearer view of the legislation concerning the development and financing of new towns. In Congress, we inspected the thick volume of pending legislation on the subject. I also visited Phil Hammer who offered his cooperation. We talked to Polish congressmen hoping for their support. We began to send out letters offering our services. Beginning in autumn, I split my working hours between the Manhattan office and teaching at Pratt. It meant spending hours in the car but the work was interesting, and I enjoyed it.

Other than that, I was designing private houses in my basement studio in New Canaan. I had little relevant experience in this domain and had to prove myself to my clients. It was very time-consuming, involving discussions with the owners, visiting sites, offering preliminary sketches (most of it unpaid) in the hopes of getting the job. Should I decide to devote myself to this kind of work, I would have to settle in some small town, give myself at least a year to become known, and write off my more ambitious plans for the future. But the truth was that what attracted me were large projects and wider horizons.

At Pratt, unrest ruled once again. Salvador Allende, the new president of Chile, became the first democratically elected Communist leader in the West. The machinations of the American government eventually led to his assassination, and our students from Latin America were vociferous in placing the blame on President Nixon and his adviser Henry Kissinger.

In order to acquaint my students with the latest achievements in building technology, I arranged a visit to the construction site of the twin towers of the World Trade Center. The papers reported that, having already exceeded by one yard in height the tallest building in the world, they were still growing. One could not but be overwhelmed by the magnitude of the task. We had all become, in a way, blasé by the sight of Manhattan buildings. However, the building site of the twin towers defied all comparison and dwarfed all previous experience. Its surface area was greater than anything previously seen by my students, and it extended further up and down than in any other building. As far as I was concerned, excluding the height aimed at here, the very magnitude of the design reminded me of certain sites in Warsaw in the unforgettable years of postwar reconstruction and of the enormous building site of the Sadd el Aali, the Aswan High Dam, extending further than the eye could reach.

The erection of the Twin Towers in such troubled times was to me a proof of the power of technological thought constantly evolving in spite of serious problems affecting the country. Being actually present at the site, bearing along eyewitnesses to the construction, impressed me more than seeing on television the cosmic drama of *Apollo 13* reaching the moon. Following a serious mishap, but due to the unprecedented presence of mind of the crew and the available technology, the astronauts returned safely home. In spite of all that, Uwe, a Danish student, who never removed his Maoist cap with its red star, whispered confidentially in my ear as we were coming back from the site, "You'll see, they won't win in Vietnam all the same."

Some of our college design lecturers were attempting to introduce new teaching methods that would be acceptable to the students. An Italian architect, who had conducted the practical summer course for our students in Florence, arrived at the school in November. The task he had set them there was to create a tridimensional design of a town of the future. They spent four weeks traveling in Italy and discussing the theoretical aspects of the problem. In the first semester after their return to New York, they were supposed collectively to make a model of such a town and present it to the visitor. The day he arrived, I accompanied him to the large design room where the Florentine group had been encamped for the last few days and nights, to see the results of their work. He asked me to participate in the discussion and give my opinion. One can imagine our amazement when what we saw on the long table was a mass of various shapes six-feet long, constructed of dry pasta: macaroni, shells, linguine, zita, farafelle, of different kinds and colors. The designers of this "masterpiece" sat with stony faces behind the table. There was no discussion.

Urban planning and design were becoming fashionable. Even John Johansen, the man who gave me a helping hand at the beginning, came to teach at Pratt. His class project was . . . a city of the future!

On another occasion, my friend, the second-year lecturer of design, a tall, handsome man with raven-black hair reaching down to his shoulders and held in place with a red headband, invited me to the end-of-semester assessment of the work of his students. The subject was the rebuilding of Manhattan in a way, which would facilitate the movement of traffic. I was truly baffled to see this design concept with Manhattan buildings hanging in the air, suspended from huge balloons.

Such incidents with my colleagues were very frustrating. Fortunately, there was a consolation: Karen, our lovely secretary, wrote me a poem for my birthday in November. She typed it on yellow card, the color of jealousy as she explained, blushing. This is the one and only panegyric that I had ever received. Embarrassed, I quote below one of the stanzas:

> I thought of the things he seem to mean
> like bigness and honesty, like something between
> the earthiest earthy that man can be
> and a duke who has caught the heart of the Queen . . .
> I thought of flair and grandiosity
> Of untamable curiosity
> But all of these things, though they ring true
> Still left me with nothing to do . . .

I believed that meeting people from outside the college would widen my students' mental horizons; particularly, as in my own student days, we had been totally deprived of such helpful contacts. The doctrine of Socialist realism was considered all embracing, and it could be improved upon only by a careful study of the history of Communism and of Soviet achievements. In our college, however, not every visit was welcome. The alienation of young people was serious and embraced many branches of science and culture. For some reason, architecture and urban planning became the focus of their tempestuous passions.

Ed Bye introduced me to a man by the name of Kaufman, one of the major New York developers. He offered to deliver a lecture, illustrated with slides, on the role of money in the building of a capitalist city. At a time when crucial new legislation was being debated by Congress, it seemed to me a splendid and topical subject. Kaufman, a tall, slim man in a silk navy-blue suit and a white shirt with gold cufflinks, presented a striking contrast to our students sprawled on the lecture theatre chairs. He mounted the podium in front of the screen and asked for the first slide. This showed the top part of his body, a yellow hard hat on his head, his sad, dark-circled eyes fixed on a bag held in his hands and marked with a black dollar sign. In the complete silence that followed, Kaufman began, "My whole life and all my enterprises have been motivated by two premises, thought by some people to be sins, namely greed and avarice . . ." No one could have predicted what followed. There was shouting, swearing; no more slides could be shown. Kaufman responded very sensibly; he took off his jacket, came off the podium, sat down among the excited students, and slowly tried to engage them in a calmer discussion. Many recalled the event later as having been quite useful, after all.

On December 14, the press reported riots on the Polish Baltic coast. Throughout the following week, we watched and read in the *New York Times* about the events in Gdańsk. Could it be the beginning of the downfall of Communism? Local Poles organized a small demonstration outside the Polish consulate. The pitiful demonstration mustered a few score of people who assembled on the sidewalk across the street from the consulate. Having done a bit of shouting, they finally handed in a petition. It seemed quite obvious that émigré Poles would not gain much in the political stakes by street demonstrations. On top of that, I had the distinct impression that New Yorkers had little sympathy for the Polish cause. Poland did not have a good press.

All this was in clear contrast to the well-planned action by Jewish groups protesting against the Soviet ban on Jewish emigration to

Israel organized by some influential groups, among others the fighting units of JDL (Jewish Defense League). These demonstrations eventually led to the Soviet Union allowing its Jewish citizens to emigrate to Israel.

The spring of 1971 brought also changes to the Pratt Institute. The institute had not been attracting new students in sufficient numbers. It might have been its location in Brooklyn, close to the sites of recent riots and associated with crime. In the nearby Fort Greene Park, lawless hordes of drug addicts and homeless people camped. The once regularly maintained lawns as well as the sidewalks surrounding the square, were now covered with filth, garbage, and broken glass, and were becoming difficult to negotiate. No wonder that the finances of the worthy institution were affected. The administration was desperately looking for additional income. One weekend, a fleet of large trucks arrived at the institute bringing personnel and equipment. This was the outfit shooting a pornographic film about a Texas university sports team, *Debbie Does Dallas*. A big scandal followed, leading in turn to changes in the management. The number of new students went up, unfortunately at the cost of a lowering of the admission standards.

At that time, two events, complementary in a way, affected my life. First, I was asked at the school to develop a new course on the role of architecture in the conservation of the environment, concentrating on the relationship between unchecked development and nature. I was to start lectures and practical exercises in the autumn. I had to prepare thoroughly for this new assignment and gain some practical experience. It would be taking me away from pure architecture, but it represented a new challenge; and this was what I liked most. After all, I thought, an architect's skills can be used in many ways. I tried to recall incidents of conflict between the preservation of nature and the inevitability of damage in the process of building. I also remembered my past observations of river pollution, one in Poland and one in North Carolina, naïve and almost insignificant though they may have been by today's standards.

A parallel event was my meeting with a member of the committee of PRUP, the Pound Ridge United for Planning. This was a committee created by the inhabitants of Pound Ridge, a town adjacent to New Canaan, though over the state line, in New York State. PRUP's objective was to find a method of developing the town, while at the same time protecting it from excessive or ill-planned building that might damage the ecological basis of their superb natural environs. They intended to operate independently from the town council, which adhered to the traditional practice of approving building applications solely on the basis of the existing building by-laws and sanitary requirements. PRUP's ideas were revolutionary and hitherto unheard-of, and their proposed new directives and regulations might have threatened the traditional American practice—in one's own backyard, one does as one wills.

The CODA office has for some months now been situated in Cos Cob, a coastal town in Connecticut. The office, which we rented, was on a promontory surrounded by moorings for hundreds of sailing boats, motor yachts, and other types of small vessels. The mighty dollar reigning here for years had left its conspicuous mark on the area. Ed's clients were discussing with him the appearance of the vast open spaces surrounding their magnificent suburban residences. They were interested in landscaping them so that not only plants would be taken into consideration but also the topography of the area. Ed specialized in converting plain fields into lightly undulating grasslands with shadow effects changing with the sun's position at different times of the day. He used only native flora in his designs; he also published albums of his nature photographs.

The representatives of PRUP had come to my new office on the recommendation of Frank H. Bormann, professor of Forest Ecology at Yale University, whom I had not met till then. During the following years of our cooperation, I learned a lot from Frank and his five-strong team. This was indeed a happy coincidence, which helped me at the same time to formulate my Environment Protection course. I lost no time in turning to the problems of Pound Ridge.

The only break I allowed myself was a short family visit to Montreal, taking my mother-in-law to the ship on which she was to sail back to Poland after a yearlong stay with us. In spite of the happy days in Montreal, visiting friends and exploring the old city with its French cultural past, it was a sad farewell. We could not tell when we would be able to see Grandma Zofia again; we were also concerned about her health, problems with which she has been obviously concealing from us. She was a very private person at the best of times. She never talked about herself nor did she ever attempt to stand out in company. Lenta inherited some of those, otherwise enviable, traits of character.

On our drive home, all the radio stations were broadcasting news of the sensational Washington story. In response to president Nixon's attempts to conceal the true state of affairs in Vietnam—for which the opposition naturally blamed him—an employee of the Pentagon, Daniel Elsberg, had leaked to the press certain secret documents describing the situation of American forces in Indochina as hopeless. These revelations would fill the columns of papers and television screens for months to come, as if suddenly an honesty bubble had burst over the land, compelling the government and its institutions to answer the questions worrying millions of people: what was this war about, and was it worth all the casualties? And the number of deaths had by now exceeded thirty thousand, with that of seriously wounded many times greater.

In the midst of these tragic events, we, the newcomers from behind the iron curtain, could not get over the unconstrained freedom of the opposition to criticize the actions of the government. With total incredulity, we were reading all the critical reports and listening to investigative journalists digging out secrets that Nixon's White House did not wish to share with the general public. For us, this was a real lesson in democracy in action. We discovered that though virtually indiscernible in everyday life, democracy came into its own in the hands of courageous individuals in times of danger and in the face of willful and lawless actions by the government. And this was only the beginning of such disclosures.

At the time, I had come across the principles of democracy even in my own neck of the woods, having for the first time come face to face with it. It was a liberating experience, even though it did not yet quite reach my conscious mind. What I understood though was that progress depended on the shaking of existing habits, often presented as laws or dogmas and defended by the forces of conservatism and blind faith.

The early 1970s were the dawn of the so-called ecological revolution. Man's unbound right to manage the Earth's resources was beginning to be questioned. It was said that this kind of attitude went back to the Bible and its assumption that man is the master of the earth and all its other living creatures. Bookshops were full of new publications devoted to the preservation of the environment. It seemed that the volunteers of PRUP, with the cooperation of CODA, would have to show how to translate the theories into action. The motive power behind the enterprise was the Trust, a group of private citizens, residents of the town, who decided to change, in a democratic way, the existing, deep-rooted mindset. This was neither easy nor unopposed by the alarmed conservative town authorities. The membership of the board kept changing; some members left and new ones stepped in. Doubts and emotions led to tensions, to defections, even to sabotage. Board members were recruited from the upper and middle classes and represented many professions and occupations. Its heart was Mary Jane Russell, a supermodel of the 1950s, whose photographs had adorned the covers of *Vogue* and other fashion magazines. Her and her husband's, Ed, vigorous fund-raising activities kept the coffers handsomely filled. This was hard work. Every couple of months some fund-raising function would be taking place in Pound Ridge; later, my presentations of our work's progress would also attract good audiences.

Then, the festering wounds of unresolved Middle Eastern political problems surfaced in the most unexpected time. While watching the Olympic Games held in Munich, we were suddenly shaken to the core by an unprecedented event. Several days before the end of the games, a commando unit of eight Palestinians took hostage a group of Israeli competitors, demanding the release of their comrades and of some terrorists from German and Israeli prisons. During the intense drama at the airport and an exchange of fire, nine hostages and five kidnappers were killed. This was the new, hitherto unknown face of the growing conflict due to the resistance of the Arab world to the recognition of Israel and its territorial conquests in the 1967 war.

Being, over a long period of time, personally present during some historical developments in that region, I felt closer ties to these events than most of my friends and acquaintances. These contacts, together with our many links to our old country, described our tri polar existence in America.

In autumn, my archeologist aunt, Maria Ludwika Bernhard, came to visit us from Poland. She was coming on the invitation of Princeton University and planning a longish stay. When I met her at the airport, Maria told me that Lenta's mother was seriously ill and that Lenta ought to go to Warsaw as soon as possible. Grandmother Zofia, as usual, had kept her personal problems to herself, not wanting to bother anyone. On top of it, she did not have a telephone, still a hard-to-get commodity in Warsaw, which made communication so much more difficult. Fortunately, we now had our new Polish passports, so it did not take long to organize Lenta's trip. Just before leaving, she took a call from Kosiński, asking her to take a parcel for his mother in Warsaw. According to him, Polish censors were confiscating all his mail, including parcels—he was considered an enemy of the state. Lenta left for Warsaw in October, her luggage full of medical supplies and other goods difficult to obtain in Poland. She arrived there just in time.

20

Doubts and New Challenges

On Christmas Eve, 1972, the editorial in the *New York Times* carried an ominous title "Which America?" It said, among other things that "The very week when American astronauts ignited the rockets of *Apollo 17* to take them back to earth, American pilots released bombs that tore asunder the skies over a peasant country in Asia. The two Americas, one brilliant, full of ideas; the other sinister, envious, fired by vengeance—both in simultaneous action . . . This is a century when millions of people had suffered aerial bombardment, while America avoided this peril. At the present moment of religious contemplation and personal resolutions, the United States and its citizens are being judged by the use to which our government puts our mighty technology. Are we the new barbarians? Which is the real America?

The year 1973 was ushered in with much tension and frustration for most Americans. After the hotly contested 1972 election, which had been for us an introduction to the workings of American democracy, Richard M. Nixon came back to the White House for his second term of office. He was elected by a vast majority and that in spite of the extensive criticism of his Vietnam policy and the violent protests against it, and in spite of the discovery of his role in the Watergate scandal. His election came as a great surprise to many people. We wandered whether this is how democracy works?

There is an astonishing phenomenon in Americans' public perception of the culpability of the president. Quite innocent misdeeds, as in the case of Jimmy Carter or George H. Bush, are more likely to lead to the president not being elected again than grave mistakes endangering the future of the country such as those committed by Nixon and George W. Bush. Nevertheless, both were allowed to complete their two terms in office.

Still a Polish citizen, I was not entitled to vote. I did, however, go with our neighbor, Dick Beckler, to his friends' rather boozy election party held in front of the television set. Dick was an amiable, slightly balding young lawyer, who had recently moved with his family to our street. The company was all Republican Party supporters and hoped that Nixon would win. With tongues loosened by beer, President Nixon's great political skills were loudly praised though, curiously, the war in Vietnam was not even mentioned. The news, arriving from all parts of the country, soon began to show clearly the extent of the defeat of Senator McGovern, the Democratic candidate. As he had promised a swift end to the war and the withdrawal of American forces from Vietnam, he was perceived as a weak leader, likely to give in to the Communists. Vietnam was still seen as part of the worldwide conflict with Communism. Many of the New York Poles supported Nixon, but I, though politically uninvolved, felt a great, almost physical unease on hearing the company's shouts of joy. I subscribed to the slogan of the day, "Let's proclaim victory and get our boys home," which in the end proved to be the best solution. Though not claiming to be clairvoyant, I was quite anxious about the future of our adopted country. As for my professional self, my commitment to the work of the restoration of old and the building of new towns seemed now a risky undertaking. The necessary decisions could only be taken by a Democratic administration in Washington, where the relevant legislation introduced at the time of President L. B. Johnson kept gathering dust on the shelves of the Congress, awaiting their debate and confirmation. The reelection of President Nixon meant further delay or worse.

Since the creation of our new company, CODA, I invested a great deal of time and energy into preparing the ground for our expected commissions. While still based in Manhattan, we found some officials at the Manufacturers Hanover Trust Company, an important bank interested in the program presented by our new firm. We felt very optimistic but, unwittingly, we might have been swimming against the current of new developments.

CODA

New York, a city sinking at the time into financial and political chaos, was more than ripe for new initiatives offering people hope, work, and a roof over the heads. Entire districts of the city had been burned and looted. In panic, owners and tenants were abandoning the still-standing buildings, leaving them to further dereliction; and the local authorities began to withdraw essential community services. The press was full of apocalyptic warnings that even if it were possible to stop people leaving their buildings, fifty thousand new dwellings would have to be provided every year for the next fifteen years to make good the losses. The situation reminded me of that in postwar Warsaw. Yet this was happening in America, untouched by war, the richest country in the world. All that was needed was a large investment earmarked for reconstruction, but the banks capable of providing the funds were waiting for a signal from Washington for an offer of a government guarantee, which was, however, not forthcoming. The *New York Times*, quoting clearly exaggerated words of some state politicians, wrote, "Housing development presents a problem so great that only an equally momentous idea could bring a solution . . . Crisis is an inadequate word—catastrophe is much more likely."

Paradoxically, many people did not see the danger inherent in the situation. Not only that, they completely ignored its existence. It made me wonder at times whether my partners and I were also given to exaggeration. My students though responded with interest to my lectures bearing on the subject. It was the response of the younger generation, which gave us some comfort. All the same, we decided to devote rather less of our time and energy to the New York problem. At least for the time being.

The Cos Cob studio and the Pound Ridge job provided me with a relatively secure base when a new, though not altogether architectural, challenge came my way. Some invisible force was pushing me in a new direction. Surprised, I kept analyzing the situation. There were two possible explanations.

I wondered whether my present impatience with some of the available jobs went back to having been spoiled by the exceptional demand for professional services offered by the rebuilding of war-flattened Warsaw, when resources were available and architects in short supply. And secondly, was it my unconscious need for new challenges that would keep my interest and passion alive? I was aware by now that, in contrast to my experience in the Socialist system, no one here in America was waiting to offer me new, interesting, totally absorbing work. That much I had understood as far back as 1965 when, fully aware of what I was doing, I had left my job at the Raleigh University for the totally unknown waters of the Egyptian projects. The attraction of the challenge was too great to be rejected. In fact, I had already then been worried over my chances of working as an architect in a new, totally unknown environment. And now, I have to admit that I did not fully appreciate the risks to which I was exposing my family. Seven years later, when I had turned fifty and when we were settled as immigrants in America for good, such concerns were only too real.

But what were the alternatives? One was a secure professorship at the Pratt Institute or a job in someone's large design office. A few Polish immigrant architects had done very well in the second kind of setting; and after a number of years, they achieved status and much recognition. But I had also heard of clleagues who were suddenly fired even from high positions and their contributions were marginalized. The labor market in our profession has always been and still is rather unstable and notorious for considerable turnover. Wave after wave of political or economic migrants was coming to our shores: Chinese, Vietnamese, Indians. The Mexican border was very porous, and thousands of illegal immigrants from all over Latin America were penetrating it. American-born students accounted now for a minority in our school of architecture.

Truly alarming signals regarding our profession were coming from all sides. One day, we sat in the lecture theatre listening to a philosopher-futurologist from Chicago projecting his anxieties as to the future of Western civilization in the twenty-first century. I was sitting next to Philip Johnson, a well-known architect and a promoter of modern tendencies in architecture, which he dubbed the International Style. When the speaker came to the future role of architects, Johnson, evidently loosng patience, turned to me and whispered sarcastically, "This is all nonsense . . . nothing will change; things may just become more difficult. The idealists have had their time. To become a successful architect, you either have to be born rich or marry an heiress. I was lucky on the first account, but generally speaking, you have to have connections in the right circles or be damn lucky."

I certainly wasn't refusing any commission to design a new building. But it would be a waste of time to describe them all. I have found over the years that no one is interested in the process of creation of an architectural design and, talking about it, one only risks becoming a bore. It isn't that surprising; after all, how many professions provide material for inherently interesting stories? Very few. Consequently, I prefer to describe incidents, which, to some extent, provided the background to the rather interesting events taking place in America of the 1970s, the America I knew.

In the spring, my mother arrived from Paris on her first visit to the USA. This put my interest in town planning and ecology to rest for a while. Instead, mother and I paid a tourist visit to Washington DC, which she wanted to visit. She was born on July 4 and, subconsciously, associated herself with the birth of the United States.

The five-hour drive unexpectedly provided an opportunity for her to tell me family stories I had never heard before. Sitting relaxed next to me on the wide, comfortable seat of our car, mother responded to some of my naïve questions by beginning to talk about her own life. I felt rather like a Freudian psychiatrist during a therapy session. But for this car journey, I would never have known many of these detailed family stories, which constitute part of my memoirs.

The next day, exhausted after our visit to the Capitol and to National Gallery of Art, we retired to a seafood restaurant overlooking the Potomac. We sat there like a couple of children with paper bibs tied round our necks by the waiter, waiting for our lobsters. "We must look like idiots," worried my mother. "I hope we don't run into anyone we know." At that very moment, we were surrounded by a small group of men. One of them was Vernon George, a member of the Phil Hammer group with whom I had worked closely on the Ottawa project. And soon they too were sitting with bibs round their necks. It is difficult not to enjoy a situation like this, the atmosphere so friendly and informal all round. And on top of it all, the lobsters were delicious.

I had a word with Vernon on leaving the restaurant. He told me that all legislation concerned with the financing of new towns was bogged down in Congress. In his opinion, the only possible source of finance for our enterprise would be private investors, and only those with huge resources. This was a solution very different from those I had encountered in Europe. I would have to learn the ways of dealing with these situations, he advised. "I think you overestimate my resourcefulness," I said. Vernon shrugged his shoulders. "You never know," he replied and told me about the first instance of a new city planned and built with private backing. This had happened recently and not far away, between Washington DC and Baltimore. Columbia, the new city for a hundred thousand inhabitants, was the idea of a very wealthy and enterprising builder and was carried out by his firm, The Rouse Corp., hitherto specializing in new shopping centers on the outskirts of big towns. The trouble was that I had not the slightest chance of meeting another Mr. Rouse and becoming involved in this kind of venture.

I suddenly felt that my entire professional strategy, on which I counted and on which so much depended, was endangered. In life, particularly in America, a solo swimmer "chasing his proverbial dream," entering uncharted waters takes his destiny in his own hands and has to expect surprises and, often, tragic failure. I had by now begun to get used to such turns of fortune; but this news was truly alarming.

Soon after our trip to Washington DC, mother returned to Paris and I went back to work. The uncertain future in my chosen profession was causing me a lot of anxiety. The papers frequently wrote about the need for new towns and of the scarcity of accommodation for people of modest means; the developments in Europe were often quoted as an example, which could be followed to great advantage.

The building of Columbia was to be the beginning of a new epoch in the growth of towns in America. Rouse had once before demonstrated his ability to shape the future. It was he who had built the first large shopping mall, thus changing the immemorial character of a town where most commercial activity used to be located at its center. Forty years later, shopping malls would come to surround bigger and smaller towns virtually all over the world.

So how had it come to pass that a new town was created in Maryland, financed entirely by private capital? Lenta and I went to have a look at Columbia's building site. I wanted to know how Rouse managed to acquire a piece of land the size of our New Canaan. One often hears that in America, anything is possible, but one does not run into thousands of acres of fine agricultural land in a most desirable area of eastern USA, between Boston and Washington, by chance. From stories told me by various people and from press material, I tentatively deduced the builder's method; it could easily have come from a Hollywood script. Here it is,

One evening, in the chosen area, several scores of agents of the firm in question entered the homes of all the local owners of agricultural land and asked to meet with the whole family. It was the time of day when people would be normally sitting down to their evening meal. As custom went, an unexpected guest would be asked to join the family at the table. After a brief chitchat about the weather, the children, or local events, the newcomer would come to the point and announce to the whole family gathered for the meal that he had come to buy their property. This, as I heard, would be followed by complete silence and, taking advantage of the surprise, the agent would reach for his large attaché case, place it in his lap and, watched by everybody, would state the sum, which he was prepared to pay. The offer was for all the land, buildings, indeed the whole farm lock, stock, and barrel. But the sale had to be completed that very evening, and the payment would be in cash. At that point, the agent would place wads of banknotes on the table. The silence would continue. The price offered was fair, the actual market price. Some owners would resist the temptation; others seemed to doubt the genuineness of the offer or the honesty of the buyer. These doubts would be silenced by some additional bundles of bills added to the ones already on the table. The agreement was signed there and then, a receipt for the money obtained. The legal formalities would be dealt with at a later date. That way, the Rouse Corporation bought in one evening all the land required for the future town. Only two or three of the farmers had resisted the offer. When Lenta and I toured the area, we noticed a few old houses scattered here and there still surrounded by trees, while road building was going on around them. All this was for me a truly American story, taken from a film script or perhaps a gangster novel. But if that were true, and if these were the methods required, neither my partners nor I had the slightest chance of applying Columbia's strategy elsewhere.

But life is full of surprises, sometimes welcome, which may, however, lead to further disappointments. When the telephone rang, at first I was not sure whom I was talking to. But it was Stephen, one of my old students, who was presently working for a building contractor in Massachusetts. He had something important to tell me. His employer had got hooked on the idea of building new towns. He had a meeting arranged with a firm of local architects and, on Stephen's advice, wanted to see me as well. I went to meet him in Springfield, the state capital. Carabetta, a stocky, energetic, middle-aged man, took me to a large room where detailed maps of a particular area covered the walls. Another man of a similar build joined us and was introduced as his deputy. After the initial introductory platitudes, Carabetta said, "Your name is what? Polish? Barzo dobzie . . . very good," he added in what was supposed to pass for Polish and laughed. "But seriously," he continued, "your friend Stephen tells me that you specialize in designing new towns. Is that true? OK. I want to build a new town in Massachusetts, in the peak area for business and traffic, between Boston and Springfield, next to the main east-west Interstate I-90. Let's look at the map," he said, leading me by the hand. Showing me the area in question, he said that he had already bid for several thousand acres of woods and meadows and, in order to avoid land speculation, had his bid legally frozen for the time being. He then questioned me about my past work and experience and made sure that I would be able to present him with a work program together with a timetable for the necessary undertakings before leaving for Europe—I had planned to spend a vacation with Klara in Poland. A long silence followed. Carabetta rubbed his hands together and looked at his companion. "OK," he concluded. "Let's do it this way. Let me have the work outline for the first phase by the end of the year. We shall settle our accounts monthly." He specified a sum, rather larger than I expected. He shook my hand, stretching his over the table, adding, "Welcome, good to have you on our team." That was all. My contact was to be with his deputy.

The trip to Europe came as a pleasant change. Lenta wasn't particularly keen on going to Poland and decided to stay at home. I was looking forward to traveling on an American passport for the first time. Besides, Klara and I had planned to begin our journey by a sentimental retracing of my movements during my service in the air force on the western front during the Second World War. Having rented a car in Paris, we followed the trail through Normandy, Belgium, and Holland to Germany. Everywhere we went, I was trying to find traces of the airfields of the 131 Polish Fighter Wing of twenty-nine years ago, as we then followed the advancing frontline. But it was a daunting task. Apart from the visit to St. Denis-Westrem near Ghent in Belgium, to which we were taken to by my old friend, Monique, tracing the old airfield sites proved impossible.

The memory of the war had gone with the wind. From Germany, we drove to Copenhagen to see old friends who had been hounded out of Poland in 1968 because of their Jewish origin—a disgraceful episode, which still mars the name of Poles especially abroad.

As we were crossing the Kiel Canal, I recalled to Klara my adventure of secretly lifting a Polish girl from a refugee camp on a nearby island of Sylt, in the first year after the war. She laughed, saying that she could not make head or tail of my wartime stories and that really I ought to write them up. After several days in Denmark, we crossed to Sweden and boarded a ferryboat for a Polish port, whence we proceeded by train to Warsaw.

As an expatriate returning to Poland after nine years abroad, I could not help but compare Poland and America with very mixed feelings. On one side, it was a great joy to rediscover the familiar sights, the well known landscapes, even streets; it was good to see and touch the furniture in the apartment of my childhood, now occupied by my paternal aunt, an artist potter. It was an emotional experience to see my old schoolmates and meet university friends, to reminisce about the time of our shared work on the reconstruction of Warsaw. On the other hand, it was disturbing to witness a kind of cultural decline, combined with inept attempts to follow the achievements of the West. I could see this everywhere: in shops, in restaurants, in offices, even in car wash points, or in watching road-building gangs. And that was the time of the so-called minor economic stabilization, when after the dramatic shipyard protests of the 1970s, the party attempted to create a kind of make-believe, state-controlled mini-prosperity. My friends seemed actually proud of these achievements and often asked me to confirm their perception. But I could not tell them what I really thought; after all, the situation was not of their making. What I saw was that, apart perhaps for some minor improvements in housing standards, a slightly better chance of buying a second-rate car, everything was just as I remembered it from the time when I lived in Poland. The press still boringly described the "struggle" for an efficient harvest to be completed on time. At least there was no mention of "struggles" with American warmongers—in a minor way this was progress.

I was rather surprised to find that no one was interested in the Vietnam War. This was something so far away that it did not impinge on their lives. When I once raised the subject, one of the company answered that one ought to fight Communism wherever one could. In private, the official American view was obviously accepted by Poles without qualms. Klara, though, was, without reservations, in a seventh heaven. She had managed to trace her friends from previous vacations and was full of joy. She quickly rediscovered a common language and shared interests with her contemporaries, which, she said, she has been missing in her New Canaan school. It's puzzling how certain cultural ties tend to remain intact—they are no doubt embedded in the unconscious mind. And anyway, who could have resisted the attractions of that vacation?

We spent one week in the State Stud Farm, where, under its director's watchful eye, we galloped on powerful stallions through forest paths or perfected our horsemanship on the large exercise field. Later, we went to a fishing village on the Hel Peninsula. The area was obviously favored by artists and intellectuals. I had never been in touch with such a concentration of talent and intellect in America, where my access to those circles was limited. Klara also met young people, children of the old Polish intelligentsia, whom she remembered from the English language course they attended together in childhood. Recalling their names, I cannot help reflecting that most of these young people had subsequently left the country in the successive regrettable waves of immigration that were draining Poland of its vital energies.

Klara in Łąck

Soon it would be time to start on our return journey, though events had not quite come to an end. We were all going back to Paris, Klara by plane and my aunt and I driving the latter's car via Wrocław and Munich. A rather amusing incident took place at the Polish-East German border; it remained in my mind as a symbol of those peculiar times. A Polish border guard approached the car to check our documents. I handed him the whole pile: my American passport, my Polish passport, Aunt's French passport and her Polish permanent residence document, my American driving license, her Polish and international driving permits, the car's Polish registration book. The poor man bunched all the papers up in one hand while attempting to inspect them and sort them out with the other. As they kept slipping out of his grasp, he decided to spread the lot on the hood of our car. The East German guard, wondering what caused the delay, also came up and, not able to understand what it was all about, kept a wary eye on us. I had a feeling that the Pole wanted to ask some question; but obviously confused, he gave up and, gathering all the documents together, passed them to me through the window. He pushed the German guard aside. "Ales in Ordnung," he said and waved us on.

This rather human response coming from an official of a hostile authority put us in a cheerful mood, which not even the sullen looks of the East German policemen could spoil.

In Munich, we stopped with a friendly couple who have both been working for several years for Radio Free Europe; and while Aunt Maria went off by train to Paris, I spent the next few days doing the rounds of museums and visiting Bavarian towns with their historical treasures. These impressions of Europe had pushed American affairs to the back of my mind. My solitary car drive to Paris during the memorable heat wave of that summer was rather tiresome. I was driving fast, leaving behind the fields and vineyards of Champagne, planning to reach Paris before nightfall; but I was beaten by the heat. There was no town or village to be seen anywhere near; but as the river Marne was quite close, I turned into a side road, hoping for a dip in its cool waters. The riverbank was high and steep, overgrown with trees and shrubs, and it was not easy to reach the water. Stripped to the skin, gripping the overhanging branches, I was trying to lower myself down the bank. The fast-flowing river beneath me was an odd shade of bright green. Suddenly, the branch I was holding on to snapped, and I fell head down the rest of the way. When I came to the surface some distance down the river, I found myself all covered with a sticky, greasy, stinking mess. I clambered back to the bank and tried to clean myself up with fistfuls of grass, though with very little success. Willy-nilly, having covered my car seat with leafy branches, I drove on and stopped at a small motel on the outskirts of Châlons-sur-Marne. In the state I was in, I could not get out of the car. Somebody handed me the room key through the window. A woman, laughing her head off, followed me to my room with various toilet articles in her hand and called out, "Faites attention . . . vous étes trés sale . . ." As I soon discovered, she was the owner of the motel. As she was kindly helping me to wash the sticky mess off my back, she still could not stop laughing. "Toutte cette merde viens d'Alsace." She was saying, "Our rivers are poisoned and full of shit; there are no fish there anymore."

The degree of river pollution in a country as progressive as France was shocking. But this crazy incident brought back to my mind the jobs awaiting me at home. I was relieved to be so forcefully reminded that my obsession with the conservation of environment was, after all, soundly based. It was, I felt, more important that striving to land new commercial commissions. It was definitely high time to go home. The dream was coming back. And I was beginning to wonder what had been going on in Pound Ridge while I was away. Were there any changes at Pratt? It wasn't long before I found that my diary was full to bursting.

As my lectures and exercises increased in popularity, I was soon fully engaged with a growing numbers of students. Luckily, I got help in the shape of a Princeton educated architect with Polish-Jewish roots, Stuart Pertz, who joined me in handling the crowd. Counting the countries they came from, I arrived at the figure of thirty-five. In the architectural design class, the level of attainment among the students was far from uniform, and the work demanded infinite patience. I set my heart on making each one of them into a great architect. To help them understand the demands of their chosen profession and the need to take into account the requirements of the environment in every one of their designs, I gave every student an individual project to work on in their own country, on a site of their choosing. The course proved to be very successful, but the additional work it created took me by surprise. On the other hand, it offered me an unexpected bonus—it provided me with ample information about the wider world. Students from Nigeria, China, India, Korea, Brazil, Argentina, and Greece debated the pros and cons of their projects with those from Israel, Syria, and Morocco, and compared the rationale of their designs with American and European students. It was a veritable tower of Babel, spiced with much laughter and joking.

At home, we were trying to get Klara ready for Yale. It was the first time she would be leaving home. In the next two years, Lenta and I would be thinking of changing our bucolic lifestyle in New Canaan for the metropolitan one of New York with all its attractions and perils. We were getting tired of life in suburbia. Lenta, now largely free of her domestic duties, began thinking of finding some interesting pursuit. One obvious solution to our problem would be to find a small pied-à-terre in Manhattan. We had a stroke of luck; we came across a whole attic under the sloping roof of a five-story house built in the 1920s and thus rated by the local authorities as a "historical monument." The building is architecturally quite unusual; it was neglected and dilapidated though, but it did have an elevator going straight to the top.

The new apartment badly needed renovation, and it wasn't long before we started decorating and equipping our new home. And it came to us just at the right time. With three different courses to run, I was spending so many hours at the institute that not having to travel at night all the way to Connecticut would be a relief.

our "pied-à-terre"

In the meantime, the staff at the school continued to change. A Scotsman, Alan Foster, became our new dean. He took to organizing small meetings in his office after lectures. He kept a handy, well-supplied bar in the left-hand drawer of his desk. Having other work to do in the Cos Cob studio, I did not take part in these libations, but I heard on the grapevine that theirs was a rather thirsty company. Alan had invited me for a chat soon after starting his job. He poured two glasses of whisky and winked. "I see from the students' assessments," he said smiling, "that you are top of their list." What he was referring to was the end-of-semester assessment of lecturers by students, introduced after the students' revolt. "It has also reached my ears," he continued, "that another honor, outside the school, awaits you. You will hear about it soon, but this is confidential stuff, and remember, I have not uttered a word," he concluded, trying to look mysterious.

The mystery proved to be the American Institute of Architects, New York Chapter's, Brunner Award. I entered my project proposal for this annual award back in the spring, and it had totally escaped my mind. The 1973 competition covered the fields of architecture, town planning, and conservation of the environment. It was exactly up my street. I chose for my subject Newburg, a historical town situated on the mighty Hudson River, about seventy miles north of Manhattan. Winning the prestigious award and the allocation of funds necessary for the presentation within one year of the strategy to help Newburg, proved to be quite an event in my professional circles. A reporter came to interview me while the local press published articles about my alleged successes, though their information was obviously second or third hand. I was the first nonnative American to receive the prize, so they all mentioned my Polish origin and, on top of it, made me out to be one of three architects responsible for the postwar reconstruction of Warsaw, not to mention that they confused this, as usual, with the rebuilding of the Warsaw ghetto alone. In Aswan, I was supposed to have been instrumental in the construction of the High Dam on the Nile. To my great surprise, I had also learned that the Canadian government had entrusted me with saving its capital, Ottawa. My "successes" multiplied from one day to the next. So much for the accuracy of some reporting.

The students at the school came to congratulate me and to offer me their help. Also, one day, unexpectedly, I was invited to one of the students' apartments to celebrate the occasion. I was no stranger to students' rooms, where I would sometimes go to help with their projects. And I had no idea that something very different was in the offing this time. I was greeted by a small crowd of students of both sexes; there was wine, cheese, and music. Suddenly the doorbell rang. Two long-legged girls came in and slowly started to undress in front of me. This "artistic striptease" had been booked as a special treat for me. Toward the end of the performance, one of the hosts murmured in my ear, "You ought to get laid, Jerzy. You need to relax after all these successes; it will do you good." He pointed to a small mirror on the coffee table with several lines of white powder. "You must know that sex is free in our school." This information had never reached my ears before, but generally speaking, I was shocked by the lack of respect for my position as their professor. I took my leave promptly and relegated the episode to oblivion. But something else had happened then; for the first time, I was really annoyed by the excessively relaxed behavior and the lack of manners of our students.

I began to observe what Tyrmand called an "insupportable psychological degeneration of American youths." In his latest book, *Notebook of a Dilettante*, he critically compared their attitudes with the wartime generation, which, in his opinion, created the present greatness of the United States and, in the process, rebuilt war-scarred Europe. Looking at my surroundings from this perspective, I had to agree with him.

On October 1, 1973, on the Jewish Holiday of Yom Kippur, Egyptian forces crossed the Suez Canal and attacked the Israeli forces. It was the beginning of the third war in this region. My two Israeli students came to say good-bye. They were interrupting their studies to return home and join the army. This was quite a contrast to the attitude of their American colleagues, whose main preoccupation was to avoid the draft. We had a little farewell party, although nobody in the class expressed support for either one side or the other. After three weeks, a cease-fire was agreed and fighting on both sides of the Canal was stopped. The Egyptian president, Anwar Sadat, gained much respect as a politician. We took a particular interest in the events, as our old friend from the Cairo days, Boutros Boutros-Ghali, a professor of political sciences at Cairo University, became a close adviser to the president. Of special interest was the fact that he reached such a position in a Muslim country, even though he himself was a Coptic Christian while his wife Leia came from an affluent Alexandrian-Jewish family. All this brought back to us unforgettable memories, and maybe even a bit of nostalgia.

Suddenly, America and the rest of the industrialized world were reminded of how unstable the Middle East was. In November, an embargo on oil exports was imposed by the oil-producing cartel. To begin with, gasoline prices at the pumps went sky-high and then the supply dwindled. With the onset of winter, drastic measures, intended to reduce the consumption of oil, went into effect. For the first time since the Second World War, long lines of motorists waited all night at gas stations for the morning deliveries. Drivers were losing patience and nerves were frayed. Brawls, arguments, and even fistfights erupted. The customary smiles were disappearing. In adversity, Americans were getting angry, not used to being deprived of their usual comforts.

In December, in order to save energy, a three-day working week was introduced in England. A photograph from the Vatican showed Pope Paul VI in a horse-drawn carriage. At Rome's airport, Arab terrorists killed thirty-one people, before commandeering a plane to Kuwait. The name of Sheikh Ahmed Zaki Yamani, the Saudi petroleum minister, was used as a common expletive in endless rude remarks about the Arabs. These hostile reactions were additionally fed by the mortifying news of another highjacking of a passenger plane, shootings of hostages, and other unheard of acts of terror.

The press demanded that Western governments concentrate their entire available technical and scientific resources to end the

Western world's dependency on foreign oil. Suddenly, as if from one day to the next, the ecological movement gained another urgent objective: the promotion of safe sources of energy without the devastation of the natural environment and without the danger of nuclear or chemical pollution. The students began designing houses equipped with primitive devices for the exploitation of solar energy. The automobile industry displayed new prototypes of hybrid electrical or battery-operated engines. New sources of energy were explored, such as those obtained from plants, from wind power and ocean waves.

Researchers in institutes of technology endeavored to improve existing techniques and explore new avenues. There were popular demands for investing funds equal to those thrown at space exploration into finding new sources of energy, other than fossil fuels. The security of the Western world seemed to depend on self-reliance in the field of energy. Radical opinions were voiced against American dependence on unstable, autocratic Arab states artificially created after WWI.

But in the end, nothing really changed; and even now, years later, our economy is still based on oil. We can only speculate what went wrong. What was missing was leadership, such as could be provided by USA, the only economic and political power embracing the entire world. Was this another unfortunate result of the American involvement in the unnecessary and expensive war in Vietnam? Or was it the lack of a direct challenge, such as in its time provided by the Soviet *Sputnik*? Or was it President Nixon's pathetic response to the Watergate affair, engendered by his own greed for power? It is possible that all these elements played their part, but the opposition by vested interests, such as the huge international industry, embracing oil, mining, and automobile companies, played a far from secondary role.

The year was ending with an avalanche of problems hitting us from all sides and over which we had no control. Some optimistic events, though, lifted the gloom threatening to engulf us before Christmas. The greatest surprise for me personally came with an article in the *New York Times*, stating, among other things, that

Poland, forever at odds with herself and her place on the map, appeared more at peace than she had been since WWII. The country depicted in the news was very different from the one, which we had known under Communism. Coming as it did against the background of the turbulent events in America, it did provoke a fleeting thought, had our immigration really been a step in the right direction?

21

Between Routine and Anxiety

My notes for the period in question show no great changes in our family's life, nothing that might have affected our day-to-day existence. Klara embarked on her freshman year in Yale. Lenta was working in an art gallery within easy reach of home, a blessing in a city the size of New York and an advantage envied by many. In contrast, I had to travel a great deal all over the place: to Brooklyn to give lectures, to our studio in Cos Cob, and to Pound Ridge. Each car journey took at least an hour one way. The fuel crisis was still hurting; and by the time winter came, the price of gasoline had gone up by 80 percent. House owners grumbled about the increasing cost of heating. There were no signs of any improvement in view as the Middle East conflict continued unabated while the enormous costs of the Vietnam War, in blood and money, were steadily mounting.

In the meantime, another kind of war—to become known as the Watergate affair—was going on between President Nixon's administration and Congress. The president hindered the progress of the investigation and categorically denied any knowledge of the burglary in the offices of the Democrats, his political opponents. His apologists trivialized the incident as a botched operation by petty thieves. But the affair blew up in the president's face when, unexpectedly, information was leaked about the existence of tapes of all the verbal exchanges taking place in the Oval Office. All this was taking place soon after the resignation of the Vice President Spiro Agnew, accused of embezzlement. He was replaced by Gerard Ford.

The noose round the president's neck was thus inexorably tightening. The legal battles about to begin held some personal undertones for us, inasmuch as Dick Beckler, the lawyer engaged to act for one of the White House defendants, used to be a neighbor and an old acquaintance of ours on Kimberley Place. He had moved since to Washington DC, where he was working for a big, influential firm of lawyers, getting a lot of government work. Beckler's name would later acquire the epithet of "pit bull of a lawyer" and frequently appear on the front pages of newspapers.

As I had discovered the previous summer, people in Europe were not particularly interested in the Watergate affair. Did this indifference stem from an instinctive recognition of the enormous self-healing power of the American polity both externally and internally? In the opinion of foreigners, the affair was no more than a temporary local crisis to be expected in a democracy. In contrast, in the USA, the affair continued to claim the front pages of newspapers for months. Most people followed the affair with great interest; but amazingly, its potential danger to the state was never raised. In spite of the political, economic, and military difficulties, and other problems facing America and the world. No question was raised of a possible threat from abroad.

From our European and particularly Polish historic perspective, it seemed that no country could survive such a multitude of problems. Yet America's position in the world was so secure that there could be no threat of invasion, no ultimatums, and no attempts at diplomatic humiliation. To us, relatively new immigrants, this was quite incredible and thought provoking. Furthermore, in spite of all his problems at home, Nixon embarked on a series of visits abroad to an invariably enthusiastic reception. In the Middle East, whether in Egypt, Syria, Israel, or Jordan, he was being met by cheering crowds. In Arab countries, such demonstrations are invariably orchestrated by the rulers; but the fact that it had happened even in such a democratic country as Israel, could only mean that Watergate was a purely American problem. Soon after, Nixon visited the Soviet Union. He drank toasts with Brezhnev, opened exhibitions, received flowers from smiling girls with pigtails and the red scarves of Communist Pioneers around their necks, and, toward the end of his visit, attended a ceremony commemorating "the Nazi massacre of 150 Belorussians in 1943," in Khatyn of all places. I was not sure whether it was a case of American naïveté and the American press not recognizing the Soviet perfidy, or whether it could be ascribed to Kissinger's Realpolitik? What hypocrisy! The 1940 massacre of thousands of Polish officers, prisoners of war in Katyń and in other camps in the Soviet Union, for which at the time the Soviets blamed the Germans, was now perfidiously presented as the murder of a handful of unknown Belorussians in Khatyn. The *New York Times* noted the fact of the visit without comment. It would be surprising if they did not know the controversy surrounding the infamous place, spelled Katyń. It was only after the collapse of the USSR that the Russian president admitted that the Polish officers, nearly twenty four thousands, were indeed murdered on Stalin's order.

In July, sports writers from the world soccer championships in Munich reported the defeat of Brazil by the Polish team. However, as soccer was not a popular sport in USA, the fact itself was not of great significance; and the only object of the exercise was to show a photograph of our foreign secretary, Kissinger, raising both arms in despair at the Polish victory. We did not have many supporters in USA at the time.

The indefatigable secretary of state, Henry Kissinger, kept circulating between the Middle Eastern, European, and Asian capitals, trying to get the Arabs and Israelis on one hand and the Vietnamese on the other to initiate some talks, agree on an armistice, or to provide some other form of diplomatic aspirin. All to no avail. Evidently, the world chose to ignore American headaches. Yet Kissinger, though publicly disappointed in the defeat of his favorite team, had never shown any disappointment at the failures of his own diplomatic efforts. Dismal news of the lack of progress in the Egypt-Israeli conflict, of the breakup of the Paris talks with

North Vietnam, and of the Soviet-engineered difficulties in the discussions regarding the reduction of nuclear arsenals were invariably accompanied by photographs of the man, pressing flesh with a broad smile on his face.

Perhaps it was only once that I saw a picture of Kissinger looking ill at ease. The photo was taken in the Oval Office. President Nixon was kneeling and motioning to Kissinger to kneel down beside him. These were the dying moments of his presidency, and the sarcastic caption questioned whether the president was humbly asking God's forgiveness or praying for a miracle.

At the beginning of August, in a televised speech to the nation, Nixon officially resigned from office. He did not blame anybody, but equally expressed no remorse for his errors or for having caused the paralysis, lasting close on two years, of the executive and legislative arms of the nation, and that in the middle of an exceedingly difficult political situation. He had engineered the crisis for his own personal reasons and in order to stay in power. Apparently, the great and mighty of this world do not recognize the norms, which they themselves wish to impose on us ordinary mortals. The whole affair was a bitter lesson in how easily power corrupts, but also that in a true democracy right eventually prevails.

A week after being sworn in as the new president, Gerard Ford pardoned Nixon and thus cut short the legal proceedings against him. Ford was now the sixth president in power during the Vietnam War. By that time, practically nobody knew why the country got into that war in the first place or how it could extricate itself from it. At the beginning of the new parliamentary session, in the traditional message to the combined Houses of Congress, the president's statement that "the state of the Union is not good," was an unprecedented admission of the errors of his predecessors. It was clear that the main reason for this bad state of affairs was the unwarranted war.

In spite of ten years of brutal warfare, carpet bombing, and enormous losses suffered by the civilian population, the leaders of North Vietnam raised a huge army, numerically the fifth biggest in the world, at least according to the American press. Four months later, the South Vietnamese armies and their American allies ceased all resistance. The American embassy in Saigon was evacuated on April 30, 1976. Refugees in their tens of thousands were taking to ships and planes. The TV screens all over the world showed the dramatic escape of the last helicopter from the embassy roof with people, terrified of being left behind, holding on to its undercarriage. The Communist victory was absolute.

For us, who put all our hopes in USA, this defeat, combined with the American loss of face especially in the eyes of her enemies, proved a tough nut to crack. All kinds of hitherto little-known matters were now coming to the fore, contributing to the general feeling of despondency. The treatment meted out to Vietnam veterans returning home became a great problem. Excepting their immediate families, they were met with complete indifference. No official "welcome home" meetings were staged, no traditional parades arranged. The question of their sacrifice split the nation. Consequently, thousands of severely wounded men and invalids took to the streets in protest marches and demonstrations.

On the whole, the situation could but leave one with a bitter taste in the mouth. And as far as I was personally concerned, as a veteran of the Second World War who returned to Poland in 1947 only to be told that I had been fighting on the wrong, i.e., capitalist side—it brought back memories.

Lenta and I were rather depressed by the turn of events; but suddenly, a chance of a new and interesting job imbued me with new energy and put an end to the joyless contemplation of the fate of the world.

22

The Maamura Dreams

Egypt Air's Paris—Cairo flight departure was already delayed by almost four hours. I had browsed through all the newspaper and magazine stands in the terminal and had drunk several glasses of wine. Now I was aimlessly pacing to and fro the whole length of the waiting hall. An attractive woman sitting along my path smiled every time I passed her. I wasn't sure whether it was my restless pacing, which was amusing her or whether she was engrossed in her own thoughts. After my umpteenth hike past her, she did, however, look up at me, pointing to the seat next to her. "Do relax. Fretting won't make us depart any sooner." Both of us laughed. "We could talk instead about the adventures, which might await us in Egypt," she added, inclining her head and sweeping back her thick auburn hair. "OK," I replied, amused. "By all means, let us play at foretelling the future. You start." She stretched out her hand. "My name is Christianne, and I am flying to Cairo to meet my husband who is waiting there . . . apparently full of longing," she laughed, looking at me aslant, her head still inclined." "Yes, but how will it affect the adventures you seem to have in mind?" "That will become clearer when you tell me what your plans there are." I was beginning to enjoy myself; this lighthearted chat was such a relief after the hours of waiting.

At last we were boarding the plane. The throng of tired and anxious passengers surged ahead, ignoring the helpless Egyptian ticket-control agent. Christianne and I, holding hands, pushed our way to the cabin and grabbed the nearest two seats. The Egyptian crew, typically unconcerned, did not intervene. Inshallah (It's all in Allah's hands). Once settled in our seats, we continued our interrupted conversation, which was turning more and more into a not altogether innocent flirtation. I learned from further conversation that her father-in-law was the head of an international building concern specializing in the erection of entire settlements of prefabricated multistory housing. Her husband had apparently just completed negotiations with the Egyptian government. "But now it's time to relax," she laughed nervously, pushing her fingers through her hair and casting a sidelong glance at me. "What a coincidence,"" I said. "I too am going to Egypt at the invitation of friends to get Egyptian architects interested in the new American building technology." "Wonderful, you must work together!" she exclaimed with childish naïveté. So saying, she turned in her seat, and put her legs across my knees. "Could you get those high boots off for me, they are rather tight." Next, she raised the armrest between our seats, rolled into a ball, put her head in my lap, whispered *bonne nuit,* and within minutes was fast asleep.

We landed in Cairo after 2:00 a.m. An old-time friend, Raouf, was waiting for me. His brother, Boutros Boutros-Ghali, was at the time minister of state in the Ministry of Foreign Affairs. I was very touched by Raouf's kindness, meeting someone at that unearthly hour at the cold Cairo airport was not a pleasure. He took me to the Omar Khayam Hotel on the Zamalek island, the neighborhood where we had lived during our stay in Egypt. The hotel itself had originally been the palace erected in 1869 by Khedive Ismail, the ruler of Egypt, for Eugenie, the wife of Napoleon III. She stayed there briefly to attend the ceremonial opening of the Suez Canal. Its interior was a bewildering collection of gigantic wall mirrors in gilded frames, massive crystal chandeliers, Persian carpets, not to mention the enormous marble staircase and the wealth of sculptured details.

Great changes had taken place in Egypt in 1974. President Sadat had turned his back on his predecessor's, Nasser's, socialism and was increasingly opening the country to foreign investors. My present journey to Egypt was precipitated by a telephone call from Cairo, which I took one day in Pound Ridge. It from was Leia, wife of Boutros, who visited with us the year before and with whom I had been corresponding ever since. She told me that she knew of circles in Cairo who were interested in my Egyptian experience and possible contacts in the USA. She suggested that I come to Egypt, where her brother-in-law Raouf would be glad to effect the necessary introductions.

At the time, people with any interest in Egypt were trying hard to find out more about the business openings offered by Sadat's program. My contacts proved to be first class. I had a number of curious, even strange, meetings with people, about whom I would subsequently get more information from Raouf. They were a bunch of pseudo-businessmen who suddenly appeared from nowhere following the fall of Nasser's Socialism; they offered contacts with dubious officials, probably the usual swindlers and impostors. I had never dealt with people like that in my previous dealings in Egypt, restricted as they had been to government agencies. Hearing my accounts, Raouf laughed. "Mais mon cher, c'est comme ca, c'est la vie [But, my dear friend, that's life]. This is the Middle East for you; everyone trades with everyone else. It's also human nature. No Communism or Socialism will ever be able to eradicate man's instinct to improve his lot by grasping any available chance. If I were you, I would explore contacts, note useful addresses and, when you are back to the US, think whether and how you could make use of any of that information." It was easy for him to offer such advice, but I was entering uncharted waters, potentially dangerous yet rather exciting, tantalizing at times.

For instance, one of my objectives was to find land for a sizeable housing development. This could be a good start for possible cooperation with Egyptian architects and for bringing in novel construction technologies from the West. Consequently, instinctively feeling my way in various meetings, but determinedly refusing to hand out the expected sweeteners and advance payments, I eventually shortened my list to a group of three architects who seemed truly interested in my proposal. Two of them had studied in Switzerland and had Swiss wives, while the third had contacts in the Ministry of Housing.

We arranged for a foursome meeting in the suburb of Maadi, an Egyptian garden city. Taher, one of my new friends, told me that we would have to deal with another layer of middlemen. "Leave it to me, don't say anything," he said. "I'll present our proposal." A jovial, portly gentleman received us in his impressive office, ordered coffee, and with a rigid smile listened to Taher's peroration. Naturally, I did not understand a word. Eventually, with a serious mien, he firmly shook my hand and passed into good English. "All right gentlemen . . . I think that Maamura will provide just the land you need to start." Then he turned to me and explained, "This is a large area at the seaside, just behind the palace of ex-king Farouk, east of Alexandria. Shall we meet there in two days time?"

Such success after only four days in Egypt! Or at least that's what it looked like. The next day, in high spirits and running down the stairs, I almost collided with Christianne. I did not even know that she was staying in the same hotel. She too was on her way to breakfast, and we joined her husband who was already sitting at a table. A handsome, thirty-something man with a mane of thick black hair reaching down to his shoulders, he looked like an actor rather than a building contractor. He and his wife had just returned from a short excursion to Upper Egypt. They planned to stay a few more days in Cairo. They were both very pleasant, and it was good to talk to them. He mentioned the constant difficulties he had been having with the authorities in finalizing his contract for starting a factory of prefabricated housing components. I had some knowledge of the industry from my time in Warsaw, even though such factories did not operate in Poland until after my departure. I had heard about their operations in the Soviet Union. I remarked that their technology had probably been brought to Poland via Moscow.

Our professional talk was interrupted by Christianne, "Perhaps we could do something, go somewhere together? Georges (she translated my name into French) used to live here and knows the city well." A good idea, I thought. "I have been invited to visit friends of mine tonight. If you are free, why don't you come along?" Our good friends, Nadia and Zohair Faried, lived nearby, on the ninth floor of a modern apartment block on the shore of the Nile. Zohair was a physician and worked in a tropical diseases research laboratory, one of several in the world run by the American Navy. He was Lenta's and my family doctor during our time in Cairo. Both he and his wife were very good-looking, with the classical features of ancient Egyptians as seen on Pharaonic frescoes. They were related to the Ghali family, and were, like them, Copts, and thus not of Arab origin.

Zohair

The Farieds' apartment was, as usual, full of interesting people. Everybody who was anybody in Cairo was there, the Ghali family, some other relations, professors at the American University, archaeologists, bureau chiefs of the main American and European weeklies, and some remaining members of the old royal family. Nadia and I reminisced on how we danced the night away on New Year's Eve 1966, which Lenta and I had hosted in our Cairo apartment just round the corner. Nadia kept looking from Christianne to me and back again. "You know," she said suddenly to Christianne with a kind of warning in her voice, "that Jerzy's wife was known at that time as a real beauty, quite legendary here in town. She was dubbed a true Miss Universe . . . *sans blague* . . . seriously." What she said was true, but why did it sound like a warning and who was it for?

Nadia

Anyhow, what could I do about it? The evening was more than successful, so we walked along the river back to the hotel in very high spirits. Christianne asked her husband for his visiting card and put her private telephone number on it. He watched patiently with a smile.

My stay in the Middle East was unexpectedly extended. My newly acquired Egyptian friends arranged a meeting for me in Beirut with representatives of Kuwaiti firms who might provide the necessary funds. My visit to that city just reinforced my wanderlust. At the time, Beirut was at the peak of its prosperity. I stopped in a smallish, elegant hotel called the Georges, just like the hotel in Lwów I remembered from my youth. It stood on a rocky peninsula overlooking the anchorage of the yacht club and an adjacent small beach, the haunt of the town's glamorous youth of both sexes.

I was sitting in the hotel's wood-paneled bar when a man whose face seemed familiar sat down next to me. But as he offered me a long Cuban cigar from his silver case, I was no longer sure. "I wonder whether you are taking me for someone else," I said. "No, not at all," he protested. "But let us now forget about all business. I am here on leave," he pointed to his dark blue silk suit. It suddenly clicked; I might have recognized him more quickly had he worn his habitual Arab dress. This was Sheikh Ahmed Zaki Yamani, the notorious Saudi minister of petroleum and mineral resources. We never mentioned the fuel crisis, but I had a feeling that I had found myself by chance in a situation rather above my head. It was an appropriate commentary to my whole Middle Eastern adventure.

The hotel's interior reminded me of the prewar 1930s style. The nearby Hamra Street, the commercial artery of the city, redolent of prosperity, lined with the best restaurants and shops, displayed goods from all over the world. The campus of the American University, where I went to visit Ed Bye's friend, was arguably the most perfect site for an academic establishment that I have ever come across. I vaguely remembered the city from nine years ago, when we had visited here as a family, but the changes since then were remarkable. The streets were alive day and night.

The meetings I had were looking quite promising. The Kuwaitis were interested in the Maamura project and gave me the addresses of their representatives in Alexandria. That was one step forward. I don't quite remember the actual chain of events and how I met in Beirut the tall, broad-shouldered American by the name of Penn. He lived in a large apartment in the city center, distinguished by its vast terrace, nestling just above the tops of blooming trees and boughs of bougainvillea.

For a change, it was he who was seeking my cooperation, though, in his words, he disposed of wide contacts in the Middle East. "Money," he told me, "was plentiful in Beirut; ideas, though, in short supply. Real estate development was an excellent investment." I knew that was true. He was amazingly frank in our conversation. But he did not have a good word for the "natives," and this did not augur well for our future relationship. He spoke of Arabs disdainfully, as if he had no understanding of the complex geographic situation and multiethnic problems contributing to conflicts in this part of the world. This attitude of certain representatives of American authorities and, in particular, of their intelligence services, would later cause great problems for the USA and leave it open to criticism of ignorance in the international forum. That put some doubts into my mind. Whence came all the contacts he was boasting of? He dropped hints about having worked at some stage in intelligence and having even been in charge of the Beirut agency. Was he a CIA agent? Interesting. Having taken early retirement, he told me, he was now looking for other work. It might be relevant. When he left the terrace, his wife came up close to me, put an arm round my neck, and asked me to pour her quickly a full glass of gin. When her husband returned, he made a rather vulgar scene. He screamed at her, and pointing his finger at her, yelled at me, "She is an alcoholic! She mustn't touch the stuff!" It certainly remained a memorable evening. Some time later, he came to see me in New York and in Connecticut; and as a result of his visit, I went with him to Baghdad. But that is another story.

In the taxi, on the way to the airport, as I was leaving Beirut, I noticed a large settlement of shacks, barracks, some buildings made of concrete blocks. A variety of rags or were they clothes? fluttered on lines in the wind. Crowds of children, mongrel dogs, and goats roamed the narrow streets. "What is it?" I asked in amazement. "Shatila," answered the cabby, "the Palestinian refugee camp. It was supposed to be temporary, but they've been here close to thirty years. It's already quite a problem, but what will happen in a few more years? God only knows."

On my return journey, I gave my mother a surprise and stopped in her apartment in Paris for a few days. The future seemed bright. I was aware, though, of my limitations. I was on my own, backed neither by an established financial institution nor by a government agency. However, the advantage lay in my complete independence, and that was an important aspect. Or was I being an incorrigible madcap?

I returned to New York a couple of days before the start of the new semester. The city was struggling to dig its way out of mounds of snow left untouched because of some trade union trouble. It had been quite a respite to be away from New York's reality. Already in the plane, on my way home, I had plans for changes in my professional life. The magic of Egypt, combined with the reminiscences of my time there, opened a floodgate of ideas. But what about Lenta? I could foresee her response. She hated change. My ideas would just make her anxious. Getting her to leave Manhattan and New Canaan would be a major problem. But then, who wanted to move out?

I needed more people to work on the Pound Ridge and Newburgh projects and hired several of my students as well as Jan Dąbrowski, a younger graduate of the Warsaw school of architecture. Having spent some years in France, Jan, with his wife Magdalena, a vivacious young woman, made his way to New York, hoping to get involved in some grand projects. He too was full of enthusiasm for the planning of new towns and became disillusioned by the dearth of opportunities, while she was determined, come what may, to study history of art. In spite of our initial skepticism, she became eventually one of the most talented curators of contemporary art at MOMA, the Museum of Modern Art and the Metropolitan

Museum, with a number of important publications and exhibitions to her credit.

My visit raised a lot of general interest in Egypt, but the majority of inquiries concerned potential work openings. I found a good contact in the international chain of Ritz-Carlton luxury hotels, whose president was ready to accompany me, together with his wife, on our planned March expedition to Alexandria. The date coincided with my two-week spring break at the institute. It was exciting to leave by helicopter from the top of the Pan Am Building in the heart of Manhattan directly to the plane waiting at the airport. There were stopovers in Paris and in Athens. In Athens, I met with an owner of a shipping company who invited me to lunch in a seaside restaurant in Pireus. He told me how his family had been expelled from Egypt in Nasser's time, even though they had lived in Alexandria for generations. In view of the changes taking place there now, he was thinking of returning to the town of his birth. "Yours is a very interesting project. As you may know, we Greeks have been investing in Egypt for generations," he said. "After all Alexandria, as history tells us, was built by the Greeks. But I have to be absolutely sure," he continued, "that this Socialism of theirs has really come to an end."

Virgil's words in Aeneid, about the Trojan horse, learned at school, came into my mind: *Timeo Danaos et dona ferentes* (I fear the Greeks even when they bring gifts). Well, it might apply to gifts, I thought, as much as it did during the Trojan War, but when the Greeks talk business, one ought to listen to them. "What do you actually mean by 'the end of Socialism'?" I asked.

"It's simple. In this kind of system, whether it's Socialism or Communism, the state organism inevitably grows a hard shell of organizations that inexorably create a huge army of employees whose livelihood and welfare are totally bound up with this shell. Socialism may die, but the shell endures. If the Maamura land has become part of such a shell, no one will be able to dislodge it. And we, the developers, may bleed to death, financially speaking, trying to get in. The people involved will not allow any change." Travel broadens the mind; what a useful addition to my education, I thought.

A week later, we knew for sure that Maamura was an inseparable part of the old Socialist shell described by the wise Greek businessman. Nobody told us, but it became quite obvious that the pyramid of interdependent interests and loyalties would not be demolished. What used to be state property was now held in dozens of rapacious hands, and none of the people involved gave two hoots about the foreign investment, which their poor country needed so much.

A month later, the civil war in Lebanon was to break out, and in the following ten years Beirut would be almost completely destroyed. And so was my dream of Maamura.

23

Scandals, Lies, Wars, and Hope

My routine work plus several trips to Egypt occupied me to the point that I tended to ignore the rather unusual events taking place in the world. In addition to the outrages perpetrated by Palestinian terrorists—as they were being referred to at the time—against Israel, mainly in Europe and in the Middle East, unexpectedly, acts of terror erupted closer to home, targeting the USA government. In Washington, a bomb placed in the State Department caused six thousand employees to be evacuated and stopped work for many hours. Responsibility was claimed by the Weather Underground, an organization hitherto unknown to the nation at large, whose aim was to overthrow the U.S. government and radically change American policy, no less. This and other groups frequently and openly advocated racism and armed action. They attracted former soldiers, anarchists, members of intolerant pseudo-religious sects, and other adventurers. They sprang up mostly in sparsely populated northwestern states such as Montana, Wyoming, or Utah, still imbued with the myths of the Wild West, cowboy sagas, and Indian wars. A new less romantic and less attractive local history was emerging, waiting in turn for its place in popular literature and films.

Similarly, New York had nothing to boast about this summer. Strikes involving the police force and the employees of the city's departments resulted in chaos in the streets and the collapse of norms of civilized behavior. All kind of louts, encouraged by the prospect of impunity, amused themselves by setting fire to the pyramids of trash in plastic bags cluttering the pavements. The plague of rats, the stench of rotting refuse, and the smoldering remains completed the picture of this capital of the Western world.

The financial collapse of the city resulted in the creation of MAC, the Municipal Assistance Corporation, a new body with special powers to reform the city authorities and to reorganize the corrupt city hierarchy. It was headed by Felix Rohatyn, a renowned financier and philanthropist. The man's origins, frequently referred to by himself, were interesting. He was born in a well-to-do family of Jewish immigrants from southeastern Poland. Their fate, and several similar cases I knew of, symbolized for me the great losses suffered by Poland as a result of war, Communism, and further waves of immigration, which all deprived the country of the pick of the intelligentsia, its crème de la crème.

For some considerable time, the question most frequently discussed was the Jewish emigration from the Soviet Union to Israel. Congressional support pushed it to the fore of American foreign policy. Kremlin's stubborn refusal to issue passports to the would-be immigrants even led, at one stage, to the suspension of economic cooperation with USSR. What never occurred to anyone at that stage was how the open American support for Israel might become a factor in the radicalization of Islam and of its political arms. It reminded us unfavorably of the Katyń question, which, having been raised in the 1950s by a Senate committee, had never led to any political action. The massacre of thousands of Polish officers seemed not to warrant any change in the American administration's accepted conciliatory policy toward Moscow. Poland has been firmly placed in the Soviet sphere of influence, and that remained an accepted fact. Israel was clearly in a more favorable situation.

Then we learned about the international conference of thirty-five countries to be held in Helsinki. In the absence of a postwar pan-European peace conference, its aim was to confirm the status quo. The immigrant circles in America criticized the Helsinki agreement as a great victory for the Soviets, and as a confirmation by the West of the acceptance of the postwar borders and of the Soviet annexation of the Baltic states. Nevertheless, the new president, Gerard Ford, wishing to use the occasion to improve his hitherto negative image, decided to embark on his first visit to Europe. On his way to Helsinki, he stopped in Warsaw, where he was apparently enthusiastically received by crowds of people all waving small American flags. I received an interesting report of the event from Izabella, our friend who gave us shelter in Providence on our arrival in America as immigrants. At the time, she happened to be visiting Warsaw with her eight-year-old son. The boy, a proper little American, also asked for his Stars and Stripes, but his mother explained to him that this time there was nothing warranting a cheering of this American president. Several passersby, hearing her explanation, also put their flags away.

At home, meanwhile, the image of the president and his administration was further deteriorating, particularly in New York, a city verging on bankruptcy. Banks were refusing to lend it any more money. Local authorities were firing staff in large numbers. In September, teachers in public schools went on strike, and roughly a million children found their schools closed. The city's treasury was empty. Over eight billion dollars were required to put the city back on its feet. The negotiations and talks with a variety of agencies presided over by Felix Rohatyn lasted well into the night, virtually to the critical hour before the city was declared bankrupt. The affair had repercussions throughout the world. There was panic on European stock exchanges. The price of gold shot up. All currency transactions stopped. New York's insolvency could have far-reaching consequences in the entire country. Was that the haven that we chose as a refuge from a corrupt world?

It was actually the teachers' union that saved the city by offering to buy New York City bonds ignored by other buyers for some considerable time. The union used dollars from its pension fund in an unprecedented and risky transaction to which the other unions also gave their support. In turn, the city undertook to introduce draconian cuts in its budget and layoffs of over ten thousand employees in its building department. Our profession's future was endlessly discussed in the school of architecture and—though in the event, the misgivings proved unduly pessimistic—our mood verged on depression.

This tense situation lasted a whole month. It was an unprecedented experience, living in a city under siege, yet besieged not by foreign armies outside its walls, but by inept officials and politicos within. In this case, so different from our Polish customs and experience, no help would come from building barricades nor mounting cavalry charges. The conflicts here involved different approaches to economic problems, namely skilful negotiations, payment timetables, valid pledges, financial guarantees. Consequently, the temporary escape from catastrophe was received with a deep sigh of relief. However, the pledged funds were still far from sufficient, and private New York banks were still refusing loans, pending a guarantee from the federal administration. Mayor Abraham Beam went to Washington DC to meet with President Ford. However, the following day, the big headline of one of New York's newspapers proclaimed, FORD TO NEW YORK: DROP DEAD! This was, obviously, not what the president had in mind; but it would appear that, reading from his Republican bible, he believed that grants or even loans with no guarantee of repayment were the worst possible kind of help. And rightly so, like giving starving fishermen fish instead of providing them with nets.

His opponents, on the other hand, went on reproaching him that during his long term in Congress he had voted against every single act of social legislation.

In October, in San Francisco, an exasperated woman attempted to shoot the president. She did not succeed; but inevitably, some political confusion followed, and the administration had to give more thought to the social ills affecting the people. After all, USA was the only industrialized Western democracy whose citizens were not covered by a general health insurance, where no secure pension awaited people after long years of work in private companies, where there were no state-endowed nursery schools, and where many other social services taken for granted in most of Europe and in Canada were missing. All this was reflected in the 1976 presidential campaign. The governor of California, Ronald Reagan, put forward his candidature and strongly criticized both the internal and the foreign policy of the administration. The gauntlet thrown down by Ronald Reagan was picked up by Jimmy Carter, the practically unknown governor of Georgia, put forward by the Democratic Party as their presidential candidate.

The New Year 1976 was greeted as a harbinger of major changes. The cup had seemed to overflow, at least in the opinion of the more liberal circles. The economic stagnation had led Kosygin, the prime minister of USSR, to declare at the Twenfty-fifth Congress of the Soviet Communist Party that in economic terms USSR had already overtaken America. This was of course pure fantasy, but it left its mark. In New York, in the meantime, one became aware of changes. The city looked better. Police patrolled the streets. Preparations were under way for the two hundredth anniversary of the Declaration of Independence on the fourth of July. Dozens of foreign sailing vessels were expected to participate in a great gala in the port of New York. They started arriving some days before the festivities and dropped anchor in the port roads. A forest of masts and rigging was visible from the tip of Manhattan. The newspapers gave full descriptions of these beautiful ships, the dates of their construction, and records of the naval schools training the young crews in the tradition of seafaring.

We were lucky, having secured a place at the windows of a high office building on the very tip of Manhattan, to have a perfect view. We watched the ships as they were passing, the Italian *Amerigo Vespucci*, Soviet *Kreuzenstern*, Argentinian *Liberdad*, Japanese *Nippon Maru*, Columbian *Gloria*, and, of course, the Polish *Dar Pomorza*, not to mention many, many others. Later, groups of sailors from various nations, in white summer uniforms, wandered the streets, an unusual sight at a time when uniforms were no longer popular and were rarely seen in the city. This was thus the happy anniversary of the birth of this great and beautiful country, which, however, had also witnessed in its history some surprisingly tragic events. Just at that very moment, we heard the results of the public opinion polls in Europe: the Republican administration had the lowest possible ratings, and the prestige of America was at its lowest for over twenty years.

A fierce presidential campaign continued in full swing. On the Republican side, President Ford kept beating off Ronald Reagan's increasingly forceful attacks; while in the Democratic Party, the list of presidential candidates was headed by Jimmy Carter. At the end of July, the press carried pictures of Carter and Zbigniew Brzeziński, whom Carter had recently nominated as his foreign policy adviser. It was a source of great satisfaction to us to see someone we had once personally known elevated to such an exalted position.

For the first time, we too were truly involved in the coming presidential election, wholeheartedly supporting Carter to the point that spotting the latter stand in an open car, I was touched to the point of tears. Up till then, I was not totally conscious of how all the scandals, lies, the evidence of daily unfairness, the unnecessary wars were causing me to yearn for change. I also fully understood that it was only in a democratic country that this kind of audacious hope had any chance of fulfillment. American Poles were quite shocked by the great gaff committed by Gerard Ford in his second televised debate with Carter. Asked about political freedom in Eastern Europe, he stated that in his opinion Poland and other countries in that region were free of Soviet domination. And this was soon after Flora Lewis, the doyenne of foreign correspondents, reported on the growing crisis in Poland. She believed that the situation has reached a point as explosive as that preceding the 1956 riots. After that, I lost any shred of trust in that Republican administration's ability to make sense of foreign affairs.

In November, Jimmy Carter won the election and confirmed Polish born Zbigniew Brzeziński as the chief of the National Security Council. That was only the second case, after German born Henry Kissinger, that the job went to a foreign-born American.

One of the first acts of the new president after his inauguration was to declare an amnesty for deserters and draft dodgers; his intention was to unite and reconcile the country still deeply divided since the Vietnam War. Unfortunately, this provoked demonstrations by Vietnam veterans. Old wounds were taking a long time to heal. As for myself, the New Year started with yet another invitation to the Middle East.

24

Abu Tartur and What Came of It

After ten years' work at the Pratt Institute, I was beginning to get restless. My contract was about to expire anyway, and I was not sure whether I wanted to continue. At the same time, I was too old and not really attracted to the idea of starting a freelance architectural practice in a city the size of New York. Perhaps once more, the adventurous side of my nature was gaining the upper hand and was propelling me to new, greener pastures. My recent Egyptian solo adventure was obviously not the way to do it. I applied to the United Nations Development Programme (UNDP) for consulting work abroad; and eventually, I was asked to attend an interview at the United Nations Industrial Development Organization (UNIDO) in the new skyscraper opposite the old building of the UN Secretariat. My interviewer was a tall, wide shouldered Barbadian who did not beat about the bush. "Abu Tartur," he said without any preambles, "is a large semicircular plateau with

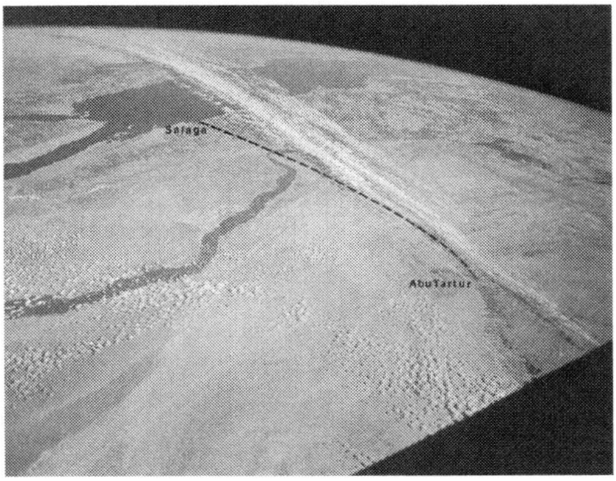

Abu Tartur

high escarpment rising over a sandy desert. Let me show you a picture of the area taken by the *Apollo* crew." He smiled, showing his very white regular teeth. Raising his index finger, he fished out from his desk drawer with his other hand a color photograph and placed it before me. It showed a segment of the globe. "Are you about to send me into space?" I quipped, getting hold of the photo. "No," he answered, "unfortunately, this office could not offer you anything that attractive. But look here," he pointed with his finger, "this might interest you. You can see the escarpment outlined by the shadow, which it is casting over the desert. It is about hundred and fifty miles west of the Nile valley. Our question is, would you undertake a month's mission to inspect local conditions with a view to designing and building of a new town to serve a planned industrial development in this area?" This sounded too good to be true. An offer I could not refuse. But what was coming next? I kept silent and waited for what was to follow. "The Egyptian government is now exploring in earnest the chances of attracting foreign capital to invest in the exploitation of the great, untouched natural resources of the country, which would at the same time provide some badly needed employment. One of the projects under consideration is the exploitation of the enormous deposits of phosphates visible even to the naked eye in the Abu Tartur escarpment. The planned fertilizer factory would provide employment for a lot of workers who, with their families, would number some thirty thousand people.

"So you are talking of building a town in the middle of a desert far from civilization to house a large number of people who would also require the usual facilities: schools, clinics, shops, entertainment, etc. Am I right?"

"Correct, but this isn't all. Following local processing, the fertilizers would be transported by a specially built railway line across the Nile to Safaga, a small port on the Red Sea some four hundred miles distant." He remained silent for a moment. "So what do you think?"

The very mention of Safaga dispelled any doubts I might have had as to this unexpected proposition. After all, this was the very town, the development of which was the project on which I had worked with my students some fourteen years ago soon after my arrival in USA. So how could I miss a chance of converting all our fantasies and ideas into reality? "Of course I agree," I said. "We thought you would," answered my interviewer, not even trying to hide his wide smile.

The day before the school's spring break, I was ready to leave. Taking a short break in Paris to visit my mother and few friends, I arrived in Cairo. I was met there at the airport by Samir, an old employee of the Aswan project, now working in the Cairo office of UNDP. He greeted me with true Egyptian cordiality, and we reminisced about our time in Aswan. By coincidence, my rented lodging proved to be a short walk from the house in which we had once lived in Cairo. "You will be comfortable here," said Samir, "much better than in a hotel crammed with tourists. Our offices are not far from here. The landlady's name is Peggy. A widow, a very nice woman . . . anyway, you will find out for yourself."

My departure for Abu Tartur was planned for a few days hence; and in the meantime, I was to attend meetings in the Ministry of Industry and in the UN offices. The industrial development of the Western Desert had been in the government's sights for some time. It was a difficult task requiring vast funds, the financial support of the West, as well as an exploration of relevant new technologies. I was told that a survey of underground water reserves and even of oil deposits had given positive results. German engineers were looking at prospects for digging a new canal connecting the great depression of Qattara with the Mediterranean Sea. I learned that a new city, simply called El Gedida, or New, had already been built in the desert. This sounded very interesting, and I was promised a visit there. Another new desert place to be called Sadat City was apparently on the drawing board. I was getting more and more excited by these projects, realistic or not, but amazing in their scope. In my free time, I kept visiting old friends and wandering through the maze of narrow lanes and alleys of our quarter. On the corner of the 26th July street I found the old Greek delicatessen where we used to buy smoked eels for our Polish style snacks with vodka. The narrow lanes running between residential buildings held small open-fronted artisan workshops of all kinds: car mechanics, tailors, cobblers, watchmakers, seamstresses, laundries, as well as the ubiquitous little cafés, the few tables of which were taken by men in their long galabiyas, smoking water pipes, engrossed in their interminable discussions. They did not seem to mind either the permanently switched on television showing locally produced soaps or the radio transmitting old hits by Um Kalsum, the Egyptian chanteuse acclaimed all over the Arab world. In spite of the ever-present noise, the city offered me the chance of relaxation I had been missing in my pressurized New York life. I could just sit down at a table here, drink a glass of freshly made lemonade, leisurely watch the bustling life around me, something I could never afford to do at home in Madison Avenue. It might also have been the exotic lure of the Middle East, which charmed me, or maybe it was the specific relationship between people and their immediate environment, which I found so attractive here.

My landlady, indeed, proved more than obliging. She would wake me every morning at dawn with a cup of tea, following the Egyptian or, being English, perhaps the old colonial custom. Fortunately, I was able to fall asleep again, but punctually, at eight o'clock, she was back with breakfast and the morning paper on a tray. Following the afternoon siesta, she would ask me to her large kitchen for a beer. This was followed in the evening by various maneuvers and beer-driven suggestions difficult to refuse. When the beer was running out, she would just lean out of the kitchen window and call resoundingly to the little café in the yard, "Yallah Ahmed! Talata bira, alatul . . ." She would then lower a basket on a length of rope and, within few minutes, three large bottles of Stella beer would appear before us. Some evenings ended thus on a very jolly note.

In the beginning of April, as I was traveling by train up the Nile valley to the southern university town of Assyût, my companion, a geologist from the Ministry of Industry, would not stop talking. He was telling me about the major projects in the offing, about the great interest Egypt was attracting now in both Western Europe and America, and about the changes which followed President Anwar

Sadat's rejection of Nasser's Socialism resulting in the country's U-turn to a quasi-capitalist market economy. He was telling me, as it were in confidence, how much yet remained to be done to get the state to relinquish its hold on all economic activity. Fascinated as I was by the landscapes rapidly changing outside the window, I listened to him with only half an ear.

The rich green of cultivated fields was crisscrossed by the dark brown lines of irrigation canals. Here and there, in the shade of scattered clumps of date palms, stood closely packed clay buildings, appearing to play piggyback with one another. Hedges of prickly pear outlined small individual fields. The mirrorlike surface of canals reflected the upside-down images of pack dromedaries and black water buffaloes. A red patch of a dress or a white pinpoint of a turban would suddenly appear in the middle of a field. As the train was slowly crossing a provisional bridge spanning a long, deep excavation in the black soil, I watched half-naked workers laying down large iron irrigation pipes: new technology invading the ancient landscape. Soon a much larger canal came into view, harboring a number of loaded feluccas with their tall white triangular sails; further down, a yellowish minaret and a brick-built villa with three arching arcades and a balcony denoted a small town. In Assyût, we transferred to a waiting car to drive in a southwestern direction to El Kharga, an oasis lying at the bottom of a great depression about sixty miles long. Having descended the desert escarpment, we continued due south. Eventually, some grayish shrubs and stunted trees appeared to be followed by plantations of low-growing date palms and isolated farmsteads partly hidden behind high mud walls. The hotel in El Kharga, capital of the Wadi El Gedid (New Valley) province, was surrounded by flower beds and shrubs in bloom. The new three-story housing blocks of the town, painted in bright colors, were buried in masses of well-kept greenery. "We have plenty of water here," my guide informed me. "Huge reserves are lying under the desert. The remains of our ancient history of dozens of millions years ago." I looked at him with amazement. "Your history?" I asked. "Yes," he confirmed in all seriousness. "In ancient times, this was a savanna full of animals."

After dinner, we went to a large and noisy lounge. A group of boys were laughing and playing games round a ping-pong table. Girls, in small groups, sat separately, talking to one another. They were all wearing long skirts, their heads covered with white scarves wound round their necks. This was something new, not seen when I was here ten years ago.

"The old Islamic tradition is coming back," said my companion seeing my look of surprise. "Young people, especially university students like these ones here, are rediscovering religion and some of its requirements rather lost in the times of pro-Western monarchy and pro-Soviet Socialism. I'll tell you more about it later, if you are interested, but let's go to bed now; we'll be leaving at dawn."

The sun was just rising over the desert's eastern horizon when we got in the car. Before taking the road to the west, we drove to the maidan, a little square in the old part of the town densely packed with houses built of sun-baked mud bricks. No windows in these houses faced outside, but traditionally opened on to the internal courtyard. The houses in the narrow alleys linked overhead; the tunnels are thus formed protecting pedestrians from the sun and from the dust blown in by the frequent sand storms. In the middle of the square was a well to which women came to draw water, which they carried home on their heads in variously shaped vessels. I was handed a mug of water. Its owner smiled widely, showing a row of white teeth in her brown face. A small crowd of people watched to see how this *khawaga*, a foreigner, would drink it. The water tasted strongly of iron. I did, though, take several sips and told the waiting audience, "Maia qwayissa [good water]," which met with general applause.

Soon after, we left the town and sped down the straight desert road. The engineer kept telling me about the enormous deposits of this desert water. "Do you realize that you were drinking water, which fell here on the savanna as rain several million years ago? The success of the Abu Tartur project is to be based on the exploitation of these water deposits. German hydrologists are already investigating them." We then drove in silence until yellow mountains of sand appeared on the horizon. Suddenly, both my companions tried to speak at the same time. The driver stopped the car. A shifting dune was blocking the road. "This is the dune belt; it's some dozen miles wide here," said the engineer. A tip of a telegraph pole was sticking out of the sand on the windward side. On the other side, one could see the rather beautiful, as if compass-drawn, semicircular edge of the dune. A steady cloud of fine dust was blowing off this edge. Apparently, a dune can move this way several yards a day. Semicircular edges of other dunes stretched on both sides of the road as far as the eye could see. "We have to find another way," said the driver. "In this area, all roads have bypasses and detours." It took us some time to get past the belt of dunes.

I spent all day on fieldwork, inspecting three possible sites for the future town on the level desert at the foot of the escarpment, examining the sites of deep wells into the Paleocene fresh water reservoirs. In the afternoon, we all met in the tent of the geologists working in the pilot phosphate mine. They told me about the deposits of this raw material, laid down about sixty million years ago when the present desert was the bottom of a warm sea. They gave me, as souvenirs, several fossilized plants, snails, and shark's teeth found during the excavations. They talked excitedly about their project and about the great benefits, the future export of phosphates to India and to the Far East would bring. They confirmed what I'd already heard, that the project was to be started in 1981. They

new city in the desert? How about there?

wished me luck and hoped that we would meet again soon when the preparatory work would begin. "Sadat too could do with some luck," remarked suddenly one of the geologists. Serious problems were apparently brewing in the country. The main one was the growth of Islamic fundamentalism; its followers fearing that the opening of Egypt to foreign capital would entail further secularization and an increased Western influence endangering Islam and its traditional lifestyle. Silence followed, as if a bucket of cold water had been thrown over us, dampening our enthusiasm. "The situation," the geologist continued after a while, "might be compared to what you encountered on the route here from El Kharga. Do you remember, you crossed a belt of drifting sand dunes? You may have had to look for a detour when your road suddenly disappeared under a mountain of sand. Sadat is facing a similar problem in trying to develop this country. He is looking forward to the twenty-first century and attempting to improve the standard of living for the millions of today's young people; when all of a sudden, he finds his route barred by a mountain of drifting sand. This sand is an inflexible interpretation of Islam, exactly as spelled out in the Koran of the seventh century AD. Religion viewed in this way would dictate the governance of the country and determine its economic development. This is a serious threat."

At noon the following day, we were on our way back to El Kharga. Three times, we had to seek new routes as all traces of yesterday's road disappeared under mountains of drifting sand.

I had to strike while the iron was hot. An opportunity on the scale of Abu Tartur was not to be despised. The problems so candidly raised by the geologist were serious, and had to be taken into consideration. I consoled myself with the thought that many more people must have shared his way of thinking. I decided to return to the problem once back in Cairo. In the meantime, my companion gladly returned to our unfinished discussion about fundamentalism. He wondered whether I knew anything about the Muslim Brotherhood, a political and religious faction, which President Nasser had tried to suppress. This reminded me of an episode I had witnessed in the past and which I now related to him.

It was January 1966, and I had just arrived in Aswan, where I set up an exhibition on the development of the town. Soon after, I came across three bearded guests who arrived to view the exhibit. They were truly interested in my incorporation in the housing design of the centuries-old traditions, of the ways the family life in a Muslim country shapes their physical environment. They were in fact, the only ones who had appreciated it. All the officials in the Ministry of Housing, and most of all, the governor of the province, could not see beyond standard housing blocks. But there was another side to the visit, my colleagues were manifestly anxious that the three men might be members of the Muslim Brotherhood whose aim was to overthrow President Nasser's regime and do away with its Socialist program. As my work at the time was closely related with this program, I was not sure whether my response ought to be one of anxiety or of relief that my original intentions were noticed.

"Let me tell you something about the origin of these revolutionary ideas in Egypt," said my companion. "This might be compared to Christianity before the Reformation, or even to American radio preachers with their literal interpretation and belief in the historical authenticity of biblical texts. What happened here, in the late 1940s, was that a contemporary literary critic, Sayyid Qutb, returned from America so outraged by the American way of life and its loose morals that he decided to reform the world by a return to the past—"

"That's rather the reverse of what Martin Luther had done for Christianity," I interrupted.

"Could be, I am not an expert in these matters," he continued. "In his book *Signposts on the Path*, Sayyid Qutb wrote words to the effects that the Western way is the greatest barbaric influence that has ever endangered our faith. That everything around us is confusion and barbarity: perceptions and beliefs, customs and morality, culture, arts and literature, laws, rules, and regulations including everything which we consider to be the Islamic culture."

"But didn't these words sound quite absurd at the time?" I asked. "Of course they did. Being seen as a product of a trubled mind, they were not taken seriously. But Nasser did not agree. He had Sayyid Qutb arrested and finally executed. Well, the man was no longer there, but his ideas survived. And now, we may be facing a problem." There followed a silence, and he looked at me for a while. Then, bending over, he whispered in my ear, "There are people, you know, saying that for some time these radical groups—I mean the Muslim Brotherhood—were financed by the Saudis and also by the American government." "What? America? CIA? But why?" I was incredulous. "Well, they say that this was the cold war strategy to weaken Nasser, who was leaning towards the Soviet camp. All history now, but it is left to us to face the problem."

When I returned to Cairo, Peggy received me in style. Incense was burning in the sitting room and bedroom. The table was set with silver and candles. Enticing smells were wafting in from the kitchen. I was tired after the journey, surprised, and not a little embarrassed by the situation. I was asked to open two bottles of Omar Khayam—the local red wine. My landlady, raising her glass, proposed a toast, "Bottoms up . . . let us enjoy life while enjoyment is not forbidden." Soon came the peak event of the evening. Peggy decided to show me how proper belly dancing ought to be performed. This was to be followed by Salome's Dance of the Seven Veils. However, the evening was coming to an end much sooner and in a rather hilarious way. But Peggy did not hold her drink well. Exhaustion took over, and I had to help her to bed. In the morning, I found her in the kitchen, bent over a bottle of Stella beer. "What happened last night? Why do I have such a splitting headache?" she asked, but did not wait for my reply.

Overcome by the rush of thoughts brought about by the impressions of the last few weeks, I began to formulate a new notion: could I approach the Egyptian government with the idea of developing, as it were, an alternative, a new Egypt? It is generally known that the territorial growth of the country is restricted to the narrow strip of land on the two banks of the Nile, from Aswan to Alexandria. The Nile valley, irrigated over millions of years with the loam-rich waters of the river, is bounded by the sheer escarpments of the Western Desert and the mountains in the east. With the population growing on an exponential scale, every new settlement takes away another piece of precious land, which ought to be under cultivation. Thus, a time may come when either the country will no longer be able to feed its population or no land will be left to house future generations. Hearing of all the varied yet uncoordinated desert enterprises, it occurred to me that perhaps I could collect all the relevant data, point out some realistic solutions, and, if possible, present the results to President Sadat. I looked at myself in the mirror and laughed. What a daydreamer . . . The President might just say, So what? How would I answer him? Well, I would address him, Mister President, as you are aware, sir, the Western Desert shows signs of the existence of former ancient cities as well as of agriculture. Life had thrived in five oases: El Kharga, El Dakhla, El Farafra, El Baharia, and El Siwa. This is confirmed by fossilized tree trunks, millions of years old, by ruins of Pharaonic temples, large early Christian burial sites, and the existence of underground reserves of potable water. Roughly over one hundred thousand people live in the area, not many as compared with elsewhere in Egypt, and there is potential for a large increase in population. Many cataclysms depopulated these parts over the millennia, but the existing water deposits maybe will provide a chance for a revival with irrigation opening the land to cultivation once more. By tradition, the Egyptians are not people of the desert. From the dawn of history, they had lived in the fertile valley of the Nile; but now with the population explosion, resources are growing scarce there. One ought to be able to recreate similar conditions for the future based on the oases of the Western Desert, wrest the land from the desert, and create a new Egypt-West for a better future. I glanced again in the mirror and patted my head.

Am I out of my mind? Gone completely mad? Or maybe dreams can come true?

I decided to talk to my Egyptian friends. A year earlier, during my previous visit to Cairo, when these ideas were just beginning to form in my head, I did mention them to Boutros Boutros-Ghali who was then, besides being the adviser to the president, the chairman of the Center of Political and Strategic Studies. The periodical *Al-Ahram Al-Iqtisadi* printed a two-page interview with me in March 1976. Now I learned that the project of developing the desert wastelands was very much alive. Boutros suggested organizing an international roundtable conference to discuss the complete project. He also told me that I ought to get in touch straight away with Dr. Abdel Rezzak Abdel Meguid, my former boss on the Aswan project and, at present, the Minister of Planning. That seemed like a propitious coincidence. Two days later, I was invited to dinner by Josephine and Magdi Wahba, where I was to meet Abdel Meguid. Magdi was the scion of an old Coptic family of great landowners whose estates were confiscated during Nasser's revolution. I had met him in the 1960s, and we had once, for fun, driven his father's old Rolls-Royce along Alexandria's Corniche. The reunion with Abdel Meguid was very emotional. We reminisced about old times, times of great hopes and even greater disenchantments. He told me that his ministry was working now on development projects for 1978-1982. He insisted that my ideas fitted very well into their strategy, and that he would shortly be in touch with me. In the meantime, I might start working on contacts with scientists, experts in engineering and regional planning who could take part in the conference. He had just two questions: would the water reserves in the oases be sufficient to last long enough and would the land be suitable for agriculture? I promised to investigate these conditions, the basis on which the success of the entire project would stand or fall.

All these new developments, the numbers of fortunate encounters, left me in a kind of daze. My priority was now, however, the writing of the preliminary report on my visit to Abu Tartur, which I had to submit to the ministry before my departure. I needed some peace and quiet. I was advised in the UN office to go for few days to Alexandria, where the tourist season had not yet begun and where I could find conditions suitable for my work as well as some relaxation at the seaside. Peggy, hell-bent on accompanying me, was causing me some problems. The small hotel on the waterfront corniche was almost empty, and the owners could not have paid me more attention. One day, I came across the office of the Polish Archaeological Mission of whose work I had been aware for some time. The director took me round their dig, which covered a large area in the center of the city. Several historical layers, down to the Hellenistic beginnings of the town, had already been uncovered; there was a fragment of a Roman colonnade, a small amphitheater, and ruins of baths with their subterranean effluent canals. The baths had been serviced by slaves who, concealed behind the walls, would hand to the bathers whatever they required through special openings. On the walls of the effluent tunnels, I saw numerous graffiti scratched by the slaves, reviling the Romans and cursing the fate, which had doomed them to forever work in such inhuman conditions. I could not escape the comparison to present day inhabitants made to live in multistory, western type housing blocks. Would they revolt one day?

Before returning to New York, I decided to have a look at El Gedida, the new desert town. It was quite a sobering experience. This settlement of several thousand inhabitants had not been built near an existent oasis, but next to a mine of iron ore. It had been put up with the help of Soviet advisers and showed clear imprints of Socialist town planning. It consisted of rows of three-story housing blocks, the usual kind of social center, food warehouses, a bakery, a school, administration buildings and mine offices, and a pumping station bringing water via a pipeline from the Nile valley. All the spaces in front of the houses were teeming with children. At school, the benches designed for two had to seat five children. Residents of the housing blocks complained of their tiny rooms having to accommodate their ever-increasing families. I was interested to note that all the available spaces between the blocks were divided into small, cultivated allotments, on which, clay brick rural huts of the type found all over the country had been erected. "How do you get your vegetables to grow so well in the sand?" I asked. "This desert is not really as barren as it looks," I was assured in reply. "All you need is water and good crops will grow." So even here, the ancient way of life of these people, somewhat altered by social manipulation, was still in harmony with the natural environment. I found it surprising, yet in a way encouraging. On my return journey, I noticed a train loaded with ore and immobilized by sand drifts; hundreds of workers, wielding spades, were laboring hard to clear the track. Another problem in search of a solution. After a series of official meetings, and many social ones, I was going home to New York, as usual, via Paris.

At home, I found Lenta rather distressed. While I was away, our Madison Avenue home had been burgled; and she had a scary encounter with a black young man who got into the apartment through a back door unwittingly left unlocked. Having safely wondered through crowded quarters of Cairo and Alexandria, I was really upset by what had happened at home. On top of it, the newspaper stories of lawlessness in New York were frightening: daily robberies, and the number of murders rising to hundreds a month. At night, in some quarters of town, the streets belonged to armed gangs, fighting murderous battles with one another. The police seemed powerless. Inhabitants of certain streets or even stretches of street, formed civil defense units and patrolled their immediate area. At the same time, the problem of homelessness reached its peak. Even in our own neck of the woods, after all a main artery of a city renowned for its prosperity, homeless people slept in all available niches and recesses, wrapped in rags or tucked up in cardboard boxes. In our house, before the renovation, the outside entry door did not have any lock. Returning home at night, we had to step over some repulsive, shaggy, dirty, and smelly individuals fast asleep. City hostels for the homeless were overcrowded. Many avoided using them, fearing rape and robbery. The situation became even worse when the temperature dropped below freezing.

With the new semester at the school, I had not a moment to spare. Among other things, I gave a lecture, illustrated by slides, about my expedition to Abu Tartur. Unexpectedly, I found the project of populating the desert criticized by two Egyptians. One of them was a student whose approach to architecture had already caused me some trouble in the preceding year. Faruk, the son of the head of the protocol section of the UN Secretariat, came from a privileged background. Overweight, longhaired, showing off his black velour suit and white silk shirt, he stood out a mile from the other casually dressed students. It wasn't quite clear how he had managed to get into the school of architecture, but I had my suspicions. All he wanted, from the word go, was to have, as the subject of his exercises, the designing of luxury palaces for Saudi sheikhs. Nothing else was of interest to him. He said to me after my lecture that he could see no reason for developing new desert towns and agriculture for the poverty-stricken rural masses. In his opinion, the future of the Middle East lay, as shown by Saudi Arabia, in the search for oil deposits while engaging American firms for their exploitation. The other Egyptian was Gamal El Zogby, a colleague, lecturer in architectural design, who saw this in terms of a cross between sculpture and abstract graphics. He supported his spatial concepts by his own inalterable philosophy. Not surprisingly, both my project of the development of Aswan and the subject of new desert cities were totally outside his sphere of interest. Gamal supplemented his income in New York by managing a restaurant in Lower Broadway. I dropped in once to sample the tasty Egyptian dishes and to watch the belly dancers. However, unwittingly, Gamal gave me an excellent idea for another argument to enrich the scope of my project, which had become my new passion. He had once explained his indifference to the great construction projects in question by some work he had read, stating that the High Dam project would eventually come to nothing: it was bound to be blocked by the enormous, unforeseen by the planners, amounts of silt brought every year by the Nile from its upper reaches. Yet in my work, I had followed the construction of the dam from the start. I knew that in order to protect the inlets to the hydroelectric turbine tunnels, an over hundred-feet-high sill had been constructed to hold the silt. And then, a thought struck me. This silt had been fertilizing

Egypt for thousands of years, while now it was being replaced by artificial fertilizers. But why should this natural bounty go to waste? Perhaps, in some distant future, the lake upstream from the dam, several hundred miles long and reaching far into Sudanese territory, would really silt over? I took to studying in detail maps of the American army land survey service and satellite photographs of the area. Eureka! I found the answer in the topography of the region: the relatively short stretch of the desert from the lake to the El Kharga oasis was sloping sufficiently to help in diverting the abundant, silt-rich waters of the lake to irrigate and fertilize the belt of future agricultural land. With renewed enthusiasm, I started working on my plans.

In May, Lenta and I went to Yale to Klara's graduation. She graduated magna cum laude. Both Klara and her companion, Erroll McDonald, have finished their courses in English literature. Having graduated a year before Klara and waiting for her to finish her course, Erroll enrolled in a postgraduate MA course.

Klara has a cheerful, serene disposition; she likes people and company and can laugh from the bottom of her heart. She is at the same time very hard working and conscientious, nothing seeming to be too difficult for her. I can now say with some pride that in spite of having forced immigration and frequent changes of environment on her, we were able to give her a first-class education and provide her with a secure home to which she always returns with pleasure. Erroll is more self-contained and takes life seriously and with a doze of suspicion. Classics, both in literature and music, are his passion. His life had been totally different from Klara's and much more dramatic. He was born in the port town of Limon, in Costa Rica. His grandmother was said to have fled, as a young girl, from Jamaica, where racial strife was prevalent. Life in Costa Rica was different; the large community of the descendants of slaves from islands under the British rule led a quiet life. There were better employment opportunities there with the building of the Panama Canal, and in on the huge plantations, and in the canneries of the United Fruit Company. Human relationships in communities of African descent are often loose and unstable. Fathers of numerous children come and go. Women are the great stabilizing factor. They maintain the family traditions and take care of all their children. Lena, Erroll's mother, came from a very large family but decided that her life would be different. She had an only son and wished to give him a better chance by bringing him up in the United States. Erroll has only one group photograph in which he can point out his father, who died young, most probably by his own hand. Lena was a seamstress and had, for many years, worked late into the night in the sweatshops of the Manhattan garment district. Erroll, being an exemplary student, received grants to the best schools but had to work after school, doing the shopping, cleaning, and cooking for both mother and him. It was not an easy life for a young boy.

Lenta and I came to Klara's graduation dressed in the European manner, in our best clothes. Lenta wore a Henri Bendel lilac silk dress, and I my summer navy blue suit. Parents of Klara's friends told us later that we had stood out in the crowd. This had not been intended, but most families arrived in their everyday clothes. It was the beginning of the American dress revolution, when the old customs gave way to a new informality of jeans, T-shirts, and sneakers. The celebrations were a rather quiet affair. BB King, the famous blues singer, received a honoris causa doctorate. There were speeches and cheers. All graduates wore black academic gowns and square caps and were holding blue balloons with the white letters YALE on them. Soon after the ceremony, Klara and Erroll moved back to New York. Errol had so many books and LP records that I had to rent a van to help them bring all their chattels into town. Erroll moved in with his mother in Brooklyn, while Klara came back to our small apartment in Manhattan.

With some help from Toni Morrison, a Nobel literature laureate, Erroll got a junior editor's job in Random House. Klara was, for the time being, staying at home, doing some small jobs, mainly for charities; nothing that would further her career. As far as I remember, she never even considered leaving home and looking for a job elsewhere in the States, as is quite a common practice here among young people. Eventually, Erroll came to her aid by getting her an interview at Random House. After several weeks of anxious waiting, she started work there as assistant editor. Thus, both of them entered the exclusive world of big publishing companies with their particular methods of selecting books and authors, and their competitive world of promotion and advertising, of profit chasing and of the envious watching of other companies' successes.

By then, Lenta and I have been living for some three years in Manhattan, while our New Canaan house was occasionally rented out, supplementing our income and allowing me to pursue my dreams. Truly, an immigrant's obligation.

With the coming of spring, work on the Pound Ridge project became more intensive; and quite often, I had to think what to do next. We were stepping onto new ground, away from traditional land planning methods. Mary Jane Russell, our principal fund-raiser, announced a series of promotional meetings. In the summer, we moved our studio to a school in Pound Ridge, leant to us for the purpose. We placed six colored maps of the town, three meters high and two meters wide, on the walls. They depicted different kinds of natural environment, of building development and of density of population. The results of our surveys were now expressed in figures, with individual plans for each of the eleven watershed basins to follow. People from surrounding towns were coming, interested in the details of our work and anxious about whether

in Pound Ridge, NY

our method of protecting the environment might affect the control landowners had over their property. I could not deny that in theory this was a possibility.

The first meeting took the form of a garden party attended by a few hundred people, with a lavish buffet arranged on tables in a large white marquee erected in a meadow next to the Russell's home. Mary Jane had found an old copper bathtub with four legs in an antiques store, and placed in it dozens of champagne bottles on ice. There were speeches; there was a raffle. There were also threats. A woman by the name of Dolores, who at one time served on our council, came up to me with a vicious glint in her eye. "Watch it, Jerzy!" she said. "Don't be so confident; you're riding a high horse, it's easy to fall." A man standing next to her added, "I strongly believe that it's dangerous to play with God's will. After all, the Bible says that God gave people the earth to do with as they wished." I was surprised to meet with such an ultraconservative attitude so rooted in religious fundamentalism and wondered whether this might prove an obstacle in the long run. Work, however, continued uninterrupted into the autumn.

In October, I prepared an outline of themes for the Cairo conference, including a list of required American experts. I presented it to Richardson Pratt, president of the Pratt Institute, inviting him to accept the patronage of the project. I also included a letter from Abdel Meguid, the Egyptian minister of planning, in which he suggested that we begin with a large scale topographic model of Egypt from the Red Sea to the Libyan border, showing all the areas covered by the study as well as those where work had already begun. He felt that it would help if all those involved in the conference could have the subject under discussion in front of their eyes. He must have remembered the success of our Aswan project presentation twelve years before. "In my opinion," he wrote, "this job ought to be finished quite soon so that it can be presented to President Sadat and serve as a kind of prototype for any future conferences in this field."

In November, President Sadat's surprise visit to Israel and the dramatic U-turn in the relationships between Egypt and Israel totally changed the political configuration of the Middle East. It seemed that, if anything, this improved the chances of my project's success. I dreamed that American institutions of higher learning and certain foundations might become involved in my project rather than governmental agencies, like USAID, weighed down by their political and bureaucratic ballast. I badly needed the support of at least my own institute before getting other ones interested and obtaining the necessary funds. All my free time after the work at the school was devoted to this project. On large-scale maps of Egypt, obtained from the U.S. Army's cartography department, I marked all the desert development sites known to me. I needed some assistance; and Ron Shiffman, our lecturer in sociology, who was also in charge of the local Community Advice Center, suggested that I talk to a young Pole whom he had recently met. He had apparently studied architecture, had no money, and was keen to work. "If you take him on I'll get him a small allowance from the center's fund to help him with his living expenses. He is a bit peculiar . . . but you will see for yourself."

It was a Saturday afternoon; there were no students at the school, as it was the time of the spring break. A haggard-looking, unshaven, long-haired young man came into my room weighed down with a large backpack and bulging bags. A large frying pan was dangling from his belt. Quietly, he deposited his belongings under one of the drafting tables and sat down on a stool without saying a word. I described my project briefly to him. He kept nodding his head. I showed him several map sections and asked whether he could help me join them together to form a whole to be placed on the wall. When I returned the next day, I could hardly recognize the room. All the tables and stools were piled together into a pyramid reaching right up to the ceiling. My precious maps, stuck together with tape, were covering this structure like a tent. A path of strewn sand led from the door to the pyramid. The rest of the floor was covered with slips of paper bearing Egyptian place names. In one corner of the room stood a table with the young man's sleeping bag and other belongings. I stood there, rooted to the floor, looking round; but the artist was nowhere to be seen. He appeared in a short while with a wide smile on his face and invited me to a feast in his tent under the table. It was then that I saw his small electric stove with his frying pan full of vegetables arranged in a colorful painterly composition. "Every dish has to provide an aesthetic experience, particularly in Egypt," he said, handing me a spoon. My god, I thought, if only President Sadat could see how the idea for the future of his country disappears in a puff of smoke rising from a frying pan! True, it had not disappeared yet, but I began to doubt whether I would be able to cope by myself.

I put up quite an impressive presentation of the project, which stretched from the school's exhibition hall to the common room. We invited the dean and the teaching staff of the engineering departments. Interesting discussions and ideas followed. Various technical achievements were mentioned, like for instance the great pipeline, consisting of concrete segments over twenty feet in diameter and presently under construction, designed to convey water from the Colorado River three hundred miles south to Arizona. Pictures of another huge pipeline, in Wyoming, were shown, which was already pumping water carrying coal dust over a long distance. "We can foresee no difficulties in pumping of water with silt," wrote the head of the Mechanical Engineering Department, P. Basch, in his letter. In January 1978, I received approval from Richardson Pratt. He advised me, however, that he has to apply to Washington for funds first. This was a great mistake. He was wrong. Nobody suggests to the State Department how to spend money on foreign aid projects, particularly as our budget of less than $100,000 was, in comparison, ridiculously low. Projects like ours concern the very nature of American foreign policy, and its priorities are within the exclusive domain of the USA government, especially as it concerns the Middle East. President Pratt's letter remained unanswered or, as I later suspected, he never sent it out. At the same time, the inertia of Egyptian authorities was discouraging. In spite of all my contacts, practically none of the people I had talked to seemed able or willing to show any initiative. Except for the Boutros-Ghali's center, no one was prepared to do anything specific, to advance funds or even to offer advice. And that in spite of their originally positive attitude to the project and the continuing interest of the press. Demographic studies based on the latest census showed that the population of Egypt, where space was already at a premium, would double to eighty million in thirty years, to be accommodated in only 3.5 percent of the country's surface area, the rest remaining a desert. From the perspective of thirty years, the project idea was sabotaged from both ends. *Nec Hercules contra plures.*

Lenta, conscious of my nervous tension, started to object to my involvement, comparing me to our dachshund chasing his own tail. She was, by then, working in a promising new gallery of modern art, started by André Zarre, a Polish art collector. The gallery ran at the time an exhibition of Polish erotic graphics. It proved very popular. I was surprised to see that our writer friend, Leopold Tyrmand, contributed to the exhibition two excellent Indian ink drawings by a Polish illustrator of children's books, depicting scenes from New Orleans brothels with well-known black jazz musicians in action. I began to brood over my choice of career. Why hadn't I taken up drawing or painting instead of architecture? Many people had told me over the years that I was talented in that field. In my younger days, I was forever sketching; and my surviving wartime drawings are a rare record of life in the Polish Air Force in Great Britain and on the western front. I was now discovering, to my chagrin, that whatever his ability, an architect or a town planner is forever dependent on others. He can achieve nothing at all without a client who has a commission to offer. These were sobering thoughts, but it was too late to do anything about them. Though in consequence, I came to the conclusion that I ought not to continue teaching a profession in which I was losing faith. My contract was expiring at the end of the academic year, and I decided not to try to extend it. I was tempted by the big, wide world. And then, as if by magic, another commission arrived from the UN.

25

Back Behind the Iron Curtain and out in the Caribbean

As I found out, my Polish experience, this time, in designing industrial projects stood me in good stead. I was offered a consulting job on St. Lucia, a Lesser Antilles island in the Caribbean. "You always fall on your feet," remarked a colleague who was at a loose end at that time, looking for work.

I was truly relieved to have a respite from the problems of deserts and of Arab bureaucracy. The St. Lucia's job involved a project for a duty-free zone in a new port, in a valley with the rather apt name of Cul-de-Sac. The entire valley, to which indeed the name applied, has been hitherto a large banana plantation, regularly flooded during the rainy season. An English civil engineer from Brisbane, Australia, was to join me on this job. Looking forward to the new assignment, I was busy completing the Pound Ridge project as well as the work on several individual houses on which I collaborated with Ed Bye. We planned that Lenta would join me in the autumn, while Klara and Erroll would come later. A vacation in the Caribbean could not be a bad idea.

Yet suddenly events took a different turn. I had a phone call from Paris from my brother, telling me that mother had a mild heart attack and was taken to hospital. He hoped that she would be well soon as she was continuing to plan her visit to the Holy Land. She died the following day. The funeral was to be held in Warsaw. He gave me the date and assured me that he would be able to come, in spite of the problems he had been having with the Polish consul for the last six months. In this period of a relative relaxation of Communist rule, his company had opened a branch in Warsaw. But lately, he himself had been repeatedly refused the visa by the Polish authorities. Mother kept warning him that dealings with Communists were bound to end badly and that he should not even try. Yet it appeared that under the new circumstances, the consular authorities have become somewhat more understanding or had a different plan.

He, together with our Aunt Maria, met me in Warsaw's wretched, dark terminal building; apparently, a new one was under construction. From the airport, we went to order flowers from a private florist. My brother, driving the small Russian-made rented car, was speeding furiously, keeping an eye on the rear mirror. "Are you crazy? Do you want to kill the lot of us?" "Don't worry, I just want to lose them," he laughed. "They think that I don't know Warsaw . . . I'll show them! The bloody secret police!" When we stopped for a while, he pointed to two cars parked on the other side of the road. "Can you see them? There they are, waiting for us." On the way back, he drove again as if acting in an American thriller, crossing red lights, suddenly making a U-turn until, eventually, we reached the hotel where we had booked a room for the two of us.

It was a sad and strange feeling to visit to Poland after a five-year absence. Warsaw looked gray, dirty, and unfriendly in the dim March light. The mood changed though, the following day, during the funeral mass at the cemetery. The church was full to overflowing; there were relatives, Mother's numerous friends, some of whom I had known since my childhood, there were also friends of mine. Oddly, for a funeral, there were many smiling faces. Mother herself must have created this spirit, she, who was always full of optimism, full of joie de vivre, in spite of her often-difficult life. After the funeral, a great crowd filled our aunt's flat. People kept commenting on mother's vitality, resourcefulness, her strength in adversity. Many of her and my father's old friends were there, going back to the interwar period, to the times of Nazi occupation, to the first years under Communism, when she was admired for her unyielding struggle with the authorities to save our inheritance. Through the kitchen window overlooking the park, still bare and gray at this time of year, my brother pointed out a few more secret policemen. As he deliberately waved his hand at them, they took cover behind trees. "Idiots," he opined loudly. "They don't even know how to covertly watch people." Having been part of the Polish Underground Home Army as a teenager under the Nazi occupation, he considered himself an expert in such matters. We left the house together with mother's cousins. As we were nearing the car, he was suddenly surrounded by several plainclothes policemen, whom we hadn't notice, and pushed into another car. He just managed to hand me his car keys. "Go back to the hotel. I will join you before long." But it was not that simple. A family council met that evening, debating what our next step ought to be. My sister-in-law phoned from Paris, crying and demanding that we procure his immediate release. Easy to say. Next morning, I was woken by the hotel reception, telling me that several men were on their way to my room. Three of them came in, smiling broadly, "Regretting that they had to disturb me." After an interrogation of four hours (who? where? for what reason?), having searched the room as well as my suitcase, and having collected my brother's belongings, for which they issued a receipt, wished me a happy return to USA, and left. One of them, with longish blond hair, turned round in the door, saying how he envied me my magic card from American Express, which he had been twisting this way and that. There was no mention of any of my former clashes with security police.

After several days, we managed to secure an interview at the military prosecutor's office. We were received by a major, who informed us that my brother's case was serious, that the investigation has not yet begun and thus he was not in a position to tell us any more. Whatever the accusation was, the fact that the case was under military jurisdiction, did not augur a speedy resolution. All we found out that he was in the Mokotów prison, so I was able to take him a parcel of food and clothing. Taking parcels to prison seemed to have been a well-rehearsed ritual in Poland; everyone was giving me advice on what to take and how to pack it.

Having left my brother's case in the hands of a well-known lawyer, I took a flight to New York with a short stopover in Paris.

In May, I completed my course of lectures, said good-bye to the school, and flew to the Caribbean. The island of St. Lucia seemed to us outsiders, was a true paradise. Similar to Martinique, just north of it, it used to be a French colony; and the towns carried French names such as Anse La Raye, Soufriere, Vieux Fort, while the volcanic peaks rising steeply from the Caribbean Sea were called Le Petit and Le Gros Piton. Waves were breaking on the steep cliffs of the Atlantic coast. The island was at the time a British protectorate, soon, though, to become independent. Our project was part of the preliminaries for that event. My English/Australian partner, Reggie Millburn, got lost in Miami airport where he was supposed to change planes; and I had to wait several days for his arrival. In the meantime, I rented two apartments for us in the converted nineteenth century barracks of the British colonial garrison.

The history of the island read like a boys' adventure story. From ancient times, the island was inhabited by various tribes of Carib Indians. The first European to see it was supposed to have been Juan de La Cosa, Columbus' navigator. In the sixteenth century, it was used as a base by Francois le Clerc-Jambe de Bois, a pirate known for his cruelty, for attacking and plundering Spanish galleys. In Napoleonic times, the island changed hands fourteen times until, following the fall of the emperor, it was taken over by the British. The people in the country spoke Creole, a dialect based on French. The indigenous Indians had either become extinct or had interbred with the African slaves and the indentured workforce brought over from India.

My partner joined me at last, and I liked him from the moment I clapped my eyes on him. He was the true prototype of an Englishman from a British movie: tall, straight as a ramrod, with smooth, well-brushed hair, and a thin moustache. His English came in short, crisp phrases, such as I had heard from British officers during the war. In fact, Reggie Miller frequently reminisced with affection about his time in the Royal Engineers. He reminded me vividly of Alec Guinness as the British commander of the prisoners of war in the film *Bridge on the River Kwai*. He never tired of telling me of the difficult winding road he had built in Hong Kong up a steep mountain. His tales were, however, relevant to his present work. To link the future industrial harbor of Cul-de-Sac with the capital city of Castries, we proposed building a new road round the steep mountain of Le Morne. Reggie started work on this project. At present, the entire traffic between the north and the south of the island was carried by the existing road over the top of the mountain—at a snail's pace.

Right from the beginning, we noticed that a slim attractive girl with a shaved head was regularly strolling back and forth, hips swinging on a balcony in front of our office windows. "She may want to attract our attention; what do you think?" said Reggie. "How perceptive of you," I replied with a touch of irony. Without saying a word, he left his desk; and within few minutes returned, holding the girl by her hand. "This is Caroline Wheatfield," he formally introduced her. The girl first turned her face away, pouting, then stretched out her hand, her white teeth glinting in a bright smile. She came back after work, asking whether we could give her a lift home. As it turned out, we all lived on the other side of town, on the hilly Vigie Peninsula. Caroline was a clerical worker in one of the municipal offices and worked in a room next to ours. The two-story brick-built old barracks housed a variety of offices such as ours. Our building stood on the Le Morne hill, overlooking the area of our Cul-de-Sac valley project. Like all such former military structures, it had a long roofed-over balcony running all round it with doors to the separate quarters. The windows were protected against hurricanes by massive black

Soufriere, St Lucia, WI

cast-iron shutters. One day, Caroline came to our building to introduce us to Brent, her six-months-old son. She eventually became our frequent guest, which irritated Elaine, my domestic help. "She no good, master," she kept saying, rolling her eyes, "she bad, bad, bad, *le chienne* . . . a bitch." The summer passed quickly, and with it went the visits, first Lenta's, then Klara and Erroll's. Whenever Elaine spoke to Lenta, she used the old colonial servile style, addressing her as "my mistress"; she was also in a good mood all that time, as, understandably, Caroline kept away throughout that period. Reggie and I took Klara and Erroll for a weekend in the hotel Dasheene, picturesquely perched above a tropical forest on a mountain saddle between two Gros Pitons peaks. We invited more young people to keep them company that, altogether, there was about a dozen of us. The hotel, totally built of round logs, offered no individual rooms, only spacious apartments, each on two or three levels, and all facing the shimmering turquoise bay, several hundred feet below. It provided all the comforts: a restaurant, a bar with its parrots, and a large swimming pool overhanging the sheer cliff. We spent time exploring the island, making excursions to hot geysers, to the tropical rain forest, where Erroll, reminded of his childhood in Costa Rica, enjoyed picking the heavy fruit off the cacao trees. In the evenings, we all danced to Bob Marley's reggae. That business in Poland, the secret police, my brother in prison, all seemed to recede, though not for long.

On October 16, I was woken up by Reggie banging on my door with all his might. "Jerzy, open the door, for Christ's sake . . . listen . . . I have news for you . . . Congratulations, old boy!" I have never heard him so excited. "What happened?" "I have just taken a call from the Government House . . . to tell you that you have your own pope. A Polish cardinal was elected pope . . . How about that?

What do you say?" Then the Messings called, insisting I came to their celebratory dinner. They were a couple from the Polish diaspora, who came to the island from Britain. He was a horticulturist, head of the epidemiological laboratory of the British banana plantation concern. His wife, who had taken part in the Warsaw Rising of 1944, had been, as I found out, a girlfriend of a childhood friend of mine at the time. Small world. The two were living now in a large house on top of a steep hill surrounded by tropical vegetation. Another guest was a Polish doctor who has lived on the island since the end of the war. He had a dark-skinned wife and a small adopted Indian son. Someone in the company remarked that the election of a Polish pope was bound to have political repercussions in Poland; but of course, we could not foresee their magnitude. So far, we hardly knew what was happening in the Vatican; but as was the Polish custom, speaking of everything and nothing, we emptied a bottle of brandy or perhaps even more than one. I remember this well as I was driving home much too fast, skidding dangerously down the narrow slippery, hairpin bends. The following day, Caroline arrived accompanied by three of her friends, all decked out in their best, their clinging satin dresses, stiletto-heel sandals, and small straw hats adorned with hibiscus flowers. They came to take me to church, to the special mass to celebrate the election of the new pope. The Catholic Church in Castries stands in the town's main square, next to an ancient wide-branched tree casting its shade over a quarter of the square. The church's interior is divided by arcades, paneled with all kinds of wood. But here ends the charm of its interior. I found the primitive, gaudy, plaster statues of saints, with their pink cheeks, blood-red lips, and blond hair really off-putting. I hoped that the new pope would bring some historical truth to Christian iconography. After all, other religions do not try to disguise their prophets and gods. Islam is proud of its Arab Mohammed, the Buddhists have their Indian Buddha, and the Orthodox Church invariably depicts on its icons a mystical dark-skinned Christ. Why is the Catholic Church ashamed of showing the Semitic features of its New Testament figures? Is it its persistent anti-Semitism? I put this question to my companions, but got no answer. Perhaps the local people did not even notice it; for them, these odd figures were not reflections of a religion but simply a confirmation of the superiority of the white race, capable even of creating its own gods. After mass, we went to Rain, the nearby restaurant and enjoyed their grilled lobster and planter's punch.

The elevation of Karol Wojtyła to the papal throne reminded me of all the events now taking place in Poland. My last visit had left me with rather unpleasant impressions. I was happy that I chose emigration. Judging from all the letters I received, my brother's case was looking serious. Aunt Maria was still not able to discover the reason for his arrest. One day, while visiting one of the local British functionaries, I met a tourist, an English construction engineer, who happened to have arrived straight from Warsaw, where he had been employed on building an office tower near the central railway station. His stories of corruption among the Communist elite who have to be bribed at every level were shocking to hear. I wondered whether something of this kind was behind my brother's arrest. Once again, Poland seemed a very distant country.

26

In Saudi Arabia on a Wild Goose Chase

The Middle East caught up with me even on this faraway island. An invitation to an international conference on "Housing in Desert Conditions" arrived by mail. The conference was to take place at the Saudi University of Dahran in December 1978, and my presentation on "The Development of the Western Desert of Egypt for Settlements," which I had sent several months earlier, had been included in the program. We returned to New York in early December to report on our Caribbean project at the UNDP head office. At home, I found another letter from Dahran University, reminding me of the dates of the conference. There was hardly enough time to tell Lenta about the rest of my stay in St. Lucia before I had to start packing again.

By this time, I had virtually given up on being involved in discussions on desert settlements. In my naïveté, I was bitter at the lack of interest and the passivity of both the American and Egyptian authorities in a matter, which not only I, but also many thinking people in Egypt, considered so important for the future of the region. My program for President Sadat of the development of the Western Desert must have got lost somewhere in the bureaucratic jungle. And, as usual, everything depended on an investment of money, which so far, no one had been prepared to undertake. I now saw the invitation to Saudi Arabia as the crowning achievement of all my past endeavors; I believed that the proverbial "sack of money" was at last coming my way. I was also looking forward to the chance of a great adventure. The recent developments in European and American town planning and housing construction were not, to my mind, directly transferable to the Middle East, as they would clash with local traditions. Particularly, as in view of the increasingly loud objections to the Western life style, this alone might inflame the growing fundamentalist, purist feelings. This might have applied to many other walks of life; but naturally, planning and building were of primary interest to me, and I saw these activities as most likely to create highly visible problems. After all, the new environment created by architecture affects literally everybody. The clash between hostile lifestyles unfolds within its walls. In the 1970s, Saudi Arabia was entering a period of unprecedented growth, fuelled by the billions of dollars deriving from the exploitation of her oil deposits. The combination of almost unlimited funds with the ultratraditional Islamic system of government and jurisdiction offered a chance of designing modern buildings, particularly in the area of public housing adapted to local customs and traditions. This could have been a true intellectual and technological challenge.

A group of us taking part in the conference went to have a look at the new, highly praised Al-Khobar housing project. In the middle of the flat, featureless desert stood several fourteen-story tower blocks. My disillusionment was deepened when the construction manager, a broad-shouldered Dutchman, proudly informed us that all the building elements were prefabricated in Holland and brought over by sea in specially adapted ships running a shuttle service. In one of the already occupied apartments, I noticed a traditional low cooking charcoal stove placed on the typical European balcony and shaded from the sun by a screen put together from plywood, sheet metal, and paper. In the bathroom, stood a bunk bed for three children. While assuring us that exceptional consideration had been given to the tenants' needs and traditions, the manager took us to see the helicopter landing pad on the roof.

At the same time, events were taking place in the country, which must have perturbed the authorities. On the second day of the conference, we were advised not to go out shopping in town as disturbances were expected. We heard on the grapevine that a public execution of some conspirators plotting to overthrow the monarchy was to take place. This was an unexpected development. There was talk about an Islamic fundamentalist faction protesting against the Western influence on Saudi Arabia's traditional lifestyle. It reminded me of my journey to Abu Tartur.

I had other reminders as well as unexpected encounters during the conference. On the day of our arrival, I was having an early breakfast when my neighbor at an adjacent table looked at my identification tag and was happy to recognize a Polish name. He called out to his wife sitting at another table, "Look Pat, what a coincidence, this is a compatriot of our new pope!" Charles and Patricia Westwater was an interesting couple. In the fifties, they worked in Pakistan where they had both gone as missionaries to organize Christian schools in rural areas; she was a nun and he a Dominican monk. Having met, they eventually chose a different lifestyle, though remaining very devout. I teased them that their marriage was the punishment for having attempted to convert to their beliefs people of a different culture and religious tradition. Charles's contribution to the conference was a lecture on his own building experience in the Pakistani desert. Pat just came along to keep him company and was telling us about her visits to the Saudi women's quarters, to which, of course, we had no access. I was also approached by another Pole. He had gone to work in Libya on a contract from Poland and arrived in Saudi Arabia on a Libyan travel document, as he would not have been admitted on the passport of a Communist country.

His story was a shock to me. I was stunned when he told us of an interesting project for using the enormous water deposits under the Libyan desert for the development of agriculture. I could not believe my ears. He mentioned that huge pipes, fifteen feet in diameter, were already being laid, bringing water from the distant oases of Tazerbo and Sarir to coastal areas. Also interesting was that, as he told me, the Libyan leader Muammar al-Gaddafi was extremely critical of Egypt and of the Gulf Emirates for refusing to participate in the project. He accused their leaders of a servile obedience to the U.S. government that, according to him, was known to block any kind of progress in Egypt and Libya, apart from help in maximizing the exploitation of their oil deposits. This information shattered my illusions. If it was true, then my endeavors of the last two years were nothing but a wild goose chase. As I was planning to stop in Cairo on my way back home, I decided to check on it.

One day, another participant of the conference, dressed in traditional Arab clothes, came up to me to congratulate me on my lecture. "Don't you recognize me?" he asked with a bright smile. "We've met in 1975 at the Pratt Institute. Do you remember?" Indeed, I didn't recognize the friendly dean of the school of architecture and planning at the King Faisal University in Dammam at first, now so differently attired. Ahmed Farid Mustafa was an Egyptian living in Saudi Arabia. I had met him three years before, while he was visiting scientific centers in the USA. We talked then about the problems of architectural design in the Middle East. Now, he was in the process of organizing for January 1980 a symposium at his university on the subject of modern architecture and town planning in Arab countries, and warmly invited me to come. My Middle Eastern adventures seemed to continue.

Charles and Patricia joined me on the return journey via Egypt. In Cairo, we all stopped at Peggy's, delighted and excited at the prospect of entertaining such a large company. It was all as before: breakfast in bed, beer bottles arriving via the window. I took my new friends on a tour of old Cairo and the Khan el-Khalili bazaars. I improvised a Christmas Eve dinner in a restaurant in the neighborhood in which we had lived in the 1960s. We attended midnight mass in a local church, which was full to overflowing. The Westwaters then went for several days to Upper Egypt, while I was invited to a party at my old friends Nadia and Zohair Faried, where, unexpectedly, I met the prime minister of Egypt.

Mustafa Khalil was a highly educated man, an engineer by profession. He must have heard of my contact with Abdel-Meguid and asked me how far I had gone in my presentation for President Sadat. He suggested I used electronic simulation methods to demonstrate the individual phases of the project—present and future. He must have noticed my wry expression and asked whether I had encountered any problems. I had to tell him the truth. "Indeed, sir. I was not able to raise any funds for the project, not a penny. Neither from USAID nor, even more strangely, from the Egyptian authorities." Our eyes met. I chanced one question. "I have a feeling that in some way the project has been blocked; by whom and why, I have no idea." Then I mentioned the information I had about the Libyan project. "Is that true?" "These are not subjects for party gossip," he said. "Write to me on your return to New York; we will see what can be done," he added, handing me his address card. I did write on January 14, 1979. I never received a reply.

In the meantime, the King Faisal University approved my contribution to the forthcoming conference, which was scheduled for December 1979. Its title was, appropriately, "The Arab Architecture for the Modern World." I had less than a year to prepare the project, so I asked two men to assist me, Charles Westwater, who had become my friend, undertook to explore the problems of faith and philosophy of Islam in relation to family and social life of Middle Eastern traditional communities, while Brent Porter, a younger colleague at the Pratt Institute, dealt with the use of solar energy and traditional Arab methods of harnessing the wind power.

Ten months later, I left New York with my team on board of a Saudi Arabian Airlines Boeing 747. We had with us fifteen large-scale illustration boards and several models of buildings in large boxes. After a twelve hours' flight, we landed in Dhahran, an impressive international airport on the east coast of the Arabian Peninsula. The subject of the symposium was the exploration of the theory and practice of the Islamic concepts of space, geometry, and symbolism. We were asked to discuss how they might relate to the lifestyle, to social structures, to the economy, and to modern building technology. All of these considerations were quite evidently missing from the Western products offered to the Arab world. The conference was attended by many people with projects prepared by large American and European architectural and engineering firms. Our presentation was chosen to illustrate a specific design for a modern urban settlement with architectural models and building methods. The symposium with its exhibition was opened by Prince Miteb, the Saudi minister of housing and public works, who called on all the ministries of the kingdom to join the enterprise and help maintain the spirit and the traditions of the great Islamic architecture. Sheikh Hassan, chancellor of Saudi Arabian universities, stressed that Islam is not only a religion of worship but a way of life and a path always leading toward scientific progress in all spheres, particularly architecture. Our presentation was a truly great success: we brought with us printed brochures in English and in Arabic, which, like the proverbial hot cakes, disappeared on the first day.

in Dammmam

Hasan Fathy, the Egyptian elder statesman of architecture, who was the guest of honor, singled out in his speech our project as the best example of contemporary residential building for the Middle East.

with Hasan Fathy

In the subsequent interview with the English language press, Prince Mitteb quoted excerpts from the bilingual captions appended to our presentation. These were minor details, but nevertheless gratifying. We were invited to present our exhibition material in Manama on the island of Bahrain and in Cairo, where our participation was to enhance the opening of the new Center for Islamic Architecture and town planning in Heliopolis. Suddenly, all seemed to be going our way. Had we found favor with some supernatural power?

However, just before leaving for Bahrain, I had a sobering experience. At the symposium, I ran into Hamdi and Ismail, the two architects who, fifteen years before, had been part of my Aswan team and who were now employed in Saudi Arabia. Our reunion was joyful, and they both gave us a hand in putting up the exhibition. They came to the airport to see us off. As we were about to leave, Hamdi took me aside for few confidential words. "Please don't hold it against me, but I feel that I ought to warn you that here, in this country, one cannot get anywhere without a large kickback for an appropriate member of the royal family. There is no doubt that your kind of buildings ought to be introduced in the entire kingdom and even beyond. They all know it, and that's why they praised it so vociferously, but all the same, the contracts will go to those companies that will pay most. Only branches of great international conglomerates can afford it, and they put up the same buildings all over the world, completely ignoring local traditions and customs. They don't know, or perhaps they don't care, that there are people here who will never forgive them and whose power is on the rise. That's all I wanted to tell you. Do forgive me, but I had to warn you. I owe it to you on account of my respect for you, our past collaboration, and my anxiety as to the future."

This conversation took place two months after the armed occupation of the great mosque in Mecca by a large unit of Islamic jihadists, in January 10, 1980, or year 1358 of Hadjira of the Islamic calendar.

27

Bayethe!

The letter offering me the post had come from Nairobi, Kenya, headed UNCHS or United Nations Center of Human Settlements. It was brief and made just two points: first that the center had chosen me for the post of director of residential Housing Construction in Swaziland, Southern Africa, and second that the government of Swaziland confirmed this appointment and invited me to take up the post. My first reaction was, where the hell is Swaziland? I'd better find out. "Swaziland . . . where is that? Never heard of it," answered my former Nigerian student when I asked him about the place.

Lenta had an interesting job at a new art gallery on Madison Avenue, which specialized in early twentieth century American art. She was very absorbed in this work, and it would have been unthinkable to tear her away from it. She was not at all keen on traveling and on all those foreign escapades of mine. She responded with silence when I broached the idea of going to Africa. But anyway, I had to find out first what it was all about. My initial contact at the UNDP offices did not furnish much information, and I needed to talk to someone with personal experience of these mysterious parts of the world. It was then that I wrote to Victor Gessler, an old buddy and architect, who left Poland in the 1960s—the time of the great Polish "brain drain"—for South Africa. He lived in Durban.

In the meantime, the UN officials gave me more information about the type of work I could expect. "They want," said my interlocutor, "someone to supervise the work of the young local technicians and to organize the 'self help' construction of a whole settlement; a project to boost the government's prestige. Would you like a word with Swaziland's representative at the UN?"

I met the two diplomats in the office of the UN mission. Reserved, distant, and distrustful, they did not say a word, waiting for me to begin. But I also maintained a silence, meanwhile having a look round. Several color posters decorated the walls. One in particular attracted my attention. It showed a smiling girl with bare breasts and a fanlike arrangement of nine scarlet feathers of some exotic bird adorning her hair; around her neck, she wore an intricate necklace of colored beads set in an interesting geometrical pattern. Pretty earrings and round pompons of bright woolen yarn hanging from her shoulders completed the attractive portrait. I moved a little closer to have a look at the details, when the two men suddenly came to life. The tall one smiled widely. "You will see plenty of that in our country," he said. "We keep performing our traditional rites all the time. We all wear our traditional clothes; we all dance. Dance is a very important part of our rituals. Weddings, births, deaths are all accompanied by dancing. Some dances are part of secret rituals; they last several days and no stranger is allowed to witness them."

"Is this a picture of such a secret ceremony?" I asked with curiosity.

"Oh, no," they laughed aloud. "This is the dress for the Reed Dance, the Umhlanga feast. Guests are welcome and anyone can take pictures. And there are plenty of subjects for photographers," he added with a wink. The ice broken, we sat down in armchairs arranged round a table. The two diplomats knew nothing about the building program. So I asked them to tell me about their country. They gave me an illustrated book and a bunch of tourist brochures. We browsed through them at home with great interest. The proposed job and the journey appeared to be rather tempting, the work being quite in line with my interests in teaching and experimenting. Moreover, this was actual fieldwork and not a desk job, unlike the work of the majority of UNDP project managers. The family's conclusion was that in view of my great interest in the post, I ought to accept it. And to be honest, there was nothing else in view at the moment, and I was not at all keen to seek new work in New York. Still, I was not decided what to do.

The Pound Ridge project was finished, and the outcome was published in two volumes with many color illustrations. One of the board members, Richard de Sola Mendes wrote even a computer program for its application.

The method of planning human settlements while preserving the natural environment, resulting from this study, "Land Use Through Ecology," would now have to wait for its historical moment to be tested and employed sometime . . . somewhere . . .

Then, came the advent of the Solidarity movement in Poland. A year after the pope's first visit to his homeland, the American press began to show an interest in events taking place in that part of the world. I was emotionally quite involved and followed these developments with care, this being the one reason holding me back from traveling to the other side of the world. I was thus taking my time in giving a definitive reply to the Swaziland job offer. But finally, a detailed and enthusiastic letter from Victor in Durban, full of praise for Swaziland, helped me to make up my mind. I sent a letter to Nairobi accepting the job. Lenta, her gallery closing for the vacations, agreed to come with me; and further decisions were to be made on the spot. Klara approved of our appetite for adventure, even more so after I promised to invite her and Erroll to spend their next vacation in Africa; this year, they had already planned to spend it in Italy. As Aunt Maria was supposed to be in

France at the time, we organized a family reunion in Paris while in transit

We planned to leave New York toward the end of July. My own books, professional literature, textbooks, instruments, and drafting materials filled two metal trunks. And following the *Polish Daily*'s appeal to New York Poles to help impoverished people in our home country, we took with us a lot of clothing to be sent on to Poland from Paris.

In the meantime, news was coming from Poland of a veritable avalanche of strikes erupting suddenly in factories and workshops throughout the country. The new danger, according to the press, was not the Polish Communist authorities, but fears rooted in the events in Czechoslovakia in 1968 and centered on the high possibility of an armed Soviet intervention. But no one foresaw what was actually to happen.

Our next step was Cairo—this was a sentimental journey—for Lenta it was after an absence of thirteen years. Our luggage had been checked and sealed at the Orly airport in Paris, these being the days of the start of international terrorism, and new safety rules were being introduced. This produced confusion in Cairo, as the customs officers wanted to open our suitcases while the frontier guards would not allow the seals to be broken. I suggested that we just took our hand luggage necessary for the few days of our stay in Egypt, while the rest could stay at the left luggage facility at the airport until our departure for the last leg of our journey. This started infinite discussions of the technicalities involved; each of the Egyptian officials had his own unswerving opinion and no agreement could be reached. Phone calls were made to other offices and to the relevant authorities. Lenta was getting anxious whether the problem would ever get resolved. I assured her that all one needed was patience and a smile on one's face. I told her of a similar situation a few months back, when my team and I had brought our exhibits from Saudi Arabia to be shown in Cairo. The whole of our project, including models of buildings, had to be assembled in Heliopolis for the opening ceremony of the Center for Islamic Architecture and to remain there for a week, before being taken back by us to New York. The customs officers at the airport, however, would not let us collect our materials on arrival without paying customs duty. "Duty? For what?" We kept asking; our credulity strained to the limit. But I would not give in. The unforgettable circus of bureaucracy, in which I had to take an active part, was such as I had never encountered before. It took three hours of negotiations, eventually involving a written request for a temporary exemption from customs duty. After I collected one hundred and sixty three signatures from a swarm of clerks, covering both sides of the application's sheet of paper, we were at last allowed to take all the exhibition material to Heliopolis. On top of this, our host had to deposit a large sum as a security deposit. I wanted to keep a photocopy of the application as a memento, but was refused permission and, at this stage, could not be bothered to argue. And even this was not the end of our problems. On departure, I had to write another application to the customs office before being allowed to load our exhibits but, on this occasion, only twenty-four signatures were required.

This time officialdom proved somewhat more efficient. Having left our heavy trunks at the Customs repository, we drove to the Mena House hotel. This hotel in Giza, close to the great pyramids, was previously a British "Rest House." I actually remembered it from my army days, when it was designated *for officers only* and thus out of bounds for me, one of the lower ranks. Visiting the pyramids has always been a magical experience for me. Some forty years had passed since I first climbed the Great Pyramid, soon after finishing my training with the Polish brigade near Alexandria. I still have the photograph taken from the top of the pyramid, showing the old Mena House with its extensive gardens. Behind them, in the distance, lay the cultivated fields of the Nile valley. The flattened apex of the Cheops pyramid could provide a foothold just for me and my three companions. Looking to the east, we could see a rocky escarpment; and at its foot, a small village of clay huts and a clump of date palms. Further to the south stood the pyramid of Chefren, the son of Cheops, with its still regular shiny apex, the finish, which, at one time, topped all the pyramids. Several hundred yards down, practically on the edge of the plateau, rested the great Sphinx, said to be the monument to this particular pharaoh. Its damaged head with its chipped nose clearly shows the anthropological facial features of the black race. Furthest to the south stands the much-smaller pyramid of Mykerinos, the third pharaoh of that dynasty. I do remember clearly the feeling of near ecstasy, of a strange lightness, which kept bringing me to this place again and again, even when I could not climb to the top of the pyramid anymore.

Toward the evening, we walked to the rocky plateau and climbed the stairs hewn in the great blocks of stone, leading to the small landing in front of the entrance to the interior of the great pyramid. We came across no tourists on the way and, in the silence, admired the orange glow of the sun sinking beyond the horizon. Somewhere below, a man in a white galabiya was riding a horse nervously stepping on the large slabs of stone.

About a quarter of the way up the pyramid, we sat down on the steps, looking at the views around us. They had changed considerably from those etched in my memory. The outskirts of Giza were now reaching the edge of the escarpment. Some buildings and barracks could now be seen on the western desert side, beginning to surround the pyramids. There were no more cultivated fields beyond it, just a dense cluster of concrete buildings with stumps of posts sticking out at the top, waiting for upper stories yet to be built. Far away in the east, where once the minarets of the old city were to be seen, a gray cloud of smog hung over Cairo. It was said that the capital of Egypt had now reached seventeen million inhabitants. "What will happen to Egypt in the years to come?" asked Lenta. "Will urban sprawl cover the entire Nile valley?" That was the question, which I hoped would have been up for discussion at the international conference proposed by Boutros-Ghali several years before. But it did not happen. There were rumors that it was the United States, which nipped in the bud any suggestion of a path of development for Egypt other than the status quo, which kept it in financial and military dependence on America, thus securing the safety of Israel. This may not be true, but the thought that this is how superpowers work is very sad. Dusk was rapidly advancing, and we were coming down the stone steps carefully and slowly. Somewhere below, in the distance, the mournful bray of a donkey sounded the lament for the passing days, for times never to return.

The next stage of our journey took us to Kenya. The driver of a microbus met us at Nairobi airport, reassuring us that our luggage would be delivered later. We left the hotel to have a look at the town. The Thorn Tree restaurant looked inviting; and indeed, the tables were set in a small garden in the shade of a big umbrella-shaped tree. "All we need is a giraffe feeding on its leaves," I quipped. "After all, this is Africa." We thus chose antelope kebab from the menu and washed it down with local beer. I bought newspapers in a nearby kiosk. The first pages were full of the Moscow Olympic Games, which had been hardly mentioned in the American press, no doubt because of the U.S. boycott of the Games, a reaction to the 1979 Soviet invasion of Afghanistan. The local papers were giving full coverage of the events; most of all, of the achievements of the celebrated Kenyan runners. In contrast, there were no photographs of Iranian girl students in their black chadors demonstrating in New York in favor of Ayatollah Khomeini's Islamic reforms and distributing leaflets; no reports of Afghan mujahadin partisans' resistance to the Soviet forces. And of course, not a word about the strikes in Poland. Moonlight, filtering through the leaves of the thorn tree, competed with the flickering candles on every table. The events in Tehran, the fate of the exiled Shah, Kabul, Kandahar, the Moscow Olympics all receded into the shadows.

The UNCHS offices occupied a rather amusing round tower block with the elevators and service accommodation placed in its central core. All the officials I had met in New York were now working in Nairobi. I received the ritual briefing initiating me into my new job and found out more about the mysteries of work in Swaziland. My predecessor was an Israeli who had already begun to build a small settlement in the capital, Mbabane. My job was to examine the existing situation and design a bigger housing settlement with improved building standards. Meanwhile, as a weekend was coming, we were advised to spend a few days in one of the safari camps, on the savanna of the Masai country.

The Masai tribesmen were tall, slim, dressed in rust-colored tunics, canvas bags hanging from their shoulders. Their skin was of a lighter hue than that of the majority of people seen in Nairobi. They wore their long hair plaited into slender braids and tinted a reddish shade. In their hands, they wielded long shepherd's staffs and were driving large herds of buff-colored and roan cattle. They crossed the path we were on and drove their herd toward a nearby gully, the lushly overgrown banks of which indicated the presence of water. Soon after, a swift herd of impalas followed in the same direction. Their orange-tan backs and white bellies flickered against the yellowed grasses each time they leapt in a dramatic arc. In the distance, giraffes and zebras were stepping majestically in the same direction. Dusk was falling and all animals were hurrying to their favorite waterholes. But it was when large families of baboons started leaping from the tall grass, barking and baring their fangs that we decided to turn back and return to our bungalow. That gave us the feel of Africa in a nutshell.

A long time ago, the Masais found their pasturelands in the Bantu country, some Bantus having moved southward, displacing the Bushmen from the southeastern plains. Thus, the Swazis, the Zulus, and the Basutos, originating in the jungles of central Africa, became pastoral nations inhabiting the southern savannas.

It was time to continue our journey. There were many empty seats on our Lufthansa Boeing 747 to Johannesburg, as the majority of tourist passengers had disembarked in Nairobi. We took the window seats on the left side in expectation of the promised spectacular views. And indeed, the Kilimanjaro massif soon appeared, lit by the strong afternoon sun. Its two snow-covered peaks appeared above a thin cover of pink clouds. I promised myself to climb this mountain some time in the future. Next, we flew over the valley of the great Zambezi River followed by the somewhat smaller Limpopo.

We touched down in Johannesburg airport after dark. The following day, my old friend Victor managed to trace us to our hotel. It was good to renew our friendship after twenty years; he had acted as a witness at our wedding. He emigrated to South

Africa in the 1960s and was now running an architectural studio in Durban in partnership with Jurek Brejowski. Victor had recently started seeing Delscey Shaw, a well-to-do widow from an English family settled in Natal province for generations. The whole lot of them became friends, visiting one another, and spending vacations together in South Broom, south of Durban, where Victor built a splendid summer residence. Such were the doings of the Polish diaspora. But that was not the end. Soon after, we were introduced to their friends, Wojtek and Mariola, who had arrived in South Africa in the same wave of Polish exodus. It was from them, who kept listening to the news broadcast by the BBC that we learned about the trouble in the Gdańsk shipyards. It wasn't known yet what the immediate cause was but sixteen thousand workers had gone on strike. As this was, in a way, a continuation of recent demonstrations and disorders, the news did not impress us all that much. From this distant perspective, events in Poland no longer had the same impact. My immediate priority was to get acquainted with the work awaiting me. And thus, after two days in Johannesburg, we boarded a Royal Swazi jet airplane bound for Swaziland. What struck me first among the group waiting at the Matsapha airport arrivals lounge was the bright smile on the dark face of a man with a big head of curly hair, who quickly introduced himself as Teshome Tsighe, my future assistant. Teshome, an Eritrean, was a building technician, one of the UN's volunteers from the Netherlands.

Matsapha airport was almost the size of Warsaw's, and that for a country of approximately six hundred thousand inhabitants was quite impressive. There was a lot of comings and goings, so it seemed that after all we had not found ourselves in the middle of nowhere. We found out later that Swaziland was also a tourist Mecca for South Africans seeking interracial adventures forbidden at home and easy to come by here. On the way to the kingdom's capital, Mbabane, lying in the hilly part of the country, we passed through the wide and beautiful Ezulwini valley. Teshome pointed out on the right the Mdzimba Mountains with their royal cave tombs and, on the left, the two conical peaks commonly known as Sheba's

Tits. Next, we passed the gardens of the Royal Swazi Hotel with its casinos. After that, we saw the gates of the Mlilwane Wildlife Sanctuary. Too many impressions for newcomers.

In the next ten days, I was getting acquainted with my new office occupying a bungalow belonging to the housing department of the Ministry of Public Works, which was our sponsor. I met my young staff and the student trainees. Lenta and I found a small apartment in the Diamond Motel in the Ezulwini valley, complete with a swimming pool, owned by an elderly Latvian couple. The two were Holocaust survivors, and Mr. Diamond remembered a few words of Polish. They must have gone through terrifying experiences, as they would never talk of those days, even though we became good friends over the next two years.

Later, I got better acquainted with this attractive country by driving to various interesting places together with Maher Abdalla, an Egyptian UNESCO expert, who had arrived in Swaziland at the same time.

It was time for Lenta to return home. For the second time since my stay in St. Lucia, we were to lead separate lives. This time, the distance made the separation even more poignant, even though telephone communication throughout the world was by that time quite easy. We made use of it even before Lenta's departure by calling Aunt Maria in Warsaw. It was she who told us that the Polish government had recognized the independent trade union, now called Solidarity. She mentioned that an electrician from the Lenin Shipyards in Gdańsk called Lech Wałęsa has become its leader and, apparently, people were joining the new union en masse. Having promised to call home every week, I said good-bye to Lenta who took a plane to Johannesburg, where she would change for a direct flight to New York.

It took me three months to get the Sidwashini-North program running. It provided for 170 individual family homes. This led to the creation of a small school of architecture and building technology, which gave me great personal satisfaction. The enthusiasm of our young students was my greatest reward. Helped by new friends from among my coworkers as well as others met on social occasions,

I began to learn about the history of Swaziland, which is a rather special case in the new postcolonial Africa.

Chris Mkhonza, undersecretary in the ministry, decided to coach me in Swazi customs. One day, he drove up to meet me dressed in the traditional costume. Around his hips, coming down to his calves, was wrapped a length of cotton with a small orange and brown design. His waist was cinched with two monkey hides creating a semblance of two aprons, one in front and one behind. Obliquely across his torso hung strings of colored beads and shells, several short necklaces adorned his neck. I had seen such colorful dress when, during Lenta's stay, we attended the yearly celebrations of the Reed Dance. Men thus dressed took part in this ritual dance accompanied by thousands of half-naked girls who, in a symbolic gesture, presented the Queen Mother with bunches of reeds several yards long for the building of the traditional fencing round her kraal in Lobamba.

"Are we going dancing, Chris?" I asked, sitting next to him in the car. "Look behind you," he pointed to the back seat. "You have to get to know our weapons." A large oval shield made of dried cow's hide with a strong wooden rod threaded lengthways through incisions in the hide lay there. There was another long staff, made of a tree branch, which ended in a round piece of where the branch joined the trunk. "This is the knobkerrie, our club, the most deadly traditional weapon apart from the assegai," he pointed to a short spear. "The assegai was introduced by Shaka Zulu, the great Zulu leader and the terror of the British," he concluded. "And no, we are not going to dance; we shall visit my family kraal. The king requires us to wear traditional dress whenever we visit our old villages. He is right; it keeps up the tradition, and it is very attractive, don't you think?"

Chris's family kraal consisted of six round domed huts, made of an outer layer of intricately woven cane laid over a similarly constructed network of wooden rods. One rectangular building, a kind of barn, had clay walls under a thatched roof. A tall reed fence surrounded the whole settlement. Small red and a blue banners fluttered from two masts placed at the entrance. Chris left the car outside and removed his sandals. Barefoot, holding his weapons, he stopped at the gate, bowed low, and waited thus outside to be called in. Afterward, he signaled me to follow him and placed his shield, club, and spear by the fence. An old woman appeared from one of the huts and, gesticulating with both hands, palms up, and bowing repeatedly. "Saubona, yebo . . . saubona," she said several times, "undzhani?" (What's the news?) She went back to the hut and came out again carrying a large black clay bowl with a small top opening. We passed it round and, standing, slowly drank the white frothy liquid—homemade beer. The woman, Chris's old nurse, brought a chair out for me and put it in the airy gazebo. It was November, almost summer. Chris went in to see his ailing mother. Later, we had a look at the barn and at the granary, full of sacks of grain and aromatic herbs. Having eaten some grilled meat with roasted vegetables, we decided it was time for a siesta and lay down on straw mats. The aroma of dry herbs and the refreshing light breeze sent us to sleep straight away. "What is the meaning of those banners?" I asked Chris on our way out. "It's a sign that fresh meat and beer are on sale here," he smiled.

The proper evening program of the local cable television began with the national anthem followed by news from the world. Before that, the screen was showing the country's mountain landscapes. In one of the close-ups, one could see a warrior running up a rocky peak wielding his shield and his knobkerrie. Raising the latter above his head, he shouted, "BAYETHE!" a kind of war cry, at the top of his voice. One evening, straight after this Swazi cry, I suddenly heard the tune of the Polish national anthem. I ran to have a closer look at the screen and saw a crowd of people singing, taking part in some kind of manifestation. Above their heads were banners with the word *Solidarność* in large red letters. A man with a dark moustache was speaking to the crowd. The newsreader explained that this was a report from Poland where great political changes had taken place, where for the first time the Communist system had to give in to the demands of citizens. Several ad followed, President Reagan briefly appeared, and finally the program changed to a local football match.

I was learning about the events in Poland from Lenta's letters and telephone conversations. The peaceful revolution was growing into a national revival movement. Friends in Johannesburg were telling me about a new wave of immigrants from Poland and the new aid committees, which were being formed to help them in finding work. According to Lenta, the same was happening in New York. Apparently, the old Communist restrictions on foreign travel were being lifted in Poland. In December, I flew home for a ten day's leave. I took with me several bottles of the fine wine from the Stellenbosch vineyards, which, due to the trade embargo on South Africa, was unknown in the USA. Our South African Airways Boeing 747 stopped for refueling on the Salt Island of the Cape Verde Archipelago near the western coast of Africa. A few sleepy passengers got out to stretch their legs and visit the duty free shop, apart from which there was nothing but desert and four hungry-looking mongrels, one with a crooked tail. In the evening, we landed in New York, in the snow-covered JFK airport.

It was Christmas, and our social life was in full swing. We celebrated a family Christmas Eve at home in the company of some of our old Warsaw friends and some new acquaintances of Lenta. There were now several journalists newly arrived from Poland working for the *Polish Daily News*. This immediately raised the standard of the paper, improving also its circulation. Suddenly, the iron curtain was no more. The *New York Times* published reports from various towns in Poland almost daily, though they had to vie for space with John Lennon's murder. Photographs of crying girls placing flowers in front of the Dakota, the big eclectic apartment building and site of the murder appeared next to those of peasants protesting in front of some shabby building in a Polish town, demanding the recognition of the rural branch of the Solidarity trade union. There were articles about NATO warning the Soviet Union not to invade Poland and so on. Continuing protests even reached New York. In January, as I was going to meet someone in the UN Secretariat, where my blue passport offered me untrammeled admission, I was stopped by several hundred protesters sitting on the ground. They were employees of the Secretariat protesting against the continuing imprisonment of their colleague, arrested in Warsaw in 1979 for alleged spying. On the same day, Lech Wałęsa had a private audience with the pope. Having extended my leave by another week, I was returning to Africa in mid-January. In New York, we had to wait for three hours after boarding the plane. The passengers looked on nervously as water jets were removing the thick cover of ice from the wings.

In Johannesburg, it was mid-summer. On the way to Swaziland, I stopped in Pretoria to see Gerd Ockert, a German architect who had his office in Mbabane and who had become a good friend. He kept going home to Pretoria from time to time to be with his wife Else and his daughter Doris, a medical student. Over our beer, we both came to the striking conclusion that Germans and Poles had a lot in common. Now Gerd insisted on showing me his prewar photo albums. Ilse brought her album too. There were small snapshots, similar to those in my mother's albums: holidays on the Baltic shore, children riding a donkey, the whole family packed tightly in a convertible car, someone doing a headstand; and on the next page, Nazi banners with their swastikas and rows of uniformed youngsters with their arms raised stiffly in a Nazi salute. "That's me," said Gerd pointing to a slim youth. "I was thirteen." "And I too wore a uniform with a swastika armband when I was nine; you can see me here," added Else. Suddenly we were all silent. Why were they showing me these photographs? I was puzzled. "Yes, so . . ." I started, not really knowing what to say. But Gerd rescued me. "We wanted you to know that our youth did not differ from that of the majority of German children. But when the war ended, when we grew up, we truly regretted having been part of that past; a past, which we abhor to this day. We decided to settle in South Africa. Unfortunately, here, we came across apartheid, another nasty form of racism. This is so painful for us, and this is what we wanted you to know."

I have not forgotten this small episode because it struck a chord with me and made me think how some family habits and stereotypes can be so differently perceived by subsequent generations. While writing these reminiscences, I have frequently been puzzled by the question of how was it possible that, having been brought up from my earliest youth in a rather nationalist right-wing milieu, I always felt discomfort and embarrassment when listening to even slightly racist, anti-Semitic, or religious opinions characteristic of this milieu. Perhaps one does not, after all, learn one's political views at one's nurse's knee.

Teshome came to see me soon after my return to Mbabane. He arrived with his girlfriend, Margaret, and wanted to know all about my stay in New York. He told me that during my absence, practically nothing had been done in our center. The festivities, the parties, the heat were not conducive to work. He mentioned that friends of his were now organizing a carnival party and wondered whether I'd join in. Well, why not? Let's go. We found quite an international crowd there, aided and abetted by local playboys and unattached black belles. They were all dancing to the rather monotonous African pop music, quite unlike the rhythmical but melodious disco music that had in the last few years conquered America and many other parts of the world. All the same, we had a good time. There was a new face there, the handsome and elegant Fred Lule, son of the former leader of Uganda who had been briefly in power following the fall of the despicable Idi Amin. Fred was one of the many political refugees then living in Swaziland and was working as an accountant in a private firm. After several beers, he started confiding his problems to me. "I haven't got enough women to be happy here," he plaintively told me. Amazed, I pointed to the dancing crowd. "But, you see, they don't want it." "Don't want what?" And then he told me. He and several friends invented a game in which points were awarded to each one of them for the number of young girls he managed to impregnate during the year. "I already have twenty three pregnancies confirmed by a doctor friend," he boasted. I found this sickening. Two years later, Swaziland, as all of southern Africa, suffered the greatest in the world epidemic of AIDS. Unrestrained promiscuity in some African countries is seldom mentioned in the Western press. I trust that, by now, all these game players have paid a hefty price for their amusement.

Two of the guests at the party I knew already quite well. Constance Khumalo and Studla Mugadi both worked for the Ministry of Public Works and were very useful in pushing our paperwork through the bureaucratic maze. This was very helpful to our project, which was nearing the phase of actual construction. Studla, though, even while helping us, defended the bureaucratic procedures as proof of Europeanization and democratization of the country's rule. She argued that the regulations put a brake on the autocratic impulses of the more conservative advisers of the king, of whom, nonetheless, both young women were very proud.

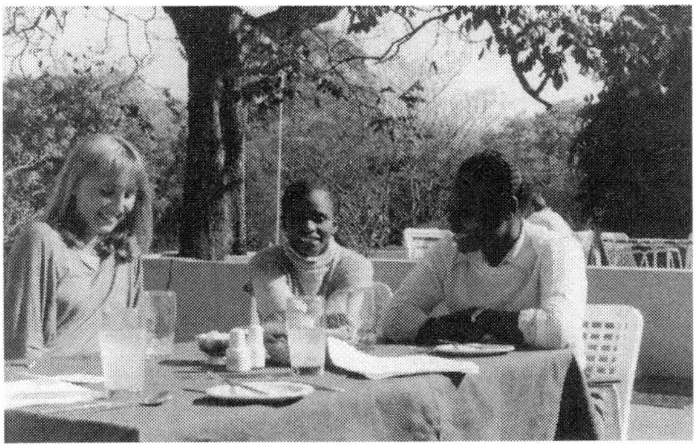

Klara,Constance and Studla

It was then that an embarrassing incident stirred the public opinion. Several human heads were found in the freezer in the house of one of the members of parliament. Soon after, the police arrested someone in South Africa carrying a human head in a shopping bag. Belief in sorcery, witchcraft, and the power of medicine men was still alive in the primitive, ancient layers of local traditions. I often heard these stories spoken in a whisper by Pumzile, our office typist, while she cast troubled glances behind her shoulder. Once she took me for a walk with her little daughter to visit a *sangoma*, a fortune-teller, living in a traditional reed hut on a steep hill above the town. A half-naked woman, wearing an assortment of amulets, with plaited copper-colored hair, kneeled in font of us on the ground. She was laying out on the sand an arrangement of small bones, stones, and other strange-looking objects, giving me a careful look from time to time. Pumzile's daughter, imitating her, began also to put down rows of pebbles. Suddenly, the sangoma swept her hand over the girl's design, causing her to burst into tears. A commotion and a lot of shouting resulted in the termination of the fortune-telling session.

I subsequently learned that the pattern of pebbles was a bad omen for me, and she had to destroy it quickly. The only remedy, I was informed, was purification by contact with a human amulet and by drinking some brown liquid from a small flask. I declined the cure for the time being, and we returned instead to town to get a large ice cream cone for the frightened child.

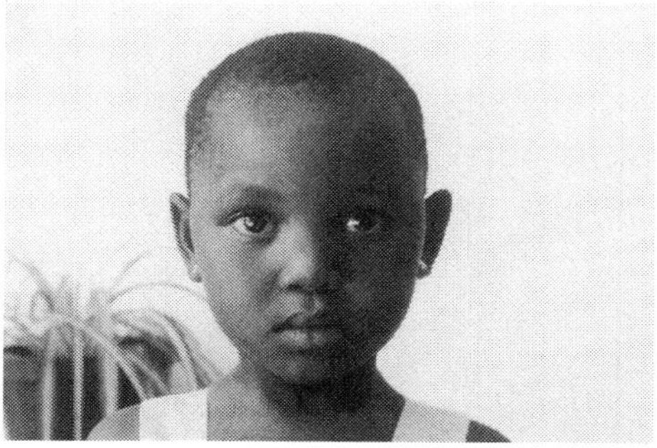

Pumzile's daughter

Sobhusa II, the king of Swaziland, was the descendant of a long line of tribal Swazi rulers. He was at the time, as I kept being reminded, the longest-ruling monarch in the world. We were approaching the sixty-year jubilee of his ascendancy to the title of Ngwenyema, the Lion of Swazi. He was widely praised for achieving the near impossible in the way he introduced what was best in Western culture without destroying the basis of local African tradition and customs. He was helped by the fact that the Swazi are an ethnically well-knit nation. I met king Sobhusa II at the celebrations of the United Nations Day. I invited the shy Constance Khumalo to accompany me; dressed all in white, she looked as good as a fashion model. The celebrations took place in the sports stadium, and we were allocated seats in the diplomatic box. Before us, in the middle of the stadium, was a richly decorated covered grandstand for the dignitaries; present already were the prime minister, the regional director of the UN, newly arrived from New York, and the local program director of UNDP. On the left stood rows of older women in traditional dress, wielding, instead

Women's dance

Sibhaca-warriors dance

of warrior weapons, kitchen tools such as scoops, ladles, and pokers. Tradition or a joke? Sitting on the grass, to the right of the grandstand, were about two dozen participants of the Sibhaca, the traditional warriors' dance, with their large two-sided drums deposited nearby. A choir of schoolgirls in school uniforms waited in front of the grandstand. The king arrived in a black Cadillac limousine with a motorcycle police escort. He wore a full dress suit and top hat. He marched briskly to his seat, raising his hat to greet the assembled company. First there were speeches, followed by a slow, rhythmical dance-past of the women with their kitchen tools. Next, the girls' choir sang traditional songs; and finally, an energetic warrior's dance was performed by men with short assegais in their outstretched hands. To the rapid rhythm of the drums, they raised their legs with great precision above their heads, to hit them next, hard on the ground. This was a splendid, proud display of male power. A reception and more dances followed. Constance insisted on completing my education with a lecture on the laws governing the royal Swazi succession, but time ran out.

young wariors

Suddenly, work became hectic in our office. Designs for several buildings were ready, and we were beginning to build on the designated site. At the same time, Chris Mkhonza and myself were chosen to represent Swaziland at an international conference on residential housing in Africa on the island of Mauritius, organized by USAID. The journey was easy, as Swazi Air maintained regular flights to the Indian Ocean island. Several days before our departure, I had a talk with the director of UNDP. He wanted to extend my stay in Swaziland for another year, as the Nairobi headquarters wanted me to take charge of a rural development program. I said that I would have to get in touch with my wife. "Fine," said he rubbing his hands, "but I have yet another task for you. The New York headquarters would like you to go to Khartoum after the conference. We have problems in our office there."

My trip to Mauritius was memorable, as, for the first time, I was representing a country at an international conference. We were taken to a hotel with an enticing name: La Pirogue. The island, once a French possession, was taken over by Great Britain after the Napoleonic wars. Now it was an independent African state. The population was quite recognizably an Indian, African, European, and Malagasy ethnic mixture. Such a "melting pot," using American terminology, produced excellent results. The official language was English; but even after 160 years, most people still spoke correct French. Chris promptly decided that the conference was not for him and, with a wide smile on his face, assured me that "this is your show." In spite of having no French, he quickly befriended a local belle, obviously for some lessons.

This is new to me, I thought, taking my place in the large conference hall behind the desk with the country's name and the Swazi flag. We were seated in the alphabetic order of countries we represented and, next to me, was the representative of Tanzania. Her name was Aichi Kenzo and, as she promptly informed me, she had a British PhD in regional planning and was the youngest daughter of a tribal chief from the southern slopes of Kilimanjaro. The conference began with dreary presentations on the achievements of individual countries; on the third day of this, we had had enough and, playing truant, took ourselves to the beach. Before long, Chris joined us too. About a mile along the coast, we came upon a charming small pension called La Perle. We came to the conclusion that this might be more pleasant than La Pirogue with its crowd of noisy conference delegates and decided to move there. It was, indeed, very pleasant until the busload with the crew of a huge American aircraft carrier, which I noticed the day before at anchor in Port St. Louis, invaded our retreat. The sailors came to the island for so called R & R or rest and recuperation. They were soon followed by a minibus with its cargo of girls; and over the next twenty-our hours, the sailors were perhaps not so much resting as actively "recuperating." As the girls booked into two rooms, the entrance to which led from the same terrace as the one to my room, I had a good view of the sailors waiting their turn either on the terrace or downstairs at the bar. Fortunately, the aircraft carrier left soon, and La Perle became pleasant and quiet again. Meanwhile, Aichi invited me to visit Kilimanjaro.

Halfway through April, I embarked on my return journey to Swaziland via Paris and New York, having discovered that the roundabout flight across three continents was much cheaper than a return flight on one continent. This gave me an opportunity to go home, as well as to find out how Solidarity was doing in Poland. Even on the main street of Nairobi, I had glimpsed a white T-shirt with the now-famous logo of *Solidarność* in red letters with the small red-and-white flag.

In Paris, I met Aunt Maria who told me of the incredible mass movement in Poland; people demanding changes in all fields of life. She mentioned some signs of anarchy, which was attributed, however, to the security forces as provocation.

The second year of my stay in Africa started again with Lenta's visit. She had been managing quite well in New York on her own, working in Syd Deutch's art gallery. Syd's wife's family originated in Galicia, in southern Poland, and one of her childhood memories was that Poles were such . . . elegant people. I was not quite sure what she meant by this. Could it be parallel to the old story of a woman of questionable reputation, about whom the best that could be said was . . . that she loved her mother?

In August, Victor and his lady friend Delscey visited us in Swaziland, having come to watch the yearly Reed Dance. The cool and windy weather this year was disappointing, and we pitied the almost nude girls taking part in the great parade in Lobamba, shivering with cold. It improved by early September for the sixtieth anniversary of the reign of Sobhuza II. The celebrations lasted four days and ended with a great parade in the Somhlolo stadium, in the presence of a number of heads of states, with Princess Margaret representing Queen Elizabeth. It included a British-style Trooping the Color with detachments of guards in red tunics, navy trousers, and white gloves and belts. Sobhuza appeared in the full glory of the traditional national costume, barefoot, wearing a crown of eagle feathers, a leopard skin round his hips, and wielding a shield and knobkerrie. Accompanied by officers and adjutants, he marched along the straight lines of soldiers. The parade was followed by traditional celebrations. Several thousand warriors entered the stadium, their spear shafts beating a dull rhythm on their huge leather shields. They stopped, facing the tribune and, joined by the king, started a slow dance, squatting and rising, singing a monotonous tune. Next came the dance of young half-naked girls and older women wearing their traditional beretlike wigs. In the evening, oxen and antelopes were roasted on great spits, and there were firework displays. The general mood of great contentment spread even to us. The evening ended with a grill supper at Iris and Maher Abdalla's, our Egyptian friends.

Trooping of the colors

Lenta and I paid a visit to Johannesburg, stopping with our Polish friends. Lenta then returned home, changing places with Klara, who came to spend her vacation here on her own, as Erroll was not keen on visiting South Africa with its apartheid and stayed behind in New York. In Swaziland, she enjoyed horse riding on the vast veldt at the Mdzimba foothills, safaris in the Kruger Park adjacent to the northern border of Swaziland, and excursions to Durban, South Broom, and the Hshushlui nature reserve in Zululand. When Klara, laden with her trophies, returned to New York, I went back with enthusiasm to my rural housing demonstration project in the beautiful, rolling Madulini area in the south of the country. The workforce consisted exclusively of women, as the men preferred to sit in the shade and pass comments about the progress of the work.

I wasn't able to even dent this African custom. Nec Hercules . . .

Madulini—Chris Mkhonza translating

I also continued my lessons of the Swati language. Constance began with great patience by teaching me to pronounce certain sounds like Kh, as in her name Khumalo. This is not pronounced like a K sound, but it starts with a difficult click of the tongue and what is even more difficult is the transition to the next letter, U. One day, as I was driving with my local secretary-interpreter, Gloria Matsebula, through rural areas to visit the local clan chief, we ran short of gas.

I stopped and asked a passerby where the nearest gasoline station was. "Uyatwolakala yini phethiloli kulerndala?" Gloria went first into a state of shock and then couldn't stop shrieking with laughter.

Sidwashini project

Toward the end of the year, we roofed over

seventy single family and semidetached dwellings in the Sidwashini settlement. Local building materials, such as large sun-dried clay and cement bricks, were produced in neighboring villages. In Mbabane, I found another task awaiting me. The minister of the interior asked me to look into the chances of expanding the capital in the twenty-first century. The problem was the lack of suitable sites on the sheer slopes on the surrounding hills, coupled with an unbridled inflow of rural population.

And so it was in Africa that the problems of planning new towns have caught up with me.

Mbabane project

On the evening of December 12, the customary tribal shout of Bayethe was followed by a special TV report from Poland: a military coup had taken place, which threatened an invasion by Soviet, East German, and Czechoslovak forces. Martial law was imposed on the country. It looked like an international crisis. The subsequent reports from London and Washington confirmed the event and showed President Reagan embracing an elderly man with tears in his eyes. This was the hitherto Polish ambassador to the USA who had resigned from his post and "chose freedom" in America.

In the months that followed, the Republic of South Africa was to admit considerable numbers of Polish refugees. Their stories varied greatly. Many had been imprisoned. But actual bloodshed seemed to have been conspicuous by its absence, unusual in the light of previous Polish national uprisings. However, there was a general feeling of a great loss. Loss of what? We did not know it at the time.

When the cooler African fall weather arrived, I was glad to have completed my mission. The only remaining task was to write the final report of the center's activity. This proved to be almost two months of hard work. Before leaving, I visited Durban to say good-bye to Victor and his partner. We drove to South Broom to the house near the beach, which is still known as Gessler House today. We got up at dawn; and while Jurek went fishing in the ocean for small salmon, I was busy gathering huge mussels from under submerged rocks. Back in the house, we feasted on our catch in the kitchen, entertained by a bunch of small monkeys frolicking in the wide branches of a nearby tree. We had no tape recorder, but we used the one in the car to listen again and again to the Polish satirical, political cabaret songs recorded before the imposition of the martial law and obtained from the refugees. We grew quite nostalgic and sad.

There were long and warm good-byes at work. I left all my kitchen and household stuff to the ladies, of whom there was quite a number, while members of the male team wished for a true masculine treat. I thus bought half a calf that we roasted on a spit. I knew that there had to be enough meat to last till morning; according to an old tradition, you have to eat as much as you can because you never know what the next day may bring. The last parting was with friends in Johannesburg. I wanted to buy a particular rug produced only by the Venda tribe in northern Transvaal, and Mariola drove me in search of it all over the city. It was the end of April 1982. Hamba kahle! Good-bye!

I spent several days again in Nairobi. They tried to talk me in the center into taking another assignment, this time in Uganda, but I wasn't sure and hesitated.

Meeting one's countrymen in exotic locations might often be a pleasant experience, though one obviously cannot choose whom one comes across. To begin with, I met a pleasant and cultivated Polish transportation engineer on a long-term UN contract in Kenya, one of the pool of experts sent by the authorities in Warsaw. He knew Nairobi and its environs pretty well; and during my several stays in Kenya's capital, we would go together to the savanna to watch lions and rhinoceros, to have meals on the large veranda of his club, visit interesting out-of-town restaurants such as the Carnivore, where local game was barbecued on long spits over a huge round fire and then carried to the tables on long iron spears and served with spicy sauces. Such experiences often lead to an immediate friendship.

My professional interest took me also to another Nairobi, very different from the one of exclusive clubs, golf links, and residences standing amidst tropical gardens. This one was swimming in the detritus of life without sewers, swarming with hundreds of naked children covered in mud and excrement. A Nairobi, where bleary-eyed young men, dazed by drugs or drink, unable to leave the hell of their hopeless existence, sat leaning against the walls of their often derelict dwellings roofed over with rusty corrugated metal sheets. Young women or even underage girls had only one way of escaping this fate, and one saw the results of this tragic exodus around the bars and hotels, which they besieged in their garish clothes. One evening, after a substantial and jolly meal, we went to investigate Nairobi's nightlife. In a dance hall called California, saucer-shaped like a spacecraft, we were immediately surrounded by a crowd of dark faces, their brilliant white teeth and eye—whites shining unnaturally in the flickering lights of colored strobes. It was still a relatively early hour and there were few guests, most of them men. Another girl brought our beer together with a second tray loaded with more bottles—"For the girls you pick," she said. Soon two burly men came up to our table and greeted us in Polish. My companion seemed to know them and was obviously not pleased to see them. Just before their arrival, he was telling me that we had already seen all that there was to see here, that the sequel to such an evening was quite obvious, and that it was high time to leave. The two newcomers were set, however, on having a good time. I don't know how they found out that I had been offered a job in Uganda, but they were trying to convince me that I ought to accept it. They introduced themselves as area representatives of the Polish Ministry of Foreign Trade. They kept dropping hints that my cooperation with them in some enterprises they'd been planning might be quite lucrative for both sides. They obviously needed someone from the outside to provide a front for their activities. I was furious. Damned impudence!

"Who are those horrid individuals?" I asked, already in the car. I was told that they were high-ranking officers of the Polish secret police, whose present jobs were a reward for having bloodily repressed a worker's demonstrations in 1976. Now we know that in the years of Communist rule, most of the Polish foreign trade was in the hands of the secret police or of people in their pay. The profit from these transactions may have gone toward financing activities not accounted for in the official budget.

For me this was the turning point. I resolved there and then not to allow myself to be drawn into situations similar to one I had managed to extricate myself from now, and fifteen years earlier in Egypt, when I was pressured to cooperate with Polish and Soviet agents spying on Americans. I soon boarded a plane to New York. It was my personal *Out of Africa*.

The direct Pan-Am flight had one short stopover in Lagos, Nigeria. The sky was clear, and we were flying along the equator over a green carpet of primordial jungle. In Lagos, a new passenger took the seat next to me. The man was Japanese; he was covered in blood and his suit was in tatters. He drank a measure of whisky in one gulp and declared that he was never going to visit Africa again. His car was stopped by bandits on the airport road, and he was robbed of all his possessions. This incident reminded me of another Africa, the one I did not know well—the Africa of corruption, of assassinations, of religious hatred, mindless racial violence, the one where sharp machetes took the place of law and order. And that was the end of my African adventure.

In 2000, while on a family vacation with our grandchildren in Poland, we stopped to visit some old friends in their summer cottage in the forest. Their daughter, who lives in Switzerland, and who was visiting her parents, told me that she had come across the two-volume report on my work in Swaziland in the library of Zurich University.

28

What? Has a New Jihad Begun?

On one of my consulting trips out of Swaziland, I took the afternoon flight from Nairobi to Khartoum and was met at the airport by a representative of the Sudan's Ministry of Housing who drove me to a hotel in the center of town. From the balcony, I could see the endless expanse of sandy, boxlike buildings, mainly two—or three-stories high with green clumps of low trees and grayish shrubs scattered here and there. Behind the hotel stretched the low buildings of the commercial quarter, its streets thronged with people buying and selling all kinds of foods. The aroma of spices wafted up to my fourth floor balcony. Right in front of me, placed at an angle to the regular grid of the streets, stood the main mosque and its surrounding gardens. The mosque itself, a modest two-story brick building, was facing northeast toward the holy city of Mecca. My musings were interrupted by the muezzin's call to early evening prayers. The voice was coming from the upper balcony of the fairly high minaret, and its somewhat hoarse quality suggested a tape recorder with a rather worn tape. Soon groups of young men started converging on the nearby sidewalk. They were all tall, slender, their heads uncovered, dressed in flared jeans, T-shirts, and the platform shoes so fashionable in Africa. Their skin was so dark as to have a blue sheen, suggesting they came from the south of this enormous country, from the provinces of Sud or Kordofan, inhabited by the, until recently, nomadic tribes of the Dinka and the Nuba. Unlike the Arab and Islamic north, the south of the country either preserved the old animistic cults or was converted to some form of Christianity by European and American missionaries.

My curiosity was aroused by the large group of people surrounding a bookseller with his wares in colorful covers spread directly on the pavement. I came downstairs to have a closer look at this mobile bookshop. Most of the books were Arabic translations of the works of Lenin accompanied by a variety of brochures, magazines, and leaflets, all bearing the sign of the hammer and sickle. This was the period of People's Republic of Sudan, ruled by Gaafar Muhammad an-Numeiry, when Islam was not much in evidence. The gardens and the shaded tree-lined streets around Khartoum University reverberated with the happy laughter of students of both sexes. Most of the women wore their day dresses covered by the traditional long colorful muslin wraps. These so-called tops went also round their heads; yet unlike the Islamic attire meant to exclude women from ordinary life and cut them off from the rest of the community, these head coverings not only provided protection from the sun but, actually, framing the girls' faces in bright color, brought out their grace and beauty. Many of the men in the streets wore long galabiyas and bulbous white turbans. On Friday, the weekly day of rest, I asked to be taken to the swimming pool and the weekend pavilion advertised in the hotel brochure. "No problem," I was assured in the hotel reception; and after some commotion lasting about half an hour, I was shown to a minibus as its only passenger. We left Khartoum proceeding in an easterly direction. We traversed a desert as flat as a pancake, with the Blue Nile somewhere to the left, and passed a building site where some two-story houses were being constructed. Scattered any old how around them were small semicircular shacks roughly thrown together from cardboard, newspapers, rags, and bits of sheet metal. Remains of old packaging, empty tins, and other rubbish shivering in the light breeze made the entire area flicker in the morning sun. Black goats roamed all over the place, bleating. My driver, seeing me taking photographs, proffered an explanation,

"What they are building here are lovely houses for members of our government. This is just the beginning. Next year, they will be surrounded by splendid gardens and that will be the time to take pictures." I laughed. "It's the shacks, which interest me more than the villas. What are they?" He looked at me with amazement. "Those hovels? That's where the workers live. Black men from the south. They like to live like that."

We now turned north and saw, on the horizon, a dense clump of trees and flowering shrubs. We soon reached a modern bungalow standing in the shade of bamboo and banana plants. Only then did my driver inform me that there were no other guests and no staff, and wondered at what time I wanted to be collected. There was nothing to be done. I was left on my own in a delightful garden on an escarpment overlooking the Blue Nile, with a swimming pool, with a luxurious but empty building in a place seemingly frozen in some recent past, where perhaps only a magic spell could bring back the chatter and laughter of some unfinished party. I knew no such spell, but I had time to reflect on the inequalities existing in this country governed by a specific form of Arab socialism and wondered where they would lead.

In the afternoon, having returned to the hotel, I went down to the foyer to have a look at the festive crowd in the hotel's café. It was a very interesting gathering. There were several Indians wearing traditional salwar kameez, their women in brightly colored saris; two Sikhs with intricately wound crimson turbans, their beards enclosed in fine-meshed nets; I noticed a couple from the southern town of Juba, whom I had met at an official reception several days earlier, he was in a pale suit, his dark forehead showing faint ritual cuts running like strings of beads from one temple to the other; she was wrapped tightly in white muslin, framing her dark face with its amazingly white teeth. There was also a scattering of Japanese tourists and their wives, weighed down by numerous cameras; and a group of Sudanese men, their brown faces set off by voluminous snow-white turbans. A receptionist inserted a cassette into the video recorder. The whole company moved over to the chairs facing the TV screen while I went out to buy some fruit at a nearby market. As

I returned, the film was already on; and I was surprised to see that it was an American one. There were cars carrying arguing couples and stopping in front of huge houses; girls dressed in scanty bikinis kept running round the pool; there were frowning men with angry faces and women with heavy makeup; someone was smashing something on the floor; someone else was leaving the room slamming the door. I had never watched American TV serials, so it took me a while to realize that what all these people were watching was *Dallas*. I can still clearly recall this group of people of different races, in their distinctive clothing, silently watching scenes from the lives of these outlandish strangers behaving in ways none of them would ever dream of behaving at home. I felt so embarrassed that I quickly withdrew to my room.

After ten days' work, my report of talks I've had with representatives of various ministerial agencies was ready; and I took it to the UN offices to be typed. Being free for the day, I went for a walk on the boulevard along the Blue Nile. I visited the impressive exhibition of early Christian frescoes from Faras and Dongola in Nubia, uncovered by Polish archaeologists and displayed in a special pavilion of the history museum. Having reached the bridge over the White Nile, I crossed to the western side. The city life here was far less animated. Individual villas, surrounded by high walls, as was the custom among most peoples living along the banks of the Nile, were seemingly scattered through the desert. From this point, the highway led straight north, bordering the Nile proper, formed by the confluence of its two mighty constituents. According to the road sign, Omdurman was just a couple of miles down the road. Now a large suburb of Khartoum, Omdurman looked like an enormous market in the absolutely flat and featureless desert, totally devoid of any greenery. I crossed it one way and then another, through the sector of mobile transistor radio repair kiosks, then between heaps of second-hand clothing, to stalls of ornate attire of all kinds, jewelry, amulets, and wonder-working medicines peddled by itinerant witch doctors and medicine men, and eventually stumbled on a large camel market with hundreds of fallow dromedaries patiently standing or lying down, oblivious of their surroundings. The trade in these animals followed ancient traditions. Small groups of herd owners and traders squatted in a circle, sipping strong mint tea, holding the small cups with rounded bottoms with three fingers, talking at length about various matters. Invited to join one of the groups, I too squatted next to the men. Omar, the leader of a large caravan, was a man of the world. He had a smattering of English and had even once been with his camel herd as far as Aswan; and so, we had something to talk about. I asked him about the history of Omdurman. I remembered the old British film *The Four Feathers* and the great battle of 1898 between the army of Arab dervishes, adherents of self styled prophet and Muslim mystic, Muhammad Ahmad al Mahdi and the Anglo-Egyptian Nile Expeditionary Force under General Horatio Herbert Kitchener. Years before, Mahdi had proclaimed a jihad, a holy war, the first one of modern times, against the Europeanization of Sudan by Britain and its Egyptian protectorate. The insurgency was meant to spread to Egypt and to Palestine. Mahdi's army took Khartoum, murdered its defender, General Charles Gordon, and all the European and Egyptian inhabitants. When Mahdi died in 1885, Gordon had become a symbol of the European imperial expansion and of suppression of the renascent power of Islam. According to Omar, we were now sitting at the exact site of the battle. Shell casings, odd bits of metal, and dervishes' spearheads were still cropping up in the sand, he said. According to him, Mahdi's tomb was somewhere in Omdurman, near the Nile; and on my way back I went in search of it. I found the site with the help of three smiling young women, each wearing a differently colored bright top.

They were all teachers and could speak a little English. They tried to talk the guard into letting me in, but to no avail. "No entry for infidels," he kept repeating.

Omdurman

Surrounded by a high yellow wall with an ornate blue-and-white cornice, it was more a mausoleum than a tomb. Looking though the green metal gate between the two tall yellow pillars, I could see in the grounds, the main building with its triple elongated silver-gray dome and smaller turrets at the corners. I assumed that this odd triple dome must have had some particular significance, but no one was able to enlighten me. I learned later that, originally, Mahdi had indeed been buried in this place, but the British, having beaten the dervishes, threw his remains in the Nile, heaping further humiliation on the vanquished.

Later the same year, while in Nairobi, I was startled by the news splashed in large letters on the front pages of papers: SADAT KILLED BY ISLAMISTS. "What? Has a new jihad begun?" asked a passerby.

I had to come to terms with the fiasco of my efforts in the Middle East. I was not the only one who had thus failed, but perhaps for different reasons. For five years, since 1975, I have devoted much of my attention and energies to pursuing this dream. I can honestly say today that this quest was not financially motivated, and there were times when I was endangering the well-being of my family. Many may think that my fascination with countries of that region was sheer madness. Twenty years later, I myself began to analyze the origins of that "madness" and, to my great surprise, I detected that the source of it lay . . . in Poland, and even more specifically in Warsaw.

My return home, after a six-year's absence on the fronts of WWII, was the first, although not yet fully conscious decision to become involved in the protection of our threatened culture and traditions. Joining in the monumental effort of rebuilding Warsaw and, in particular, in the reconstruction of the old buildings of its historic district was, in a way, a reaction against the foreign ideology of Communism with its diktats affecting our living environment. What I gained from that experience were two principles, which I tried to follow wherever possible in my life as an architect working in foreign lands, namely, respect for local, indigenous traditions of communal living, and preservation of the natural environment. One may doubt whether they stand a chance, with the accelerating pace of globalization in the twenty-first century. Nevertheless, at the time they beguiled me to the point of obsession. While working in the Middle East, I came across vestiges of a great civilization corrupted by the imposition of foreign rule and thus by foreign models. On the surface, one might have gained an impression of normality: religion was not affected; commerce, the life-blood of the Middle East, prospered; agricultural development was progressing at a leisurely pace; bureaucracy was, as always, maddening—a possible inheritance of the Ottoman Empire or perhaps even going back in Egypt to the time of the Pharaohs; the cities were densely populated and overcrowded, but nowhere was the strain more visible than in the clash between the proposed new settlements and the ancient traditions of communal life. In my calculations, such conditions affected then about 80 percent of the people inhabiting the region. I thought that I had a chance to do something different; but, through no fault of mine, I failed. My sincere desire was to avoid, if possible, the imposition of alien lifestyles on developing countries. Unfortunately, my dream failed in the Middle East. There were many possible causes, from vulgar commercialism and private greed to attempts of imposing foreign political systems and, finally, the enormous gulf, which opened between Western civilization and the long-dormant hatred of its manifestations in the Muslim world.

29

To Survive in New York

It was an entirely new situation for me to come back to New York with no further work in sight and with no plans for the immediate future. I was not sure now whether I had made the right decision in refusing the mission in Uganda. But I had to return to New York. Lenta was getting impatient and tired of my long-lasting absences. Moreover, in addition to the surfeit of African experiences, the incident with my countrymen put me off further escapades in that area. This incident, which at the time I had almost immediately forgotten, was now coming back with rather mixed feelings. So why did this episode go on playing on my mind even after my return home? There is probably no simple answer. But as soon as I was back in our apartment, I had to ask myself, What next? And I made the emotional decision not to do any further work sponsored by the UN, even though the situation was making me anxious. I could not afford to be without work for more than six months.

Halfheartedly, I applied for the post of dean at the school of design and architecture in the city college, the main department of New York City University. Soon after that, Lenta and I went on holiday. As it happened, we had recently run into Andrzej Wirth, an old friend from our Warsaw days. He had been lecturing comparative literature for many years in top universities in America and in Berlin. Not long before, he had been appointed director of the new Institute of Experimental Theatre at the University of Giesen, German Federal Republic. He and his second wife, Josephine, invited us to their new house on Pawleys Island, South Carolina. We were glad to accept the invitation and decided to combine the trip with a sentimental visit to Raleigh, where our American adventure had begun some twenty years before. On the island, we were joined by Klara who brought me my mail with the bad news: the job of dean I had applied for had gone to a black applicant. I wondered whether he was better qualified or whether the choice had been dictated by the program of affirmative action, designed to create a "level playing field" for racial minorities. And sunning myself on the hot sands of the beach, I suddenly found myself out in the cold. We were going back to New York in a rather somber mood.

It beggars belief, but, literally, as we were crossing the threshold of our Manhattan apartment, the telephone rang. On the line was Adelle, the secretary of Arol, a building developer I knew. He wanted to meet me as soon as possible. I had worked with him on a number of interesting projects for the redevelopment of some run-down outer suburbs of the city in the 1970s. He did not know whether I was back in America and was trying to trace me.

studio work, Bronx, NY

He was the managing director of a family owned firm, which was at the time buying out or leasing large postindustrial properties in the hope of rebuilding them some time in the future in more favorable economic circumstances. Arol was a handsome engaging man in his forties, with a good head of dark hair and a bushy beard. At one stage, he had contemplated an academic career and kept referring to his experiences at an Arizona college. When we first met, he had just taken over the management of the firm from his father, David, an energetic businessman born in Odessa whose dream now, at the age of seventy-six, was of becoming an actor in gangster films.

"Good to see you, Jerzy!" called Arol greeting me warmly, once we got together. "You are the answer to my prayers; we have a great new project for you to work on. We have acquired four blocks along the East River, in Spanish Harlem. These are the premises of the last remaining metallurgical works in Manhattan. They were very busy during the Second World War, producing parts for tanks," he continued excitedly, "but closed down after the Korean War." "But what do you intend to produce there?" I asked with interest. "We are going to convert these buildings into the latest generation television studios . . . absolute state of the art. There is a great shortage of such facilities in New York. Besides, father hopes he will meet some film producers, perhaps land a good part . . . God bless him!"

And thus, an interesting new job began. First I had to get acquainted with the subject then to find the best way of adapting the existing, virtually historical, buildings for their new use. After a year, a powerful industrial concern, Procter & Gamble, became interested in the new studios, where they were hoping to shoot their advertising films for television, which were known as soap operas. These shows continue to this day, but they are not being shot in our studios, which were never finished. Two years after the construction began and having spent over thirty million dollars, the client suddenly pulled out of the project. As always happens when contracts are broken, a court case followed. Both sides claimed compensation reaching hundreds of millions dollars. And thus, the work of my team also came to an end. Ten years later Arol won the case, but lost the lease on the studio grounds. Before, however, his father did manage to play the part of a dapper, intimidating gangster "godfather" in a film directed by his younger son. The film, shot in our unfinished studios, was a total flop and met with hostile reviews. The unfinished buildings would wait for twenty years for the next wave of prosperity, while its naked walls continued to haunt the drivers of cars speeding along the riverside FDR highway.

In spite of the unforeseen failure of our project and its painful financial consequences, the 1980s gave rise to a number of pleasant memories. Once the Polish borders were thrown open during the Solidarity period, large numbers of gifted Polish artists, writers, musicians, and others invaded New York. This intensified after the declaration of the "state of war" in Poland. Many New York homes, ours included, opened their doors to the newcomers who were arriving virtually penniless. Fortunately, the International Rescue Committee, in which Barbara, the wife of the editor of the *Polish Daily News*, held an important position, provided financial aid and other assistance. She and her husband held also numerous meetings for the new arrivals and refugees in their own home. For the first time, we witnessed the plight of real refugees. In most cases, they arrived without money, without experience of life in a foreign country, and, at best, with only a basic knowledge of English. Most of them had no particular skills and had to look for odd jobs.

With so many newly arrived writers and scientists, fresh life was breathed into the Polish Institute of Arts and Sciences, PIASA, which started running series of lectures and meetings. Soon the work of some of the artists would be discovered by the New York newspapers and magazines. No week would pass without their contributions appearing on the op-ed pages and front covers of prestigious publications.

I managed to get a commission, financially not particularly attractive, for one of them; it was for a huge billboard advertising the Bronx Terminal Market, one of the city's main fresh food wholesalers. The market, under the management of Arol, was situated along and under the main highway leading north from New York; and thus, over a period of months, hundreds of thousands of drivers must have noticed the panorama of Manhattan and its skyscrapers, all apparently built of vegetables: cucumbers, corn cobs, zucchinis, carrots, and parsnip. I am not sure whether this allusion was properly appreciated.

One of the accidental immigrants was Janusz Głowacki, a well-known author and playwright with a playboy fame, who was energetically trying to break into the most difficult theatrical market in the world. He succeeded and had his first play staged in the Public Theater. It was quite unprecedented for an unknown foreign playwright, but it succeeded, and other plays and world acclaim would follow.

A special session devoted to the heroes of resistance in Poland took place in the packed auditorium of the New York University, in the presence of the Nobel laureate Czesław Miłosz. Amazingly, a telephone connection was allowed for an interview over the loudspeaker with one of them, Adam Michnik, jailed at the time somewhere in Poland.

These were thus the unforgettable years when we had the chance of getting to know all those talented Polish people at last liberated and introduced to the rest of the world. Unexpectedly, the press was now full of praise for the achievements and attitude of Poles. We could be proud of our compatriots. In the middle 1980s, many other authors became also highly visible in the press and in the field of essays on cultural affairs. Lenta wrote about this phenomenon in the *Literary Notebooks*, a Polish quarterly at that time still published in Paris,

> . . . Books by Brodski, Michnik and Konrad, Brandys, Kundera and Konwicki, the poetry of Miłosz, Herbert and the youngest of them, Zagajewski, remind us that civilization—so fragile and yet so valuable—is these days like a city under siege, its survival depending on its inhabitants' constant striving. The philosopher, Leszek Kołakowski, invited to give the yearly 'Jefferson Lecture' in Washington, was the first ever non-American speaker. This may be one of the first indicators of the interest the American intellectuals are now taking in the thinkers of Central and Eastern Europe . . .

There were moments when I regretted not having become an artist, a free spirit, creating and interpreting my own vision of the world. Yet this world was not an easy patron of the arts, money and the markets being the chief driving forces. The status of an immigrant was not particularly welcome by some. Some time later, a number of Polish artists, having dipped their toes in foreign waters, did eventually return to a liberated and democratic Poland where, having gained experience abroad, they thrived and enjoyed a wide recognition.

Incidentally, in the course of my work, I got the opportunity to compare the two Polish milieus: on one hand those talented individuals leaving the still-oppressed country and on the other the ones who represented the old Polish immigration. It is probably an unfair comparison, one—as the saying goes—of comparing apples with oranges, but I could not resist indulging in such an analysis.

At the time, I was working on another interesting project, with a greater emotional content: the old four-story building of the Polish Army Veterans Association of America was to be replaced with a taller new building, provided the enlargement could be approved by the building authorities. The new premises would house a number of Polish institutions now scattered throughout the city. The idea originated with Bolesław Wierzbiański and the group behind the Polish-language *Daily News*. I was asked to lead the project. We wanted to create a modern cultural Polish center in the heart of New York—quite a challenge to the problematic Polish sense of unity and ability to work in unison and organize. This was the first time that I became professionally involved with a Polish émigré body.

Historically, the Polish emigrants had arrived in America in two separate and different waves and remained, generally speaking, as two distinct groups. The first group was the descendants of the economic migrants of the turn of the nineteenth and twentieth centuries, who were predominantly of peasant origin. They congregated mainly round parish churches and thus were often rooted in rather outdated but familiar ways of thinking. During WWII, a new organization, the Polish American Congress, was formed and took upon itself the role of representing the Polish community in the United States. It created links with many local organizations and found out that an insurance business was quite a lucrative way to raise funds—nothing wrong with that. But this was also how the Polish American Congress was perceived in Washington and, as it was seen as having access to a large number of potential Polish votes, was given some importance before elections. During the war, Congress occasionally ventured into political initiatives in matters concerning Poland. Its political weakness, however, was the failure to secure the ear of influential people, and its lack of understanding of the workings of the American political machine was well demonstrated by the events of 1944. At the time, when the postwar borders of Poland were in the balance, President Roosevelt invited representatives of the Polish American Congress to the White House. He assured them of the friendship between our two countries and posed with them for a photograph in front of a large map of Poland within her prewar borders. He reassured them that USA would respect the integrity of their country and brazenly asked for Polish votes in the coming election. This took place well after the Tehran and Yalta conferences, where the Western Allies, and Roosevelt in particular, had already secretly agreed to major border changes in favor of the Soviet Union. The Poles, not aware of these agreements, massively voted for Roosevelt. I presume that the members of that Polish delegation did not remember the words spoken at another time by England's Lord Palmerston, "We do not have permanent enemies, we do not have permanent friends, we do have permanent interests."

The second large émigré group consisted of veterans, their families, and the former inmates of Soviet and German prison and concentration camps. This wave of immigrants who had already begun arriving toward the end of the war and who were opposed to the new order in Europe under Communism, included many well-educated people of the prewar Polish intelligentsia. We, who had arrived in the 1960s, were at the tail end of this wave. The third wave of arrivals started to reach America around the 1980s, prompted by the relaxation of travel restrictions during the ascent of the Solidarity movement.

The two original groups lived their separate lives, had little in common, their paths rarely crossed except for an occasional marriage or the gathering for the annual Pulaski Parade. During the forty years of our life in USA, I can't recall a single occasion when a representative of the Polish American Congress approached me with an offer of cooperation, sought my participation in a political initiative, or even suggested I joined the organization as a paid-up member. The truth is that I never sought such contacts. The only exception was when I became a member of the Polish Army's Veterans Association. Now there was at least a purpose: work on the new building project.

The association was created after the First World War by veterans of the so called Blue Army, which was formed in 1917 by Polish volunteers from France, Belgium, and USA, and which, under the command of General Haller, fought in the Polish-Bolshevik war of 1919-1920, and which later distinguished itself by liberating, from the Germans, the province of Polish Pomerania with its Baltic coast. Its New York home at 17 Irving Place was the headquarters of several outposts scattered throughout the country, which then grouped few surviving veterans of both world wars. Any decision concerning the New York building had to be ratified by all the outposts, in spite of the fact that a great majority of the veterans never used it. This made introducing any changes rather difficult, particularly as the aging board members were also weary of innovation, their ingrained old habits and their apathy in the face of any challenge often impeding my work. At long last the board managed to arrive at a decision. After three years of talks and vacillation, I was commissioned to provide an initial design for the conversion in order to get estimates and explore the chances of obtaining a bank loan.

The ceremonial presentation of the design took place in the association's assembly hall, its tables crammed with Polish delicacies. It was followed by a period of quietude, as if a general fatigue had overwhelmed the members of the board. The reason lay in the need to make a decision to apply for a loan from one of the many banks involved in financing thousands of building projects in New York. The vacillation continued, and valuable time was running out. All around, building work was in full progress while the Poles were on the verge of losing possibly the last chance of acting together for the common good. Some time later, the board decided simply to redecorate the old building and to rebuild the ballroom as a concert hall and bar, with a view to their commercial use. The hall is now used for profitable pop and rock concerts. The fragmented Polish cultural activities in New York had to find other premises. In a similar context, one of the Polish political commentators wrote,

> "Political and social pragmatism has never been our forte. American Poles lack the group instinct necessary for securing success. The laudable achievements of individuals are never matched by Poles working together as a group. Private interests prevail as a rule. I am always left with feelings of loss and regret when watching the lack of ability for creative and constructive action, and the inability to exploit existing historical chances. And thus, Poles lose face in America, and the spectacle is painful to behold".

This was written, however, several years before the collapse of Communism in Europe, when Poles played such an important leading role. As for myself, after four years of frustrating meetings and fruitless discourse with my compatriots, I had enough. I felt that, other than facing a mortal threat from the outside, Poles were reluctant to engage in any productive cooperation. It may have been a harsh judgment and too much of a generalization, but that was how I felt at the time. After the fiasco of establishing a Polish Cultural Center in Manhattan, I felt as if suspended in a void. It may have been in a way a pleasant feeling, but one I was psychologically not prepared for.

At the end of the eighties, I decided to end my professional career as an architect/urban planner. After forty years of successes, failures, and fascinating adventures, a time has come to relax and stop searching for new projects to work on. To continue in the rat race, in which some of my friends were still engaged, was suddenly not for me. Brutal competition between small firms or individual designers led to absurd situations, where scores of architects vied for the same commission. Moreover, the methods employed by the more persistent competitors were not always strictly ethical.

I am referring of course to the New York Metropolitan area, just recovering from the crisis of the late 1970s. Suddenly, I felt no longer attracted to struggling to find contacts in the business world, to seeking the support of city authorities, to ingratiating myself with social organizations. Public design competitions no longer fascinated me as an adventure; the passion has gone out of the challenge. Anyway, I did not have the financial resources to sit out protracted negotiations and long-term tenders.

My interest in planning and construction of new towns turned out to have been an unrealistic dream, which had fooled many people in my profession. As in many other domains, America did not follow the European beaten track. The new direction for the country's development was not devised by visionaries of the future and was not supported by scientific papers and big ideas of intellectual elite, as had happened before the war in Europe. Here a new trend, called now exurbia, would be emerging over the next two decades, driven by the preferences of ordinary people buying their houses or apartments, and forcing the building industry to offer them a range of solutions to choose from. Democracy in action caught up with and overtook the prestigious and slightly arrogant profession of a town planner. There will be no more new towns and no more of suburbia surrounding them. What is being built today by private developers on the vast open spaces of this continent is a compilation of all known forms of human settlements, with their innumerable choices and variations, provided solely to meet the demands of prospective residents. What emerges is a nation of people residing in constantly improving villages, each proclaiming to offer a modern living style, supported by an unprecedented expansion of technological inventions.

At the time, though, I was not aware of this. Unexpectedly, however, chance led me toward a new and totally different path, mainly by having become involved in Polish affairs, lately commendably promoted by the publishers and editors of the *Polish Daily News*.

30

The Dawn of a New Poland

The twenty-fifth anniversary of Bolesław Wierzbiański's journalistic and publication career was celebrated in one of the ballrooms of Manhattan's Hilton hotel. Around the tables sat the cream of New York's Polish society. As soon as I entered the banqueting room, I came face to face with Jerzy Kosiński. This was our first meeting after quite a long break. Even though we were virtual neighbors in Manhattan, we did not see each other frequently. In the meantime, he had become an internationally recognized author. His first novel *The Painted Bird* was followed by several more best sellers; and he received the National Book Award, the most prestigious American literary prize. Films were made based on his scripts, and he even acted in one of them. Articles about him appeared frequently in the press; and in no time, he had become a member of the international jet set. Now, as he was attending a purely Polish celebration in New York, he must have had his reasons for doing so, though I could not guess what they were. For some time now, Kosiński has been criticized in certain Polish circles for the anti-Polish attitude he was supposed to have adopted in *The Painted Bird*. He himself kept rather aloof and did not respond to these charges. He kept insisting that the book was based on his own personal experience and he kept reiterating it at his readings, lectures, and other public appearances. According to his story, at the beginning of the Second World War, at the age of six, he got lost and was eventually sheltered by primitive and cruel peasants in a remote village. Once the book had been translated and published in Poland, doubts were raised as to the veracity of his account. True, he had a vivid imagination, and an author's fantasy is often interpreted as a lie. I saw this imaginary account of his life as an innocent fable, one, which accounted for the success of his book.

A band was playing on the podium, speeches were being made, and Kosiński was one of the speakers. These were followed by dinner and dancing. It was the latter, which I found rather amusing. It always amused me to see that whenever Poles step onto the dance floor, they seem to go back to the times of the polonaise, with their deep bows, their meaningful glances, their passionate clasps. No sooner had I remarked on it to Kosiński than I spotted him doing just that while dancing a sentimental tango with his life companion, Kiki.

"I wouldn't laugh at it if I were you," he responded. "These tunes carry a true emotional charge and revive old memories, some good, other tragic, but all certainly important." I could hardly believe my ears. But he was serious, and all I could do was chuckle.

Yet his response made me wonder. I had always seen Kosiński as an exemplary citizen of the world, devoid, the same as I, of the so-called ethnic urges. Was I mistaken? This particular episode may appear to be a curious introduction to my description of the coming epoch-making events. But it was the accumulation of just such minor, seemingly meaningless, personal occurrences, which made me think of their deeper significance as harbingers of the coming momentous changes. From our New York perspective, it presaged our own growing interest in Polish affairs, both local and the ones taking place in Poland and filling at the time pages of the world press. Eventually, these changes would lead to the downfall of Communist rule in Poland and in the rest of Central and Eastern Europe, as well as in Central Asia.

From that time on, I kept seeing Kosiński in various places and under different circumstances. One day, when visiting us, he spoke at length and with great passion about the need for the Polish community in USA to achieve a higher profile. At the time, the press was full of reports of the restoration work being carried out in Ellis Island and of plans for creating a Museum of Immigration there. That tiny island at the entry to New York port had played a major historical role as the gateway to the New World and is embedded in the collective memory of millions of new American citizens and their descendants. Over twenty million immigrants, most of them at the beginning of the twentieth century, disembarked there and passed through its border controls. Kosiński was sounding me out on his new idea. He thought of creating an organization to take over one of the island's many halls and dedicate it to all those Poles who had come from the three parts of Poland, partitioned as the country then was between Russia, Germany, and Austro-Hungary. Those newcomers would have been registered as citizens of these countries. That, he felt, had now to be rectified. "We would need considerable funds for this purpose," he said, "but I do have ways and means." Another of Kosiński's favorite subjects was the bringing to public attention the centuries-old history and cultural achievements of Polish Jews. He had rather radical views on the recent history. In his opinion, stressing the Holocaust as the most important event in the history of European Jews was counterproductive, as it completely overshadowed the centuries of coexistence of Poles, both Christian and Jewish, in the vast Polish territories. He invariably added that the Holocaust had lasted four years and was a problem created by the Germans, while the mostly peaceful Polish-Jewish coexistence—apart from the religious intolerance created mostly by the Catholic Church—developed peacefully for close to a millennium. "This is a unique story, a historical fact that had produced an exciting brand of culture, now destroyed by the war, and not encountered anywhere else. It is high time the world learned about it!" he kept repeating. These were strong and fascinating arguments, and I was quite prepared to support them.

Soon after, a new organization, the American Association for Polish-Jewish Studies, was set up by a group of Polish Jews, all academics, based in Cambridge, Massachusetts, and dedicated to the study of the history of Polish Jews and their culture. Kosiński managed to raise large funds from his rich friends to finance the association and was elected president of its board. One of the association's first actions was to co-opt some non-Jews to its founders' board. A meeting was organized in the Fifth Avenue apartment of a wealthy widow, and a fairly large number of New York Poles came to hear about the program of the new organization. The aims of the association were presented by Irena Pipes, born in Warsaw, and wife of Richard Pipes, Harvard professor of Russian history and adviser to President Reagan. She reported on the progress of the new Oxford publication, *Polin* (meaning "Poland" in Hebrew), and annals of historical documents edited by Prof. Anthony Polonsky, then of London University. Kosiński, in a passionate speech, presented the whole range of his ideas for the future. He stressed the need for choosing the first project and for raising the required funds. He insisted that a center of Polish-Jewish culture ought to be created in Poland. There were some who considered this initiative worthwhile, though possibly premature, as no suitable contacts had yet been established with the Polish side.

* * *

"Jerzy!" Kosiński was shouting so excitedly on the phone that I had to hold the receiver away from my ear. "Kiki and I are flying to Israel next week. You must come with us. There is a wonderful opportunity to build a new center on the shore of the Sea of Galilee!"

"What center? Where?"

"The Center of Polish-Jewish Culture and Civilization in Poland. You know, we'd talked about it before."

"Well, yes, but that was to be in Poland."

"Yes, yes in Poland too, but that can wait; if we start in Israel, it will be accessible right now to people from all over the world . . . Just think of it, a study center on historic events combined with rest and recreation on a historical lake in a country so full of history! A unique opportunity!"

The departure of our Pan-Am flight to Tel-Aviv was already overdue when a further delay was announced. A group of orthodox Jews traveling with us insisted on saying their prayers, which had to be said at that particular time, or they would not be able to start their journey—no details were offered.

Kiki, born in New York, educated in England, member of the von Frauenhofer family of German barons, has been Kosiński's partner for a number of years and, later, became his second American wife. She was the epitome of a highly organized modern woman. For years, she has been the principal organizer of his extensive social contacts. She also told us that she edited and endlessly retyped the manuscripts of his books. As we waited for our departure, she browsed through her documents and the letters of recommendation to our contacts in Israel. I listened with great interest to the suggested program of our journey, as there had not been enough time to confer before. I learned now that from Lod airport, we were to travel to Tyberias on the Lake of Galilee. On the way back, we were to stop in Jerusalem for official talks while Kosiński was going to give lectures and attend press conferences. Meanwhile, our copassengers went on with their prayers, standing between the practically empty rows of seats. Covered with their prayer shawls, they rocked rhythmically to and fro—that went on for another half an hour. At last, the prayers were finished and our departure was announced.

"We ought to have a safe flight after all that," said Jerzy.

At the Lod airport, we were met by a small army of journalists and photographers. After some short interviews, cameras flashing, we were rescued by a man who cleared the way for us, shouting at the obstructing spectators, and finally leading us to the arrivals hall. Irena Pipes was waiting for us there and introduced us to several people who were to accompany us on our journey to Galilee. That evening, in the hotel in Tyberias, I had an emotional meeting, which took me back to my first arrival in Haifa, many years ago, at the beginning of the war. As on that former occasion, I was now approached by an old couple; the man spoke to me in Polish, smiling shyly, as if embarrassed, "Is it true that you are Polish?"

There was something endearing in his approach. "Yes, I am," I replied "and you must be from the city of Lwów."

He looked at me with surprise, his hands trembling, and whispered, "How do you know?"

"I recognize your accent," I said. "I had a good friend from Lwów. He was the head of the department of microbiology at the Warsaw University."

He turned to his wife with tears in his eyes. "You see, it's so many years . . . and yet I haven't lost it . . ." He pulled himself together. "And what was your friend's name?"

"Dobrzański."

"Yes, I remember . . . There was a Dobrzański Pharmacy in Lwów."

"That's right; his father's. And his mother was Jewish," I added.

The following day, we played tourists and went round places, some of which I had visited in 1941 with my wartime Polish school in Tel Aviv. Later, as part of a larger group, we went to the lake's shore to view the site offered for our purpose by an Anglo-Jewish organization. From the end of the paved road, we had to walk, making our way through dense reeds. It was getting wetter and wetter; the terrain was becoming quite marshy. As the other side of the lake with its steep Golan Heights came into view, we found ourselves in a true bog. When one of us sunk in knee-deep, we turned round and went back the way we came.

"Well, they've taken us for a ride," decided Jerzy. It became obvious now that our project would have to wait for a more suitable site. But this did not change our happy mood. The next day was a Saturday; and as public transport did not operate in Israel on the Sabbath, Irena Pipes, another member of our group, and I hired a Palestinian taxi and drove along the Jordan River via Jericho to Jerusalem.

From my window in the King David Hotel, the whole panorama of the Old City spread before me with its old walls and the Jaffa Gate. The golden cupola of the Dome of the Rock shimmered in the distance. It was from there, according to the Muslims, that the prophet Mohammed ascended to heaven. And the Jews maintain that on that rock, Abraham was prepared to sacrifice his son Izaak. Not far from there, during the first Crusade, the Christian knights burned all the local Jews in their synagogue, alive. Some historic site!

In the evening, Kosiński, Kiki, and I were received in the guesthouse of Teddy Kolleck, the mayor of Jerusalem. There was Shimon Perez and other Israelis I did not know; and to my surprise, the guests included a delegation from the Jagiellonian University in Kraków headed by the rector, Prof. Józef Gierowski. They had come to attend the special Polish-Israeli symposium in connection with the Center for Jewish Culture, which had recently been opened in Kraków. With our plans for a center in Israel drowned in a bog and for the one in Poland forestalled—even though its opening was welcomed news—we felt disappointed for the second time in one day. Mayor Kolleck promised to get me a guide, an art historian, to take me round the old city the following day.

In the evening, we attended a public meeting for Kosiński, organized by an English-language newspaper, in the large lecture hall of a nearby hotel. The meeting proved very popular, soon only standing room was available. Suddenly, a group of people started screaming that he had kept silent on the Jewish question, and then noisily questioning the veracity of his assurance that *The Painted Bird* was not an account of the persecution of a little Jewish boy by Polish peasants. There was confusion, lots of shouting, until Kosińki went up to the press table and called out loudly to the noisy group at the back of the hall, "There is one thing I can tell you without any doubt . . . Had the fate of Jews depended on Polish peasants, none would have perished at the time of war!" Silence followed, no one stirred in the hall. All this happened three years before the world learned about the wartime murders of Jews in Jedwabne and other townships in eastern Poland by their next-door peasant neighbors. Just as well that Jerzy did not live to hear those revelations.

In October 1988, Lenta and I decided to go to Poland and witness, first hand, some of the changes that were actually taking place there. Lenta had not been back to the country for seventeen years, while my last visit was ten years before. This latter visit, for my mother's funeral, ended with the arrest of my brother by the secret police. No wonder that we were feeling anxious; trying to guess what might await us in Poland this time. However, contrary to our expectations, it became a lovely and sentimental journey. Yet we were shocked by the impoverishment of the people we met, by the meager food supplies, and by the ramshackle state of the places of our overnight stops—they could certainly not be described as hotels. As an architect, I was particularly angered by the appalling living conditions in the huge, dismal housing developments that we visited. The tiny apartments with their miniature rooms had insufficient heating, poor quality sanitary fixtures, balconies that were not even decorative and so small as to be practically useless, yet cluttered up with overflowing miserable belongings. I was left with the sad impression of neglect and total lack of management. Even to this day, these hideous blocks are a constant reminder of the past years of Communism. In a country once proud of its renowned school of modern town planning, the socialist building methods had scarred the environment of historic townships and, haphazardly encroaching on the countryside, damaged the once beautiful rural landscapes. Could the situation be remedied? My architect colleagues were resigned to the fact that no change was possible while the present political system was in existence. Somehow, I was not ready to subscribe to this pessimistic view, though I had not the slightest chance to influence the destiny of the country.

It was several months after our return to USA that increasingly fascinating news began to arrive from Poland. The pressure of public opinion and the legalization of Solidarity, an independent trade union, forced through by its members, broke the back of the old system of oppression to the point when it suddenly lost its power and had to face spontaneous opposition. However, the extent to which the old system had been corroded by its inherent corruption was largely misunderstood by the opposition, which failed to press for unconditional surrender. All the same, the peacefully negotiated compromise resulting in power sharing between the governing Communist party and the ad hoc constituted group of its inexperienced opponents was an unprecedented historical event. It was presumably arrived at in good faith. The celebrated compromise, arrived at during the so-called Round Table conference, reverberated around the world.

The changes in Poland had their repercussions in New York among the people we knew. The publisher of the *Polish Daily News* and an émigré political activist of long standing went to Poland for the first time since the end of the war. He was one of the observers at the conference and witnessed the signing of the compromise documents. Having returned to USA, he wrote words that I remember to this day, "The events taking place in Poland and all the resulting changes must be credited solely to the people there. Émigré groups had nothing to contribute . . ." Zygmunt Nagórski, a well-known publicist and political commentator, wrote in one of the publications, "The events in Poland demonstrate the insignificant role played by the political émigré circles. In truth, we numbered some several hundred individuals, most of us working for organizations financed by the USA. What we achieved was like footsteps left on a sandy beach, washed away by the next new wave."

Some years before, Leopold Tyrmand had written in a similar vein, "Political exiles, with their didactic and accusatory role, have now moved into the shadows of history, unnoticed by the world . . ."

Every day brought fresh news from the other side of the former iron curtain, keeping us in front of our television sets and compulsively reading newspapers and magazines. Changes were taking place even in the Soviet Union. Perestroika and glasnost, initiated by the party secretary, Mikhail Gorbachev, have taken on a momentum of their own. In Czechoslovakia and Hungary, protest meetings denouncing the Communist rule were organized for the first time. Without the slightest exaggeration, the eyes of the world were focused on that part of the continent, now, at last, dubbed Central Europe by the media.

At the same time, changes were taking place in our family. Klara and her life companion, Erroll, decided to get married now that their professional careers were already well established. After some research, they decided to get married in the Unitarian Church, open to all, without too many questions asked. Its complex of imposing neo-Gothic buildings occupies a high hill overlooking the Hudson, and its magnificent tower can be seen from the highway running along Manhattan's western shore. The preliminaries having been dealt with, all that remained was to send out invitations. Now, one could only count the days, not many, exactly one month. Several days before the wedding, my brother with his family arrived from Paris bringing also Aunt Maria Bernhard, the retired professor of classical archaeology at the Jagellonian University in Kraków. We all gathered on the terrace of our apartment with a welcoming glass of champagne, the sun setting behind the skyscrapers of Manhattan. After two days of relaxation and socializing, the great day arrived. Having negotiated all the courtyards and cloisters, we entered the chapel, already full of guests. There were many black faces among the congregation. As I approached the altar with Klara on my arm, I suddenly realized that the priest was wearing a red robe. It was a woman! Welcome, modern times.

The reception was held in the house and garden of the young couple's friend. As the father of the bride, I had to give a speech; I spoke about the inter-continental and interracial links as the future of our civilization. There were other speeches, followed by dancing in the garden. Someone was playing a saxophone, solo. We returned home, by now rather tired, and all we could do was to order a pizza. The young couple had rented a suite in a fashionable hotel and invited their close friends for further celebrations. The following morning, they flew to Morocco for their honeymoon.

I began to prepare for my next trip to Poland. A new, unexpected chapter was opening in my life.

Beginning with the spring of 1989, I saw a lot of Kosiński, who was at the time totally absorbed by his new idea of building American-style houses in Poland. However, he knew absolutely nothing about the subject. My reports after I returned from Poland just fed his enthusiasm. He hoped he would be able to secure the considerable funds necessary for the purpose. In the meanwhile, to kick-start PARC, the Polish American Resources Corporation, he invested a substantial amount of his own money into this new venture. Five people became the founding members: he himself, his wife Kiki, a banker friend of ours, myself, plus a man whom Kosiński had met by chance and who wormed his way in by assuring everybody of his business contacts.

Carried by the wave of euphoria created by the political and social changes in Poland, we felt very close to our compatriots; after all, we were all members of one great, honorable family, united by their will to dump the remains of the thoroughly rotten system onto the scrap heap of history (as once described by Lenin in a rather different context). We did not anticipate that this "spring cleaning" would be associated with a universal plunder of state, communal, and private property by the old Communist rulers joined, in this endeavor, by a new class of con men, fraudsters, and swindlers taking full advantage of the turmoil and of the lack of experience of the new class of politicians. Several months before Kosiński went to Poland, where he was now well known, his books having been translated into Polish. He had talks with a number of ministers to inform them about the new building methods of family homes, which had been demonstrated to him that winter by a developer in Colorado. His meeting with the prime minister resulted in his getting a letter of intention and a promise of help in starting a modern construction enterprise. Everybody felt that the industry was overdue for changes. Also, the president of the National Bank of Poland promised that PARC would be granted a license to open, the first in fifty years, foreign private bank in Poland. Some very strange and unexpected circumstances accompanied these events. It became obvious that the former Communist dignitaries, now threatened by the climate of rapid changes, were willing to facilitate the growth of business enterprises, hoping to feather their own nests in their guise of new capitalist converts. In the meantime, and already for some time they have been "privatizing" state property, appropriating it for themselves or passing it on to friends and relatives.

Such were, more or less, the origins of the new business elite in the newly independent countries. In some ways, the process resembled the birth of fortunes of American millionaires of the nineteenth century, when the capitalist system was acquiring its modern form, though the two backgrounds were rather different. Yet even now, the general opinion both in America and in Poland is that the first million was rarely, if ever, gained in an honest way.

Our executive director, once an organizer of pop music concerts, suddenly stepped into the role of a "banker." Short of stature, portly, with the remains of his hair tied into a scrawny ponytail, he now treated himself to a proper haircut and acquired expensive Italian suits, charging them to the company. He ordered many volumes of cheap publications, such as an encyclopedia of business and a dictionary of banking, which used to be sold by door-to-door salesmen. He subscribed to the *Wall Street Journal* and the *Financial Times*. When I looked at all this with a certain amusement, he said, "So what? I've just moved from show business to money business." I began to have misgivings.

But the prospect of establishing a Western style bank, the first in Poland since the beginning of the Second World War, was beginning to look interesting. It was called AMERBANK (American Bank in Poland). The Kosińskis were trying hard to find investors to raise millions of dollars as the necessary initial capital. They managed to secure a contribution from a big New York bank, friends invested some money, and they hoped to raise the remainder in Poland.

In this intoxicating atmosphere, I became the director of housing development, unpaid to begin with, and began to formulate a plan of action, in theory only, as no money was yet available for the purpose. My first task would be to explore the actual conditions in the country.

The credibility of our new enterprise was enhanced by the participation of Witold Sulimirski, a genuine banker, an elegant and worldly man, one of the five board members of PARC. When *Gazeta Bankowa* (Banking Gazette) published on its first page an article by an outstanding journalist, accompanied by a photograph, in which he appealed to Sulimirski to return to Poland to save

Polish banking, it seemed that for us sky was the limit. Our office on the corner of Broadway and Fifty-Seventh Street soon became the meeting place for a number of Americans and Poles from the New York area, as well as from Poland. Many of these Poles were relatively new immigrants who had left Poland during the hard times of the final stages of Communism, and who have not quite yet settled in USA. They were looking for work and would be happy to return to Poland as representatives of a reputable firm that will give them the prestige so far missing from their lives.

One acquaintance, who was married to the sister of the former tsar of Bulgaria, said that Bulgarians were closely following the developments in Poland. Any news of interest from outside boosted our enthusiasm. One day, a Polish Gypsy group came to the office, inquiring about the possibility of a loan to start a dance and song troupe. In return, they offered to publicize our activities during their tours of the Americas. There were others who came out of curiosity, interested in the new firm, perhaps the first of its kind in the USA; a harbinger of major changes expected in Poland. They wanted to stress their personal involvement in these changes by being in touch with us. This was really moving and reflected the great wave of optimism sweeping over us all at the time. Such meetings were really impressive, although they camouflaged the great naïveté of not only our visitors, but also of ours, the future directors of the firm, which intended to marry American resources with the enormous needs of Poland. As the whole story of my life shows, I was again, not for the first time, on cloud nine of unbridled optimism.

High Noon—Solidarity poster

It was very interesting at the time to meet people newly arrived from Poland. The mood of the country, following the recent elections and the great victory of the Solidarity opposition, reached the peak of optimism. We had the celebrated Solidarity poster, which took its inspiration from Gary Cooper's movie *High Noon* hanging on the wall of our office. This was soon joined by a preelection poster, brought over by the newly elected senator, a childhood friend of mine, showing himself, as were all the Solidarity candidates, photographed individually with Lech Wałęsa; this invariably impressed visiting American businessmen.

At the time, many representatives of the new Polish authorities, members of the government and of parliament were visiting USA. I was quite perplexed to hear of some of the political factions emerging from the supposed monolith of Solidarity. Apparently, the Wałęsa group of political innovators was already disintegrating. New names were being mentioned of people never heard of before, of demagogues, troublemakers, initiators of suspect political theories either untested or dragged in from the prewar period and long past their sell-by date. For us this was sad, incomprehensible though maybe inevitable given the situation. Soon after, Wałęsa's declaration of "war at the top, peace at the bottom" initiative, so tragic in its consequences, finally gave the coup de grace to Polish historical unity. Brutal political methods in a country yearning for peace came to the fore once again during the presidential election campaign. The shocked people could not believe their own eyes when they saw the axe-swinging presidential candidate, Lech Wałęsa, threatening his political opponents. One wonders whether this outrageous behavior influenced the subsequent course of the political life of the country. Or maybe it just reflected the decline of the requisite political culture and confirmed the degradation of values in a society poisoned by the bane of Communism.

What I was dreaming of was to obtain access to the magnificent building sites still held by the old venal Communist housing cooperatives. These sites were supposed to be allotted to our American style housing, for which AMERBANK would provide generous credits. We had other ideas as well of new forms of economic activity based not on cooperation with Communist authorities, as all business had to be done before, but based on totally different principles. Thus, my branch of PARC was to be called AMERDOM; others would be named AMEREXPORT, AMERDRINK, AMERSPORT, AMERFOOD, AMERFILM, etc., to which someone jokingly added AMERSEX.

All the same, I was preparing for my next trip to Poland full of almost childish optimism. My arrival in Warsaw coincided with the inauguration of the first democratically elected government. I met a number of interesting people and saw some good sites for housing construction and that was of special interest to me. They were still in the hands of the old administration, which, as I soon found out, had no intention of allowing any outsiders in. Though, to tell the truth, I have so far made no offers to them. It all brought back to my mind the experience of the Maamura project in Egypt. Similarly, in Poland, the old petrified layers of Communist business interests and established mutual dependencies were keeping out all newcomers who might stake any claim on their empire. This was happening in spite of the fact that these properties came into their possession without any financial investment and that they held no title deeds for them. I also had a look at some factories providing building materials, tools, and machinery. Practically all needed a complete overhaul and most would have to be adapted to new technology. What I saw before me was a country economically ruined; and this had happened in the previous dozen of years under the rule of Communist barons who were always boasting that they had made Poland the ninth industrial power in the world. Many of my interlocutors still believed this fairy tale.

Several friends of mine, now members of the new government, were telling me of the huge problems, which had to be solved before such mundane questions as housing construction could find a place on their agenda. A member of the cabinet told me, without beating about the bush, that building would now be the domain of private investors that the state had to get its finger speedily out of this particular pie. "If you have the necessary capital, do start by all means; but bear in mind that none of the ordinary citizens here have any money. No one has savings; all just lead a hand-to-mouth existence." Another old friend had now been given the green light to prepare the legislation necessary for the monumental job of decentralizing the administration of the country. Local authorities would have to be established as the first step to democratic government from the bottom up. The country was being strangled by the catastrophic inflation inherited from the last Communist government. In the near future, the new minister of finance, L. Balcerowicz, would salvage the country's financial health by the shock imposition of a free market without any transitional period. This brave though rather unpopular decision gained Poland and her new government wide recognition and the approbation of the whole democratic world. Balcerowicz's American adviser, Jeffrey Sachs, was later to try out the same method in many other countries, where, however, it would prove less successful than it had been in Poland. Important events were taking place at government level. And they were filtering through and could be seen literally at street level, where small private traders were now operating in any available space. Neither I nor anyone else I knew could fully appreciate the significance and scope of these changes. It was the first time that the world had witnessed the bloodless metamorphosis of a powerful political system, based on the entrenched control of all its citizens and maintained through secret policing, into a democratic one based on the rule of law. Now, looking back on it, we realize that mistakes had been made, that unnecessary statements had been issued, and that some awkward explanations could have been better phrased. These hiccups would, years later, be resurrected by various political demagogues and used to serve their private ambitions. They could not, however, obscure the image of the great historical achievement contributed to by the entire nation. Whether that great chance would later be fully exploited would depend on the maturity and attitude of politicians and of the Polish nation. But that is an altogether different question.

When I returned home, still giddy with the events in Poland, I felt that I was no longer an immigrant but a citizen of a free world. I was irritated in New York by the lack of any improvements for the better. This was obviously a rather superficial response, no doubt related to the comparison of the sudden and enormous changes of a whole system of power with the slow moving development of the two-hundred-years-old American democracy. When I shared my feelings with Lenta, she just laughed at my having been bewitched by Poland. She had just finished writing an essay for her series "Kartki z Metropolii" (Notes from the Metropolis) for the Polish *Zeszyty Literackie* (Literary Notebooks). She showed me an excerpt, to help me to keep some balance in my comparison of the two worlds:

> . . . A hot and rainy summer always reminds me of the fact, that around us stretches in all directions a city, largely unknown to us, which practically in front of our eyes has metamorphosed into an international metropolis of success—and of an incomprehensible decline. In this capital city of music and ballet, of big publishing houses, of a stock exchange, of one where works of art worth millions of dollars change hands, millions are also being made from dealing in drugs. Nowadays even children of tender years—many of them born with AIDS—sell crack cocaine in the streets. Above this mighty ocean of civilization—with all its successes and its miseries—the floodlit arrows of skyscrapers hit the night sky and old trees lean from the park over Fifth Avenue, exactly as painted by Childe Hassam, the gentle landscape painter of the early twentieth century . . .

Thus, whatever the rate of changes, some of our plans had to be altered; and the question of housing in Poland had, for the time being, to be shelved. The priority of our small but ambitious group was now the establishment of AMERBANK in Warsaw. The first step was the finding of suitable premises and the appointment of an experienced person to the position of the bank's president. To begin with, we opened a small interim office in a building, which also housed the head office of the State Conglomerate of Power Industry and Oil Deposits, one of bank's shareholders. Several failed attempts to rent suitable permanent premises brought to light an unforeseen difficulty: the legal ownership of all buildings rebuilt after the war in Warsaw or nationalized in 1945 still remained to be settled and there were no owners listed in the Land Registry that we could sign a contract with. This seemed to apply to most office premises. The lawlessness of Communist rule was thus coming to light in the most unexpected ways. Eventually, however, we managed to locate a relatively modern building with a recognized owner. It was, by an irony of fate, the previous seat of the Polish-Soviet Friendship Society. Lenin could be heard turning in his grave.

Finding a prospective Polish-speaking manager for the bank, someone with experience abroad, capable of organizing the bank from scratch, proved a much more difficult proposition. It was quite interesting to interview the applicants for the lower-grade jobs and hear them expound their ideas on the organization of the various departments of the bank. Even though my knowledge of banking was limited, I could see straightaway that many of the people we were dealing with were, at their best, simple frauds or, at their worst, swindlers aspiring to join the class of international financiers. The few I remember, when engaged for a probationary period, immediately found glamorous female companions, obviously on the lookout for a better life. With the job went attractive apartments rented from the old Communist big shots in the neighborhood referred to as the Bay of Red Pigs. The owners of these apartments had moved by then to their own newly built luxury mansions in exclusive outer suburbs; how they had come by the necessary funds remained a mystery.

The unfilled vacancy for the position of the bank's president was creating a problem, particularly in view of the approaching official opening of the bank. It was inevitably delaying the remodeling of the new premises suitably located near the aptly named Bank Square. Eventually, after several wasted months, someone had recommended an old friend, resident in London. The man was interviewed by Kosiński in New York and made a good impression both as a person and as a professional banker. He was appointed president of AmerBank.

I received the message of his arrival on the eve of my departure from Warsaw. I quickly organized for him a presentation of the rebuilding plans in one of Warsaw's hotels. The following day, I was to attend a meeting in New York in connection with the furnishing of the new premises; so I had to acquaint our new president promptly with the overall picture, as well as ask him several pertinent questions. However, time was passing, he did not get in touch, and it was only late in the evening when reception informed me that our president has finally booked into the hotel. I met him in his apartment, where drinks and a light supper were prepared to refresh him after the presumed hardships of his journey. The tall, presentable man of over fifty greeted me with a friendly smile. He seemed rather surprised by the reception and by the rebuilding plans spread out before him. "What are they?" he asked while pouring himself a glass of whisky. He settled himself in an armchair to listen to my explanations. When I asked him whether he had not been told in New York about the rebuilding plans, he made a wry face and shook his head. "I had no idea, and you know, on the way here I had to stop in Paris . . . a lady friend, you understand, was waiting for me. And you know what women are like . . ."

"I do, yes, but I need your reply to several questions," I insisted. "It is the problem of appropriately locating the individual departments of the bank for their easier cooperation. And this is connected with . . ." He got up, flipped through several drawings, returned to his armchair, stretched his legs, drained the rest of his whisky, and turned to me with a smile. "I am really sorry; but to tell you the truth, I know absolutely nothing about the organization of a bank."

The first meeting of the American and Polish shareholders was accompanied by another sumptuous dinner at the high class Ambassador restaurant. On a superficial level, it appeared that everyone was happy, and a mood of optimism and unity of purpose prevailed. Being in some way detached, I was able to observe the behavior of our Polish guests. They seemed a motley collection of haphazardly assorted individuals whose background and origins of their fortunes nobody knew or had bothered to check. It seemed to me that we were offering them an opportunity for large-scale money laundering. There were some who were holding shares as managers of firms—still in state ownership—involved in foreign trade. Others, nouveau riche traders, had come into their money by selling such things as cosmetics in Moscow or engaging in a semi-legal cross-border trade in clothes and textiles with East Germany, Lithuania, or Ukraine. One of the guests was whispering to his neighbor about the profit one could make smuggling cigarettes and alcohol, while someone else was insisting that better gains could be made in Belarus, though he did not specify the merchandise.

I have no idea who got this group of investors together, and who had been distributing positions. While clinking champagne glasses with Kosiński, I remarked that at first glance the gathered company, with their mysterious pasts, would make a perfect cast for a thriller on the rebirth of capitalism. He was not at all amused, but frowned as if I had hurt him. Being only an occasional visitor to Warsaw, he was not really acquainted with the background of the affairs I was trying to introduce him to. With his hand round my shoulders and raising his glass once again, he said, "Let's look at it from another angle. Could we have expected anything like this several years ago? Look, we are in Warsaw, we are drinking champagne at a meeting of shareholders of an American bank in Poland. No one is spying on us; we can say whatever we want. Could we have expected anything like this?" A tear appeared in his eye. And I too was moved.

Soon after, a new president of the bank was appointed. He was an American, a handsome and well-dressed man, who had recently returned from the Far East where, as the rumor had it, he had been establishing a Dutch bank. Our American shareholders had also sent us an energetic young woman by the name of Joyce whose job was to curb our rapidly growing expenses. Joyce was a highly qualified accountant who had previously worked in investment control in the American Express Company. She quickly uncovered gross negligence and unaccounted-for expenditures.

The new president of the bank began very quickly to be seen in the company of a very attractive woman, who was soon spotted driving round Warsaw in the bank's official black Volvo. This liaison would end a year later with a major scandal involving gambling and a casino; as a result of which, both protagonists would disappear from the public scene and from the wagging tongues of Warsaw's notorious gossips.

I mention these events, as they give a good picture of some aspects of the new Polish reality in the process of transition. This was a period of raptures, of tragedies, of absurdities. We, Poles living abroad, tried to help in any way we could, considering it our duty to contribute to the rebuilding and stabilization of the country. It would not come amiss if the sentiments of those days, enriched by the experience of our pioneering efforts, returned once again.

In the meantime, the bank's new board began to develop its professional commitments, while the building work was put out to tender and eventually granted to a Yugoslav firm, presently redeveloping the silver tower in Bank Square. The new premises were scheduled to open in the first half of May. It was Lenta who, coming to Warsaw for the celebration, brought the shocking news that in New York, on the night of May 2, 1991, Jerzy Kosiński had committed suicide. We had no idea what tragedy prompted Jerzy to take such a drastic step, and, to boot, on the eve of the opening of the bank of which he had been the initiator and the true soul of the venture. Our festive mood was shattered, but we decided, nevertheless, to carry on as planned. Our resolve was reinforced by the arrival of Kiki, who insisted that Jerzy would want us to proceed.

Now that Kosiński was dead, reams were being written about his mysterious, fascinating, and dramatic past. The reason for his sudden suicide is, to this day, a subject for speculation. Many authors peruse his books and try to find an explanation in his writings as well as in his life. The Polish Institute in New York recently published an extensive monograph on Kosiński in the quarterly, *The Polish Review*, which reports many attempts to solve the puzzle. I have my own suspicion, but that should remain untold. We may only wonder, why did Kosiński choose death at the very moment of the opening the American Bank in Poland, his amazing last crowning achievement, an enterprise so different from his other ones, which had brought him fame in the world of literature?

The bank operated reasonably well for several more years, though, as usual, not without scandals at the top. The bank's first Polish president ended behind bars after several years, while the vice-president escaped abroad. Finally, AMERBANK was bought by one of the German banks and that was the end of our venture in Poland.

I am describing those attempts simply to put on record the good faith of Poles living abroad who tried to prop up the newly established free market economy in the old country. They were offering their enterprise, their command of foreign languages, and their contacts in the capitalist world—all the skills extinct under the state-controlled economy of the People's Republic of Poland. Some succeeded; others, like myself, only partly so. What one is left with, though, are the memories, together with the satisfaction, of having taken the decision to face the stormy waters, and of having been part of the great changes taking place in the transition period in Poland.

31

The Folly of the Twenty-first Century

The time has come to end my memoirs of the twentieth century. Unexpectedly, for an amateur writer, I went ahead and remembered much more than I would have expected when I set out, shyly, nine years ago, to record my reminiscences. The title of the book carries a hidden question. Has our immigration to America, at the time imposed on us by circumstances, been the right choice? Generally speaking, I believe that the answer is yes.

But it has not always been easy. Having finished my chronicles, I remarked half in jest that I had experienced five battlegrounds: the beginning of the Second World War in Poland in 1939, the war in the Libyan Desert in 1941-42; the air war on the western front in Europe in 1944-45; the period of Stalinism in Poland; and, finally, the immigration to USA. The latter period was our longest struggle for survival at a time of great turmoil, social unrest, the tragic war in Indochina, racial uprisings, and assassinations. At first on my own, and later with my family, we luckily overcame all the trials and tribulations of that dangerous era.

In 1989, soon after the collapse of Communism, when I went to the newly democratic Poland, I was surprised to feel almost at home. But to return to the old country for good would not be an easy decision. The older one gets, the more difficult it is to face being uprooted yet again. But even for younger people working in the liberal professions or employed in businesses and various institutions, the decision may be just as or even more difficult. No words of encouragement were coming from the home country; no one in any official capacity said come back, give us a hand, tell us how problems such as ours would be dealt with in the West.

I can't help wryly smiling while writing these words. For how many such hopes of a joyous return proved to be a flash in the pan? How naïve were those who entertained this idea? Nobody, either in Poland or among Poles settled abroad, could envisage the consequences of such a radical change in the political system, happening practically overnight. Nobody gave a thought to the difficulties, of incorporating into the process the possible returnees from abroad. Thus, in the end, only a small number of retired people, plus perhaps a few enterprising businessmen, did decide to go back. From amongst our friends, a number of artists did return; and for them, the move was fairly easy.

Many, including ourselves, set up a second home in Poland to which one could now easily commute, the old fear-inspiring frontier controls having been swept away. And somehow, the hidden question of the title of my memoirs has lost its relevance.

It is forty years now since we came to settle in America. It was a period of great changes throughout the world, greater and faster than in any previous period of history. For the first time, the world became a "global village," all parts of it interdependent and united by the constantly flowing rivers of information. Television has brought to our homes instant pictures of events and developments in distant lands. These could then be imitated or adapted in other parts of the network in an unprecedented exchange of experiences. And now, the Internet is continuing the process at an even faster rate.

Many epoch-making developments either originated in America or had an American connection: the arms race between the communist East and the democratic West; the spectacular space contest and the landing of man on the moon; the growing conflict in the Middle East; the Vietnam War; the questionable U.S. support for political dictatorships in Africa and South America; the cold war in Europe and in countries of the third world; the demise of Communism to mention only a few. To this list of major political developments, we have to add new achievements in science and technology such as the discovery of the genetic substrate of life; the exploration of other planets and of space by man-made robots; the continuing development of computers, cellular telephones; the cloning of live organisms and tracing, through the DNA, the origins of human race back to Africa only few million years ago. And yet man's achievements were not confined to these domains. America has become the driving force in the spread of Western civilization, leaving the old Europe behind, at least for the time being.

The 1960s till the end of the century were an exceptional period in the history of the USA. The political, economic, social, and cultural changes taking place in America were almost instantly spreading abroad. Digested and adopted by other cultures, they ricocheted back in due course, inevitably affecting, modifying, and enhancing their original source. Due to the instant transmission of information, this process acted also in reverse, from its sources in the rest of the world to America. This applied to all domains of human activity. The future augured to be problem free. The historian, Francis Fukuyama, became an instant celebrity with his book *The End of History*. Such was the state of affairs at the start of the twenty-first century.

At home, I often argued with Lenta about the varying perceptions of "Americanization" of the world. At the time, she was writing an essay about New York for *Zeszyty Literackie*, a Polish literary magazine, and this included a passage, which now reads as a prophecy for today:

> . . . I look at the city, standing on my terrace, I see only height and grandeur: skyscrapers, those soaring temples of capitalism and the once triumphant economy. Even today, though somewhat abated, it is still admired by some and hated by others. It was beneath such walls, as if they represented an inimical religion, that a bomb was recently placed. One can't help thinking of an abstract distant

> future: what will these lofty towers stand for, those traces of a secular faith in humanity? Will the old convictions, power and the puritan self-assurance, known to us from history books, suffice? On the cover of the Washington publication "The New Republic" several terrestrial globes spin round the White House—a different war raging on each, civil, tribal, religious—the face of the century to come. And yet there is talk of hope in town. Of attempted reforms, of a desire for better justice, of the young, new president, Bill Clinton, promising change. And perhaps we carry with him the burden of each day of his term—the conflict between races, the chasm between the rich and the destitute, the depressing war in the center of Europe, perhaps not just for us (Poles), but affecting all. I see Manhattan from my terrace as if from reels of old films depicting battles won by the West . . . And on the streets below, I walk amongst the multilingual crowds. Their millennium, approaching fast, crowded and uncertain of its hopes . . .

And then, on September 11, 2001, came the suicidal attack on the twin towers of the World Trade Center in New York. Suddenly, the West was directly and immediately confronted with the unresolved grievances brewing for years in the Middle East. All the achievements of the West were shaken that day by the Islamic suicide fanatics attempting to destroy the symbols of Western power, epitomized for them by America and the World Trade Center. In order to recruit followers and suicidal assassins, the Islamists turned to the exact interpretation of holy book of Koran. Not many people understood fully the seriousness of the challenge at the time. America, the only remaining superpower, responded in the time-sanctioned way by armed intervention.

I had also been witness to many changes occurring at that time in the Middle East, which eventually surprised the Western world with the present-day crisis. Previously, with the Soviet Union dominating Europe, the West knew what it had to deal with. In contrast, the West has been largely ignorant of the dangers emanating from the Middle East. The Muslim world, through its leaders, basically rejected Western, mostly unfamiliar, democratic institutions, and with its ancient hatred of Western dominance and its way of life, turned to insurgency and terrorist tactics compensating for the lack of large military establishment and sophisticated weaponry. But the result was unlike any historical precedent—this time the presumed enemy remained dispersed and hidden.

Attacks on Americans and on their halfhearted allies most likely will continue. It is the fast spread of the ideology of hatred directed mostly at the unresolved Palestinian-Israeli conflict, at the presence of an U.S. Army in the Muslim Holy lands, at our democratic institutions and at our way of life, which drives these attacks and helps them to succeed. Now, several years after 9/11, the Western world is less safe than it was before. The fanatics attack in unexpected venues, catching security services unaware, and gravely testing the credibility of the "war on terror" rhetoric. In the Middle Ages, European crusaders used religious rhetoric to recruit fighters against Muslim infidels. This time, in reverse, it is the Muslim insurgency, which uses religion as its weapon against Christian infidels.

It is always risky to attempt to describe topical events while writing a memoir. What seems to be true today may be disproved tomorrow. But because the outcome of the war faced by our civilization is so uncertain and still evolving that I am prepared to take the risk and finish my reminiscences by including several comments on the ongoing war in Iraq and Afghanistan. After all what happened yesterday is already a part of my memoir. These concern mostly USA, the country in the forefront of the war, but other countries are also vulnerable and under threat.

I am fully aware that in the near future, the situation, so dangerous today, might change for the better. But the lessons of history are clear: great powers make mistakes which eventually might lead to their demise. What complicates the situation immensely is the fact that the US government concocted stories and used blatantly false information to make the case for attacking Iraq, rather than secure its initial gains in Afghanistan. The lies were then fed to the media, and were spread around the world with no regard to truth. In an almost unbelievable twist of logic, highest government officials quoted these press reports as facts and the reason for their risky decisions. In the age of instant global communications most Americans believed in these lies, for the first time in recent history, antagonizing sections of its own population as well as the rest of the world. The USA is still an immensely powerful country; and what looks like a rush over-adventurous policy may tomorrow prove, to have been right. Who knows?

The difficulty in conducting this kind of war is that the enemy is elusive—here today, gone tomorrow. This is not a situation with which modern armed forces, such as those of the USA, however powerful, can easily cope. Under the disapproving gaze of the rest of the world, in the absence of any third party able to seek diplomatic solutions, the military option is taking upper hand. But the army, with its latest technology, equipped and trained for combat with another technocratic power, at a distance, is practically helpless against an individual enemy no different from any passerby in the midst of an urban crowd yet capable of inflicting enormous damage.

The concept of a small volunteer army of experts seems to be failing. America has no armed reserves to speak of. About one hundred fifty thousand soldiers serve in the Middle East. Every year, the recruitment figures keep falling below the requirements while the casualties are rising. The problem is that in spite of the government's campaign, which keeps emphasizing the global threat to us all, nothing has actually changed in the daily life of the citizens of this country.

Every great power had until now an absolute right to act in a way, which would best serve its own interests. Only America was considered an exception as the ostensible savior of its allies in both the world wars. Yet this time, the aims of her dangerous policy are kept under wraps. From the very beginning, the reason for invading Iraq was presented to the population in a series of lies. The first was the need to preempt a nuclear war about to be launched. The next one was the presumed link between Saddam Hussein and al-Qaeda terrorists, then it was the introduction of democracy. This last explanation seems to be most bizarre, bordering on childish naïveté. For America's enemies, who use religious and nationalistic rhetoric as a means of recruiting its fighters, the idea of a democracy is tantamount to sacrilege. "We do not want our Islamic nation to be either socialist or democratic . . . Islam and democracy are opposites, which shall never meet . . . Democracy means that people govern themselves. Islam recognizes only the rule of God and his law . . ." quotes, Alaa Al Aswamy, a contemporary Egyptian writer, from an overheard sermon in a mosque. This does not bode well for the spread of democracy in the Arab world. Having failed on all these accounts US government substituted another objective: containment of the insurgency by a supposedly temporary police action. So what was the true purpose of launching this disastrous war? Financial gains? Oil? Military bases? Policing a civil war?

Moreover, this is the first international conflict in which no bonds have been established between the professional armed forces and the country's civilian population. And so far, this war has hardly affected anybody in USA, apart from the families of American dead and wounded. The only acknowledgements of the soldiers' sacrifice are the bumper stickers with the slogan SUPPORT OUR TROOPS. And even that seems to be a call for only moral support, as no organized action seems to be in the offing. Only families of individual front line soldiers go to the trouble of sending them equipment required in the hopeless partisan warfare, seemingly neglected by the Defense Department. A reader's letter appeared in a newspaper: "It is now hard to imagine our grandparents who used to 'dig for victory' in their gardens and were buying war bonds to help the country. We do not even bother to salvage scrap metal; we drive about in Hummers or other cruiser motorcars, which consume vast amounts of gas, which we import at great cost from people who hate us . . ."

The gap between the action abroad and society's attitudes at home was emphasized by Rudolph Giuliani, the mayor of New York, when within hours of the attack on the WTC towers, he appealed in his broadcast to New Yorkers to return to normal life.

He called for shops and restaurants to remain open, for theatres and cinemas to continue their performances. It did seem to have been the right decision at the time, though there were people who considered it excessively casual. There were no calls for sacrifices, no appeals to the public other than to continue their daily business was made.

Yet some reactions went perhaps too far. Returning home on 9/11 with the smell of smoke still fresh in the air, I passed La Goulue, our neighborhood French restaurant. The tables on the pavement outside were packed, diners enjoying their meal, celebrating somebody's birthday, laughing and joking. And this was taking place six hours after the terrible event, in the same city, only a few miles from the buildings where nearly three thousand innocent people had just lost their lives.

Acknowledgments

Memoir writing is, as I discovered, a risky undertaking, unless one gets the chance of verifying the described events. In my case the risk had been magnified by the diversity of the events reported, their historical perspective, as well as by the great number of characters gracing these pages, some unwittingly, some even posthumously.

The fact that my war-time notes, drawings and photographs survived through the sixty years of my truly nomadic life was an incredible piece of luck. However, it wasn't just my memory and those saved materials which helped me to complete my task. The three volumes of my memoirs, were first published in Poland by the publishing house MOST, in the years 2003-2004-2007. Consequently my thanks go to many of my old and present friends, witnesses of the events and of the times described, as well as to the unexpected commentators for their invaluable support and help in adding fragments which contributed to making the memoirs a more complete whole.

Finally my repeatedly re-written Polish manuscript has found its way into the hands of readers. I had worked on it over a period of many years.

I am greatly indebted to my son-in-law, Erroll McDonald, for editing my own first translation of the war-time part of my memoir into English and for writing a new version, fragments of which filled in some gaps in my story and have been preserved in the present text.

For the translation of the whole of my memoir from Polish into English I wish to thank Danuta and Stefan Waydenfeld, a couple of my very special friends and contemporaries, whose life stories in part corresponded to mine. Deported with their families, among hundreds of thousands of Poles, into the depth of the Soviet Union and saved by the diplomatic action of the Polish Government-in-Exile in England, they travelled through the Middle East and Italy, where Stefan served in the Polish Second Corps and Danuta in the Polish Red Cross. Soon after the war they married and settled in Great Britain. With Danuta's help, Stefan described his wartime story in The Ice Road, published in Edinburgh in 1999, and in Poland in 2004. Their help over a number of years and our long and friendly conversations and correspondence relating to various parts of my manuscript proved an invaluable contribution to the present English edition of my memoir.

Further valuable help came from my Egyptian-Canadian friend. Medhat Shaheen, Cambridge and London educated architect, who read all the versions of my manuscript with meticulous care, noting even minor mistakes and, unexpectedly, correcting even my aviation terminology. He described his life in From Bedroom to Bedroom & Beyond, published in Canada in 2005, all of this in contrast to the Islamic, Arabic-speaking culture of the country of his birth, Egypt.

Lastly we arrived at the problem of the graphic design for the book cover. How does one visually present the reminiscences of a somewhat reluctant immigrant to the New World? How does one sum up many decades of a life lived through the extraordinary events of the 20th century?

For finding the answer I wish to thank Janusz Kapusta, an artist of international repute, with an interest in philosophy and in mathematics, and the discoverer of a unique geometrical shape, known as the K-Dron.

Special thanks is due to Czesław Czapliński, renowned photo-journalist, writer and author of the cover portrait.

Made in the USA
Columbia, SC
18 May 2020

97572601R00271